P9-CQQ-005

NOV   2014

THE JEW WHO
DEFEATED HITLER

THE JEW WHO DEFEATED HITLER

★ ★ ★ ★

HENRY MORGENTHAU JR., FDR, AND HOW WE WON THE WAR

PETER MOREIRA

Prometheus Books

59 John Glenn Drive
Amherst, New York 14228

Published 2014 by Prometheus Books

The Jew Who Defeated Hitler: Henry Morgenthau Jr., FDR, and How We Won the War. Copyright © 2014 by Peter Moreira. All rights reserved. No part of this publication may be reproduced, stored in a retrieval system, or transmitted in any form or by any means, digital, electronic, mechanical, photocopying, recording, or otherwise, or conveyed via the Internet or a website without prior written permission of the publisher, except in the case of brief quotations embodied in critical articles and reviews.

Prometheus Books recognizes the following registered trademarks and trademarks mentioned within the text: Bugs Bunny™, Donald Duck®, Gallup®, and Lockheed Martin®.

Cover image © Corbis
Jacket design by Nicole Sommer-Lecht

Inquiries should be addressed to
Prometheus Books
59 John Glenn Drive
Amherst, New York 14228
VOICE: 716–691–0133
FAX: 716–691–0137
WWW.PROMETHEUSBOOKS.COM

18 17 16 15 14   5 4 3 2 1

Library of Congress Cataloging-in-Publication Data Pending

Printed in the United States of America

For Stephen Bagworth
With the Greatest Respect

When the final history of the Roosevelt Administration is written, it will be said that Henry Morgenthau, next to his chief, did more for the war than any other one man in Washington.

—Syndicated Columnist Drew Pearson
July 30, 1945

CONTENTS

★ ★ ★

PROLOGUE

★ ★ ★

The scrapbook recording the Morgenthau family's 1938 summer vacation in France lies in a cardboard archive box in the Franklin D. Roosevelt Library and Museum in Hyde Park, NY. Its dark, Depression-era cover has weathered the years badly, and the newspaper clippings stuck to its rigid pages have yellowed. Yet it chronicles a seminal event in the family history. Henry and Elinor Morgenthau took their three children to Europe each summer, always in grand style due to the income they drew from their families, who were wealthy New York businesspeople. On this particular trip, the Morgenthaus and their Scottish maid, Janet Crawford, crossed the Atlantic in three first-class cabins aboard the Dutch ocean liner *Statendam*. What made this trip special was that the Morgenthau children were entering adulthood, Europe was simmering with tension, and Henry Morgenthau Jr. was being hailed for the first time as a statesman.

The Morgenthau children—Henry, who was twenty-one, Robert, nineteen, and Joan, sixteen—were now old enough to enjoy all that Europe offered, and the spirit of adventure was accentuated by the brewing of a nascent war. Their father was convinced their steward aboard the ship was a German spy because of his accent and manner. Later, the boys spent late nights reveling in Paris. Languishing on the rocky shores of the Côte d'Azur in southern France, the family mingled with the film star Marlene Dietrich, the author Erich Maria Remarque, and the vacationing family of Joseph P. Kennedy, the American ambassador in London. The paths of the two Democrat families would often cross in the ensuing years. Robert Morgenthau would one day organize John F. Kennedy's presidential campaign in the Bronx and would be with Robert Kennedy on November 22, 1963, when the call came in that the president had been shot in Dallas.[1]

The thing that really stands out in the scrapbook was the adulation Henry Morgenthau Jr. received in Paris. He had been secretary of the Treasury for almost five years, but this was the first time he was treated abroad as a man who influenced events. His greatest achievement had been the Tripartite Pact of September 1936, a treaty with France and Britain that aimed to reduce the harmful volatility among the three countries' currencies. Morgenthau had been regarded as a lightweight until he sealed that pact—a feat few thought possible. More recently, he had been the main player in talks to stabilize the French franc, which was being battered by a faltering economy, a capital drain, and growing defense spending. And the French that summer made sure Morgenthau knew how much they appreciated his efforts.

The newspaper *Excelsior* ran a front-page photograph of the Morgenthaus being met at the Gare du Nord by US ambassador William Bullitt on July 24, and the coverage continued in all the major papers, even those outside France. The *Daily Mail* in London ran a photo of Elinor and Bullitt leaving the Élysée Palace after a meeting with President Albert Lebrun. Outside the French Treasury, on the bank of the Seine, Morgenthau was photographed by one paper surrounded by France's leaders. In another, he was pictured addressing platoons of reporters. The *Financial Times* and other papers reported on the splendid banquet that Raymond Patenôtre, the minister of national economy, held for Morgenthau in the beautiful state dining room of the Quai D'Orsay. The press covered his meeting with Finance Minister Paul Marchandeau, the dinner with the prime minister and other cabinet ministers at the American embassy, and his luncheon with Foreign Minister Georges Bonnet.[2]

"That sort of social function isn't at all to my liking, but I couldn't help feeling proud at the high esteem in which the French hold Henry," Elinor wrote to her parents. She was also proud of her children, who conducted themselves with such dignity at the formal dinners. "To see little Joan sitting next to the head of the Bank of France and talking with the air of a grown person was quite a sight," she said.[3] Certainly the whole family felt proud of Henry's celebrity. "It is a grand change for you and, no doubt, you will realize what a following you have abroad," wrote his father, the original Henry Morgenthau, from Murray Bay, Quebec, where he had listened to radio broadcasts relayed from a transmitter in Nova Scotia. "I hope you will enjoy it to the fullest."[4]

Henry Morgenthau Jr. was indeed enjoying himself to the fullest. He was relaxed and jolly in his meetings with the French leaders and even with the journalists who followed him everywhere. He had received two substantial checks from the family funds before he left the United States, so he was flush with cash. And it had been three weeks since he had suffered from a migraine headache, a debilitating affliction that often drove him throughout his career to recline in darkened rooms. He was even more upbeat about the stability of France and her currency. "The French feel a little more optimistic and I think that their feeling is justified," he wrote his father from Antibes. "Things have picked up here and their government is more stable." At the end of the letter, he noted that there was one aspect of the vacation that was troubling him: "I get a great many letters for appeal from refugees but I can not do anything to help the poor things."[5]

After they finished relaxing on the Côte d'Azur, the Morgenthaus traveled up the eastern border of France and into Switzerland for the final leg of their journey. They ended up in Basel, the country's third-largest city, located on the banks of the Rhine at the juncture of the Swiss, French, and German borders. From this ancient commercial hub, the Morgenthaus could gaze across the river and see Germany. One day, Henry III told his father he wanted to walk across the bridge and go into the country. His father was shocked by the statement and asked why. The young man simply said he wanted to be able to say he'd set foot in Germany.

"Oh, Henry," said his father. "You don't want to set foot in Germany."[6]

Even without the letters he'd received from oppressed German Jews, Henry Morgenthau Jr. was well aware of the hell that was unfolding across the river. Germany was now in its sixth year of Nazi rule, and Führer Adolf Hitler was rearming, expanding, and oppressing his enemies. Since seizing power in early 1933, he had renounced the Treaty of Paris, which prohibited German rearmament and demanded reparations. Then he'd brought in the Nuremburg Laws of 1935, depriving Jews of German citizenship and outlawing marriage between Jews and other Germans. He had taken over the Rhineland in March 1936 and annexed Austria in March 1938. And now, in the summer of 1938, he was insisting Germany be given the Sudetenland, the industrial portion of Czechoslovakia with a substantial German population. A man of Morgenthau's acumen, especially a Jewish man, could not ignore the Nazi menace germinating nearby.

The lurking Nazi menace even appears in the family's vacation album. Tucked in the back of the scrapbook is a small article from an unnamed French paper, noting that Morgenthau's visit to Europe had drawn the attention of Hitler's chief propagandist, Joseph Goebbels. The article, dated August 25, 1938, reported that *Der Angriff*, Goebbels's official publication, had launched a violent front-page attack on Morgenthau. The article called him "the real chief of a wide Judeo-Bolshevik conspiracy" against Germany and her friends and said the secretary was engaged in "mysterious intrigues" during his trip to France. "Mr. Morgenthau did not come to Europe for a rest, as he pretends, but [was] charged with a special mission by Mr. Roosevelt," said *Der Angriff*. "Moreover, it is he who, behind the president, holds the power."[7]

Of course, *Der Angriff* had frequently attacked the Jews who surrounded President Roosevelt for years and would continue to do so until 1945. But until 1944, it rarely singled out Morgenthau. The Nazi media frequently mentioned that Roosevelt had surrounded himself with Jews, but it usually referred to them as a group. Besides Morgenthau, the circle included financier Bernard Baruch, Supreme Court Justice Felix Frankfurter, speechwriter Sam Rosenman, Congressman Sol Bloom, and even New York mayor Fiorello Henry La Guardia, whose mother had Hungarian Jewish lineage. If the Nazis gave one Jew prominence, it was Baruch, who had led the War Industries Board in World War I. And the right-winged media on the Continent could take the issue of "International Jewry" to comical heights. In October 1938, the Fascist journalist Giovani Preziosi wrote in the magazine *La Vita Italiana* that the Jewish International was planning to take power in the 1940 US election. Baruch would be president, he wrote, and the cabinet would include Albert Einstein as vice president, Herbert Lehman as secretary of state, Henry Morgenthau Jr. as Treasury secretary and Leon Trotsky as secretary of war. Walter Lippmann would be secretary of the press.[8]

Americans also noticed the unprecedented preponderance of Jews surrounding the president. Several wags, such as poet Ezra Pound and farm leader Milo Reno, referred to the New Deal, Roosevelt's recovery program, as the "Jew Deal."[9] Some called the government "the Rosenbaum Administration." But what is difficult to understand for people born generations later is that the Nazis actually believed their own propaganda. The men surrounding Hitler were sick sadists whose ravings about an international Jewish conspiracy seemed ludicrous to reasonable people. But the Nazis themselves actually believed there was an international Jewish conspiracy, and a substantial body of the European population agreed with them. In one of history's cruel coincidences, Jews gained unprecedented political power in the United States just as the Nazis were coming to power in Germany. When Roosevelt aligned himself with the British and later entered the war, it served only to vindicate the Nazis' conviction that an international network of Jews was at work against their country.

Of all the American Jews frequently cited by the Nazis as being part of this conspiracy, only Morgenthau held an executive position and wielded the power necessary to fight the Axis. The thesis of this book, as the title suggests, is that Morgenthau's role in the war was utterly crucial to the Allied victory to a degree that history has not appreciated. He was certainly the most powerful Jew in the world while Jewry faced its greatest peril since the days of Moses.

I admit the title *The Jew Who Defeated Hitler* somewhat overstates the case. No single person—not Stalin, nor Churchill, nor Roosevelt, nor any soldier—defeated Hitler. The single biggest reason that the Nazis fell was the Soviet acceptance of suffering and casualties in order to withstand the German onslaught. More than twenty million Soviets died in the war, three times the number of Germans. I'd argue that the second-biggest reason for the Allied victory was that the industrial might of the Allies tripled that of the Axis. "The Allies possessed *twice* the manufacturing strength (using the distorted 1938 figures, which downplay the US share), *three* times the 'war potential' and *three* times the national income of the Axis powers, even when the French shares are added to Germany's total," writes Paul Kennedy in *The Rise and Fall of the Great Powers.*[10] (War potential is the segment of the economy that can be used for waging war.) The Allies were certain to win, regardless of the excellence of the German military leadership, simply because they had three times the economic clout and could devote a larger portion of their economy to manufacturing arms and financing their forces.

And who was the main administrator harnessing the economic might of the strongest member of the alliance? Henry Morgenthau Jr.

Historians have tended to downplay his role because he is viewed as a yes-man to Roosevelt, so Roosevelt has gotten the credit for Morgenthau's work because academics assumed he was simply doing the president's bidding. What's more, Morgenthau was never an easy historical study. Oh, he wanted to be remembered by history. He even wanted to handpick the historian to write his biography. He went to pains to set up a recording system in his office—similar to that of Richard Nixon—and had a pool of secretaries to transcribe all meetings and phone calls. He frequently had stenographers come to his house if he met people there in the evenings. He filed away every document that crossed his desk, an archive that eventually became known as the Morgenthau Diaries. These official documents and his personal papers totaled one million pages. As early as May 1941, Morgenthau hired a Treasury underling named Joseph Gaer to assemble material for a planned biography. He agreed to pay Gaer $6,500 per year from his own pocket for the work, which fell by the wayside as war broke out.[11] After the war, he called in Arthur M. Schlesinger Jr. to help him write memoirs for *Collier's* magazine. In 1954, Morgenthau asked the Yale historian John Morton Blum to write the story of his years with Franklin Roosevelt. The ensuing project consumed twelve years of Blum's life and resulted in a three-volume work titled *From the Morgenthau Diaries*. The greatest omission in these works is the role of Elinor Morgenthau. Henry Morgenthau Jr. made certain his wife's remarks were rarely recorded, likely to protect her privacy, and refused to discuss Elinor with Blum during their long collaboration. Morgenthau's own legacy suffers because of this. Elinor Morgenthau was brilliant—her mind was analytical, her opinions cogent and precisely expressed. Yet little of Elinor's advice has been recorded. The Morgenthau story would be all the richer if we had a stronger appreciation of her influence.

Morgenthau proves a challenge as a historical hero. He was not made of heroic stuff. In a time of great military feats, he was a bureaucrat, and his greatest strength was his ability to make governments act. He was thin skinned and would often snitch to the president about his cabinet colleagues. He was inarticulate—so much so that it is all but impossible to convert his discourse into readable quotations. His diction was a tangle of incomplete sentences, malapropisms, and meandering dependent clauses, all overlaying his own brand of Runyonesque New York street talk. He was also the ultimate multitasker, frequently engaged in five or six different sets of simultaneous negotiations, lasting for months or years, involving several countries. He oversaw the most unwieldy of government departments, and because of this, historians have a hellish task in stringing together a storyline in the Morgenthau biography. There are simply too many threads. He set the budget, negotiated exchange rates, issued bonds, oversaw the coast guard and the Secret Service, and maintained public buildings. He even had more responsibility for monetary policy than his modern successors. And those were simply the responsibilities *within* his portfolio. He frequently took on other jobs because he didn't think other secretaries were doing their job properly. Quite often, Roosevelt agreed with him. (And on a few occasions, the president brought in other people to do the work of the Treasury because he didn't like what Morgenthau was doing.)

The Jew Who Defeated Hitler will sidestep this chaotic administrative workload by focusing on Morgenthau's efforts to help defeat Germany, Japan, and Italy. It is the story of the American who raised more than $300 billion in debt and taxes to battle the greatest combination of power and evil the world has ever seen. As perspective, consider that the Roosevelt government spent $33.5 billion in the five years of the New Deal, the Roosevelt administration's program to overcome the Great Depression. It was a program criticized for creating so much public spending that it might bankrupt the country.[12] The war against the Axis was the most expensive human undertaking ever, and the man most responsible for financing it was Henry Morgenthau Jr. It is true Morgenthau did little without FDR's approval, but this book will show that Morgenthau urged Roosevelt to prepare for war while the president was still waffling. He was the early architect of the US airplane program, he was instrumental in rearming Britain after Dunkirk, and he exceeded expectations in raising hundreds of billions of dollars at low interest rates. And he was the driving force behind the War Refugee Board, which helped to rescue about 200,000 European Jews. He did all this even though he had little formal education, was considered stupid, had to battle enemies within the administration and Congress, and faced anti-Semitism. This is the story of how Morgenthau led the Treasury to finance the dismantling of the Nazi juggernaut and how his final gambit led to his inglorious political downfall.

CHAPTER ONE

BATTLING THE AGGRESSORS

★ ★ ★

Henry Morgenthau Jr. was growing frustrated that his two most brilliant aides just didn't understand what he was hinting at. It was late on Tuesday, October 11, 1938, and the Treasury Department's chief counsel Herman Oliphant and Harry Dexter White, the director of monetary research, had come to Morgenthau's wood-paneled corner office to persuade him once again to recommend that the president impose countervailing duties on Germany and Japan. They knew Morgenthau supported such a policy. All senior Treasury officials hated the rightist aggressors, and nobody more so than the Treasury secretary himself. Even Morgenthau's secretary, Henrietta Klotz, who was silently taking notes at the meeting, hoped the department could do something to halt the extremists' steady advance. And yet as Oliphant and White outlined their plan, the secretary kept suggesting there was a problem, obviously hoping that they would pick up on what he wanted.

Oliphant told the Treasury secretary that the president had the authority to impose a 50 percent duty if he found a country discriminated against the commerce of the United States. And under section 338 of the Tariff Act, he reminded Morgenthau, the Treasury had already found eleven to thirteen instances of Germany discriminating against the United States. Morgenthau heard him out and focused on one question: Why? Why impose these duties on Germany and Japan and not on other countries?[1] The two men across the desk from him fumbled for a response, even though they were widely considered to be intellectual heavyweights compared to their boss.

Morgenthau perplexed many in Washington because he seemed dim-witted but ran arguably the most efficient department in the capital. Historian Arthur Schlesinger Jr. was not alone when he pondered how the man could possess such a simple mind yet be such an able administrator.[2] The forty-eight-year-old Morgenthau was six feet one inch tall and bald; his pointed nose and pince-nez glasses gave him a birdlike appearance. He had gained a moderate girth in adulthood, despite walking two miles to work each day. "He is slow-thinking and slow-speaking," wrote Joseph Alsop and Robert Kintner in the *Saturday Evening Post*. "He has an exasperating habit of repeating statements which he thinks important, occasionally stutters and is always forgetting names. When his memory fails him, he snaps his fingers and utters a sort of low cry, intended as an appeal to his companion to supply his deficiency. He is self-conscious without being self-confident, a born worrier and inclined to be suspicious."[3] In the middle of World War II, *Time* would write: "His eyes light up behind his pince-nez when he shakes a stranger's hand. But his shyness is so painful that he can never relax. Only a few men like Franklin Roosevelt have known the human warmth that lies behind Morgenthau's deaconish mien. Most others have decided, after a time, that he is suspicious, autocratic, a real cold fish."[4] Former National Recovery Administration head Hugh S. Johnson tagged Morgenthau with the nickname "Henry the Morgue," accentuating the secretary's lugu-brious features.[5] (Johnson assigned similar nicknames to most members of the Roosevelt circle, so Frances Perkins became "Franny the Perk," Harry Hopkins "Harry the Hop" and Harold Ickes "Harold the Ick.")

Yet Morgenthau was a forceful character, rarely backing down from a fight with a peer. He often pouted if Roosevelt berated him, but he would also tell the president things the chief didn't want to hear. He was known for his ethics, largely because he refused to offer patronage positions to undeserving Democrats. He and his wife were known to have one of the soundest marriages in official Washington, and their children were univer-sally admired. If Morgenthau did have a moral shortcoming, it was that he enjoyed the perks of high office. He was criticized in 1933 for spending $1,406 of public money to install a shower and a cooling system in his office when he ran the Farm Credit Administration.[6] He would have the officers of the Secret Service (then a division of the Treasury) pick up his wife in New York and drive her to Poughkeepsie, and he liked the use of his twin-engine Lockheed coast guard plane to fly to Dutchess County on the weekends at a time when air travel was still the preserve of relatively few.[7] Seven months after the attack on Pearl Harbor, he had the Treasury general counsel contact the Office of Price Administration, which oversaw war rationing, to explain that Morgenthau needed extra gasoline for the Plymouth station wagon on his farm because he used it, among other things, to visit the president.[8] But these were mere bagatelles for a man whose ethical values were so strong that his staff often said they joined the Treasury because of its idealism.

Oliphant had been with Morgenthau longer than any of the other Treasury personnel (other than Klotz), so the lawyer was the one who now pushed the countervailing-duties issue. A shy, tireless man whom *Time* magazine described as "grey-locked, hollow-eyed," he suggested the president could draw a distinction between trade from Germany and Japan on one hand and the rest of the world on the other. He was supported by White, a compact, Harvard-trained economist who had joined the Treasury in 1934. White had a gruff manner that offended many colleagues, but he was known to have a profound intellect and was respected throughout Washington. "They're discriminating against our trade and possibly by the imposition of that additional duty . . . [we] may help them to abandon that practice and thereby in the long run increase our trade," he suggested, trying to make Morgenthau see how the duties would benefit the United States.[9] Though they had worked on this brief for years, Morgenthau still asked Oliphant and White why he should make such a recommendation to the president. The two aides came up with answers, and Morgenthau battled back, demanding better reasons for the recommendation.

Finally, the counsel stated the real reason they were having the discussion. Oliphant said he would like duties to be imposed against Japan because it would be decisive in helping China in its escalating Asian war. "And I would do it in the case of Germany because it might very well be decisive in the struggle between that grisly thing in Europe and the sort of institutions we know about."[10]

Oliphant had said it. They were going after the two most potent aggressor states because the Treasury officials believed they threatened the entire world, including the United States. For the five years the Democrats had been in power, they had watched the right-wing dictatorships expand at a frightening rate. Just the day before, German troops had completed their occupation of the Sudetenland in Czechoslovakia, the result of the embarrassing acquiescence of Britain and France at the Munich summit in late September. In the two years before that, Germany had seized Austria and the Rhineland. Italy under Benito Mussolini had invaded Ethiopia in 1935, gaining control of the African nation in 1936. In Spain, Generalissimo Francisco Franco's Loyalist forces were into the endgame of their bloody civil war. The democratically elected Republicans were clinging to two coastal areas in eastern Spain, and the news of the appeasement at Munich had broken their morale. Across the globe in Asia, Japan was moving at will through China. The island nation had been expanding since it occupied the Korean Peninsula in 1910 and had captured Manchuria, in Northeast China, in 1932. Since 1936, the Japanese occupation of China had advanced as it captured Peking (now Beijing), surrounded Shanghai, and committed the horrendous massacre in Nanking in December 1937.

Of all the members of Roosevelt's cabinet, Morgenthau was most aware of the frightening advance of right-wing extremists. He hated the Nazis with an all-consuming passion. No doubt the fact he was Jewish contributed to this hatred, though a more important factor was his abiding love of democracy and American liberty. As a minority who lived in considerable luxury, Morgenthau had always believed his family could enjoy such a station in life only in a country that guaranteed personal liberties as the United States did. He was consistent throughout his life in his admiration for democratic countries and contempt for totalitarianism, except for a blind spot to the evils of the Soviet Union. He had been warning about the perils of German, Japanese, and Italian aggression in and out of cabinet for years, more so than any other secretary. On December 20, 1936, Morgenthau delivered a speech to the Federation of Brotherhoods of the Temples and Synagogues of Baltimore, calling for America to rededicate itself to the preservation of democracy and freedom. "In 1936, there are any number of lands which have rejected democracy without having tried it, or have experimented with it and then pronounced it wanting," he said. "And even in countries possessed of long sustained democratic traditions, there are those who insist that ours is not the best pattern for social living." He added that the need to preserve democracy was especially important for minorities, who can thrive and practice their religions and traditions within a democratic system.[11] Morgenthau delivered this speech ten months before Franklin Roosevelt gave what became known as his Quarantine speech in Chicago, in which he called for a policy to "quarantine" aggressor states as an alternative to the neutrality so prevalent in the United States. By any measure, FDR's speech was restrained, but it resulted in an uproar by isolationists, who accused the president of trying to draw Americans into another European war. Hamilton Fish, the ranking Republican on the House Committee on Foreign Affairs, called it "dangerous, hysterical and inflammatory."[12]

Roosevelt continued to scheme privately against the aggressors, but his cabinet in late 1938 included only two fervent antifascists: Morgenthau and Secretary of the Interior Harold Ickes, both officially responsible mainly for domestic issues. The secretaries with foreign-affairs portfolios were Secretary of State Cordell Hull and Secretary of War Harry Woodring, a confirmed isolationist. Hull was by no means an isolationist. In fact, he had devoted his tenure in the State Department to increasing US trade with other countries. Given that his wife, Rose, was Jewish, he also understood that brutality was the essence of Nazism. But he was ferocious (as much as this silver-haired, soft-spoken gent from Tennessee could be ferocious) in his devotion to the Neutrality Acts. First enacted in 1935 and renewed annually, these acts prohibited the United States from dealing arms to combatants in a foreign conflict and, in effect, all but prevented the country from aiding the victims of aggression.

It would be wrong to say that Morgenthau disliked Hull or that they were members of different factions. There were no factions in the Roosevelt cabinet largely because the president never allowed any to develop. In fact, the president never let any secretary feel secure enough to form his own faction. But Morgenthau and Hull had profound differences of opinion on foreign policy, which was, after all, Hull's bailiwick. "Despite the fact that he was not at all fully or accurately informed on a number of questions of foreign policy with which he undertook to interfere, we found from his earliest days in the Government that he seldom lost an opportunity to take long steps across the line of State Department jurisdictions," Hull wrote of Morgenthau in his memoirs. He hinted that Morgenthau's motivation was often that he was "emotionally upset by Hitler's rise and his persecution of the Jews" rather than a rational belief that Nazism threatened the United States.[13]

Now Morgenthau's two senior advisers wanted him to go to Roosevelt to say the president had the option to impose duties on the commerce of the aggressor states. Morgenthau told Oliphant and White bluntly that it was a waste of time and that they couldn't penalize these countries just because they didn't like their governments. He didn't have to add that they all knew the State Department would block any optional policy to set the tariffs.

"What I'd hoped you'd say, what I'm begging for you to say, is that it's illegal not to set. See?" he said. "Now if it's just a question of judgment, of aims, I can't get anywhere. But if you say to me that as Secretary of the Treasury the law directs me . . . then I have something to work with."[14]

Morgenthau had a tendency to fumble for his words, and he often sputtered out confusing phrases like "illegal not to set." Often when instructing his staff, he talked around a subject, on and on, rarely stating categorically what he wanted but always letting them know what he meant. It frequently took several sentences for him to convey his meaning. He now said he had only so much influence with the president, and White finally understood, saying he knew the secretary wouldn't get to first base with an optional proposal.[15]

They agreed Oliphant and White would examine the matter again, but before they broke up, Morgenthau wanted to read out something White had handed him before the meeting. It was a draft letter the economist and his wife had prepared that weekend that they hoped the secretary would sign and hand to the president. Morgenthau now began to discuss it then read it out loud.

"The events of the past weeks have brought home to all of us the increasing effectiveness of the forces of aggression," the note began; it then went on to document the heinous advance of dictatorships in the past five years. It made quite clear that the aggressor states were a threat to the United States and that only the US government under Roosevelt had the wherewithal to stop them. The letter finished with a passionate appeal for Roosevelt to act.

"Mr. President, I beg that you will not let pass this historic opportunity of a first effective economic measure against aggression, this great moral gesture so sorely needed in a world in which 'appeasement' has superseded morality," concluded the letter. "I have never felt more sure of the wisdom of an investment; I have never felt more sure of its urgency."[16]

When Morgenthau finished, they all congratulated White, and Morgenthau's enthusiasm began to grow. He realized the potential of the letter. He knew Roosevelt in his heart of hearts understood the United States had to stand up to the aggressor nations. What he needed was a call to action. But Morgenthau also knew what the letter was missing. He directed White to rework the letter to include two proposals—first, to extend credit to China; and second, to use the US reserves of gold to help develop Latin America. He noted that if Germany's neighbors contained it, Hitler would have to come to the New World for the raw materials needed for his armament program. By increasing its presence in Latin America, the United States could influence decision making among the southern governments and deny Germany that market. Then Morgenthau revealed the true intelligence of his proposals. He knew that two senior State Department officials, Herbert Feis and Stanley Hornbeck, wanted to aid China, and another faction gathered around Under Secretary of State Sumner Welles wanted to bolster US influence in Mexico and South America. Morgenthau told his aides that they could gain support from the two largest blocs within the State Department by uniting these policies, and in doing so they might be able to outflank Cordell Hull. It was a clever stroke—the type of gambit that demonstrated Morgenthau was cleverer than his reputation.

Morgenthau was now upbeat and ready to fight the State Department. In a more cheerful mood, he told Oliphant, White, and Klotz that the previous night he and his wife had eaten dinner with two other Roosevelt advisers, Tommy Corcoran and Ben Cohen, usually identified with the left wing of the party, the group often hostile to Morgenthau. They'd discussed the growing international problems, and Morgenthau had spoken of the need to confront aggressors. Corcoran, known as Tommy the Cork, proposed that they assemble a group of fifty hawkish senators and make them a unified force with Morgenthau at the center. Morgenthau graciously declined, likely because he would do nothing to jeopardize his standing with FDR. Corcoran understood but added that Morgenthau had the type of unified department needed to fight the burgeoning enemy. "He was kind enough to say that in the Treasury I have the most loyal group of any other department in Washington," Morgenthau told them. "He said, 'You've got the nucleus; you have—you're the only department that has the nucleus.'"[17]

Morgenthau knew that nucleus was sitting in that wood-paneled office with him. Oliphant and White were probably as brilliant as any civil servants in Washington. And in Klotz, Morgenthau had a completely stalwart adviser whose value extended far beyond her work as a secretary. At the center of it all was Henry Morgenthau Jr. himself. He was the one controlling this crucial engine of government at a critical moment in the history of not just the United States but also the world. Few people realized it, and none would have believed it possible a decade earlier. For in his first four decades, it looked as if Henry Morgenthau Jr. would never amount to much of anything.

Henry Morgenthau Jr.'s eldest sister, Helen, once described him as "a disappointing kid brother who didn't amount to much."[18] Though he was a big, athletic boy who had no shortage of friends, he was a weak student with little drive. Had the condition been known at the time, he probably would have been diagnosed as dyslexic. And the pressures to succeed were immense, given his father and namesake's remarkable successes in business, politics, and diplomacy.

The senior Henry Morgenthau was born in 1856 in Mannheim, Germany, where his father, Lazarus Morgenthau, ran a cigar-manufacturing business. Shipping mainly to the United States, the business thrived until 1862, when Abraham Lincoln imposed tariffs on tobacco to help finance the American Civil War, and the Morgenthaus' market collapsed. In 1866 the family moved to New York City but struggled as Lazarus frittered away their savings on foolish business ventures then slowly descended into insanity. When Henry Morgenthau married Josephine "Josie" Sykes on May 10, 1883, he hired two Pinkerton National Detective Agency operatives to follow Lazarus and apprehend him if he showed up at the ceremony or reception.[19]

After graduating from Columbia Law School in 1877, Henry Morgenthau began to invest in real-estate deals. In 1890, he headed a syndicate that bought an option on sixteen city blocks in the neighborhood of 181st Street in Washington Heights. The options cost $50,000 and valued the lots at $980,000. Then in May 1891—the same month, coincidentally, that his third child and only son, Henry Jr., was born—the syndicate subdivided the lots and auctioned them off for $1.49 million. Morgenthau had made more than ten times his money in less than a year, and suddenly the media and business community took notice of the young émigré.[20]

Morgenthau continued his shrewd investments, usually in real estate but also in industrial companies, such as Underwood Typewriter Company. He formed the Central Realty Bond and Trust Company in 1899 to combine finance and real estate in a single vehicle. The company's stock doubled in three months. Two years after it was formed, its annual profit equaled the original capital investment. "The formation of the company, its plan of operations and its success are attributed to its president, Henry Morgenthau," said the *New York Times* in August 1902. "He has been known for several years as a shrewd, far-seeing real-estate operator and attracted public notice by the great success of his auction sale of the Morton Bliss tract on Washington Heights in 1891 and in numerous subsequent real estate transactions."[21]

He was also known for his philanthropy and was a leading advocate of proper urban planning to replace the slums that housed growing hordes of immigrants. He prided himself on the quality of his developments, such as Hunt's Point in the Bronx. As a longtime supporter of the Democratic Party, President Woodrow Wilson appointed Henry Morgenthau Sr. ambassador to Turkey during World War I. He led the US protest against the Armenian Genocide during the war and served in other diplomatic missions.

The only disappointment in his life seemed to be his son, Henry Jr. The big, rambunctious kid couldn't get along at the prestigious Phillips Exeter Academy, where he found the work difficult. "I have just got 'C plus' in an algebra examination which I [thought] rather good," he told his parents in a letter after returning to school from the Christmas break in 1906, no doubt failing to bring joy to his successful father's heart. He eventually left the school.[22]

He later dropped out of architectural school at Cornell University. After falling in love with farm life during a stay at a ranch in Texas, he studied agriculture at Cornell, only to drop out again. All his life, the younger Henry Morgenthau lionized his father while trying to escape his overbearing control, and he sought to escape his father's meddling by becoming a farmer, according to the family memoir of Henry III. He bought a thousand-acre spread called Fishkill Farm, with a mature apple orchard and a cattle operation, located just south of Poughkeepsie. It was an hour and a half by train up the Hudson River Valley from New York. He adored the land and people of the area, a hilly landscape of farmland and hardwood forest. He relished the bucolic joy of riding his horse through his apple orchard at harvest time. The price was $55,000, and his father—whose meddling Henry Jr. was supposed to be escaping—put up half the money.[23]

In 1916, Henry Morgenthau Jr. married Elinor Fatman, a vivacious Vassar College graduate who had grown up in his New York City neighborhood. Henry Jr., his wife, Elinor, and their three children lived a dual life through the 1920s, dividing their time between New York and Fishkill. In addition to running the farm, he also published a magazine, the *American Agriculturalist*, which he purchased during this period. In his Washington career, he presented himself as a gentleman farmer, which served him well in his first federal job as the head of the Farm Credit Administration. What he failed to tell people was his farm lost money just about every year he owned it, and by the end of 1932 it had produced a cumulative loss of $168,690—three times the initial capital he and his father had put into it.[24]

The magazine was a money drain as well. "It is not much of a business that produces $185,000 and costs $200,000 to do so," the elder Henry Morgenthau wrote his son.[25] The fact was that Henry and Elinor Morgenthau got by on the family money, including a hefty inheritance Elinor received after 1926 and money Henry received regularly from family trust funds. (When Elinor died in 1949, she was worth about $2 million; whereas her husband's net worth was about $360,000.[26])

Throughout the 1920s, one of Henry Morgenthau Jr.'s main occupations was acting as business agent for his father, looking after his real-estate concerns in greater New York, and acting on his behalf in several business dealings. The family even had a peripheral role in the event that some people believe sparked the great crash of 1929. In 1927, a Morgenthau-led group bought a company called Photomaton, which pioneered the first photo booths. Capitalizing on the craze for these booths and their instant photos, the syndicate listed the company below ten dollars a share, and it hit fifteen dollars in four months, leading Henry Jr. to advise selling some stock. "This would put HM & Son on Easy Street," he wrote his father. "We all have to take our hats off to you on Photomaton." Expansion proved expensive, and the syndicate in January 1929 agreed to sell Photomaton to a company owned by British investor Clarence Hatry. On Friday, September 20, as the Americans waited for the deal to close, Hatry and three partners were charged with a massive fraud in London and the stock of the companies he controlled were suspended. The Hatry scandal sparked a huge sell-off in London and Berlin the following Monday. The nervous selling spread to New York, and the markets did not recover. The crash came one month later, and some historians said the panic really began with the Hatry scandal.[27]

The letters between father and son through the 1920s show that the elder Morgenthau was semiretired and either traveling the world or looking after his ailing wife. His son took care of his New York interests. And in turn, Henry Jr. drew on the family resources throughout the 1920s and even during his time in government. In 1938 alone, Henry would receive checks from one fund worth $6,000 (about $99,000 in 2013, when adjusted for inflation) in addition to his salary and perks as Treasury secretary.[28]

★ ★ ★

While his best friends—such as *New York Times* managing director Arthur Hays Sulzberger, American Metal Company vice president Harold K. Hochschild, and Sullivan and Cromwell partner Alfred Jaretzki—had successful careers in New York, Morgenthau amounted to little until he began to work closely with Franklin Roosevelt. No one knows when they met, but by the mid-1920s, they and their wives were close friends, and the Morgenthaus were devoted workers in their neighbor's political endeavors.

The lone son of James and Sara Roosevelt, Franklin Delano Roosevelt was reared in the virtually aristocratic environment of old New York families, attending Groton School and Harvard College and vacationing in Europe with his parents. Though trained as a lawyer, he followed his calling as a politician early, entering the New York State Senate just shy of his twenty-ninth birthday in 1911 and being named assistant secretary of the navy two years later. He was one of the bright young prospects in the Democratic Party, though some assumed his political career was over when he was struck with polio at age thirty-nine and could stand only with leg braces thereafter. The disease did nothing to dampen his ambition, and he was voted governor of New York in 1929. The Morgenthaus were also stalwart workers and contributors when Roosevelt successfully ran for the presidency in 1932, defeating Herbert Hoover.

They were an odd pairing: Roosevelt was smooth, dapper, and charming; whereas Morgenthau was tall, ungainly, and inarticulate. They shared a common patrician outlook, a liberal idealism, and a love of rural life among the gentry. No doubt, in an age of considerable anti-Semitism, the son of a German Jewish immigrant was heartened to have such a close friend who was not only gentile but also a member of an old New York family. They also possessed complementary senses of humor. When the Roosevelts came calling at Fishkill, Morgenthau would help the driver carry his guest in his wheelchair up the front steps. Roosevelt knew Morgenthau was ticklish and would poke his giggling host in the ribs throughout the whole exercise.[29] In cabinet meetings, the two men exchanged notes with silly jokes, the meanings of which only they could understand. Even social cards had a playful air. On the invitation to his fiftieth birthday luncheon in 1932, FDR typed:

```
       ELINOR I WANT TO KNOW
     WHAT MAKES HENRY ARGUE SO
   DON'T HE GET A CHANCE AT HOME
   TO MAKE HIS OPINIONS KNOWN?30
```

It is difficult to overstate the impact Franklin Roosevelt's approval or disapproval had on Henry Morgenthau Jr. Diary entries from Morgenthau frequently mention the president's mood, whether he was kindly, harsh, indifferent, or sarcastic toward his friend and underling. It's wrong to say, as many have, that Morgenthau was a yes-man or that he served in government only to win Roosevelt's approval. *Wall Street Journal* columnist Frank R. Kent, in March 1939, compiled a list of "complete Yes Men" within the Roosevelt circle and named Morgenthau first (though Kent would also praise Morgenthau for his courage in standing up to the president three weeks later).[31] Morgenthau had his own agenda and worked tirelessly to achieve it, and he would fight back when the president belittled him. But it is no exaggeration to say he yearned for Roosevelt's approval and grew depressed when he suffered the president's wrath or that Roosevelt's disposition had a deep psychological impact on him. Neither had had a brother growing up, and there was a fraternal relationship between them, with Roosevelt always playing the role of older brother.

In December 1938, Morgenthau broke his toe and phoned FDR's secretary, Missy LeHand, to ask if the president had a spare cane he could borrow. FDR was on the phone immediately, asking about his injury.

"What are you kicking about?" the president jeered.

"I am kicking the furniture about."

"Did you really lose your temper? Whom did you miss?"

"I was just walking bare-footed across the room and ran into a piece of furniture." Morgenthau went on to explain that he was now wearing a moccasin, as his shoes wouldn't fit and it would be three weeks until the injury healed.

"You can't come to the Diplomatic dinner and reception in a moccasin!" said the president.

"Well, I promise to have it all healed by the time the King arrives," said Morgenthau, referring to the visit of King George VI and Queen Elizabeth, which had been recently announced for the coming June.

When they hung up, Morgenthau thought for a moment and turned to Henrietta Klotz, who had recorded the conversation. "You know, I am just a baby about it," he said. "Part of the reason I sent for the cane was because I wanted the president to know that I had broken my toe."[32]

There was one final trait that Franklin Roosevelt and Henry Morgenthau shared: the complete obsession with advancing the career of Franklin Roosevelt. A tireless worker and a great organizer, Henry Morgenthau was known in 1938 as Roosevelt's closest confidant. He had been shocked to be omitted from cabinet when his friend took office in March 1933, but he took on the Farm Credit Administration, which was charged with refinancing the nation's farms. It's easy to forget what a crucial job this was. Agriculture was the largest industry in the United States but had been in decline since the early 1920s, and farm foreclosures were rampant. Morgenthau consolidated and reenergized the federal apparatus for agricultural lending, and within eighteen months, the FCA refinanced one-fifth of the farms in the United States.[33]

By late 1933, Morgenthau had positioned himself as a key member of FDR's inner circle. It appeared certain by that time that the administration would need a new Treasury secretary. The incumbent, William Woodin, had worked with Roosevelt on landmark financial reforms in a short period—recapitalizing the country's banks, establishing the Securities and Exchange Commission, creating deposit insurance, and beginning work on the creation of Social Security. But now he was terminally ill and his department was at odds with a key provision of the New Deal—the government's purchasing of all gold in the United States at a price set by the president. The new president wanted gold to rise because of a theory that the rising gold price would lead to higher prices for other commodities, which would benefit farmers. The Treasury peerage considered government gold purchases unconstitutional, but at Morgenthau's urging,

Herman Oliphant unearthed a Civil War–era law that allowed it. Morgenthau was the president's closest ally in the gold-buying scheme. Each morning, he'd go to the president's bedroom, where Roosevelt would set the price of gold, up a few cents most days but dropping it the next to foil speculators. One day he set the price at $33.21, joking that he chose it because three times lucky seven is twenty-one. Morgenthau went along with the plan wholeheartedly, and it may have helped him take control of the Treasury when Woodin retired in late 1933.[34] Though proponents of low inflation favored the elevation of Under Secretary of the Treasury Dean Acheson, Roosevelt surprised the nation in November by choosing Henry Morgenthau as acting secretary. The media and other observers were baffled by the appointment of a farmer to the government's top financial post—a seeming Jeffersonian ensconced in Hamilton's office. "Henry Morgenthau Jr. is just about the most obscure Secretary of the Treasury this country has ever had," began a largely flattering profile in the May 1934 issue of *Fortune*. Still, the article also noted he was a "humdinging executive."[35] Most observers assumed that the president simply wanted a yes-man in the post. "Mr. Roosevelt intends to be his own secretary of the treasury, just as he has shown himself his own secretary of state, and in this picture Henry Morgenthau, by reason of his supreme faith in the leadership of Franklin Roosevelt, is held to fit with perfection," wrote John Boettiger in the *Chicago Tribune*.[36] *Time* magazine would later report that one of Morgenthau's own sisters wrote to her son: "I can't understand why the President appointed your Uncle Henry. . . . He knows that Henry knows nothing about finance."[37]

Morgenthau's tenure began badly. He tried to appoint family friend Earle Bailie as a special assistant but had to withdraw the nomination because Bailie's brokerage firm, J. and W. Seligman, had been involved in selling Peruvian bonds that defaulted.[38] And Morgenthau was accused of censorship by decreeing that only he and public-relations officer Herbert Gaston could speak to the press, restricting media access to Treasury officials.[39] By the time the word *acting* was removed from his title in January 1934, the storm had passed and Morgenthau began to run an efficient Treasury. He attracted and promoted sterling administrators, and his Treasury was known not only for its efficiency but also for its ethics. He developed a method of implementing policy: devising it with his staff, selling it to Roosevelt, gaining broader support, and then implementing it efficiently. And he had Herman Oliphant, one of the smartest liberals in the government.

The two men had actually met at Roosevelt's inauguration in 1933, when Morgenthau was feeling rejected after being excluded from cabinet. As compensation, Roosevelt had appointed him the head of the Farm Credit Administration. He asked Oliphant, a native of Indiana, to join him. Oliphant had been a liberal professor of law at three leading universities—Chicago, Columbia, and Johns Hopkins—and had acted as counsel for striking transit workers in New York City and protested the execution of anarchists Sacco and Vanzetti. He had a creative mind, which Morgenthau himself often described as "ingenious."[40]

That Oliphant was regarded as the brains behind Morgenthau was highlighted at the 1937 Gridiron Dinner, the annual gathering of the Washington press corps. One skit featured a newspaperman posing as Morgenthau and another as Oliphant. Other journalists shouted out questions about taxes, prefacing each with the words, "Mr. Secretary." After each query, Morgenthau stood silent while Oliphant delivered the answer. Then Morgenthau repeated Oliphant's answer word for word, pausing occasionally for prompting from Oliphant.[41]

During the New Deal, Oliphant devised the excess-profits tax on corporations, one of the administration's most controversial economic policies. In a time of high taxation (the maximum personal tax rate was 75 percent), the administration charged that family-owned businesses avoided taxes by retaining profit within their company and paying for as many of their household expenses as they could through their corporations. Oliphant devised a means of taxing these "undistributed profits," which intensified the business community's enmity toward Roosevelt and suppressed the private sector's ability to invest in economic growth. The National Association of Manufacturers, in August 1937, charged that the tax stymied plant expansion and replacement, as such investments were often financed through retained earnings.[42] Congress weakened the tax in

1937. With the controversy over the tax, Oliphant became a figurehead for the heavy-handed side of the Roosevelt administration so hated by the business community.[43]

In the Treasury, Morgenthau's triumphs were numerous, including the Treasury's bond program that raised the billions needed to finance the New Deal and did so while keeping interest rates on the bonds below 3 percent. He grew as a statesman, and his crowning glory came in 1936 when he brokered the Tripartite Pact, a currency-stabilization pact between the United States, Britain, and France. A series of financial crises in the 1920s and 1930s had caused wild currency fluctuations, shaking all major economies. Other statesmen since World War I had tried in vain to craft a similar deal, but Morgenthau was the first to succeed. "With the world drifting on a dangerous tide, it seems improbable that one of the few to cast out an anchor should be this man," wrote the *Saturday Evening Post*. "But Henry Morgenthau snatched the tripartite agreement from the turmoil of the French Crisis."[44] On the fourth anniversary of Morgenthau's appointment, a reporter for the *Wall Street Journal*, which was certainly no booster of the Roosevelt White House, wrote, "He has come to be regarded by many of those who know the Washington scene best, as one of the most influential executive officials on matters of important, basic government policy."[45]

What the press, and indeed few in Washington, appreciated in 1938 was that Morgenthau and Roosevelt had recently endured one of the nadirs of their relationship, and the year was a difficult one for the Treasury secretary. In fact, Morgenthau had threatened to resign months earlier because the president had imposed a budget on him with which he heartily disagreed. The United States had slipped into recession that year, and Morgenthau believed the best cure for the malaise was a balanced budget and revitalized performance by private enterprise. But on April 11, Roosevelt and a handful of left-leaning advisers told Morgenthau they had decided on a public-works budget of $1.45 billion beginning July 1—worth about 17 percent of the total fiscal 1938 federal budget. Morgenthau was outraged and let influential congressmen know he estimated the move would inflate the federal deficit, which he had been trying to shrink, to about $3.5 billion.[46] In fiscal 1937, the deficit had been $2.6 billion.

Two days later, Morgenthau entered the Oval Office to air his grievances. "Mr. President," he said, "I am going to say something that is one of the most difficult things that I have ever had to do, but if you insist on going forward with this spending program I am seriously thinking of resigning." The two old friends calmly discussed the matter, and at the end Roosevelt told Morgenthau he had done a "magnificent job" as Treasury secretary.[47] The president did not back down on his budget plans, and Morgenthau did not resign. He no doubt believed the president needed him to help combat the Nazis and run the government, and it was also likely that he had no other prospects if he left the administration.

The deteriorating international situation also added to Morgenthau's stress level that year, as he thought the State Department was handling it badly. In particular, the two departments were at odds over the nationalist government of General Chiang Kai-shek in China, which had been asking for financial aid for years. On December 10, 1934, Morgenthau received a letter from H. H. Kung, China's minister of finance and Chiang's brother-in-law, asking the United States for various forms of aid, including financial assistance to support his currency reforms.[48] Morgenthau had long sympathized with Chiang, whom he grouped with the band of democratic leaders threatened by the aggressor nations, even though Chiang had never stood in an election. The Chiang clan continued to request aid over the years and, in late June 1938, asked for a loan so it could purchase US flour and cotton. Morgenthau worked hard to agree to the request, but he needed State Department approval to extend the loan. Secretary of State Cordell Hull refused, insisting that the United States under the Neutrality Act could lend money to China only if it made the same offer to Japan. Morgenthau—as he had done for years—helped out the Chinese by buying silver from them, but the situation was deteriorating rapidly in China and the country needed American help. Roosevelt told Morgenthau he supported the loan but wanted him to secure State Department approval before the government granted it. Oliphant proposed ways to issue the loan using such agencies as the Commodities Credit Corporation and the Export-Import Bank, but Hull could not be convinced.

The request dragged on and represented one of the low points in Morgenthau's often-troubled relationship with Hull. He had railed against Hull in staff meetings and had pressured State Department underlings. He'd even badmouthed the secretary of state to Roosevelt himself. During a private discussion on September 19, Morgenthau slipped this into the conversation: "You know, Mr. Hull, as represented to the public, is about one-hundred percent different than the real Mr. Hull." The president knew Morgenthau was referring to Hull's image as an honorable Dixie aristocrat, yet he agreed readily. Encouraged, Morgenthau ventured further by saying, "You know last June or July you put up to him this question of assisting the Chinese and he followed his usual policy by trying to wear us out and then do nothing." Again, FDR agreed, saying, "That is right." Yet another three weeks passed after that, and still the State Department had not approved the loan to China.[49]

As the Sudeten Crisis reached its climax, Morgenthau wanted more and more to help China, but he was unable to circumvent the stubborn secretary of state. "We might just as well recognize that the democratic form of government in my lifetime is finished," he told his staff with an air of exhaustion on September 22. "There is a bare chance we may still keep a democratic form of Government in the Pacific, but only a bare chance." When his staff pressed him to push the president harder to force Hull to approve the loan, Morgenthau declined. "In the first place [Roosevelt]'s in no frame of mind and physically I am not in shape to go to him," he said. In closing, he added, "I'm all played out."[50] A week later, Neville Chamberlain of Great Britain and Édouard Daladier of France gave in to Hitler at Munich, and Morgenthau was crippled by a wave of migraine headaches. The matter of the loan to China—like so many other Treasury efforts to battle the aggressors—had yet to be resolved.[51]

Henry Morgenthau Jr.'s close relationship with Franklin Roosevelt was complemented by his proximity to the president. The neoclassical Treasury Building—an imposing structure with a towering, eight-columned portico facing Pennsylvania Avenue—lies adjacent to the White House. The president could call his confidant at a moment's notice. The president was rumored to make a practice of phoning Morgenthau and yelling, "Henry, come hold my hand," and hanging up.[52] No other secretary's office was so close to the Oval Office, giving Morgenthau an advantage over his rivals during cabinet disputes. Other members of the Roosevelt inner circle suspected Morgenthau went behind their backs to snitch on them to the president. As often as not, their suspicions were correct. If that wasn't enough, Fishkill Farms was about an hour's drive from Springwood, the Roosevelts' Italianate mansion in Hyde Park overlooking the Hudson River. Henry Morgenthau would often drive through the birch and maple forests to visit the president when they were both at home.

On the evening of October 17, 1938, with the autumn colors turning, the Treasury secretary made the short jaunt north to Hyde Park to meet the president. It was the time of year Morgenthau adored, for he loved to ride horses amid the trees bearing ripe apples on his hilly farm. But on this evening he was nervous, as he had to show the president the letter that Harry Dexter White had crafted. White had written an eleven-page version, then expanded it to eighteen pages, and finally whittled it down to three pithy pages.[53] As he traveled to Springwood, the secretary wondered what the president's reaction would be. Would he dismiss the message and, with it, the plans to take a stand against the aggressor nations? Would he keep the letter? Would he throw it away?

Once they were settled down, Morgenthau began reading the letter to the president, who listened intently. "I know you are firmly convinced as I am firmly convinced that the forces of aggression must be stopped," he read. "By whom if not by us?"[54] White's words began to hit home. The president was soon interrupting Morgenthau with interjections like, "Grand," "Fine," and even "Bully." Then the president took the letter, read it carefully for himself, and kept the document—a point Morgenthau thought significant.[55] The secretary's timing was splendid. Other advisers, such as Bernard Baruch, had been urging a rearmament program. So Morgenthau caught the president just as he had been mulling over the country's military requirements and discussing the need for increased aircraft production. "Certainly, I got the most hearty reception from the President," he told a dozen staff members two days later.[56]

Though the United States was woefully under-armed and under-staffed on all fronts, aircraft production was a high-profile item in the arms program, largely because no one completely knew its military potential. The last time the United States Army (the air force would not be a separate service until 1947) had fought air battles was the Great War, in the days of Sopwith Camels and Fokker Triplanes. Aerial technology had advanced several generations in the ensuing two decades, so military aircraft were now made of metal, able to reach speeds of 250 miles per hour, and drop devastating payloads of bombs with some accuracy. In Spain, the German air force of Hermann Göring had displayed the brutal power of aerial bombardment, most famously at Guernica. But the Spanish Civil War was a small, land-based conflict and held only clues of the potency of air power. Military experts were divided on several aspects of aerial warfare: how effective air power could be in supporting an advancing tank battalion; whether air power could render naval power obsolete; whether aerial bombing could sink a battleship; and whether a civilian population could be bombed into submission. What was indisputable though was that the United States' air power was lagging behind most of its potential allies and enemies.

Just that week, *Time* magazine reported that naval experts had estimated the air fleet of the seven largest powers, and the United States placed sixth in terms of number of aircraft with 2,700 to 3,000. The Soviet Union led with 5,000 to 6,500 planes, including bombers, fighters, transports and reconnaissance planes; followed by Germany (4,000–4,500); Italy (3,700–4,200); France (3,200–3,500); and Great Britain (3,000–3,500). The United States exceeded only Japan, which was estimated to have something more than 2,500 aircraft. No one knew who had the most-advanced aircraft, though the average Soviet plane was believed to perform at about 30 percent the rate of its US counterpart. And it was understood that the German air force was becoming the most advanced in the world because it was producing about one thousand planes per month. That compared with fewer than three hundred per month by the United States and a combined total of one hundred per month for France and Britain. "Göring has been to the European war plane what Ford was to the car," wrote *Time*.[57]

What was shocking was that *Time*'s figures were more optimistic than those of the government. The White House secretly estimated the number of military aircraft ready for battle in Europe to be 1,500 to 2,200 for Great Britain and less than 600 for France. It believed Germany had 5,500 to 6,500 first-line planes and 2,000 second-line planes, while Italy had 2,000 first-line and 1,000 second-line planes. The army agreed with the White House's figures, though it estimated the Germans had 1,000 to 2,000 more airplanes than the administration's estimate.[58]

Now Roosevelt was ready to act to narrow the gap and even exceed the German program. Though officially neutral, it was becoming obvious the United States had to rearm in an increasingly bellicose world simply to defend itself. Convening a meeting at the White House a few days later, he told Morgenthau and other insiders he wanted to raise US aircraft production to a previously unthinkable number—15,000 planes per year. To achieve that, the United States would have to almost quintuple its aircraft-manufacturing capacity. With Morgenthau struggling to grasp all the implications, Roosevelt began to reveal the broad outlines of a plan. Private industry could continue to produce about 3,000 units per year, and the government would manufacture about 12,000. The president estimated it would require eight factories to be built around the country, operating around the clock. They'd be built on the outskirts of major cities where the government could find personnel with the needed trades. He figured the program would create employment and reduce relief payments by about $900 million. The Treasury would need about $3 billion to pay for the aircraft program, and $2 billion of that could be covered by a special national-defense tax.[59]

The numbers seemed suspect to Morgenthau, who believed Roosevelt was greatly underestimating the cost of each airplane. It didn't really matter. What he was absolutely euphoric about was that the president was ready to rearm America—and that Morgenthau and his Treasury would be a key component in FDR's war machine.

CHAPTER TWO

THE FRENCH MISSION

★ ★ ★

Within days, Morgenthau sat down with Budget Director Daniel Bell and Under Secretary of the Treasury John W. Hanes Jr. to examine the budgetary implications of the airplane program. He explained that the country now had a production capacity of about 3,600 airplanes a year, and the president wanted to more than quadruple it to 15,000. About 80 percent of the total would be manufactured at eight new, government-owned plants built near large cities like Philadelphia, Boston, and New York. The president proposed spending $3 billion on the airplane program, supported by $2 billion gained from a new defense tax. Total federal-government expenditures for the year were $8.4 billion, so the expenditure was substantial. But the president also assumed the project would create about 100,000 jobs, so the $1.45 billion funding for Harry Hopkins's Works Progress Administration would fall to about $500 million.[1]

Soon they were engaged in a discussion typical for this wood-paneled office on the southwest corner of the Treasury Building—a penetrating examination of economics and geopolitics, peppered with occasional pinches of Washington gossip. Morgenthau habitually assembled his staff here for this sort of analysis and banter, with the faithful Henrietta Klotz taking notes. He called it the 9:30 Group, because they met daily at 9:30 a.m. The office was the central nervous system for the biggest financial organization in the world, the US Treasury, and the secretary's desk was usually littered with documents on the department's various endeavors sent in from every corner of the globe. Portraits of two previous secretaries of the Treasury, Albert Gallatin (who served from 1801 to 1813) and Roger

Taney (from 1833 to 1834) gazed down on the proceedings. To the right of the desk was a broad window from which Morgenthau could see into the Oval Office. Visitors often noticed they could see silhouettes passing before the window of the president's office or flash bulbs popping if an event was being photographed. Morgenthau's windows were adorned with elegant curtains, and he'd installed blackout blinds, obviously so he could darken the room when he suffered a crippling migraine headache. Behind him was a door to his private toilet. If an important phone call came in during a staff meeting, he would extend the cord into the washroom and take it in private.[2]

Indulging in a touch of gossip, Morgenthau said Harry Hopkins, the administration's top relief organizer who was soon to be secretary of the Department of Commerce, was in Hyde Park discussing the airplane program with the president, even though the army and navy secretaries hadn't been told of it yet. A favorite of the president, Hopkins was witty and affable, and his record in job creation made him one of the bona fide New Dealers. Though they had rarely if ever clashed, Morgenthau considered Hopkins "flamboyant," by which he meant slightly shallow and shifty. The uncharismatic Henry the Morgue always seemed a tad jealous of his colleague's charisma, and the members of the Treasury believed their department deserved more credit than it got for financing the government's social programs. Now Morgenthau told his underlings Hopkins's main aim was to reduce the unemployment rolls before the next election, though he didn't want anyone to say he was playing politics with the unemployed. Turning to Klotz, he said Hanes and Bell were the ones responsible for funding work programs before Christmas in the previous two years, whereas Hopkins was the one who would lay the people off later.

"The fellow that's always taken the initiative the last two years to lay the people off is Hopkins," he said. "Mrs. Morgenthau said last night, 'It never enters his mind, what about these poor devils on the rolls, do they need work or don't they?'"[3]

"He's never thought in the last two years about the people, always in terms of projects," agreed Bell, an Illinois native who'd been running the Bureau of the Budget since September 1934.[4]

They debated whether the airplane program costs were realistic, and Morgenthau told them he was excited about the program. He felt he'd gotten his health back after feeling worn down around the time of the Munich Agreement and that he would soon be meeting with Army Chief of Staff Malin Craig to discuss the military's needs. It was part of Morgenthau's effort to nurture relations with the military and understand their spending needs. He told his staff he was "going to school" with General Henry Arnold, known as "Hap," the head of the air force, and he felt he'd grown especially close to General Craig. Morgenthau was flattered at one recent dinner party when Craig gestured to the Treasury secretary and told his wife, "In my old age I have finally found a man who is thoroughly honest and whom I love."[5]

Before the staff meeting broke up, Morgenthau broached a subject that had been on his mind, asking the advisers to keep it within the confines of his corner office. A few days earlier, the president had told him that the French government was sending a mission led by businessman Jean Monnet to build an airplane plant in Montreal, Canada. The French were worried about their arms factories being destroyed or captured by the Germans in the event of a war, so it made sense to establish their plants in Canada. They would need some help—certainly technical, possibly financial—from the US government and had enlisted the help of US ambassador to France William Bullitt to open doors in Washington. Morgenthau had agreed to meet with Bullitt and Monnet the coming weekend.

Suspicious by nature, Morgenthau had asked Harry Dexter White to look into the Monnet proposal, and White reported back: "On economic grounds, the proposal has very little merit."[6] Morgenthau had also checked with two other people whose opinions he valued immensely—his wife, Elinor, and his nineteen-year-old son, Robert. His son, still a college student, had seen one weakness with the plan, saying it was fine that Canada and Britain were now US allies, but there was no guarantee it would always be the case. Morgenthau did not say what his wife's reaction to the plan was (he rarely revealed his wife's opinions). But it's a fair bet he took her advice to heart. Their eldest son, Henry III, claimed that Morgenthau's closest advisers were his father and his wife. And if people underestimated the intelligence of Henry Morgenthau Jr., few did that of his wife. Her brilliance was recognized throughout Washington. "To sit and chat with Mrs. Henry Morgenthau is to enjoy a rare mental treat," wrote a reporter for the *Christian Science Monitor* early in the Roosevelt administration. "She possesses one of the keenest feminine minds in the country today."[7]

Born within a year of each other, Elinor "Ellie" Fatman and Henry Morgenthau Jr. grew up in the same New York neighborhood on West Eighty-First Street. Like the Morgenthaus, hers was a prosperous German Jewish family, though the Fatmans had nowhere near the wealth of Ellie's maternal cousins, the Lehmans of banking fame. Henry III said one reason his mother was so ambitious was that she had been raised in the financial shadow of her wealthy relatives. In fact, he said she bore a "lifelong resentment" of the Lehmans, though she was devoted, especially as a girl, to her cousin Herbert Lehman, who would succeed Roosevelt as governor of New York.

A graduate of Vassar College, Elinor spent her early adulthood in amateur theatre and volunteering at the Neighborhood Playhouse, an amateur troupe affiliated with the Henry Street Settlement, which delivered social services and arts programs to New Yorkers. She and Henry were married in April 1916.[8] Though she had been an athletic youth, she had gained weight as an adult, especially around her face. With deep-set eyes and an olive complexion, she accentuated her husband's lugubrious image when they were photographed together. She took an interest in politics, writing letters to papers in Dutchess County as early as 1921 to protest the state of schools, including the neglect of testing of their wells, the paucity of books, and the lack of support by the community. While her husband's syntax was garbled, Elinor's rhetoric was striking in its clarity.[9] Had she been born in a later age, it might have been Elinor, not Henry, who competed in the national political arena. But as a woman in upper-crust New York early in the twentieth century, she chose to support her husband, raising their children and working with him in Democratic politics in New York. By 1924, she was working with Eleanor Roosevelt and her circle of intimates on the women's division of the Democratic organization for New York State. Eleanor Roosevelt's letters from these days attest to the warmth between the two women and show the matronly Elea-nor's worry about her driven friend. "You must not get so tired," Eleanor chided Elinor in one 1926 letter. "I think you are a brick when you feel ill to do any work of this kind," read another undated missive. And another: "I am sorry you feel so miserable and nervous and I do hope you can have a little rest."[10] The fact was Elinor Morgenthau suffered an afflic-tion as severe as her husband's migraine headaches—excessive menstrual bleeding, which often left her floored with exhaustion. It was during these campaigns in New York State that Elinor and Eleanor fell out—almost irreparably. In October 1928, Henry Morgenthau was working as advance man for Roosevelt, and on one trip, his wife accompanied him, only to find that Eleanor's friend Nancy Cook had already arranged the event. Nancy Cook and Marion Dickerson were Eleanor Roosevelt's closest friends at the time, and Elinor Morgenthau resented them greatly. Henry Morgenthau, likely at Elinor's urging, complained to FDR, and the fallout almost cost his wife the friendship of Mrs. Roosevelt. In the exchange of letters between the various women that continued for almost a year, Eleanor Roosevelt let Elinor know she was "amazed" by her complaints and that "somehow I always forget how tragic things seem to you." The incident eventually blew over, but it highlighted the thinness of Elinor Morgenthau's skin.[11]

Once Henry Morgenthau was ensconced in the Treasury, Elinor became an invaluable political asset for her husband. She moved easily in Washington society, conversing with newsmen, royalty, and statesmen, and she even held her own when placed next to Albert Einstein at a White House dinner. She had a calmer temperament than her husband and would frequently cool him down when his temper got the better of him. She participated regularly in the events Eleanor Roosevelt organized for the "Cabinet Ladies," and as the wife of the Treasury secretary, she held the third-most prestigious place among them. Second place was held by Rose Frances Hull, wife of the secretary of state, another Jewess celebrated for her intelligence. The *New York Times* even noted that at White House social gatherings, Mr. and Mrs. Morgenthau were known to "do the Vir-ginia Reel in the East Room of the White House with the President calling the figures."[12]

Early in Roosevelt's administration, Elinor told the *Christian Science Monitor* her abiding passion was pacifism—odd considering she was married to Roosevelt's most stalwart hawk. She was also an avowed liberal (the *New York Times* said she contributed to "the human side" of her husband's job[13]), and counterbalanced the advice the secretary received from his father, who was more aligned with the business world. When Henry Morgenthau Jr. outlined his political philosophy at Temple University in June 1938, Elinor was at his side, asking journalists afterward if they would agree that it was a very "liberal speech."[14] After Joseph Alsop and Robert Kintner ran their three-part profile of Morgenthau in the *Saturday Evening Post*, Kintner wrote Morgenthau to thank a few people including Elinor, whose help was "invaluable."[15] She read Morgenthau's briefing papers on Treasury business, commenting sometimes not only on the subject but also on the quality of the staff member's analysis.[16] One Sunday after the war began in Europe, she attended a meeting at which the Treasury brass debated whether the Johnson Act—a 1934 act that barred loans to countries that had defaulted on their World War I loans—prevented the United States from extending short-term credit to democracies buying American-made armaments. At one point, the brainy Harry Dexter White asked her whether she believed the concept of cash-and-carry purchases would allow a ninety-day credit. "Not as written in the original statement but it would be written in this proviso," she responded, obviously pointing to a certain clause. "When I listened to the President the thing was to be bought and paid for; that was my interpretation." Concluding, she summed up a point the Treasury officials all agreed on: "Cash is not credit."[17] Just as Morgenthau let few of his staff call him "Henry," he always referred to his wife at staff meetings as "Mrs. Morgenthau" rather than "Elinor."

Morgenthau hosted Bullitt and Monnet for a dinner at his farm on October 22, 1938. Just two months earlier, the ambassador had hosted the Morgenthaus during their celebrated French vacation and had thrilled the Morgenthau boys with his mischievous spirit. But Monnet was more of a mystery, and Morgenthau was suspicious of the Frenchman and the plan for his financially desperate country to build overseas munitions plants. France had twice been forced to devalue its currency in the past two years, and Morgenthau understood her economic plight as well as any American. He tried to steer the conversation toward the financing of the project, but Bullitt kept returning to the operational side.

"Let's take it for granted that you could overcome all technical difficulties," Morgenthau finally said. "How much do you think the plant would cost? Twenty-five million dollars to build?"

"No," Monnet responded. "Fifty million to one hundred million dollars."

"How are you going to pay for that?"

"Frenchmen who have their money over here will subscribe to the stock," said Monnet.[18]

Morgenthau was incredulous. The French had been removing money from their country for several years as the threat of war grew. So he wondered aloud why any Frenchman would assume France would still be around to buy the planes if Monnet was so worried that he moved his money offshore. They bickered about the pricing details, and Morgenthau insisted the French did not have sufficient money to invest in such a project.

"Mr. Monnet, we figure that during the last four years, there must be at least four billion dollars in gold that has left France," he said. "Just as long as that is abroad, and what little money is left continues to leave France, there isn't any use talking about building aeroplanes or anything else. You people have to devise means and method whereby you get this money back."[19]

Morgenthau told Monnet point-blank that the government of Édouard Daladier had to issue decrees under which citizens would be jailed unless they repatriated their money. It would probably mean imprisoning two thousand people and discharging two-thirds of the cabinet because ministers kept their money offshore. Surprisingly, Bullitt and Monnet liked the idea, though the latter said only two or three people would need jail time.

"Mr. Monnet, if you don't do something like this, your country is through," Morgenthau said as the meeting ended. He repeated it twice for emphasis. "It's impossible for you to continue with the bulk of your capital abroad."

Bullitt and Monnet returned the next day, and the latter was profuse in his thanks to Morgenthau. The secretary once again encouraged him to jail people with money overseas, starting with Foreign Minister Georges Bonnet. Morgenthau said he had never seen Bullitt so enthusiastic about anything.[20] Days later, Morgenthau put feelers out through his network of businessmen and diplomats abroad to try to learn more about Jean Monnet.

Through the autumn, the Japanese continued to seize key regions in China, capturing Canton in the south on October 21 and posing a renewed threat to Hong Kong. Wuhan, a city four hundred miles west of Shanghai, where Chiang Kai-shek's government had retreated, fell on October 27. As a result, the government fled to Chungking, a depressing city on a rocky bluff overlooking the Yangtze River in the center of China. In Spain, the republican army was being beaten back by Franco to the northeast corner of the country. After a German embassy official was shot by a Jew in Paris, Germany exploded in the worst pogrom yet witnessed under the Nazis. Organized by Goebbels, the SS (*Schutzstaffel*) ran amok through the country, burning and vandalizing synagogues and Jewish-owned businesses and murdering dozens of Jews. The rampage became known as *Kristallnacht*, or the Night of Broken Glass. The sheer brutality of *Kristallnacht* galvanized public opinion around the world—especially in the United States—like no other event in almost six years of Hitler's rule.

By coincidence, the German savagery took place the day after the midterm elections in the United States, in which the Democrats lost seventy-two House seats to the Republicans. Morgenthau had spent election night in New York in the suite of his boyhood friend and *New York Times* publisher Arthur Hays Sulzberger. The party was packed with anti–New Dealers aglow with the Republican sweep. Morgenthau hung around just long enough to learn that his wife's cousin Herbert Lehman had been returned as governor of New York, then he left in dismay. Days later, he agreed with Cordell Hull that, "It could have been much worse [but is] as bad as I care to see it right now."[21]

Roosevelt understood the American people's outrage at the Nazi brutality and felt bolder now that the election was out of the way. He recalled the US ambassador from Berlin and issued his sternest statement yet against the Nazis, condemning their thuggery and saying that twenty countries in the Western Hemisphere would cooperate on defense. The *Baltimore Sun*, in its front-page article, said the president's message was understood in every quarter of Washington to mean that the United States would meet force with force if any power "turns resentful or covetous toward the western continents." One reporter at the press conference also asked the president whether he would recommend to Congress a loosening of immigration restrictions, and he answered he would not.[22]

Immigration policy and how to handle refugees were controversial issues because of anti-Semitism and because the Depression-weary country worried immigrants would take jobs from native-born Americans. What many Americans did not know was that immigration from Germany, mostly of Jewish refugees, had increased dramatically between 1933 and 1938. Exact figures are not known, and estimates of German Jewish immigrants to the United States from 1933 to 1938 range from 46,000 to 102,000.[23] Many Americans would have been appalled by the figures, given the prevailing anti-Semitism. When asked by pollsters in March 1938 whether they believed Jews held too much power in the United States, 41 percent of respondents replied yes. The number rose to 55 percent by 1946.[24] Such prominent individuals as industrialist Henry Ford, expatriate poets Ezra Pound and T. S. Eliot, and broadcaster Father Charles Coughlin publicly spoke of their distrust of Jews. Even within government, bigotry was a powerful force. "The Hebraic influence in the administration is very strong," former budget director Lewis Douglas wrote in his diary in March 1934. "Most of the bad things which it has done can be traced to it."[25]

Morgenthau naturally felt the difficulties of being Jewish in the United States, but he and his family worked endlessly to rise above them. The elder Henry Morgenthau told his son that anti-Semitism had always existed and always would and that the Jews simply had to accept it.[26] Henry Jr. and Elinor raised their children as Americans, not Jewish Americans. In fact, in their early years, the children did not even know they were Jewish. When a child asked five-year-old Henry III what his religion was, the lad didn't understand the question. When he asked his mother later what it meant, she replied, "Just tell them you're an American."[27] Yet no Jew could escape completely the pain of bigotry. When he worked for Roosevelt in Albany, Henry Morgenthau Jr. fired a chauffeur who called him "that Jew," "Kike," and "the dirty Jew from New York" behind his back.[28] Sometimes he used his religion to his advantage. For example, when he really needed to convince Roosevelt that he was speaking in earnest, he would remind the president that as a Jew he could seek no higher office than the position he held, so he was not taking a stance based on personal advancement.[29]

It's difficult to fully assess Morgenthau's opinion on the plight of European Jews before World War II. He rarely, if ever, broached the subject in his recorded discussions with his staff, and he steadfastly insisted he held his position on behalf of all Americans, not just Jewish Americans. Henry III would later write that both Elinor and Henry Morgenthau Sr. urged him not to become entangled in Jewish issues. Yet Henry Morgenthau Jr. *was* the most powerful Jew in the administration, and he and the president sporadically discussed the need to find neutral countries willing to accept Jewish refugees. There's no record of them talking about raising immigration limits within the United States, and Morgenthau tended to tread cautiously when urging settlements in Palestine. Great Britain, whose empire included Palestine, resisted Zionist demands to allow European Jews into the Holy Land because of protests from Palestinian Arabs. Morgenthau and Roosevelt focused discussions on virgin land that was economically and politically suitable for Jewish settlements.

On November 16, Morgenthau called the president to congratulate him on his condemnation of Germany and broached the refugee subject. He said someone named Constantin Maguire had suggested to him the settlements should be allowed in British Guinea and French Guinea in return for settling outstanding war debts of Britain and France.

"It's no good," responded the president. "It would take the Jews from twenty-five to fifty years to overcome the fever." He suggested the Cameroons, a former German colony now a possession of France.

They discussed various ideas, such as drawing up a list of former

German colonies where they could settle Jews. Morgenthau said the lands should be rich in natural resources, and the president mentioned countries with good climate and agricultural potential. Maybe, they agreed, they should write off about $500 million in war debts in return for the settlements. And Morgenthau added one criterion that his wife had insisted on: that these lands be open to refugees of all races, not just to Jews.

"The temper of the people today [dictates that] we can make this a political refuge for all creeds—I think the public is ready," Morgenthau recorded in his diary later. "The point is the President has this. Nobody is helping him. I am going at least to do the spade work."[30]

The spade work involved searching the globe for a suitable location, and Morgenthau enlisted the help of Dr. Isaiah Bowman, president of Johns Hopkins University, who gathered other academics and geographers (one of whom Morgenthau personally paid $100). They produced a short list of countries that would accept refugees that included Nicaragua, Guatemala, and El Salvador, eventually recommending Costa Rica. When Morgenthau forwarded that information to FDR, he noted that Costa Rica needed $5 million to cover settlement costs. But the president insisted that the settlement be within a British colony, probably because of the influence the United States exerted over the United Kingdom. By December they had come up with a vague plan that would cost $500 million over five years to rescue about half a million German Jews, to be spread throughout several British colonies, including Palestine.[31]

Meanwhile, the Treasury staff pressed on with policies to punish the Nazis and their accomplices, and many of these files were handled by Herman Oliphant. The general counsel worked with the heads of the military on a plan to manufacture aircraft and to prevent profiteering by private manufacturers.[32] The public had been outraged by arms profiteering in World War I, and the ethos of the New Deal demanded it not be repeated in the coming war. Oliphant also drew up customs rules for goods from Sudetenland entering the United States. Customs officials would no longer allow Sudeten products to be marked "Made in Czechoslovakia." When importers protested there had been more leniency when Austria was annexed by Germany, Oliphant replied it was a different situation:

there was no longer a country called Austria but there was still an independent country called Czechoslovakia.[33] And he prepared a memo saying the United States would probably have to impose duties on German goods because of the way that country treated US trade.[34]

Morgenthau continued to keep up the pressure on the State Department to approve a loan to the nationalist government in China, which Chiang's representative repeatedly demanded. Oliphant came up with a new plan, this time for the Chinese to sell tung oil, or wood oil, a key ingredient in paint, to various US companies. The income from those sales would be used to service a new loan from the US Export-Import Bank, worth about $150 million. Though Morgenthau wanted to help the Chinese, he could not grant the request as long as they were in perpetual retreat from the Japanese. "There are all these rumors about General Chiang Kai Shek and, frankly, I don't know whether I can or cannot recommend this, because I don't know what Government there will be in China to do business with," he told Chinese emissary K. P. Chen and ambassador Hu Shih in late October.[35]

As the Asian military situation stabilized, Morgenthau moved ahead with the tung-oil plan, which Roosevelt again approved as long as the State Department went along with it. But Hull and his staff prevaricated, insisting the plan had legal problems (which Oliphant solved) and violated the Neutrality Act. Following a cabinet meeting on November 11, Morgenthau suggested he accompany Hull back to the State Department offices to sign the appropriate papers, but Hull said he had to go meet the Italian ambassador. "I tried to get Hull again at five o'clock and he was playing croquet," Morgenthau recorded in his diary.[36] When Hull left Washington in late November, Morgenthau pressured Assistant Secretary of State Sumner Welles to approve the loans, insisting it was the president's wish that they do so. In one of their arguments, Welles struck at the heart of the situation when he responded that FDR had never told the State Department that he wanted the loan approved.[37] Roosevelt had a long history of overruling his cabinet members, and if he had really wanted the loans, he would have instructed Hull to approve it back in July. Morgenthau, of course, placed all the blame for the delays on Hull and his team, and none on the president.

The State Department finally approved a $25 million loan in December, and Morgenthau was responsible for organizing it. Former secretary of state and Republican Henry Stimson wrote in a letter to Morgenthau: "At this time when you may be receiving criticism as to the action of the Export-Import Bank in making the loan of $25,000,000 to China, I think you are entitled to the strong support of those citizens who believe that that action was wise and necessary. I am one of those."[38]

To outline plans for the coming arms program, Roosevelt called senior Treasury, State, Justice, army, and navy representatives to a conference at the White House on November 14. He opened by saying the Western Hemisphere was vulnerable in both its northern and southern continents for the first time since the Holy Alliance of 1818 and that the supreme power of Germany had reoriented the United States' international relations. If the United States had had five thousand planes and the ability to produce ten thousand more, he said, Hitler could not have taken the stand he did on Czechoslovakia. The United States needed enough planes to defend the Western Hemisphere and the political will to build up large armies. The group agreed that Roosevelt would ask Congress to approve the production of twelve thousand airplanes a year and the capacity to double that amount. He assumed the government would need to build seven factories at a cost of about $70 million.

Morgenthau was assigned to a committee on procurement rules, and the all-purpose Oliphant was to work with the army and the navy on writing the most cost-efficient contracts with private suppliers. Morgenthau was removed somewhat from the rearmament process for the time being. His most crucial task was working with the French Mission on a deal to supply first-line planes.

The French plane purchase was a task layered with complications, involving negotiations between the Treasury, the White House, the army, the State Department, private corporations, and a foreign country in unrelenting financial crisis. As well as the neutrality laws, Morgenthau had to adhere to the Johnson Act, which forbade credit to France because it had defaulted on World War I loans. And at the center was the mysterious Jean Monnet.

Throughout November, the secretary had waited for France to declare that it would reverse the flow of capital, but no declaration came. Roosevelt and Morgenthau both agreed they were sick and tired of the French government, whose authorities suppressed striking workers in Marseilles with bayonets. Monnet had chosen as his legal counsel Sullivan and Cromwell, the firm that was suing the US Treasury on behalf of Spanish general Francisco Franco over purchases of silver from Republican Spain. Still the French did nothing to reverse the flow of capital. "If the French don't really do something to get control of their own situation, I think they're through, and I think it's only a matter of months," Morgenthau told his staff.[39]

All that came was word that Monnet would return to the United States in mid-December, accompanied by three aviation technicians. They arrived bearing a letter from Prime Minister Daladier, saying the French government would like to buy one thousand planes from the United States and asking for delivery to begin in July 1939. FDR encouraged the discussions, and Sumner Welles gave his blessing to the talks, which the French demanded be kept secret. Monnet still wanted to make the purchases through a Canadian-based corporation and was hoping the United States would grant such a company credit of up to twelve months. Morgenthau told him to go to a commercial bank because the US Treasury could not lend him money without violating the Johnson Act.[40]

The internal differences within the US government mushroomed when the army and navy were brought into the talks. The military did not want the French orders for planes interfering with their own requirements from private manufacturers. Nor did it want France or Britain—foreign countries—armed with the best of American technology. In fact, US law prohibited foreign representatives from even seeing secret military devices or weapons. FDR had some sympathy for the soldiers' point of view. Morgenthau had none. "Think about it again," Morgenthau said to the president. "If you want them to be our first line [of defense], let's either give them good stuff or tell them to go home, but don't give them stuff that the minute it goes up in the air it will be shot down."[41]

He was also outraged that the army still had not placed orders with private factories, many of which were idle or producing under capacity. Morgenthau was even exasperated by the private manufacturers, such as Allison Motors, which was a subsidiary of General Motors but had the capacity to produce only three hundred airplane motors a year.[42]

Morgenthau believed French orders would actually increase capacity in the system and drive manufacturers to develop the machine tools needed to ramp up production.[43] But he didn't want to jeopardize the relationships he had developed with the generals. And maintaining good relations throughout the War Department was almost impossible because it was divided into two camps constantly battling one another. The first was led by Harry Woodring, the secretary of war and arch-isolationist. He publicly advocated strengthening the regular army, national guard, and reserves but fiercely opposed sending aid to Britain, France, or other allies. His nemesis was Assistant Secretary Louis Johnson, who was more amenable to arming the Allies, though he also drew the line at allowing France access to secret weapons.

By December 21, Morgenthau had produced a list of three planes, comparable to the latest German models, that the French should be allowed to test—the P-40 pursuit plane manufactured by the Curtiss-Wright Corporation with Allison Motors; the Douglas attack bomber, still in the possession of the Douglas Aircraft Company at Santa Monica; and the Martin Bomber model 166, now in production for export only.[44] The president okayed the request, and Morgenthau hoped to proceed with the inspections in the new year, not realizing the tragedy he would suffer before the next business day.

★ ★ ★

Colleagues later noted that Herman Oliphant was feeling under the weather when he left the office on December 21. At six the next morning, Henry Morgenthau's phone rang. It was Oliphant's family. Herman had had a serious heart attack. Morgenthau had him admitted immediately to the naval hospital in Bethesda, Maryland, where they placed him under an oxygen tent. He was diagnosed as having a blood clot, and the doctors said it would be a few hours before they would know the outlook.

Morgenthau was grave when he told the 9:30 Group about their colleague's condition. In the middle of the meeting, Oliphant's associate, Ed Foley, walked in. "Come in, Ed," said Morgenthau. "Ed, I guess you'll have to carry on because it will be three months before Mr. Oliphant is with us—at least three months—and they said may—well, we don't know."[45] It was one of those instances when the staff knew what Morgenthau was trying to say but couldn't articulate. They also knew the Treasury was operating without one of its most able members.

Later that day, Harry Woodring and George Marshall came to the corner office to explain why the French program would interfere with their own. Before they arrived, Louis Johnson called and started off with a chatty tone, twice wishing Morgenthau a Merry Christmas. Then he mentioned that Boeing had been preparing a four-engine bomber for the military at a cost of $400,000, but the army decided it didn't want the plane. So Boeing had signed an agreement to sell it to the Japanese government for $800,000. As he prepared for the meeting with Woodring and Marshall, Morgenthau had a flurry of calls with Christian Peoples, who was the head of the Procurement Division, and the president, trying to scuttle the Boeing sale to Japan. Eventually, they agreed to scrap the Japanese sale and let the French buy the Boeing bomber for $400,000.[46]

Woodring showed up with a memo stating that once the army ordered a plane, the first unit was generally not delivered for nine months, and only about forty could be produced in the first year. "An order at this time for one thousand planes for a foreign government would prevent fulfillment of our ten-thousand plane program within the time limits now assigned," said the memo. "The foreign orders could not be cleared through the American plants in under eighteen months."[47] They agreed the French Mission would be shown no planes with secret weapons until all parties agreed they could be delivered without interfering with the American program. The meeting broke up amiably, if inconclusively.

Morgenthau was uneasy battling the entire military establishment in partnership with Monnet, a man he knew so little about. At a December 28 meeting, Morgenthau lost patience with the shadowy Frenchman when he explained the Canadian companies buying the planes would be financed with $250,000 of capital put up by the directors. If the directors declined to do so, Monnet said he would put up the money himself. Morgenthau asked why, and Monnet responded: "Frankly, I do a lot of things in this affair that I should not be doing."[48] Morgenthau and other Treasury officers pressed him to name the directors, but he was unable to do so. What would the directors receive for their investment? Only interest and repayment of the principal, he answered.

Morgenthau bluntly said he was worried about the arrangement violating US law, and he would prefer the French government establish a branch office in Canada to buy the planes. "I will do business with a certified, authentic agent of the French Government, but I am not going to do business with a dummy corporation," the secretary said. He noted the British had openly bought two hundred Lockheed and two hundred North American Corporation planes recently with no problems.

"Let's be perfectly frank," said Morgenthau. "There is so much secrecy over such a simple operation. Either the French have or have not the money. If they have I would like to see some of it on account of all this discussion. It seems to me you are making the thing as difficult for yourself as possible."[49]

After the meeting, he told his staff, "I don't want anything to do with any phony corporation." Then he added: "I could not have been any blunter, could I?"[50]

Rumors began to reach Morgenthau saying Monnet operated a company in the Far East that received highly preferential rates because of Monnet's links with people close to Chinese finance minister H. H. Kung. He heard Monnet had influenced a manager at the Paris bank l'Union des Mines, and the result was that the bank lost 360 million francs. And a former J. P. Morgan partner said Monnet had talked Morgan and French investment bank Lazard into investing 20 million francs in a bank in Cognac, and it lost 10 million francs.[51]

On December 30, Woodring demanded in writing that the Treasury guarantee that the French had the money to pay for the planes before any

French officials were allowed to inspect them. Morgenthau immediately phoned Woodring to say he could not possibly issue such a guarantee and demanded the letter be withdrawn. As he frequently did when he fell out with other government officials, he told the president of the spat.[52]

"Our mutually good friend, Ambassador Bullitt, has put me in an almost impossible position," Morgenthau told Monnet in a meeting on New Year's Eve. "I mean, I find myself now in the position that the whole United States Army is opposed to what I am doing and I am doing it secretly and I just can't continue, as Secretary of the Treasury, forcing the United States Army to show you planes which they want for themselves."[53] He showed the French emissary a newspaper photograph of Chinese official K. P. Chen being lauded by crowds in Detroit because the nationalist government had promised to buy one thousand American-made trucks. Morgenthau said he could do the same for Monnet, but the French would have to go public with their plans.

As Morgenthau prepared for a Florida vacation in early January, he forcefully pressured Monnet to state publicly France's intention of buying American planes. "The United States Treasury can offer no more cooperation until a public statement is made in regard to this mission," he said in a January 2 phone call with Monnet, repeating the same message six times before the call ended.[54] The secretary obviously assumed he would return to Washington two weeks later with the veil of secrecy drawn.

★ ★ ★

In Boca Raton, Florida, Morgenthau was laid low with migraine headaches for the first few days, but he was soon fishing for tarpon in the South Atlantic. Every day or two, he checked in with the office by phone, where John Hanes took charge in his absence.[55]

With the affable Hanes running the department, the 9:30 meetings were a bit more relaxed, and the Treasury men ribbed Budget Director Daniel Bell about his wife's anger now that her husband was spending all hours preparing the president's budget address. "Boy, she was sore last night," William McReynolds told the group after running into Mrs. Bell, then mimicking her he said: "I'd be better off not to have a husband; he's no use at all; I can't find him; he never comes home." Bell laughed along, telling them he'd eaten only one meal at home in the previous week.

His broad, flaccid face often breaking into an infectious grin, Bell was known to lighten the mood of the Treasury meetings, but behind the gentle wit was a dedicated career civil servant whose knowledge of fiscal matters was unsurpassed in Washington. Just as the Treasury's role in conducting the war was all but forgotten, Daniel Bell's key role at the Treasury has been buried beneath the notoriety of men like Harry Dexter White and Herman Oliphant. Bell was more a centrist and a pragmatist than his more famous colleagues. He had joined the Treasury in 1911 after scoring well in the civil-service exams at the age of twenty. He left to join the Tank Corps in the Great War then returned, working his way up the bureaucracy while completing degrees in law and commercial science.[56] He had become the director of the budget in September 1934, after the conservative Lewis Douglas resigned in disgust over Roosevelt's fiscal plans.

The president revealed the fiscal 1940 budget at the White House on January 5, and the press immediately highlighted the drastic rise in defense spending, which would likely require moderate tax increases. Amounting to $1.32 billion, the *New York Times* called the defense allotment "the greatest peace time appropriation in the history of the nation." It was $309 million, or about 30 percent larger, than the previous year's defense budget. The message did not mention new airplanes but said $270 million would be used for two battleships, four cruisers, eight destroyers, eight submarines, one seaplane, and modern ship repair. There were already six battleships under construction. The navy total was $721 million, up $161.8 million from the previous year, whereas the army total rose only $5.1 million to $510.8 million. It was the type of spending announcement that reinforced the impression within the army that Roosevelt—who had been the assistant navy secretary in World War I—always favored the maritime service over the land forces.[57] For the Treasury officials, the most important words uttered by the president when he delivered the budget to Congress were these: "Our full energies may now be released to invigorate the processes of recovery in order to preserve our reforms and to give every man and woman who wants to work a real job at a living wage." Hanes believed the real message in those lines was that economic recovery now had precedence over the social reforms of the New Deal.[58]

On January 7, acting general counsel Ed Foley reported to the others that he had visited Herman Oliphant, who had looked better than Foley had expected. His face had become fuller and he had some color. Foley said he believed Oliphant was under the impression he would soon be back at work. "He told me it was fortunate for him the secretary was away because it would give him a chance to get some rest," said Foley. "I was afraid he was going to ask me."[59] Foley didn't have to state he was worried Oliphant would ask him about returning to work.

Herman Oliphant died four days later. With Morgenthau away, Hanes arranged to have a Treasury delegation present at the old attorney's funeral. Morgenthau wanted to attend, as long as it was held in Washington. Otherwise, he thought it would be an "overdue tax on his strength," according to Foley. It turned out the family chose to have the service in Herman Oliphant's hometown in Indiana, a trip from Washington that involved changing trains three times. Morgenthau missed the funeral but issued a statement commending Oliphant's brilliance and loyalty. Gutzon Borglum, the sculptor famous for carving the presidential faces on Mount Rushmore, flew to Washington to take a death mask, which he would mold into a bust for Oliphant's widow.[60]

When Morgenthau returned to Washington, the French government still had not publicly announced its intention to buy American planes, much less measures to tackle its economic problems. Though Woodring and Johnson showed rare unanimity in opposing the sale, the president saw the logic of the deal, so they were ordered to cooperate. The army successfully blocked the French purchase of Pratt and Whitney's state-of-the-art P-40 pursuit plane, so they had ordered 150 P-36s and were pondering whether to raise the order to 250. They were also examining bombers produced by Douglas Aircraft Company and Glenn L. Martin Company, though the army did not want them to have access to the Douglas models.[61]

Harry Collins, who was taking over the Treasury's Procurement Division, told a meeting of Treasury officials on January 16 that the army just didn't understand how the French orders could boost production capacity. Their order could allow Martin to order tools for manufacturing and add one million feet of factory space. Another official added that Allison could increase its capacity from three hundred engines per year to five hundred with French and British orders. Morgenthau wondered aloud where Louis Johnson got the authority to buy planes for the military. Already the Treasury's Procurement Division had some power to make purchases for the military, and now Morgenthau—rarely averse to taking on the duties of other departments—was wondering whether his department should oversee all procurement for the military. "If the President wants somebody to do the job, we could do it for him," he said, and he prepared a memo saying so.[62]

Later that day, Roosevelt told the Treasury and military officials at a White House meeting he wanted every effort made to furnish the French with planes. Ambassador William Bullitt, also attending the meeting, said the French were particularly interested in the Douglas B-7 light bomber, even though Woodring said it had many secret elements and that it was built partly with government funds. Selling it to the French could prove embarrassing to the president, said Woodring. What he didn't need to say was that neither Congress nor the public were aware of the negotiations with the French, and news of the talks would likely excite isolationist ire. FDR made clear he wanted the French to see the B-7.[63] As the meeting broke up, Morgenthau gave the president the memo recommending that the Treasury take over the procurement of aircraft.

Three days later, Johnson informed the Treasury that he would cooperate with the French requests, and General Hap Arnold signed an order for the French technical advisers to view the Douglas attack bomber in Santa Monica, California. They would have access to the plane and its secret weapons, and they would be able to go on a test flight.[64]

By Monday, January 23, things were proceeding as they should with minor irritants. When Collins met with Assistant Secretary of War Louis Johnson, he was required to stand at attention for two minutes before being invited to take a seat. But the French were testing the Douglas bomber in California and were meeting representatives from both Curtiss and Martin. Overall, Morgenthau seemed pleased, as he felt sure the French would sign a contract within twenty-four hours.

Then in the afternoon, the calls came in from the West Coast. The French team inspected the attack bomber, and one technician, Paul Chemidlin, went along on the test flight. In the course of the maneuvers, pilot John Cable banked the plane and went into a spin at five hundred feet. Losing control of the plane, Cable ejected, but his parachute failed to open. The bomber crashed in a parking lot near the Los Angeles Municipal Airport, demolishing nine automobiles. Ten bystanders were injured by flying pieces of wreckage. Rescue teams dragged Chemidlin from the rear cabin of the bomber before it burst into flames. He escaped with a broken leg, severe back injuries, and minor head wounds. Cable was killed instantly.

Later that day, the Associated Press ran a story on the crash, including the fact that a member of the French air ministry had been on board.[65]

CHAPTER THREE

THE GATHERING STORM

★ ★ ★

The atmosphere was grim when Morgenthau chaired the 9:30 meeting on February 6, 1939. The secretary had been suffering migraine headaches since the plane crash in California two weeks earlier, and there was none of the jocular chitchat that often opened the meeting.

"I just want to say this for the benefit of this group," Morgenthau began. "That what I have done for China, what I have done buying silver for Spain, what I have done to assist the French [to] get planes—I am delighted I was able to do it; if I had to do it, I would do it all over again." Repeating himself several times, he said anyone who disagreed with him should come out and say it now. "I don't want anyone connected with me who doesn't believe in Henry Morgenthau Jr., and who doesn't believe in what he is doing," he said. Then he closed by saying: "I see extremely difficult times ahead of us, and I don't want anyone who isn't as closely associated as these people are here with me."[1]

"I'm a thousand percent with you in it," said John Hanes. "I think you're absolutely right. I'll go down with you if it means going down; we'll all go down."

"I've always felt we have a group here—they'll see me through thick and thin, and on that basis I can go along and not worry," said the secretary. "I mean, as long as the Treasury gang sticks by me, I'm all right." He had hoped to spend the previous two weeks focusing on economic recovery. But instead he had spent them fighting the White House, the military, even public opinion.

"It's going to get dirtier and dirtier and I just want to know that I've got a team with me through thick and thin; and it's going to get pretty damn thick," he said. "I mean, I've never seen the weather so thick."

It had taken a few days for the storm to erupt over the plane crash. The focus of the media in late January 1939 was not a plane crash in California but a regime collapsing in Barcelona. Franco was finally crushing the last bastions of resistance by the Spanish Republic, so a third major country in Europe would now be run by a Fascist dictatorship. Then on January 28, the *New York Herald Tribune* ran a front-page story with the headline, "Treasury Let French Agent Ride Bomber." The story, which also appeared in the *Washington Post,* said the revelations came in closed sessions of the Senate Military Affairs Committee, and Morgenthau guessed immediately that General Hap Arnold was the source. Morgenthau's first call was to War Secretary Woodring, who claimed he knew nothing about the matter. "I'm not going to forget it after Arnold has done this," Morgenthau told him. When Committee Chairman Morris Sheppard called to ask Morgenthau to testify, the secretary agreed and asked immediately who had blamed the Treasury. Confidentially, said the senator, it was Arnold.[2]

If there was one bright spot that week, it was that the French had actually placed an order for US planes: 115 Martins, 100 pursuit planes from Curtiss, and at least 100 bombers from Douglas—all on an expedited delivery. They planned to buy the engines from Pratt and Whitney, which would now be able to rehire workers who had just been laid off. Collins told Morgenthau the total order could eventually rise to 400 bombers and 100 pursuit planes, but the French had started with a smaller order in the interests of time.[3] Roosevelt, a master at handling newsmen, seized on this good news and immediately announced that the French were buying planes, creating employment for idle workers. He also said he'd ask Congress for an appropriation of $50 million so the army could buy 575 planes. The *New York Times* noted, however, there was a "serious conflict" between FDR and senior military officials and quoted Democratic senator Bennett Champ Clark of Missouri as saying he would fight the French sale.[4]

Morgenthau's testimony before the Senate committee was intentionally bland. Apologizing for speaking quietly because of his recent illness, the secretary explained that the French mission was an accredited group representing France, and he was involved because the Procurement Division was in the Treasury. He read out Collins's memo from his meeting with Johnson, as well as Arnold's note that gave permission to the French team to view the attack bomber.[5]

Days later, Morgenthau tried to explain his side of the plane scandal to the president at a morning meeting. At first, Roosevelt pretended he didn't want to discuss it, then he berated Morgenthau for having a "terrible row" with Woodring after a recent meeting at the White House. One of the dichotomies of Roosevelt's executive style was that he constantly created divisions in his inner circle, but he also demanded the appearance of harmony among all major players. Morgenthau explained that he had never even raised his voice with Woodring. Secretary of the Navy Charles Edison had asked him after the meeting if he was happy with the cooperation he had received from the navy, and Morgenthau replied, "Naturally so." Johnson and Woodring were standing nearby, and Johnson had asked if he was happy with the army's cooperation. Morgenthau simply said, "No." FDR continued to rebuke him, but Morgenthau stood his ground, which could not have been easy because of the deep effect Roosevelt's displeasure always had on him. Morgenthau went on to say he had merely carried out Roosevelt's wishes and had done in a few months what would have taken the army a few years.

"Well, you know I have plans to clean up that situation," said the president. It was an open secret within the administration that Roosevelt was planning to fire Woodring or Johnson or maybe both, but he hadn't found the nerve yet.

"Mr. President, you can take six months or a year to clean up some other situations in other departments but in the case of the War Department it is a matter of days," replied Morgenthau, "because for your international speeches to be effective, you must be backed up with the best air fleet in the world and, if we are going to do that it is a matter of days to get things in order."[6]

Just as the plane furor subsided, the exhausted Morgenthau was rocked again on February 5 when he was the subject of a diatribe by the demagogic radio commentator Reverend Charles Coughlin. Notably anti-Semitic and sympathetic to Hitler and Mussolini, Coughlin's syndicated broadcasts had a following of millions. He claimed Morgenthau had attended a meeting in Paris with the half-Jewish William Bullitt, the Jewish former French prime minister Leon Blum, and the Jewish Soviet foreign commissar Maxim Litvinov during the Morgenthau family vacation in Europe the previous summer. The obvious implication was that Morgenthau was part of an international Jewish conspiracy. The truth was that Morgenthau had been on the Côte d'Azur, more than four hundred miles from Paris, when the alleged meeting took place, and he had not spoken to Litvinov since 1933. The more damaging claim by Coughlin was that Morgenthau was operating the $2 billion stabilization fund—established by Congress to prevent undue fluctuations in the dollar, franc, and pound—not for Americans but "for the benefit of British and French international bankers who reap the rewards of imperialism." Morgenthau interpreted this as Coughlin calling him a traitor. It had particular bite because some congressmen had claimed the United States could end up subsidizing the French plane deal if it led to a depreciation of the franc, and the United States–backed stabilization fund had to come in and support the French currency.

Morgenthau sought legal advice about suing Coughlin but ended up writing the priest in protest, demanding a retraction, and copying the letter to George Cardinal Mundelein of Chicago.[7] He again warned "the Treasury family" that the political atmosphere was dirty and was going to get dirtier. Anyone who was not with him completely should consider his options, he added. At noon the following day, Assistant Secretary Wayne Taylor came into the corner office and resigned. It turned out he was a closet isolationist. Although their meeting was cordial, Taylor's resignation letter (which would have to be released publicly, as it was addressed to the president) opposed such policies as loans to China and the "secret" airplane purchases by the French. In several meetings, Morgenthau convinced him to remove the offending paragraphs before the administration accepted the resignation.[8]

Taylor was one of several assistant secretaries who had resigned in Morgenthau's five years at the Treasury. It was a little black mark against the Treasury, but Morgenthau and his circle took such pride in the department that even a small black mark hurt. To Morgenthau, Hanes, Oliphant, White, Klotz, Bell, and the others who strode past Alexander Hamilton's statue as they entered their office each morning, the Treasury was not simply a government department. The Treasury exemplified the best of government service, and in the idealism of the Roosevelt administration, there could be no higher calling than government service. The rest of Washington revered the Treasury. Even Cordell Hull admitted Morgenthau had "an excellent organization in the Treasury Department."[9] In September, Harry Dexter White had told a visiting journalist that the public would be amazed if it "really knew what the secretary had done to promote world stability, world peace, and how much he was doing, but unfortunately the things he was doing and had been doing were of such a confidential nature that nobody could know until some day possibly history would write it."[10] White also once bawled out an underling, Edward Bernstein, because he went to meet a British treasury representative at a nearby hotel. "Remember that when you are representing the Treasury, it doesn't matter who it is who wants to see you, he comes to your office, not you to his office."[11]

Morgenthau's references to the "Treasury family" underscored the familial bond among them. Though most were economists, they never saw their roles in government as the dry processes of finance but as part of a grand movement for the betterment of Americans. Many were drawn to the Treasury Department because they admired Morgenthau's idealism, ethics, and anti-Nazi stand. One official, John Pehle, would later say he and his colleagues were attracted to the department because of its idealism. "It was an organization that went into all sorts of things that weren't the Treasury's business primarily," he said. "The Secretary just encouraged this."[12] Indeed, they believed their economic work was an essential part of the country's fight against Nazism. One day during their discussions, Morgenthau mentioned all the forced labor in the Soviet Union, and Ed Foley replied that they had to make the capitalist system in the United States work or the nation could end up with a Communist system.

"That's why in one sense, the Treasury is the greatest arm of defense," said Harry Dexter White.

Foley agreed: "It's the greatest weapon the United States has—the Treasury."[13]

Soon Morgenthau and his staff turned their attention to the economy, the fiscal situation, and Morgenthau's long-held ambition to balance the budget. "In his heart, he no more believes the nation can spend itself rich than he believes a man can drink himself sober," wrote the *Wall Street Journal*'s Frank R. Kent, Washington's most perceptive journalist on economic matters. Sadly, Morgenthau had never succeeded in balancing the budget. The federal deficit had reached $4 billion in 1936, and they had brought it down to $1.2 billion in 1938. Then the "Roosevelt Recession" gripped the country, and the president was convinced it was due to the decline in deficit spending.[14] As a result, the federal debt, which had stood at $22.5 billion in 1933, had risen to $40 billion in 1939. It was forecast to rise almost to the legislated debt limit of $45 billion in fiscal 1940, and the administration would soon have to ask Congress to raise the debt limit.[15] Behind closed doors, Morgenthau tried to impose some fiscal sanity on the government, but between the White House, the circle of New Dealers, and Congress, he had never been able to. In some circles, he had the same free-spending reputation as the rest of the administration. When he mentioned in a 1937 speech to the Academy of Political Science that he wanted balanced budgets, someone in the audience burst out laughing. Morgenthau assumed the fellow was drunk, but it still shocked him.

Now in February 1939, he and his staff were trying to push through Congress a budget they hoped would continue to lift the country out of the 1938 recession and prepare it for the global war. The cost of the pending war for all democracies weighed heavily on Morgenthau's mind. The secretary never found out how France could afford the $65 million it planned to spend on American airplanes, and even the fiscally conservative government of Neville Chamberlain in Great Britain was doubling its defense spending to about £800 million, or almost $4 billion. The defense appropriation in the most recent budget proposed by the White House had been staggering. "Now this whole armament program is the curse of the whole world and it's the curse of all the Treasuries," Morgenthau told Daniel Bell on February 21. He pondered making a speech to call for disarmament talks, but Bell reminded him he might have difficulty convincing Germany and Italy.[16]

Morgenthau knew the most effective way to finance the war was to get the US economy out of the rut it had been in for almost a decade. The national income—a figure the government tracked closely in those days—had been $79 billion in 1929 and had fluctuated between $46 billion and $69 billion during the Roosevelt administration. It was expected to be $64 billion in 1938, which would produce government revenue of about $5.5 billion. After running a few models, the Treasury calculated it could collect $8 billion and almost balance the budget by increasing the national income to $80 billion.[17] The "$80 billion national income" became a rallying cry for the administration. Hanes said the president should announce the goal publicly, saying, "I think it would engender more confidence in the business structure than anything we've done here at all. And I'm crazy about it; I think it's real."[18]

The problem, of course, was how to achieve it.

The staff formulated a plan to achieve the $80 billion income figure by removing "existing deterrents to private industry" and ensuring nothing new endangered the recovery of private business.[19] It seems today like fundamental economic planning, but it is easy to forget how thoroughly the New Dealers distrusted the business community. Franklin Roosevelt came to office disparaging "unscrupulous money changers" in his inauguration address, using a term attributed to Jesus in all four Gospels to convey the dishonesty of financiers. The relationship between the administration and the business community had never improved. When the National Association of Manufacturers drew up a list of causes for the recession of 1938–39, it included "excessive, unsound and frequently unfairly administered taxes" and "uncertainties created by frequent expressions of public officials voicing hostile attitudes toward business and investors."[20] Most of the newspapers that opposed the administration did so because of its hostility to business. "Business has been terrorized," thundered an editorial in February 1939 in the *Chicago Tribune*, owned by the New Deal's most vocal opponent, Col. Robert R. McCormick. "Bureaucrats armed with power to destroy enterprises and hamper their operations have been turned loose as if to discourage any one from making an effort to get ahead."[21] Beneath such strident hyperbole lay the belief by a broad swath of the business community that Washington was hostile to its endeavors.

Morgenthau's efforts to convince the president to make peace with business were aided by Hopkins's appointment as secretary of commerce in 1938. It helped that the Roosevelt favorite was now mingling with businessmen, hearing their concerns and forwarding them to the president. The other positive development was the elevation within the Treasury of John Hanes.

Blessed with attractively rounded features, blue eyes, and an affable manner, the North Carolina native worked in the family tobacco business before entering C. D. Barney and Company on Wall Street in 1920. Seventeen years later, following the death of his wife, he chose to help the country by joining government, first with the Securities and Exchange Commission, then the Treasury. He and Morgenthau soon formed a tight bond, and Hanes was one of the few Treasury men to call him "Henry" rather than "Mr. Morgenthau" or "Mr. Secretary." Elinor worked to get Johnny Hanes III into Deerfield Academy, where the Morgenthau boys had studied. Henry Morgenthau Jr. at one point wrote his father to ask for advice on a property deal Hanes was considering in Purchase, New York.[22] Hanes supported the administration, but never wavered in his belief in private enterprise as the solution to the nation's ills. In private, he would say that it took an investment of $7,000 of invested capital to put one man to work, and from 1924 to 1929, private industry invested $450 million per month—a total injection of $5 billion per year into the economy. "What have we done since 1929?" he once asked some congressmen. "We have supplied less than $50 million a month. The result is a lag in our investment of over $3.5 billion a year." His mission in the administration was to lure private investment back into the economy.[23] "Hanes, like Secretary Morgenthau, very emphatically is a budget-balancer," said Joseph Alsop and Robert Kintner in their column The Capital Parade. "He is also a believer in the importance of business confidence."[24]

Hanes liked the column and even mentioned it to Morgenthau, drawing a sharp—and customarily wordy—rebuke from the secretary, warning of what can happen when influential journalists dub someone pro-business: "I want you to know that [*New York Times* Washington bureau chief] Arthur Krock hates the President and he and his group will do everything they possibly can to build you up in order to show that you are the man that has the businessman's point of view, and they will reach the point where they will have you on the one side and the President on the other—you, saying 'this is what business wants; this is what the country wants, and Hanes is the fellow to put it through,' but with the President on the other side directly opposing you." Morgenthau warned his young charge that he had to watch his step and not let himself be held up as the champion of business standing up to the president. "When the President's machine goes to work on a fellow, God help him!" said Morgenthau.[25]

Morgenthau and Hanes formulated a plan to simplify the tax system, especially for business. Hanes long wrestled with the problem of whether the government needed to lower taxes (and thereby boost business investment) or raise them (to lower the deficit). In the end they came up with a plan to roll back the surtax on wealthy individuals to 60 percent from 90 percent. It would still be higher than the 25 percent level of the Hoover administration. They also wanted to lower corporate taxes to a range of 17 to 22 percent.[26] They still had to convince the president that this was the best course of action.

"Mr. President, you may be surprised," said Morgenthau at one of their regular Monday lunches in March. "I am going to tell you I want to see a boom in the stock market."

"That's all right," replied Roosevelt.

"Because rising prices in stocks does influence the executives of business and we have just got to get a boom," added the secretary. He later told his diary that, to his surprise, the president agreed with him.[27]

One day, Morgenthau was asked a question about some policy at a press conference and responded with his own question: "Does it contribute to recovery?" That, Hanes realized, was the key. He had cardboard posters printed up and distributed to all the senior offices within the Treasury. Soon all of Morgenthau's inner circle had "Does It Contribute to Recovery?" placards on their desks. Morgenthau offered to give the president one, believing the president was a convert to their cause.[28]

Meanwhile, the Treasury took what action it could to make life difficult for the aggressors and to prepare the country for the coming conflict. The Treasury continued to pursue countervailing duties against goods from Germany, and the State Department continued to block these efforts, saying the resultant trade war would not only hinder American trade but also impact the Intergovernmental Committee on Political Refugees. The committee, which had been struck by thirty-two countries at a conference at the French resort of Évian-les-Bains, was hoping to secure German cooperation in pursuing a solution for the refugee problem. Never one to hope for enlightened cooperation from the Nazis, Morgenthau dissented, but Cordell Hull persuaded the president to postpone a decision on the tariffs. They were still waiting for the attorney general to rule on the legality of the United States imposing countervailing duties on Germany.[29]

On March 7, Morgenthau buttonholed Assistant Secretary of State Sumner Welles to press for tariffs on Germany. "I can see your position," Welles told him. "It is obligatory for you to do it, but it puts this country in a terrible position."[30] The implication was crystal clear: Morgenthau was conducting policy as a Jew whereas Welles had the interest of the whole country at heart.

"I must carry out the law," Morgenthau said, interrupting him. "I cannot, as a Jew, stop and think 'is this good or bad for the Jews?' I have told you this before." He added he would resign before he would conduct policy in such a way.

Henry Morgenthau Jr. never wavered from his insistence that his opposition to the Third Reich sprang from his patriotism as an American and not from his reaction to Nazism as a Jew. In fact, he and his wife often worried about the public impression that he would create by identifying himself with Jewish issues or making statements against the Nazis. He'd once told his staff he would prefer to place duties on Japanese rather than German goods because he didn't want Hitler using him as the reason for the next act of German aggression. He imitated Hitler saying: "I have to fight because the American Bolsheviks, that Jewish Secretary of the Treasury, is trying to strangle me economically and I have got to fight that."[31] In the same vein, he apologized to Jewish groups when they asked him for help, saying he could not do anything for them that he would not do for other Americans.

Yet he pressured the attorney general to make a decision on the countervailing duties against Germany and then against Italy. He had White prepare a memo on how the United States could deprive the aggressors of badly needed war materials, especially petroleum.[32] He questioned the legality of the Munitions Control Board allowing arms manufacturers to make shipments to Germany, arguing that it violated the Treaty of Versailles, which restricted Germany's militarization. He was strident enough that Hull phoned the president to complain, and FDR let the Treasury secretary know his rival had called.[33] In the end, Morgenthau succeeded only in having the government impose duties on Italian silk and other textiles, though even these tariffs were delayed.[34]

In China, the Japanese had captured most of the coastal areas, so the latest problem was how to actually ship what little material China could afford. Though goods were flown in from Hong Kong by an airline half-owned by the Chiang family, the main route was the mountainous Burma Road. Not only did the Japanese frequently bomb the route, it was also plagued by the corruption and incompetence of the only trucking company on the road, which was owned by Chiang's brother-in-law, the influential multimillionaire T. V. Soong. American shipments were piling up at Haiphong in Vietnam because of the problems in shipping through Burma. Morgenthau suggested to K. P. Chen, the Chinese representative in Washington, that these problems could be overcome by forming an international transportation commission. It would comprise Chinese, French, British, and American representatives and a "very important American as general manager" to serve as "the dictator of transportation." He explained that the Chinese buying process was superior to its transportation, and that had to change. "And there won't be this idea of Mr. Soong having a private transportation company," said Morgenthau. "'Out the window!' as we say. He just can't have it. He can't be blocking the roads; can't have gasoline; this is a government proposition. Trucks, railroads, everything is pooled." Chen said he would forward the suggestion to Chungking.[35]

Of course, the aggressors continued their expansion. On March 13, Germany seized the remaining Czech portion of Czechoslovakia. Slovakia became a Nazi puppet state. It exposed the Munich Agreement to be the sham that Roosevelt and Morgenthau always knew it to be. In Britain, Chamberlain was chastened, knowing the next act of German aggression would bring about a pan-European war. Morgenthau looked into freezing all the Czechoslovakian money on deposit in the United States, and Roosevelt urged him on. It amounted to $3 million. The government didn't pursue it wholeheartedly.[36]

The US rearmament program and French purchases proceeded. Morgenthau asked Roosevelt's permission to bring in four business executives to serve as dollar-a-year advisers to the Treasury. The president questioned one candidate, financier Earle Bailie, whom Morgenthau had tried unsuccessfully to appoint as assistant secretary in 1934. And FDR opposed the suggestion of Edward Stettinius Jr., the chairman of US Steel, worried that he would let the copper price rise as soon as war broke out. He suggested a few alternatives, including Leon Henderson, a left-wing economist. "I think the President is wrong and hope to convince him," Morgenthau later told his diary.

What Roosevelt did want was Morgenthau to act on a suggestion from Joseph Kennedy that the Treasury, the Securities and Exchange Commission, the Federal Reserve, and other agencies ensure the New York Stock Exchange be prepared for the extreme volatility that would occur once war broke out. Morgenthau assembled a meeting on April 12 with Federal Reserve Chairman Marriner Eccles, Agriculture Secretary Henry Wallace, and other officials, including Herbert Feis, the levelheaded economic adviser from the State Department. Feis, the Harvard-trained author of several books, often had the undesirable task of being the go-between for Hull and Morgenthau. They discussed how war would affect not only the stock exchange but also other markets, like commodities and foreign exchange, and late in the afternoon FDR called and gave them a 5:00 p.m. deadline to give him recommendations. As they reviewed their options, Feis interrupted and said he should report to Secretary Hull. Then he asked for his next comments to be erased from the record and yelled at everyone that they were pushing him around and acting like Fascists. While the others sat in stunned silence, Morgenthau said they were carrying out a job requested by the president, but Feis insisted they were dealing with things of which they had no idea.[37]

"I'm sorry to have been so semi-dramatic," said Feis. Babbling on, he concluded: "But I'll tell Mr. Hull."

"Think you can find your way?" asked Harry Dexter White.

"I find my way in a world that looks slightly different to me from the one that I entered." He stormed from the room.

"That gave us the relief that we needed," said Morgenthau. "Anybody want a drink?"

As the others laughed heartily, Morgenthau opened a bottle of sherry. They reached the deadline, agreeing that they should keep the markets open if possible and not invoke exchange controls unless absolutely neces-sary. Morgenthau briefed the president at the White House, including the tale of Feis's strange behavior. When the group reassembled at his office at 5:40 p.m., Morgenthau called Hull to brief him and then called Feis to invite him to join them all for a drink.

When Feis entered, it was well past six o'clock. "Having a little drinkie?" asked Morgenthau.

"Just a little one," answered Feis.

Handing him a sherry, Morgenthau told him they were only making plans, not commitments. Proposing a toast, he said: "Well, here's to peace anyway, in the war, in the world and between State and Treasury."

At the white-tie Gridiron Dinner that spring, one after-dinner skit featured a reporter dressed in a dragon suit, slumped, exhausted, and bandaged, with a few arrows sticking out of his rump. An announcer's voice boomed through the darkened dining room: "The Gridiron Club presents King Arthur and his knights and wizards of the Round Table, who are confronting a grave emergency. Their pet dragon, named Business, after providing them with six years of rare sport, is about to expire."

On to the stage walked two knights, morosely studying the wounded dragon.

"Sir Henry Le Morgue, I fear we have beaten this old dragon, Business, until he's all in," said the first knight. "It looks like he is going to die on us."

"Yes Sir John of Hanes," replied the journalist playing Morgenthau. "That's what I've been telling King Arthur. But it doesn't seem to bother him a bit. He just smiles."

"He's spent six years trying to kill that dragon. Just between ourselves, even the common people are getting fed up with this abuse of poor old Business."

"See! All he needs to make him healthy is—appeasement! Even if he is a vicious beast, and not to be trusted, we'll certainly need him in 1940. If he dies, we won't have anything to save the common people from."

"King Arthur listens to those crackpot wizards—Eccles the Echo, Tommy the Cork and Benny the Cone. And how they hate the old dragon!"

Morgenthau loved the skit and secured a transcript that he filed into the Morgenthau Diaries. It was humorous relief from what was becoming a serious and very public disagreement between himself and his president.

Roosevelt had hated the Morgenthau-Hanes plan when they'd outlined it to him in March, calling it a "Mellon plan of taxation," a reference to the conservative Treasury secretary of the previous administration, Andrew Mellon. The president didn't like lowering taxes for the wealthy and didn't trust the business community to generate jobs. "I think that sign on your desk, 'Does it contribute to recovery?' is very stupid," he said flatly to Morgenthau at one White House meeting.[38]

As the seasons changed in Washington, Roosevelt was learning to detest two words that were becoming commonplace—*appeasement* and *recovery*.

Appeasement had taken on unseemly connotations since the agreement in Munich and now often referred to the administration's overtures to business. The *New York Times* reported the president didn't like the word and was looking for a substitute.[39] The left wing of the Democratic Party, including FDR, also disliked the term *recovery*—and the blue cards that bore the word— because they thought it meant abandoning relief programs to encourage business expansion. "The blue card was immediately denounced to the President by the die-hards," wrote the *New York Times* columnist Arthur Krock. "They said it was an open flag of surrender to the 'reactionaries' and to the bitterest partisan critics of Mr. Roosevelt's Administration."[40]

Morgenthau and Hanes were soon isolated into one faction that wanted tax revision to encourage private investment. Another group, led by Federal Reserve chairman Marriner Eccles, Tommy Corcoran, and Benjamin Cohen, opposed any changes to the tax system. Roosevelt leaned toward the Eccles camp, but Morgenthau refused to buckle under. In fact, he asked the president for permission to address a congressional committee to put forward the case for tax reform and prepared the remarks. In mid-April, Roosevelt and Morgenthau were getting along splendidly because the president was focused on a public warning he delivered to Hitler and Mussolini to halt their aggression. (Hitler dismissed the warning with a defiant speech in the Reichstag.) But as they focused more on the domestic economic problems, tensions mounted between 1500 and 1600 Pennsylvania Avenue.

At their lunch on April 25, Morgenthau asked the president when he would like to see the tax-revision speech. About June 15, the president replied and let out a hearty laugh. It was the date the king and queen of Great Britain were due to end their visit to the United States. "Well," said the president, "you spoiled everything. We had everything in nice shape for a month and now you keep saying the Treasury has a program." Morgenthau countered that he'd said only that he was ready to make a statement if requested. He wanted to discuss the statement, but FDR jokingly said he was busy with royalty until June 15. Finally they agreed Morgenthau could give him a draft statement to look at.

As Morgenthau, Hanes, and the Treasury intelligentsia drafted and redrafted the statement, the division within the Roosevelt circle became more public. Within Congress, Democratic senator Pat Harrison of Mississippi led the movement to add tax-revision clauses to a routine tax-extension bill that had to be passed by the end of the fiscal year. Roosevelt said the one had nothing to do with the other, and he was being assailed in the press for not showing leadership and restricting the Treasury from doing so. "What is needed and what is possible is not a series of little measures accompanied by verbal assurances, but an action, as decisive as his embargo on gold in the spring of 1933, which will cause the resumption of private investment," wrote columnist Walter Lippmann in a column Morgenthau showed to the president. "The only thing which will bring that about quickly is to offer investors and speculators the inducement of profits large enough to overcome their inertia and their fears."[41]

Morgenthau, meanwhile, received some of the best media attention of his career. In a column noting the secretary's "courage and character," Frank R. Kent of the *Wall Street Journal* noted Morgenthau had never received great press, so it was only fair to give him credit now. "Instead of curling up and saying, 'yes, yes Mr. President,' Mr. Morgenthau is sticking to his guns," wrote Kent.[42] Morgenthau, Hanes, and the longtime Treasury public-relations man Herbert Gaston pulled out every stop to win these plaudits. The *New York Times*'s Sunday magazine ran a glowing profile of Hanes on April 9.[43] Shortly afterward, Hanes (who was also lobbying Republicans and moderate Democrats on Capitol Hill) traveled to New York to persuade the *New York Times*'s editorial staff to profile Morgenthau himself. On May 5, Krock phoned Morgenthau to tell him the results of Hanes's trip were "100 percent successful."[44] A pleasing portrait of Morgenthau appeared in the Sunday magazine of America's most influential paper on June 4. It noted that Morgenthau, in five and a half years, had matured from "inexperience and overcaution to practical mastery of perhaps the most important single administrative position of any government in the world."[45]

The tension between Roosevelt and Morgenthau heightened when details of the Treasury plan were reported in several papers in early May. Morgenthau warned his staff he was "in one of the most delicate positions I have been with the White House on this tax matter."[46] The essence of the plan was contained in a single sentence in the draft speech: "We are all familiar with the fact that our National Income and the employment of our people are dependent upon the prosperity of private enterprise."[47] On May 3, Morgenthau spent one hour and forty-five minutes going over each word with the president. FDR demanded changes but accepted 95 percent of it, and the central message was left intact. The final twenty-five-page draft said taxes had to be discussed in the broader framework of the country's fiscal ambitions and laid out four priorities for the economy: (1) to promote private enterprise and investment, (2) to attain full business recovery, (3) to sustain sound private finances, and (4) to ensure equitable tax distribution. "Full attainment of these objectives is made more difficult by a new and ominous development in world affairs—the armament race now gripping the important nations of the world," said the text. "Great Britain in the coming fiscal year is spending $3 billion on armaments, or almost 50 percent of its national budget; France is devoting over 40 percent of its national government expenditures to the same purpose; Italy, 50 percent; Germany probably 60 percent; Japan over 70 percent."[48] Hanes and Morgenthau were feeling confident they could reform the tax system.

Then came Morgenthau's Monday luncheon at the White House on May 8, at which the president "went at me" for two hours and twenty-five minutes, according to the secretary's diary submission. "Henry, supposing this country is a $67 billion country, and that's all it's ever going to be," Roosevelt said at one point. "What's your recommendation?" Morgenthau said he had never approached the economy that way, so he didn't have a recommendation. They went back and forth, and finally FDR said: "Well, how about going after balancing the budget and raising $2,000,000,000. Have you such a program?" The secretary responded, "Yes, we showed it to you in October, 1938. It's all done. Hanes, Bell and I were over there in October, 1938, and presented it to you." Roosevelt struck down his tax reforms one by one, and at the end Morgenthau told him it would be best if he did not go up to the Hill at all.[49] All of Washington found out about it a few days later, when the press reported that Roosevelt had changed his mind. Kent wrote that Morgenthau and Hanes no doubt felt betrayed and humiliated. "In effect, after having been privately patted on the back they now have publicly been kicked in the pants," he wrote.[50]

Morgenthau and Hanes retreated and regrouped—but they did not surrender. They met May 9 with North Carolina congressman Robert Lee Doughton, longstanding chairman of the House Ways and Means Committee, and committee member Jere Cooper of Tennessee. The two Dixie Democrats were sympathetic to tax revision and were mystified by the president's about-face. Usually a stoic fellow, Henry Morgenthau Jr. poured out his heart to his visitors, revealing his passionate patriotism as the reason for the tax fight. Often repeating himself in rambling sentences, he made clear he was fighting to bring back prosperity to the United States. "All I am interested in is to really see this country prosperous and this form of government continue, because after eight years if we can't make a success somebody else is going to claim the right to make it and he's got the right to make the trial," he said. "I say after eight years of this administration we have just as much unemployment as when we started."

His guests agreed, adding the country had built up an enormous debt as well.

"I want it for my people, for my children and your children," continued Morgenthau. "I want to see some daylight and I don't see it. And that's why Hanes and I are making this fight, and if we are successful he and I will contribute more out of our pockets than others because it will hit us the hardest. If they take our suggestion, to take our money or leave it to them after we die, it hits Hanes and me relatively more than anybody in this administration. Nobody can be more unselfish than we are."[51]

On May 12, there was a White House meeting that Hanes was conspicuously not invited to. Soon, the *Chicago Tribune* reported that Roosevelt and Morgenthau had "sharp words" about the tax plans at a White House conference on May 15. Morgenthau, it said, was still trying to push the plan, but the president didn't want to see it. When the secretary tried to back up his arguments with statistics, FDR replied that he didn't want the figures because they were not honest. "Morgenthau reddened, according to observers, and in a choked voice said he didn't like to be accused of dishonesty by his chief," said the report, adding that the incident may have had Morgenthau considering resignation.[52]

Resignation rumors had been aired in the media throughout Morgenthau's career, but this time there was some truth in them. He continued to discuss the tax reforms with his staff, Doughton and Cooper, and even Harry Hopkins, who said some people in government simply didn't want a private-sector recovery. Hopkins over lunch one day added the two of them had been sandbagged by the hard-core New Dealers. Smiling, Morgenthau responded that Hopkins had often been the one in the past stabbing him in the back over relief funding. "Harry, you did a good job on me yourself," said Morgenthau, brushing aside Hopkins's protests to the contrary. When he detailed the exchange in his diary, Morgenthau added: "When I tell that to my wife she will say, 'Henry, I am proud of you.'"[53]

Soon Hanes and Morgenthau began to argue in private, and Hanes said angrily one day he knew of about forty elected politicians on the Hill who "will stand with me on a fight on the tax program." He then added, "I do not like Mr. Roosevelt."[54] On another day, Morgenthau asked Hanes to take his place at a cabinet meeting while he was out of town. Hanes refused.[55]

Finally, Morgenthau turned for advice to one member of the Roosevelt circle he trusted unconditionally: Eleanor Roosevelt. Washington insiders knew the Roosevelt marriage was more practical than passionate and that there were two circles of influence within the White House, one orbiting around Franklin Roosevelt and the other around his wife. They had almost divorced in 1918 when she found his love letters from his mistress Lucy Mercer (later Lucy Rutherford). Therefore the men who were close to the president often ignored his wife, believing she was of no political value to them. But Henry Morgenthau understood that the president, who could simultaneously agree with and disregard any adviser, took what his wife said to heart and that one way to influence the president was first to influence his wife. What's more, he genuinely adored the First Lady and helped her whenever possible.

Eleanor Roosevelt enjoyed the prestige of her position but also strove to use it to benefit all Americans. She was, in essence, the agony aunt to a troubled nation, fielding thousands of letters from desperate people during the Depression. She would ask friends—including the Treasury secretary—to aid her downtrodden pen pals. Each week, her letters poured into the Treasury. She forwarded Morgenthau a fifty-two-page, single-spaced handwritten letter from Hazel N. Worl of Alhambra, California, an arthritis victim who wanted Mrs. Roosevelt's help in getting $300 she had in the shuttered Union Trust Bank of Cleveland. W. W. Borm of San Francisco wrote in 1935 to say she had in desperation spent her stepmother's collection of one hundred dimes from 1894, and now her happiness depended on replacing them before her stepmother returned from a trip. Often Eleanor Roosevelt asked Morgenthau to help correspondents find work, such as M. I. Raphael, of Cambridge, Massachusetts, who in 1936 wanted to get into the diplomatic service but was too old at thirty-seven. Many letters were remarkably personal. "Dear Henry, I have advised these young people to get married at once," Eleanor wrote Morgenthau in response to a request from Miss Geraldine Horton of Hopewell Junction, New York. "Nobody needs to know when they actually were married. I wonder if it would be possible to get the boy a job with a salary on which they could get along after the baby is born."[56] Morgenthau helped out where he could.

Though other Washington insiders resented Morgenthau's intimate relationship with the president, few realized that he nurtured his ties to the First Lady just as effectively. In fact, the entire Morgenthau family showered Eleanor Roosevelt with affection, especially Henry's parents. The First Lady's voluminous correspondence is replete with thank-you letters to "Uncle Henry" and Josie Morgenthau for the gifts they sent for Christmas, Easter, birthdays, anniversaries, and just when they felt like it. In 1935 alone, in a display of genuine affection no doubt tempered with self-interest, the senior Morgenthaus sent their son's boss's wife a hat in a hat bag in January, buns for Easter, a birthday present in early October, a scarf shortly afterward, flowers in the third week of November, candy a week later, and a dressing gown for Christmas.[57] Throughout the years, they had inundated the First Lady with boxes of fruit, a necklace, pewter, and flowers. In December 1941, Uncle Henry told her he didn't know what to get her for Christmas, so he wrote her a check for $100 ($1,538 in 2012 US dollars). More checks followed in subsequent years, and Eleanor always donated them to worthy causes.[58]

These two families were linked across the generations. They hosted one another for Christmas and Thanksgiving dinners, had watched each other's children grow up, and reveled in the young people's success. As a prank and proof of their families' close ties, Henry Morgenthau III had shown up with a friend at the White House the past New Year's Eve to prove to a friend he could get the president's autograph. When Henry Morgenthau told Eleanor Roosevelt in May 1939 that he was thinking of resigning, that in fact Franklin might want him to go, he was talking of a possible schism between two houses that would have rocked both.

"Told her how Franklin had been bullying me, brow-beating me and being thoroughly unpleasant," he told his diary after their meeting on May 18. She made excuses for the president, saying he had not been feeling well lately and was taking it out on people he knew could take it. "I said I was beginning to think that the President was trying to get rid of me and as far as I was concerned I would be tickled to death to go home," he dictated, adding that she understood how he felt.

During their hour-long meeting, Morgenthau ended up reading her the tax statement, which she heartily endorsed. In fact, she agreed to "lend her name to it." He departed, leaving the paper with her. As he left, she said, "I am sure, Henry, that the President is not trying to force you out."[59]

Morgenthau, of course, did not resign. He decided, as he had a year earlier, that his future was with Roosevelt and that he was determined to help the president defeat the Nazis. As Frank R. Kent wrote: "The general feeling is that his devotion is so doglike that it is not in him to break with the President, even over a matter in which principle is involved."[60] Arthur Krock later wrote that John Hanes was also considering resignation but was dissuaded by two people, one of them Morgenthau.[61]

Morgenthau kept meeting with Doughton and Cooper and in late May announced that he and congressional leaders agreed on a tax program that would "definitely" contribute to recovery. Asked the reason for the progress, he replied: "The answer is that there is good will all around."[62] By early June, Kent was writing about Roosevelt's "surrender" as the president reversed his decision and allowed tax reform to proceed. It simplified the tax system and even scrapped what was left of the excess-profits tax. It did not, however, lower tax rates significantly.[63] The matter was settled by the time George VI and Queen Elizabeth landed in the United States in early June. It was the first time a reigning British monarch had set foot in America, and the British government hoped it would strengthen ties with the richest country in the world on the eve of war. Yet Great Britain worried about the traditional republican resentment of the Crown and also that Americans believed that the real queen was Wallis Simpson, the American divorcee who had caused the abdication of Edward VIII three years earlier. The trip proceeded flawlessly. Henry and Elinor Morgenthau attended a state dinner at the White House and sailed up the Potomac to Mount Vernon in a yacht with the royal couple. They also enjoyed a barbeque in Hyde Park, at which the king tried a hot dog and delighted his guest by asking for another.[64] Morgenthau had a full-color film of the king and queen's visit to Hyde Park made and even had Eastman Kodak make five duplicates, one of which he sent to the royal couple in London via Joseph Kennedy.[65]

As the Treasury finalized the tax-revision plans, Morgenthau immediately set about rebuilding relations within the Roosevelt circle. On June 4, he called Harry Dexter White to his house and asked him to prepare a spending program featuring "self-liquidating projects," which meant those that would finance themselves through user fees. They included housing programs, toll roads, bridges, tunnels, and the extension of foreign loans to increase trade—the sorts of projects Morgenthau had campaigned against through the spring when he was urging the country to move toward a balanced budget. "Mrs. Morgenthau later joined the discussion and expressed herself as being strongly in favor of the Secretary's ideas," wrote White, indicating Elinor was likely the prime motivator in this plan.[66] The Treasury team went along with the $250 million program. Even Hanes accepted the secretary's rationale that it was better to propose a modest program before a larger one was foisted on them.[67] The conservative press, which had hailed Morgenthau during the tax-revision battle, mocked him for suddenly adopting a relief program. But this storm was tepid compared to that of May. It was now the summer of 1939, and the Morgenthaus were planning their traditional summer vacation in Europe, which would carry on into September.

CHAPTER FOUR

THE PHONY WAR

★ ★ ★

Henry Morgenthau was in Finland, the official segment of his Nordic sojourn, when the news came that rocked the world. He and his family had crossed the Atlantic aboard the great French liner *Normandie*, landing in London. They vacationed in Norway and Sweden before traveling to Helsinki to thank the Finns for being the only country to repay their World War I debts. During their stay in the country bordering the Soviet Union, Soviet foreign minister Vyacheslav Molotov and his German counterpart Joachim von Ribbentrop signed a nonaggression pact in Moscow. Keen Soviet watchers might have noticed that Molotov had replaced Maxim Litvinov in May, and now the reason was obvious: Stalin could not have sent a Jew to negotiate with the Nazis. Now that the threat of an attack from the East was stifled, Hitler signaled his intention to seize Poland.

With the world in crisis, Roosevelt summoned his cabinet to Washington, and Hanes attended in lieu of Morgenthau. He even had a private lunch with the president on August 31 and had never seen FDR so worried about anything as he was about the situation in Europe. When the discussion turned to financing the war, FDR cautioned that he did not want to ask Congress to raise the $45 billion debt limit and tossed about various ways to avoid doing so.[1] The next day, Hanes attended a somber cabinet meeting, at which they tried to digest the news that German tanks had rolled into Poland. "There is no use talking facts with you because you're as familiar with them as I am," Roosevelt told his cabinet.[2] He added he believed the State, Treasury, and War Departments were as prepared as they could be. Hanes had already outlined the steps the Treasury was taking to respond to the crisis and said publicly that the Treasury would not issue bonds or notes in September.[3] "The President was obviously much impressed by Mr. Hanes's outline and his manner of stating it," said Arthur Krock, citing a cabinet member who witnessed the presentation.[4] FDR told Morgenthau he was pleased with Hanes's performance in the crisis, though he added that Hanes took too many notes at the meetings—a faux pas in the Roosevelt cabinet.

Once the news of the Soviet-German pact broke, Morgenthau dashed to Bergen, Norway, where he and son Robert left the family and boarded the coast guard cutter *George W. Campbell*. The ship made twenty knots through choppy seas and sailed directly into a hurricane. It was thrown about so wildly that the coast guard aide assigned to the secretary broke his arm. Robert Morgenthau would later say his father was "utterly fearless" during the four-day crossing to St. John's, Newfoundland, where a coast guard flying boat was waiting to carry him to Salem, Massachusetts.[5] Morgenthau finally landed in Washington worn out but ready to work on September 4.

The German attack on Poland was the most devastating display of military power the world had ever seen. The term *blitzkrieg*, or "lighting war," immediately entered the English language to describe the Germans' coordinated offensive of air bombardment, motorized units, and infantry. Britain and France declared war on Germany, but the immediate conflict was concentrated entirely in Poland. Shortly after the German invasion, the Soviet Union attacked Poland from the east, grabbing as much of the country as it could before it was consumed entirely by the Germans. Reports were surfacing of the atrocities by both the Germans and the Soviets in Poland, including the bombing of harmless villages and the murder of civilians. The bestiality of the Germans was beginning to harden the Roosevelt cabinet in its determination to oppose the Nazis. At an October 5 cabinet meeting, Attorney General Frank Murphy passed Morgenthau a little note saying: "For the first time in my life, at my age, I am hating. I hate the Nazis, I never hated anybody before in my life."[6]

Morgenthau immediately took charge and turned his attention to a dizzying number of problems. Within a day, he announced that he was bringing in three executives—Earle Bailie, Randolph Burgess, and Tom Smith—from Wall Street to serve as dollar-a-year advisers. The next day he forced out a few men on the customs side and appointed another New Yorker, Basil Harris, as his principal adviser on emergency shipping issues. Herbert Gaston was promoted to oversee all of the Treasury's enforcement agencies—the Secret Service, the coast guard and the Bureau of Narcotics. Roosevelt, meanwhile, appointed Edward Stettinius, chairman of the J. P. Morgan–controlled United States Steel Corporation, to the head of the War Resources Board, which was to oversee industry through the coming war. He had opposed a Stettinius appointment months earlier, but something had to be done to overcome the feuding between Woodring and Johnson. The board now comprised all businessmen, including three affiliated with Morgan interests, and no labor representatives. Speculation grew that FDR was abandoning the New Deal in the interest of fighting the war. Morgenthau even broached the possibility of bringing in Nelson Rockefeller, the grandson of Standard Oil founder John. D. Rockefeller and a prominent Republican, to be assistant secretary in charge of the Procurement Division. "You don't want to get too many of those kinds of people in," replied the president, saying it might work if it was balanced with the appointment of a liberal. "You know, there has even been some criticism of the people you brought in."[7] He added they had to be careful that J. P. Morgan and Company, which acted as agent for British and French purchases during World War I, did not end up controlling the war purchasing. At one point, the president had Sumner Welles call Morgenthau and tell him to advise the Finns that the best way to get a loan would be to avoid J. P. Morgan and use Dillon Reed, another Wall Street firm.[8] In October, the president announced that the War Resources Board would file a single report and then disband. "We are not setting up any war boards or war machinery and, as far as I am concerned, I hope we never will," Woodring told reporters.[9]

On September 11, Morgenthau told his staff he was still looking for assistant secretaries for the Procurement Division and the Bureau of Engraving and Printing, and he still needed to appoint a director of the US Mint.[10] Procurement was a perennial problem. The division had been led by Christian Peoples, who was too fond of the bottle for Morgenthau's liking. The competent Capt. Harry Collins was working his way into the position, but Morgenthau wanted a senior person who could get things done. At one point, he suggested that the president second Peoples to work with the army and navy on airplane procurement.

"In other words," said Roosevelt, "you would rather have Peoples drunk on the White House staff than the Treasury."

"Yes, and that's not so funny because it's true," replied the secretary.[11]

The main problem for Morgenthau was that the Treasury was too big and unwieldy, that it was not simply the financial arm of government but a massive tangle of divisions, many of which had little relation to each other. It included customs, the coast guard, the Secret Service, as well as procurement. Henry Morgenthau Jr. had such varied tasks as leading monetary policy with the Federal Reserve, overseeing the Treasury Art Program, managing the stabilization fund, and directing the Congressional Budget Office. In 1935 he had overseen the tax-evasion case against his predecessor Andrew Mellon, a politically motivated action in which Mellon was exonerated. And in 1939, a great part of the secretary's energies were spent on the prosecution of an antitrust case against the interests of Amadeo Giannini, the chairman of the Bank of America in San Francisco. Morgenthau had a network of Treasury representatives around the world who reported to him regularly as well as his own intelligence operatives through the Secret Service, the coast guard, and informal sleuths. He often said that he had more than enough to keep him busy conducting such a vast empire, and he was happy to leave other jobs to other people. Of course, he didn't mean it and often crossed into the duties of other portfolios.

During a military crisis, Morgenthau's duties expanded vastly. First, a conflict invariably affected the financial markets and exchange rates, which he had to monitor. Second, it often required a response from the US banking system, such as freezing the funds of an occupied country. Third, Morgenthau usually worked quietly to buttress the finances of countries opposing the Axis. Fourth, there were new responsibilities, like paying for war materials or preparing the coast guard for paramilitary duties. And finally but by no means least significantly, Morgenthau would usurp the duties of other departments to make sure things got done the way he and Roosevelt thought they should be done.

In the fall of 1939, the Treasury had to make sure the government had enough money to operate smoothly. It would eventually have to sell some bonds, and fortunately the debt markets were stable after war broke out. In the first week of September, the yield on long-term Treasury bonds rose from 2.19 to 2.40 percent, representing a mild sell-off. While Morgenthau was away, John W. Hanes, Marriner Eccles, and George Harrison, the chairman of the New York Federal Reserve (whom Morgenthau thought was trying to usurp his job) had decided the country needed a cash position of at least $500 million. If the Treasury continued with its usual financings, the Treasury would have $1.6 billion by December 1; if not, it would hit that $500 million threshold on that date. Morgenthau and his staff worried they would have to pay a higher rate to attract borrowers if they issued during a time of so much uncertainty; if they waited too long, the market would know they needed to do big issues and would demand higher rates. Throughout the autumn, they continued to debate how and when the Treasury should enter the market again.

The task that took up most of Morgenthau's attention was the crying need for ammunition on the part of Britain and France. He knew the combined arsenals of Germany and Italy put those of the democracies to shame and that the Germans were demonstrating ferocious fighting prowess. He also knew, all too painfully, that France was on the verge of financial ruin, Britain wasn't much better, and both had initiated arms programs far beyond their means. They needed help, but powerful forces in Congress were determined to restrict America's ability to aid the democracies, trying to ensure the United States was never drawn into the war. Under the Neutrality Acts, enacted in 1935, 1936, and 1937, American manufacturers were barred from exporting arms to belligerents during conflicts, so the outbreak of war in Europe had essentially initiated an arms embargo. Using his considerable political skills, Roosevelt set about persuading a special session of Congress to soften these provisions so that the democracies could buy arms on a cash basis. Of course, that raised the question of how to define cash. The Johnson Act of 1934 forbade loans to countries like France and Britain that had not repaid their World War I debts, and the administration and Congress agreed that the new neutrality legislation would allow a ninety-day credit for commercial shipments. In November, while Morgenthau was relaxing on a ten-day holiday at La Osa Ranch in Arizona, the president issued a new neutrality proclamation that allowed arms sales to belligerents on a cash-and-carry basis, meaning that they had to pay with cash and then carry the material on their own ships. It also allowed American manufac-turers to legally ship arms to the Axis powers.

The administration's aim was to help Britain and France, and it had to do so quickly, before both were annihilated by the Nazis. Poland by mid-September was a lost cause, and US intelligence reported the Axis out-gunned the British and French by a colossal margin. Ambassador to France William Bullitt told Morgenthau that Germany was estimated to be pro-ducing 1,200 planes per month, whereas the French and British between them could produce only about 600.[12] (Actual aircraft production in 1939 amounted to 8,295 units for Germany and 7,290 for Great Britain.[13]) Aside from the Luftwaffe, the German army had about ninety-eight divisions, comprising 1.5 million crack troops and a fleet of 2,400 tanks. The British Expeditionary Force had four divisions and fifty light tanks. The hopes for a defensive stand rested in the French army, which numbered 900,000 men and had access to five million reservists. Harry Dexter White also prepared a report for Morgenthau showing Germany was most likely self-sufficient in terms of oil.[14] One reason the War Department had opposed the plane deal with the French was because of fears that the United States would ship one thousand planes to France only to have them fall into the hands of the Germans when France fell. "I really believe that there is an enor-mous danger that the German Air Force will be able to win this war for Germany before the planes can begin to come out of our plants in quan-tity," Morgenthau dictated into his diary after a meeting with the president in November. "I think we should encourage the French and the British in every possible way to place the largest conceivable orders. If, before those orders are complete, the French and British shall have been defeated, we shall need the planes for our own defense."[15]

So the question became how many dollars or how much gold could

France and Britain get their hands on to rearm and narrow the alleged gap with Nazi Germany. The answer was: not much. "England is busted now," Ambassador Joseph Kennedy wired to Washington, while Montague Norman, the venerable governor of the Bank of England warned that all Europe was doomed, regardless of who won the war, because all the world's gold would be held by the United States.[16] Together Britain and France owned about $15 billion in gold, American securities, and US real estate. Half was owned by Britain, a quarter by her Dominions (independent members of the empire), and a quarter by France.[17] Most of this would have to be sold off to come up with the cash needed to pay for a bona fide arms program, and there were limits to how much it could pay the Americans given that Britain was spending about $4 billion a year on armaments at home. And the gold and securities would have to be sold in a way that did not depress the market. Since 1933, the US government had held all the gold in the United States, and the last thing the administration wanted was for gold to plunge due to the Allies' selling. Similarly, the US government did not want its debt or equity markets to slide if the Allies suddenly sold their holdings.

As they set about trying to aid the democracies, the administration was plagued by squabbling between officials, demands of isolationists, concerns about profiteering by industrialists and financiers, even its own ill-conceived ideas. On the return trip from Europe, Morgenthau had devised a plan to buy the state-owned cruise liners *Normandie* (on which he had just sailed to Europe) and *Queen Mary* from France and Britain, respectively. The proceeds, he reasoned, could be used to pay down their remaining war debts, allowing them to seek fresh credit from the United States. When he arrived in Washington, he told the president of his plan, and FDR replied with a big smile that he had been thinking the exact same thing and how they thought similarly even though they were thousands of miles apart.[18] ("That's lovely," exclaimed Henrietta Klotz when Morgenthau told the Treasury staff of the amazing coincidence.[19]) The British and French were less delighted with the proposal. The ambassadors of both countries responded that these ships were national treasures and the Americans should not be poaching their finest assets during a crisis.[20]

One early problem was that Joseph Kennedy believed he should lead the negotiations from London, that his position would be undermined if he could not counsel the British on the disposal of their securities. "That is what the President definitely doesn't want," Morgenthau told his staff. But Kennedy kept on advising the British, often shifting his opinion on when or how they should sell gold or securities. Morgenthau led the talks with the allies and was annoyed at the Bostonian's persistent meddling in the negotiations. Gradually the British began to liquidate their holdings, selling $50 million of gold at the end of November.[21] To facilitate the purchases, Morgenthau encouraged them to open accounts with the Federal Reserve of New York and to establish US-based purchasing corporations, as the Chinese had done.

The French at the outset were far more aggressive and efficient in their purchases, and the Americans had more diplomatic problems with the British. The French benefited from the plant expansions they financed earlier in the year and carried on by ratcheting up their purchases after war broke out. Morgenthau and Roosevelt helped wherever they could. When they learned the French had a desperate need for searchlights, they ordered that half the production of General Electric and Sperry Company be channeled to the French, even though the US Army had existing orders still to be met.[22] By September 12, the French had spent $159.3 million in the United States, including orders for 3,030 planes and 2,250 engines, while the French naval attaché was negotiating for 100 torpedoes.[23] Their purchases continued in late October, ordering $3.1 million in trucks and parts from White Motor Company of Cleveland, $10 million with Douglas for motors, and $9 million with Curtiss-Wright for propellers.[24] By early November, Morgenthau told both British and French representatives that he doubted the British could buy an engine for six months unless they also paid for factories as the French had. "The French have been very fore-sighted and now they are profiting by it," he told them.[25]

Throughout the autumn, the Treasury and the French and British representatives scrambled to arrange a structure that would allow the two desperate democracies to capitalize on the might of America. Eventually they came up with a proposal for a joint purchasing body whose chairman would be Jean Monnet. Morgenthau approved of the choice, though he warned the president of the strange rumors he had heard about the Frenchman and his business dealings.[26] By November, the French and British governments had the key personnel in place. The two main players would be a Frenchman named François Bloch-Laine, whom Morgenthau and Roosevelt had met before and didn't trust.[27] The English representative was someone new to Morgenthau, a Canadian businessman named Arthur Purvis.[28]

Purvis was born in Scotland and his speech still bore traces of a Scottish brogue. He was a refined, well-read, well-built man whose blue eyes shone beneath a pair of heavy, black eyebrows. Though he had studied music at the University of Edinburgh, he had spent his career in industry and government, tackling the unemployment problems the Depression had caused in Canada. The British industrial giant Imperial Chemicals Incorporated had sent him to Canada, and he became one of the country's leading industrialists. He and Morgenthau held their first introductory meeting in the corner office on November 29, and Morgenthau was immediately charmed by his guest. He was also pleased with the news that Purvis was wrapping up talks to open an account with the New York Federal Reserve to allow purchases in the United States. Morgenthau seemed even more tongue-tied than usual as he told the new emissary, "Mr. Purvis, I want to assure you you are still—you have my—how shall I say it, anything that comes strictly—any Treasury matters of course I am going to do everything we can to help."[29]

The next day, the Soviet Union launched a devastating assault on Finland, a country Morgenthau had visited only three months earlier. Morgenthau immediately sought Roosevelt's approval for forgiving the remaining war debt, which amounted only to $180,000, and arranging further credit for the Finns. However, Cordell Hull worried that the assistance to the Finns would upset isolationists in Congress. Once again, Morgenthau was the most activist member of the cabinet in foreign affairs.[30]

Now that the war had started, Morgenthau remained peripherally involved with the Jewish-refugee issue. He corresponded as early as 1939 with Stephen Wise, head of the American Jewish Congress, on the persecution of European Jews; in the ensuing years, he corresponded and/or met with the National Jewish Welfare Board, the Refugee Economic Corporation of New York, citizens working on resettlement projects in the Dominican Republic, and other groups. In October 1941, he donated one hundred dollars to the Jewish Welfare Board.[31]

In the first week of June 1939, that file intensified as friends from New York called to plead with him to help 938 Jewish refugees aboard the German ship *St. Louis*. Sailing from Hamburg, its passengers had hoped to land in Cuba while their visas to the United States were sorted out. But on reaching Havana, they learned neither Cuba nor the United States would allow them to disembark, and they would most likely have to return to Germany. Late on June 5, Morgenthau broke from his policy of avoiding Jewish issues and called Cordell Hull to see if anything could be done. If it were a matter of money, Morgenthau said, something could be worked out with private Jewish organizations.

Hull's wife was Jewish, so he understood the brutality of the Nazi regime. But some high-ranking State Department officials were understood to be anti-Semitic, and Jewish organizations had criticized his department for thwarting efforts to help Jews flee from Hitler's expanding empire. Hull sympathized with the passengers of the *St. Louis* and had called the Cuban ambassador and the president that afternoon. He'd hoped the refugees could be offered tourist visas for the US Virgin Islands, but such documents demanded that they have a definite home to which they could return. So they were helpless.

The next day, Morgenthau told Hull that friends in New York were in touch with Cuban officials, but the Cubans were demanding too much money to grant the refugees entry to the island country. The problem was never resolved, and the ship eventually returned to Hamburg and her passengers to Nazi domination.

In mid-June, Morgenthau again broached the subject of Jewish refugees with the president over lunch. The president said flat out that the

London-based Jewish Refugee Committee was getting nowhere. He mentioned that the president of Paraguay had told him he could accept about five thousand refugees. However, if the international community found homes for German Jews, Roosevelt said it would have to do the same for Jews from Poland, Hungary, and Romania. It would have added up to four million or five million people.

Harold Ickes phoned in October to tell Morgenthau he was outraged the State Department had refused to grant exit visas to four hundred American Jews who had been accepted to study medicine in Scotland. The students were willing to travel to Britain because the quotas in American universities prevented them from studying in the United States, but the department ruled that it was too dangerous for them to be even in Scotland once war had broken out. Together, Ickes and Morgenthau convinced the State Department to grant the exit visas.[32]

Stephen Wise—a leading opponent of Nazism and an old Morgenthau family friend who had actually married Henry and Elinor—wrote in November asking for help on behalf of a refugee advocate, Rev. Dr. John Maynard. Jewish men who had escaped Germany and landed in France were being detained as enemies of the state rather than being allowed to continue to their destination. Couldn't Morgenthau, he asked, request that the French ambassador do something? Morgenthau sympathized. "However, I feel that I shall have to stick to my rule that while I am Secretary of the Treasury, I cannot do the kind of thing that Dr. Maynard asks of me." Understanding the secretary's position, Wise replied, "I know, dear Henry, that my request is a little outside of your problem—of wiping out the slight indebtedness of our country—but I know that you will not be unequal to the task, too."[33]

By mid-September, Morgenthau believed economic conditions had improved enough that the government could sell bonds. He personally was in a strong position because the president had told cabinet several times he had confidence in the Treasury.[34] The fiercest resistance to bond sales came from the Federal Reserve, and Morgenthau fought the central bank tooth and nail, still piqued that its members had tried to grab power while he was in Europe. On September 18, he told the president they needed to raise money, though the president wasn't convinced. He didn't want to ask Congress to raise the $45 billion limit on the national debt, and he believed he didn't have to. Morgenthau learned that Marriner Eccles had told the president late in the summer that bond issues weren't needed. Rather, the government simply had to issue silver certificates—that is, securities backed by the government's holding of silver—and sidestep worries about rising debt levels. It was a spurious plan because the silver holdings paid the government no income, so the Treasury would have to meet the interest payments from its own resources. Though it was supported by the White House economic adviser Lauchlin Currie and to some extent Harry Dexter White, Morgenthau had little faith in such financial hocus-pocus; in fact, he had little time for Marriner Eccles.

A Mormon banker from Utah who'd become a millionaire by age twenty-two, Eccles was the most left-wing chairman of the Federal Reserve ever, with no clear contest for the runner-up. Some credited him with being the true architect of the New Deal, more so than Maynard Keynes, and he was often named as the leader among the New Dealers urging more government spending. He stated openly that he did not want strong industrial growth because that could spark inflation. "He has an almost fanatical belief in the soundness of his own theories and has worn out most of his friends talking about them," Frank R. Kent wrote of Eccles. "As a matter of fact, though he is personally agreeable, genuinely able and possessed of many good qualities, he is not a man of many friends, either in or out of the Administration. Mr. Morgenthau and he, for example, do not get along at all."[35] Their harshest falling out had occurred at a September 9, 1937, meeting when Eccles, after a long, pointed discussion, wondered whether Morgenthau supported a policy of desterilizing gold (allowing banks to reduce the amount of gold that backed paper money) simply because he wanted to relieve the Treasury of some gold. "There's never any use in talking to you, Marriner," Morgenthau exploded at him. "It's an insult for you to ask me a question like that. It's an insult."

"You get irritated every time I come here and present anything, and I'm getting as tired of it as anybody else," Eccles shot back.[36]

Their relationship was fraught again in the autumn of 1939. As early as mid-September, Morgenthau privately complained to the president about Eccles and the Federal Reserve banks and opposed their plan to delay bond issues.[37] Morgenthau often took liberties trespassing in other officials' territory, but he reacted sharply when someone meandered onto his patch. He didn't like Eccles making recommendations on the bond program—clearly the purview of the Treasury, not the Federal Reserve—and he and Hanes both took umbrage when Eccles suggested publicly that taxes on moderate-income individuals and large corporations be raised to finance defense spending.[38] Hanes bit back, publicly criticizing the proposal and once again earning the disapproval of Roosevelt for airing grievances outside the cloisters of the White House.[39] Morgenthau knew the president had faith in his ability to run the Treasury, and now he wanted to perform one task at which he was a master—he wanted to do a big-bond issue.

When Henry Morgenthau took over the Treasury in 1933, many were expecting this unproven farmer to mess up. The joke in Manhattan high society was that only Roosevelt could find the one Jew in New York who knew nothing about finance and make him Treasury secretary. In particular, the Treasury had to issue a staggering $1.5 billion—a 7 percent increase to the existing national debt—in bonds by the summer of 1934 to finance the New Deal. Few believed this novice could perform such a feat, certainly not without offering high interest rates to attract buyers. He raised the funds with no problems. In fact, throughout the New Deal, Morgenthau had never had a bad issue of bonds or notes. The interest rate on these bonds rarely if ever crept above 3 percent, and all sold out on the day of issue. It is easy to underestimate how difficult it is to issue bonds, for the issuer has to assess not only its own needs but also the demands of the market: How much appetite is there for new bonds or notes? What duration do institutional investors want to buy to fill holes in their portfolios? Is the appetite for issues from the Treasury or from a government agency? What interest rate is the market willing to pay? Will the market accept new debt or just the refinancing of maturing bonds and notes? Certainly it helped that the Treasury did not have to compete with many corporate issuers in the weak economy, as businesses were not financing expansion.

It also helped that interest on government bonds was tax-free—a substantial incentive for wealthy individuals in the days when the income-tax rate was as high as 75 percent. Morgenthau was also blessed with a superb staff. And he was far, far more knowledgeable about business than the public perceived. Certainly the financial media had come to respect his dexterity in bringing bonds to the market. "Skillfully combining the investment and speculative features afforded by Federal issues of securities, Secretary Morgenthau yesterday was able to chalk up another outstanding success in the deficit financing and refunding," the *New York Herald Tribune* had written in December 1938, the last time the Treasury had raised new money.[40]

Now he wanted to raise more funds in an atmosphere dominated by uncertainty over whether fighting would erupt on the French–German border. Press reports said Hitler would propose a peace treaty with the democracies to consolidate his gains in Poland while avoiding a bloody conflict with the other great powers. Morgenthau told the media in late September that the Treasury would be more active in the market soon, then he prepared the president on October 9 for large issues.

"All right," replied Roosevelt. "But how about issuing some more silver certificates?"

"Well, let's keep that for a rainy day," said Morgenthau, adding in his diary later, "He certainly sticks to his ideas."[41]

Soon the Treasury raised money for government agencies like the Reconstruction Finance Corporation and the Commodity Credit Corporation. Morgenthau felt the time was right for a bigger issue, even though the Treasury by late November still had a large reserve. He learned November 20 that Roosevelt wanted an issue of silver certificates to avoid asking Congress to raise the debt limits, and the two argued over financing the next day. "I had quite a difficult time with the president over getting him to agree to my doing some $500 million new money financing next week," Morgenthau dictated into his diary. When the talk turned to silver certificates, Morgenthau said he was "sick and tired of all this monkey business." They argued about the failure of the New Deal to solve unemployment and about John Hanes criticizing Eccles. Morgenthau eventually said he wanted to build up money going into an election year, making sure there were no financial problems during the campaign.[42]

On November 27, the Treasury floated a $500 million issue of new money bonds that matured over nine to eleven years. The interest rate was 2 percent. The offering sold out in a day.[43]

One other form of financing that Morgenthau approved of was US government savings bonds, and the Treasury wanted to increase their sales to diversify its sources of funds. In the first half of September 1939, the government sold $24 million of these bonds to individuals—an increase of 42 percent over the same period a year earlier. One official urged Morgenthau to advertise more to increase sales. "A million dollars a year, for two years, spent in magazines and newspapers and backed up by our great direct-by-mail campaign not only would sell more and more Savings Bonds and keep them sold, but bring tremendous and varied good that would stand our country in good stead in this dark hour of World history."[44] It was just one possibility the Treasury was studying.

The Treasury team knew it had to devise a fiscal strategy for the war, but it wasn't entirely sure what was needed. "I feel that the Treasury can make a real contribution toward maintaining our democratic form of government through its tax recommendations," Morgenthau dictated into his diary. "The program I have in mind is not a program of war taxes. It is a tax program of national defense for a neutral country in a war-torn world."[45] The important point is that his fiscal plan was essential to perpetuate the form of government he loved. On September 20, Hanes penned a thoughtful memo advising a special tax package be prepared in case the United States was drawn into the war. Yet he also urged that no extraordinary measures be taken to disrupt economic growth as the country adjusted to a war economy. He said if Congress "keeps its hands off wartime taxes, that the revival of private enterprise in all its implications, which I shall not here detail, will multiply federal revenue, increase the national income to over eighty billion dollars, and thereby contribute to the solution of our great problem—the balancing of our federal budget."[46]

Morgenthau and Roosevelt believed it may be necessary to increase taxes on middle- and lower-income groups but did not want a wartime boom that rewarded only the wealthy. "Doesn't Hanes mean that if business gets better, our income will be so much better that we won't have to raise taxes?" Roosevelt asked Morgenthau at a private meeting in late September.

"Absolutely."

"Well, I am very fond of Johnnie Hanes but Johnnie just does not understand," Roosevelt continued. "If you take a plebiscite today as to whether the people would rather have price fixing by fiat or excess profits tax, it would be an overwhelming vote for excess profits tax. The people don't want to see individuals or groups profiteer."[47]

Roosevelt continued to believe in the excess-profits tax despite the evidence it had drained the economy of private investment. To the president, it was more important to prevent great increases in personal wealth than to strengthen the businesses that would be needed for the industrial production of the war economy. And Morgenthau agreed with him.

"Well, strictly between us, Mr. President, I have not told this to John Hanes, I have asked Magill and Shoup [two Treasury officials] to prepare a memorandum for me on excess profits tax, to be ready on the first of October," said Morgenthau. "The way I see it, we need excess profits tax."[48] Years after he left office, Morgenthau still portrayed the excess-profits tax as a just fiscal measure. It is also possible he was simply ignoring the damaging effects of this tax because he agreed with Roosevelt that it was more important to prevent the rich from getting richer than to improve the overall economy.

Budget Director Daniel Bell in early November took a first stab at a proposed wartime budget and projected that within twenty-four months of the United States entering the war, defense spending would more than triple to about $10 billion, but other budget lines like public works and relief would plunge dramatically as the work force was drawn in to the military. Overall, the budget would swell to about $14.4 billion, more than 50 percent above the 1940 budget level. It was also about two and a half times the $5.6 billion the Treasury was expecting for revenue in 1940.[49] By December, they had completed an extensive study on what taxes could be increased to raise additional revenue.

On December 12, the president and Treasury secretary were sitting in the Oval Office, discussing the problem of taking gold from allies who were going broke, when the president outlined his financial plans for the coming year. He said he hadn't yet received all the budget figures for the 1941 fiscal year, but he wanted the Treasury to plan on a deficit of $2.6 billion. He did not say so, but Morgenthau had to assume that would push the national debt up toward $50 billion—certainly above the limit of $45 billion. FDR went on to say he wanted his budget message to Congress to show the national debt would be lower on July 1, 1941, than it had been on January 1, 1940. To achieve that and meet the rising defense expenditures, he said, the Treasury had to come up with $4.6 billion in assets that could be liquidated and whose proceeds could be channeled into current expenditures.

"When the last Administration moved out, those bastards left us with $125 million in the Treasury," said the president. He had obviously not yet decided whether to reoffer in 1940 because he told Morgenthau there was no reason to leave the next administration—especially if it were Republican—any more than that. That meant they could use about $1 billion to $1.25 billion of money now held by the Treasury for current programs. He proposed raising roughly $1.25 billion to $1.5 billion from the sale of silver certificates—an idea Roosevelt would not drop. Then he told the Treasury secretary he could extract a further $1 billion from the stabilization fund, a $3 billion pool of money that the United States, Britain, France, and other countries had built up to preserve the stability of major currencies. Morgenthau had pledged repeatedly over the years that the treasury of neither the United States nor any other country would touch this money other than to stabilize currencies or retire debt.

Dumbfounded, Morgenthau asked him what he was expecting for revenues in fiscal 1941. The president's answer of $6.6 billion exceeded the Treasury estimate by about $1 billion. "I don't think it's going to be anything like that," he told the president, referring specifically to the revenue projection.

"Well," said the president, "not only do not any two departments agree, but no two people in the same department agree." And so he proceeded to chronicle the conflicting predictions he had received from various parties.

Morgenthau calmly explained that for the past five or six years the Treasury had been accurate in its revenue estimates. Then he added that the president's plan would still leave him with a big deficit, even though he may disguise the worsening debt picture.[50]

"I personally feel . . . this is the worst thing he can do for himself," Morgenthau told a confidential meeting that included his closest advisers other than Hanes.[51] Morgenthau told them he would try to remain "detached" in his description of the meeting, but he found it difficult. "He has not done this thing during the time he was in and it would give the Republicans the ideal campaign issue as between financial sanity and financial something else," said Morgenthau. "All that Mr. Dewey has to do is go out and campaign on honest bookkeeping. And it doesn't accomplish anything! The deficit isn't any smaller!" Concluding, Morgenthau said: "He's trying to make a 40-inch waist go into a 28-inch corset, but when he got through there is still the 40-inch waist."[52]

There was a possibility Roosevelt was floating the idea to gauge Morgenthau's reaction, but the secretary said he believed the president's mind was made up. He wondered who was feeding him such plans. He authorized his officials to begin preparing documents that would prove conclusively that the plan simply would not work.

Had Morgenthau been the yes-man that so many portrayed him to be, he would have gone along with the president's harebrained scheme. That would have diminished the government coffers just as the world was preparing for the greatest global conflict ever, increased borrowing costs, violated international agreements, and decreased the government's economic credibility. Would Roosevelt have pursued such a policy? He had in the past, such as the excess-profits tax and the government buying of gold. In those plans, Morgenthau had been his willing accomplice, arguably his yes-man. However, Morgenthau had matured in his position, and he moved swiftly and effectively to dissuade the president, and the plan never reached fruition.

Roosevelt's scheme might have been the final liberal straw that broke Hanes's conservative back. On December 22, the White House announced his resignation. It was an amicable parting, and both the president and the secretary praised him publicly for his work. Arthur Krock noted in a Boxing Day column that conservative Democrats in Congress were heartily saddened by the departure because they had found in Hanes a member of the administration who understood their economic aspirations. "This strength was formed by a rare combination of ability, personality and character, a combination which won the regard of the president and some of his strongest critics alike," wrote Krock.[53] Frank R. Kent wrote the same day that in seven years the administration had had five different under secretaries of the Treasury. One, Morgenthau, had been promoted to secretary, and the four others quit because of policy differences with the president. (Kent neglected to mention that one, Dean Acheson, was still a senior administration official in the State Department.)[54]

Hanes maintained his friendship with Morgenthau after he returned to the private sector, but he switched his political allegiance. By the election campaign of the following fall, he was an executive member of the National Committee of the Democrats for Willkie, a group of disillusioned Democrats actively campaigning for Roosevelt's Republican opponent, Wendell Willkie. Hanes even addressed an October luncheon meeting of the Manhattan women's division of the United Republican Finance Committee, held at the Hotel Roosevelt (which was named for Theodore, not Franklin). He told the audience that he resigned from Treasury because he had come to believe that "the country was being handled by a lot of incompetents." Morgenthau clipped out the *New York Times* report on the speech and filed it with his personal papers.[55]

CHAPTER FIVE

THE ASSISTANT PRESIDENT

★ ★ ★

Harry Woodring and Louis Johnson didn't agree on much, but they were unanimous in their displeasure with the liaison committee in which Henry Morgenthau Jr. had a prominent role.

A former governor of Kansas, Woodring was the strongest isolationist in the cabinet. His objective was to strengthen the regular army, the national guard, and the reserve corps and to balance defense spending between personnel and procurement. But his critics—and there were many—sneered that he had led military procurement for years and still the military was undermanned and under-armed. As early as 1936, the year he was appointed to the cabinet, Harold Ickes noted that he understood "Woodring does not stand high in the president's regard."[1] Morgenthau considered him ineffective and hard to deal with. So did Louis Johnson, the Virginia lawyer serving as assistant secretary. "Only when absolutely necessary do they speak to each other," wrote *Time* magazine in October 1939. "When official business requires them to communicate, they do so in writing or through harried subordinates. Mr. Johnson despises Mr. Woodring. Mr. Woodring distrusts and despises Mr. Johnson, who for 27 months has gunned for Mr. Woodring's job."[2]

Roosevelt knew he had to settle the situation, likely by firing Woodring. But he hated to fire a faithful lieutenant, and Woodring could deliver the Kansas delegates at the convention, should FDR run for the presidency again in 1940. So with Europe embroiled in an expanding war, the War Department was dysfunctional and the government had no sound procurement structure to oversee the pending arms buildup. Roosevelt therefore established a liaison committee on December 6, 1939, to work with English representative Arthur Purvis and his French counterpart René Pleven in securing matériel for the hard-pressed democracies in Europe. The committee's chairman was the acting director of procurement in the Treasury, Capt. Harry Collins. Morgenthau did not at first have an official position on the committee, but in fact he provided the muscle often needed to get through the bureaucracy to ensure French and British orders were filled. The committee's power lay in Morgenthau's ability to bring concerns directly to Roosevelt and bypass both Woodring and Johnson.[3] Woodring objected to the committee, arguing to Roosevelt that the Army and Navy Munitions Board was handling the matter competently and there was no need to bring in the Treasury. He wanted the War Department, not the Treasury, to decide what the allies would receive, and Johnson agreed with him. Roosevelt sided with the Treasury. "I think you fail to realize that the greater part of such purchases is not, in the strict sense of the word, munitions—probably well over 50 per cent of the purchases will consist of articles of raw and semi-raw materials which are primarily of civil use," the president wrote Woodring.[4]

Ignoring the War Department's complaints, Morgenthau went to work with Purvis, who he grew to like immensely. First, they agreed the Treasury would help the British with such matters as helping to prevent arms manufacturers from raising prices for foreign buyers. The Vinson-Trammel Act of 1934, designed to encourage naval construction, restricted the profit on arms contracts for the War Department, but the rules were vague for foreign orders. Morgenthau had his staff vet the terms for the British orders.[5]

While he prevented profiteering by arms producers, Morgenthau knew he needed private industry to meet the requirements of the war, and he hoped to work with industry to iron out the sundry small problems that were delaying projects. As early as September, for example, Morgenthau learned the navy was a year behind on the construction of six battleships simply because a manufacturer was unwilling to invest the $6 million needed to make armor plate, largely because of complications over depreciation on equipment.[6] One key shortage was smokeless powder, a modern propellant used in firearms and artillery. The US Army had too little of this compound, and the entire country had the capacity to produce only 6,500 tons annually. Purvis concluded that the British alone needed 32,400 tons each year, not to mention 12,000 tons of TNT. To meet the immediate need, Morgenthau, with Roosevelt's support, pressured the army to give powder and TNT to the British. The army complied, but only after the navy agreed to lend the land-based service some of its supply. Purvis and Pleven proposed spending about $20 million to build new US capacity on the condition that US manufacturers lend their skill and designs to simultaneous construction in Canada with an annual capacity of 12,000 tons. Louis Johnson came out strongly against the proposal, saying the United States had to focus on meeting its own obligations before contributing to plants in Canada. "Once the Allied Purchasing Mission has given firm contracts to increase production in this country over and above what it is now by twenty thousand tons . . . we would be very glad to give the Canadian government whatever assistance they need," Morgenthau told Purvis. The British agent was forced to agree to the plan.[7]

One day in late January 1940, Morgenthau and Roosevelt sat down to sandwiches in the Oval Office and were enjoying a pleasant chat when Roosevelt offhandedly said, "I definitely know what I want to do." Morgenthau knew he was referring to an unprecedented third term as president. Rather than state what decision he had reached, Roosevelt babbled on about possible convention sites, such as New York, Philadelphia, or Chicago. Finally, Morgenthau refocused the conversation, saying: "Just what did you mean when you said that you definitely knew what you wanted to do?"

Again Roosevelt did not give a straight answer but told the story of one consultant to the administration who delivered to the president a message from his wife: "Keep on just as you are but keep your mouth shut." Morgenthau interpreted that as a strong hint he planned to run again.

"You know, Mr. President, you can count on me always," said Morgenthau.

"I know that."

"When I have lunch with you I want you to be comfortable and, therefore, I do not keep bringing up the third term issue."

"Well Henry," said the president, "it has gotten so far that it is a game
with me. They ask me a lot of questions, and I really enjoy trying to avoid
them." He paused and then added, "I do not want to run unless between
now and the convention things get very, very much worse in Europe."[8]

Roosevelt frequently mentioned to Morgenthau that he was worried
about the developments across the Atlantic, though Finland was the only
active theater as the moment. The only action the Allies were experiencing
was the Nazis' relentless U-boat campaign, which was wreaking havoc on
shipping. The Brits were starting to call it the "Phony War," but Roosevelt
felt sure the situation would deteriorate quickly and severely. Even in Asia,
there was little actual battle as the Japanese consolidated their holdings on
the coast and Chiang Kai-shek struggled to operate out of his landlocked
base in Chungking. The Burma Road was still proving an inefficient means
of transportation for the strapped government. The Chinese now wanted
a $75 million, ten-year loan backed by 100,000 tons of tin. Jesse Jones, the
head of the Export-Import Bank, which would have to issue the loan, was
unwilling to lend more than $20 million, and Morgenthau began to nego-
tiate yet again with the Chinese representatives.[9]

Having lost Herman Oliphant and John Hanes within a year, Morgenthau moved to strengthen his office. Daniel W. Bell, the budget director,
was promoted to under secretary of the Treasury, the sixth in Roosevelt's
tenure. Bell lacked Hanes's ties to business and wasn't as brilliant as Oliphant or Harry Dexter White, but he was dependable, hardworking, moderate, and loyal, and he knew government finance thoroughly. "I've been
around here about six years and I've seen you teach a lot of under-sec-
retaries, and it's about time you reaped the harvest of twenty-eight years
of faithful service," said Morgenthau.[10] He also brought in an innocuous
businessman named John L. Sullivan from Manchester, New Hampshire,
whose links to his home state were especially valuable in an election year.
Though Morgenthau was known for not hiring flunkies from the Democratic Party, he wasn't above using his staff for party work. A week after
announcing his appointment, Morgenthau sat Sullivan down in private

conversation and told him the president wanted him to do some organi-zation work in New Hampshire, the first state to choose delegates to the coming convention.[11]

Morgenthau pressed on with his primary duty of financing the govern-ment and the war effort. On January 3, the president delivered his annual budget message to Congress, which proposed a 7.4 percent decrease in expenditures for the year ending June 30, 1941, of $8.4 billion, including $1.8 billion in defense expenditures. "This is an increase, of course, over the current year, but it is far less than many experts on national defense think should be spent, though it is in my judgment a sufficient amount for the coming year," said the president.[12] By this time, Roosevelt had backed off his plan to raid the stabilization fund. The budget message began the negotiations with the two houses of Congress, the outcome of which would determine the final budget. Roosevelt told Morgenthau five days later he was happy with the response it drew and realized he still had a lot of horse trading to carry out with Congress before he got the budget he really wanted. "We sure have them fooled!" he told Morgenthau.[13]

By mid-January, the British, French, and US militaries were all increasing their armament orders, and Morgenthau was pressuring the president and the bureaucracy to do more to accelerate deliveries. He wanted the presi-dent more involved to map out the army's and navy's needs for 1940 and 1941. The army in early January had a contract for 524 Curtiss-Wright P-40s, whose delivery would begin in March. The French had an order of one hundred of the same planes, but their deliveries were not to begin until July. The president on January 8 asked Morgenthau to ensure that twenty-five of the army's planes be diverted to the French between April and June, and the army could take twenty-five of the French planes when its order began in July.[14] "I did a magician's trick for you," Morgenthau told Pleven, "pulled 25 planes out of the hat."[15] Morgenthau demanded government officials make the airplane orders a priority. When Pa Watson, Roosevelt's appointment manager, bumbled after being asked to schedule a meeting among the president, the liaison committee, and army and navy aviation representatives, Morgenthau lost his temper. "Well listen, I don't know what else he's got but this is damn important," he bellowed. "Do you know what this program involves? One point two billion dollars, and listen, fella, this is Allied money that is going to build up our airplane industry so that the Army and Navy will be on its biggest feet. I don't know of any cheaper way of doing it."[16]

Not only did Morgenthau have to battle the military over the foreign orders, he was also trying to stop the State and Agriculture Departments from trying to convince the Allies to buy American agricultural products. He thought it a misuse of their precious capital. What's more, his role of helping the Allies had never been announced publicly. By late January, Morgenthau had had enough and urged White House press secretary Steve Early to release a statement about his position working with the Allies. He complained that Louis Johnson "was dishing out . . . dirt about me, namely that I was more interested in the Allies than I was in my own country." He added: "The whole War Department . . . has fought us to a standstill on this thing." He deeply resented the assault on his patriotism because he was doing what the president had asked him to do.[17]

The White House announced on January 22 that Morgenthau would coordinate aircraft purchases for the military and the Allies, and the secretary explained at a press conference that the reason for the appointment was that the pressure for orders from France and Britain had become so great. "And don't let anyone tell you I don't look after our own interest first," he told the reporters. The article in the *New York Times* explained that Morgenthau was charged with solving the problem of how to expand aircraft production without letting the foreign orders interfere with those of the US military.[18]

The job of airplane procurement became easier when the British in February said they would begin to sell off their US securities. By the end of April, the British raised a total of $310 million through two tranches of securities sales, and the markets were stable throughout. The only downside for Morgenthau was J. P. Morgan handled the sale.[19] "Recent developments have served to emphasize the importance of Secretary Morgenthau's position in relation to the expansion of aircraft output to meet the heavy orders on hand from the British and French," said an article in the *Wall Street Journal*, which noted the secretary's role in overcoming shortages in certain machine tools.[20] He identified the shortage of machine tools—that is, the devices needed to shape the metal into parts for engines—as one of the key problems in expanding aircraft production. For example, Pratt and Whitney had ordered 700 different machine tools needed for existing orders but had received only 150 of them. Morgenthau met on January 30 with representatives of the National Machine Tool Builders' Association to work out a means for overcoming these problems—the first time an intermediary between the airplane and the machine-tool industry had attempted to find solutions. One difficulty, he discovered, was that the machine-tool makers were overwhelmed with orders from the United Kingdom, France, Japan, and Russia. He convinced them to cancel or postpone the Japanese and Russian orders so the domestic and Allied contracts could be met.[21]

In early February, Morgenthau toured the plants of Pratt and Whitney in Hartford, Connecticut, and Wright Aeronautic Corporation, at Paterson, New Jersey, and afterward he hailed their growth of the airplane industry as the largest industrial expansion that had taken place in the United States in several years. The two plants he visited had expanded output by 50 percent even though they had received only about one-quarter of the machine tools they had ordered. And the expansion had been paid for entirely by the foreign orders.[22] The Allies were now gearing up for a big order; Morgenthau was able to report to Roosevelt in mid-February that he believed existing orders could be met. Yet the success of the program did nothing to end the interdepartmental sniping.

After Roosevelt returned from a holiday sailing aboard the *USS Tuscaloosa*, a six-year-old, 9,975-ton *New Orleans*–class heavy cruiser, Morgenthau was able to tell the president on March 3 that the economy seemed to be picking up. Freight rates were rising, and the Allies had just told airplane manufacturers to prepare for a big order. He also asked to be allowed to raise money as soon as the economic and military situation was expected to sour in the spring. Then the secretary added that Johnson was still "all the time trying to undermine me through the press"[23] and that Hull and Wallace were urging the Allies to buy pork products even though the priority should have been on arms purchases. Roosevelt was jocular through the meeting, but beyond question Morgenthau was beginning to feel like he was the only senior official in Washington helping democratic allies check the advance of the dictatorships.

The British and French together wanted to buy at least five thousand air frames and ten thousand engines and were willing to buy twice the number of each. Only a year and a half earlier, the United States had the annual capacity to produce only seven thousand aircraft, and Roosevelt's talk of producing fifteen thousand planes a year seemed like a fantasy. Now capacity had increased to more than twenty-one thousand.[24] Employment at aircraft and engine manufacturers had doubled to seventy-five thousand in the twelve months to April and was expected to reach 100,000 that summer.[25] The United States was now able to exceed Germany in producing the key component in modern warfare.

★ ★ ★

Morgenthau and Bell arrived at the White House on March 4 for a perfunctory meeting with the president and White House economic adviser Lauchlin Currie on the Treasury's regular financings. When they walked into the waiting room, they found Marriner Eccles ready to join them. Currie, a dyed-in-the-wool New Dealer originally from Nova Scotia, had obviously wanted liberal reinforcement while dealing with the Treasury secretary, so he had called in the chairman of the Federal Reserve. After a brief discussion, Bell and Morgenthau ascertained the other two had been talking about using the gold in the stabilization fund to redeem some maturing securities. Morgenthau reminded them again the stabilization fund money could not be used without the approval of Congress, and both Eccles and Currie agreed.

But once they were with Roosevelt, both Currie and Eccles argued the

Treasury should hold off on refinancing until it knew what the new tax receipts would be. They also argued in various ways that the stabilization-fund gold could be used rather than going to the debt markets—if not now, then later. When Morgenthau asked Roosevelt whether he favored financing now or later, the president said he didn't want to become entangled in the details. He asked them to discuss the matter among themselves in the cabinet room.

Morgenthau later said Eccles "made one of his long-winded speeches," admitting the matter was the sole responsibility of the Treasury but feeling duty-bound to share his opinion with the president. Currie said he didn't feel he should apologize to anyone for airing his views. Morgenthau said he got the impression his two opponents simply felt they had to use this gold for something to stimulate the economy. What they didn't know was White had lobbied Morgenthau for forty-five minutes that morning to take the same action with the stabilization-fund gold. Morgenthau was worn down. He was sick of people interfering with the facet of his job at which he excelled.[26]

"I take this very personally," he later told a few staff members. "I was asking the President to decide. He was putting me in a position that I had to ask him to decide whether he was going to follow the Eccles-Currie school of thought or whether he was going to follow my advice."[27]

In front of Eccles and Currie, he dictated a quick note to the president saying that Eccles preferred using the stabilization-fund gold in the near future, even if that meant refinancing only some of the maturing securities. The note spelled out that Morgenthau wanted to refinance all of them immediately. "I cannot take the responsibility of having such a large amount of government securities hanging over the Treasury at this time," he concluded, asking for FDR to okay his funding plan before 4:00 p.m., when the president had a press conference. He read the note twice to Eccles to make sure that the central banker agreed with the summation of his views.[28]

"Well, that's the same as resigning if you don't get it," said Currie, referring to the conclusion.

"I don't threaten to resign," said Morgenthau, overlooking the fact that he'd done so at least once in the past two years.

By 2:45 that afternoon, FDR had signed off on Morgenthau's financing plan.

Morgenthau had fought off the New Dealers, but the problems with the War Department showed no sign of abating. The Army Appropriation Bill had been handed over to a congressional committee for study, and General Hap Arnold and other military spokesmen frankly testified that they believed the foreign orders were interfering with the domestic-airplane program. Several congressmen said that the foreign orders were creating demand, which in turn was driving up labor costs at some plants—a claim denied by several administration officials. On March 12, Morgenthau marched into the Oval Office armed with aircraft-production statistics and told the president point-blank that Johnson and Arnold were ruining his effectiveness. The statistics showed how dramatically production had risen, and they included the number of people now employed in airplane manufacturing. And Morgenthau quoted Lauchlin Currie as saying the aircraft program was "the most important thing in Washington" not just in military terms but also as an instrument of economic growth.

Morgenthau told his staff the president was impressed with the stats. FDR called in Pa Watson and Steve Early and said Morgenthau would head the aircraft program because he, the president, didn't have the time to meet with all the parties involved. "The fellows Johnson and Arnold don't like it and they are doing everything they can to sabotage it and they have to stop it," said Roosevelt. When Steve Early, who'd worked in the War Department, warned of how obstructionist Arnold could be, Roosevelt replied: "If Arnold won't conform, maybe I will have to move him out of town." FDR instructed Early and Watson to order Johnson to say publicly that he approved of the aircraft program, of the foreign participation in it, and of having the secretary of the Treasury in charge of it. And Arnold was no longer allowed to speak to the press.[29]

"Well, the President was swell," Morgenthau told his staff. "It shows that when the President wants to he can take two hours and get a thing straightened out. That's what he can do when he wants. He did not do that for me last year."[30]

The staff filed out, and only Henrietta Klotz remained behind to record Morgenthau's final thoughts on the day. In confidence, he revealed he had also told the president that day all that he had gone through for him with the French Mission fiasco and how he "got crucified up on the hill for a month" because of it. He said he never understood why the president had been angry with him for a month or two after the plane crash in California.

When Morgenthau finished, Roosevelt had looked at him and said: "Well, you would have to give me more details. I can't remember."

It was the first time Morgenthau had brought up his rough patch with FDR a year earlier, and the only response he got from his best friend was that he did not remember.[31]

Louis Johnson agreed to reign in Hap Arnold and to go to Capitol Hill to explain the benefits of the airplane program. Early advised the Treasury secretary to use "a little soft soap" in his dealings with Johnson, who he believed sincerely wanted to work together on the armament program.[32] The War Department that afternoon put out a statement saying the Curtiss P-40 pursuit ship, powered by its sophisticated Allison liquid-cooled engine, would be sold to Britain and France. The *New York Times* said the result was "a political tempest of the first magnitude."[33] The House Veteran and Military Affairs Subcommittee immediately announced hearings on the purchases, calling Woodring, Johnson, Marshall, and Arnold to testify. Morgenthau publicly said he welcomed the inquiry, adding that his relationship with the military was "perfectly all right." He hosted Woodring and Secretary of the Navy Charles Edison at lunch on March 14, and the latter publicly stated the foreign orders had neither interfered with nor raised the price of his domestic orders.

The controversy lingered until Roosevelt a week later publicly praised the purchase of aircraft by the foreign powers. He told a press conference that the Allied airplane program was primarily responsible for tripling capacity for airplane production in the past year. The next day, the congressional committee ended its hearings, mainly influenced by the president's support of the purchasing program.[34] By mid-April, the public was well aware of the foreign purchases, and the Associated Press reported that the British and French together had placed an order for more than 1,500 planes at a cost of more than $120 million. Purvis also told the news service that additional contracts would be signed in the near future.[35]

★ ★ ★

Given their partnership in crushing Poland, the Soviet Union and Germany were largely considered as allies, so the pending collapse of Finland was perceived to be simply another democratic country being flattened by the superior totalitarian force. "I don't know where we could spend $50 million to better advantage than to give it to the Finns to fight our battle to keep these fellows from getting to the Atlantic," Morgenthau told his staff early in January. "Because once they get to the Atlantic God help England and then we are in the soup."[36] Working with Roosevelt, who publicly condemned the Soviets' "dreadful rape of Finland," he planned to lend $50 million to the Finns and forgive any outstanding debts they had. However, he soon learned there was not enough support on the Hill for a loan to Finland. Roosevelt asked for congressional support, but Congress dithered as Finland weakened. The Finns officially surrendered on March 13, 1940. In five years, the aggressors had consumed the Rhineland, Austria, Czechoslovakia, Spain, Poland, and Finland, and had eaten into huge swaths of China.

Six days after Finland surrendered, Morgenthau sat down to lunch with Roosevelt and the president broached a subject he admitted might sound a little "cockeyed." He wanted the Treasury to devise a program that would give one dollar a day to everyone over sixty years old or who became sick. He said it would cost about $2 billion and could be financed by an increase in the payroll tax. "It may be cockeyed," Morgenthau quoted him as saying later that day. "I don't say there is anything to it, but I want you to study it." He added: "We have to do something like this."[37]

Nothing became of the matter. But it's worth noting that as the world inched ever closer to a global conflict, Roosevelt was asking his financial and procurement czar to sidetrack himself with an election-year social program that would have increased the $8.4 billion budget being debated in Congress by 24 percent and increased the taxation on businesses.

★ ★ ★

Roosevelt told Morgenthau he chatted with Woodring on March 19 and that the War secretary vowed to withhold secret devices from the Allies. When Roosevelt asked him to name the devices, Woodring could come up with only bomb sites, and Roosevelt let him have it "with both guns."[38] While Morgenthau was vacationing at the Cloister, a luxurious resort in Sea Island, Georgia, Roosevelt told him during a March 31 phone call that "Pa had to get very angry and tell them [obviously Woodring and Johnson] that if they did not get together some of them would have to leave Washington." He also told Morgenthau that he was very pessimistic about the situation in Europe and that something would likely happen within thirty days.[39]

It took only ten days for that prophesy to be fulfilled. On April 9, Hitler seized Denmark and began an initial assault on Norway. Within twenty-four hours, the Nazis had captured most of the Norwegian ordnance and had a firm hold of southern Norway and all of Denmark. It allowed Germany unfettered supply routes from iron mines in neutral Sweden, from which the German forces received most of their iron ore. To challenge the Nazi occupation, the Allies landed forces in northern Norway on April 14.

Roosevelt was outraged—"hopping mad," as Morgenthau repeatedly dictated into his diary—that the Brits had not prevented the Germans from marching into Norway. As he had with the previous acts of aggression, the Treasury secretary responded by freezing the assets of the occupied countries to make sure the Nazis couldn't get them. He also ordered customs to hold in port all ships due to sail to Scandinavia. He worked with his liaison committee on a new DuPont powder plant, reversing a decision by Collins to locate the plant in Canada.[40] They had gone through these defeats before, but there was something different about this one. The smaller countries were fast being gobbled up by Germany and the Soviet Union, and it was only a matter of time until it was the turn of Britain and France.

On the night of April 18, Morgenthau had a drink with Franklin and Eleanor Roosevelt in honor of his twenty-fourth wedding anniversary. They had good reason to celebrate for the French and British that day had finally announced their order for 1,500 warplanes. There is no record of Elinor joining them—it may have been that she stayed home because of her declining health. Four days later she would check in to the hospital under an assumed name and undergo surgery.[41] But during drinks, the war in Europe dominated the conversation.

"If things get worse I suppose you have to wait until after the convention to get rid of Harry Woodring," Morgenthau said, according to his diary.

"No, if things get worse I will form a national cabinet," replied the president, surprising his guest. A national cabinet would involve bringing Republicans into cabinet.

They bandied about names. Roosevelt said he was thinking about appointing John Gilbert Winant, a former Republican governor of New Hampshire who was more enthusiastic about the New Deal than many Democrats. William Bullitt could be the secretary of the navy, and Frank Knox, another Republican from New Hampshire, would run the Commerce Department.[42] It was obvious that Roosevelt had decided finally to get rid of Woodring and possibly Edison in the navy. One name that was not on his list of people to fire was Louis Johnson. As the weeks went on and the crisis deepened, the president and the secretary bandied about names. Morgenthau thought Winant a poor choice for War secretary and suggested Interior Secretary Harold Ickes or New York mayor Fiorello La Guardia. Roosevelt kept casting his net wider and wider, proposing the name of someone called "Simpson." Morgenthau responded with disbelief and later dictated into his diary: "I mentioned this at home to Mrs. Morgenthau and Ruth Schmuck is a great friend of Simpson and she told Mrs. Morgenthau that he is violently anti-Roosevelt and makes the most sneering, dirty remarks about him whenever he gets the chance." The suggestions kept coming but there was still no action, and by the end of April the British were evacuating their troops from Norway. "You just got to do something about your War Department," Morgenthau told Roosevelt at lunch on April 29.

"You are right," said the president. "You are right."[43]

The retreat from Norway was the final political crisis of the Chamberlain government. Neville Chamberlain won a vote of nonconfidence in the Commons but by such a slim margin that it was clear his government could not go on. He invited the Labour Party leader Clement Atlee to form a national government with him, but Atlee declined. On the night of May 9, Chamberlain resigned and the nation learned he would be succeeded by the sixty-five-year-old Winston Churchill, a pugnacious veteran of so many governments that his tenure in the Commons stretched back to Gladstone. He had previously held such posts as first lord of the admiralty and chancellor of the exchequer, and he was best known for his unwavering opposition to the Nazis. Hours after he was sworn in by King George, the Germans launched a devastating attack on neutral Netherlands and Belgium. The western front was finally erupting into warfare.

Roosevelt called together representatives from the military and the State and Treasury Departments a few hours after the German tanks began to rumble into the low countries. Morgenthau came to the "somber" meeting armed with the data on the Dutch, Belgian, and Luxembourgian holdings in the United States. He also had other loose sheets showing the various expenditures needed to equip the armed forces. He and the military had begun to examine what it would cost to fully clothe, arm, and pay an army, and he had preliminary figures showing that it would cost about $30 million to pay for fifteen thousand enlisted men. Still other loose sheets of information detailed figures such as the number of blankets in the Civilian Conservation Corps. (Morgenthau thought these blankets, 400,000 in stock and 855,000 on order, could be given to the army.) But he understood that there were too many scattered pieces of information being fed to the president. He needed to get the big picture on how to equip and pay for an army that could combat the three million German soldiers that were involved in the offensive in the Low Countries.

After the meeting, Morgenthau approached General George Marshall and asked him a pointed question that arose from the data that had been trickling into his office: "I understand that you could put into the field today, fully equipped, 75,000 troops."

"That's absolutely wrong," shot back Marshall.

"Well, how many could you put in the field?"

"Eighty thousand."[44]

Morgenthau arranged to meet with Marshall the next day, a Saturday, so they could go over a budget for the army. He was less accommodating when Woodring approached to say he would help the Treasury secretary in any way possible. Morgenthau knew the War secretary's days in his post were numbered, and he was brutal with his old nemesis. He asked if Woodring was criticizing him and then told Woodring that the War secretary's own budget officer didn't know what he, Woodring, was talking about.[45]

Morgenthau and Budget Director Harold Smith spent the weekend cloistered with Marshall on a military budget. The general had assembled plans for an $850 million budget to recruit, clothe, and equip a 750,000-man regular army. The figure was equivalent to about 10 percent of the entire 1941 budget the president had submitted to Congress five months earlier and was in addition to the government's multi-billion-dollar airplane program. But Morgenthau, like Marshall, believed it was entirely appropriate given the strength and experience of the enemy. He also learned over that weekend that Woodring, Johnson, and Marshall had brought a similar proposal to Roosevelt in September, in the days after the Polish invasion, and the president had brushed them off. "The President has to take a great deal of responsibility that the Army is in as bad shape as it is," Morgenthau dictated into his diary.[46]

On Monday, May 13, Smith and Morgenthau accompanied the senior War Department personnel to the White House to present Marshall's plan to the president. It did not take long for Johnson and Woodring to bicker over the funding, and Roosevelt rejected the proposal quickly. Morgenthau got the impression the president simply was not familiar with the problems facing the regular army and began to argue in favor of Marshall's proposal. After he mounted what he described as a strong argument, Roosevelt suggested he butt out. When he persisted, the president turned to him with a mixture of a smile and a sneer and said, "I am not asking you. I am telling you."

"Well, I still think you are wrong," said Morgenthau.

"Well, you filed your protest."

Marshall held his ground, and eventually Roosevelt began to see the logic of his argument. It was a victory for both the military and Morgenthau. Between the meetings throughout the day, the brass approached

Morgenthau constantly, with Marshall asking for advice on future dealings with the president. And at one point, Woodring, Johnson, and Smith all called on Morgenthau to take the lead in cobbling together the financial plans in the arms program.

"You better do this, because after all you really are the Assistant President," Johnson said to him.

Morgenthau replied that if Johnson wanted to ruin his effectiveness completely, all he had to do was to say that out loud.

"Oh, I won't say it to anybody, but that's what you are."

Protest as he might, Morgenthau did dictate the incident into his diary the next day and also revealed he was considering recommending to the president that he strike a committee made up of senior army, navy, and commerce personnel to oversee the arms program. And Roosevelt could "possibly make me Chairman so I can make sure the program is coordinated with the Allied Program."[47] Yet he had grave doubts about the president's airplane program.

"He has come up again with the idea nobody is ready for," he told William McReynolds, a Treasury official who had been seconded to the White House. "He wants 50,000 planes a year, just like that, which means, according to the War Department's first figures, building thirty plants of a million square feet each." He then launched into a long rant about the need for a committee on aviation, the difficulty in getting machine-tool producers on board, and the fact that not a single US plane at the time could take on a German plane. "I have never seen such a mess," he concluded.[48]

By this time, the Allied program was thrown into doubt because no one knew if the Allies would exist much longer. The Germans were marching steadily westward, taking the Netherlands. On May 13, Churchill told the British people in a BBC address that he had nothing to offer them but "blood, sweat, toil and tears." He also said his government's policy would be to "wage war against a monstrous tyranny, never surpassed in the dark, lamentable catalogue of human crime."[49]

With his masterful political judgment, Roosevelt sensed the collapse of the smaller democracies was increasing American hostility to German aggression. On May 16, just three days after he had argued against Marshall and Morgenthau's rearmament plan, the president sent a message to Congress requesting an appropriation of $896 million for an accelerated arms program. It was an astonishing figure, given that only five months earlier the president had submitted a budget that had asked for $1.8 billion in military expenditures, and that had been interpreted by most pundits as an excessive amount. "The ground forces of the Army require the imme-diate speeding up of last winter's program to procure more equipment of all kinds, including motor transport and artillery, tanks, antiaircraft guns and full ammunition supplies," Roosevelt said. "It had been planned to spread these requirements over the next two or three years. We should fill them at once."[50]

Morgenthau that night told his staff he felt good about the president's message, but he was tired of having to fight everyone to get anything done. Johnson and he had had a harsh exchange after the president's address, with the assistant secretary for War making it clear he would cooperate with Morgenthau but only because the president told him to.[51] "You have to fight Woodring, Edison, Johnson, [Under Secretary of the Navy Lewis] Compton and all the rest of the stuff," Morgenthau told his staff, explaining that he couldn't simply give the president a plan while the military people just talk about getting things done. "And if he had a Secretary of War and Navy, I would not have to do it." He added that Roosevelt wanted him to continue to do the things he had been doing, such as coordinating the aircraft program and the orders from the allies. He asked his staff to give some consideration to one matter that had been bothering him: private manufacturers held the patents on their designs, so the production of each plane was limited to the capacity of the designer's factory. Morgenthau asked his staff to look into whether the manufacturers could license out their patents and thereby increase capacity.[52] All these tasks were taking on a new urgency. For by this time, the German army was advancing again, and it was doing so against the perilous democracies of Western Europe.

CHAPTER SIX

AIDING BRITAIN

★ ★ ★

U sually so jocular, Ambassador William Bullitt's tone was desperate as it reached Morgenthau through a crackling undersea cable on May 20, 1940, and described the horrors in France. Between three and five million refugees were trudging from the German frontier to Paris, the ambassador said. The French army was too busy fighting a rear-guard action to defend its citizens. Bullitt's report that German soldiers were willfully machine-gunning children confirmed what Americans read in the newspapers. The American press had more reporters in France than in Poland, and the reports of German atrocities against America's oldest ally resonated with the public. "The German tactical plan is manifestly to sow terror everywhere," said the *New York Times* on May 21. Motorized units dashed into towns to create panic, wreaked havoc, then retreated. The Luftwaffe spread its bombs over a wide expanse—rather than in concentrated areas—simply to muddle the enemy. The result was massive civil upheaval and slaughter.[1] Morgenthau had erected a map of Europe in the corner office and could see how the Nazis were now advancing. The British Expeditionary Force was pinned against the English Channel at Dunkirk, and the Germans were breaking through the resistance in Belgium and heading for virtually undefended Paris. "All this does is make me sick at my stomach," Morgenthau dictated into his diary that evening. "What's a person going to do? Got hard enough times here."[2]

Already overworked, Morgenthau responded with a flurry of tasks. He had J. Edgar Hoover, the young head of the Federal Bureau of Investigation, ensure wire taps were installed at the German embassy.[3] He fielded a French request to assume an order of 144 Vanguard planes bound for Sweden—not a popular country as it supplied iron ore to the Germans.[4] He moved immediately to get $20 million to the French and increase the shipment of goods. He initiated the new standards for airplane makers. All the while, as the Nazis poured deeper into France, he and Roosevelt negotiated with Congress on the 1941 budget and the arms-appropriation bill. Roosevelt off-handedly told him one day there was no hurry on some matter with the airplane program because "after all we will not be in it for 60 or 90 days." In his notes, Morgenthau underlined the final four words. The president believed the country would be at war as early as mid-August 1940.[5]

The vicious German advance began to erode isolationist sentiment across the country, even in the Midwest, which felt buffered from European and Asian strife. "There may be little left in the Middle West of the comfortable idea that this is merely another European war that can have little effect upon us," wrote syndicated journalist Raymond Clapper.[6] When famed aviator Charles Lindbergh told a radio audience the United States was in no danger of an assault from Europe, isolationists like Republican presidential aspirant Robert Taft applauded the speech, but moderates scoffed.[7] "I am absolutely convinced that Lindbergh is a Nazi," Roosevelt told Morgenthau a few days later.[8] It all meant Roosevelt had actually *underestimated* popular sentiment when he submitted his military-appropriations bill. Congress began to proceed rapidly in approving the president's request.

America could not help but notice the Germans' vast military superiority. Hitler on May 20, 1940, had invited three American journalists, including Pulitzer Prize–winner Louis P. Lochner of the Associated Press, to witness his air assault from the German side of the front. Lochner's report said the Germans proved "war has been revolutionized by the air force." The methodical German assault began with aerial-surveillance planes that returned with photographs to determine Allied troop strength, armaments, and movement. The Germans immediately responded by bombing key points, including towns, if necessary, to disrupt the troops and destroy infrastructure. Amid the resulting confusion, motorized ground forces attacked to add to the chaos and inflict casualties.[9] Legislators in Washington now focused on the need for more planes. "As the debates proceed, the emphasis shifts more and more to air defenses, and it is obvious that this phase of the European war has captured the imagination of Congress," said the *New York Times*.[10]

On May 24, the British cabinet approved a massive evacuation at the Belgian port of Dunkirk, hoping to remove about forty-five thousand of its stranded troops. By June 2, a flotilla of small and large craft had evacuated almost 340,000 troops, converting an unqualified debacle into a qualified debacle, then into a propaganda boon. Though the Brits boasted of the miracle of the little boats, its army had lost thousands of men and the Germans had captured a trove of arms. Italy, led by Benito Mussolini, finally declared war on both France and Britain, posing new threats to British control of the Mediterranean. On June 5, the Germans outflanked the Maginot Line and began their final assault on France. Hitler's empire would soon stretch from Poland to the Atlantic with a strong ally in Italy and a sympathetic government in Spain. All of Washington was galvanized into action. "Not since the United States entered the [First] World War has an American President been so completely supported by all political interests, with the possible exception of the days of economic emergency when this President first entered office," wrote Arthur Krock in the *New York Times*.[11] Most important for Morgenthau, the Battle of France transformed the entire budgetary debate in the United States.

Morgenthau was the key administration official in both the budget and the young aircraft program. The president wanted to accelerate fundraising and arms production but still stressed that he wanted no millionaires created through the arms industry.[12] He worked to bar legislation that would severely loosen the restrictions on profits in naval contracts.[13] The president, Morgenthau, and congressional leaders admitted they would have to raise taxes, which would prove difficult in an election year and also risked quashing the nascent recovery. By the time Belgium collapsed, Morgenthau had agreed with Senate Finance Committee Chairman Pat Harrison to raise the debt limit with both the administration and Congress sharing the blame.[14]

Congress set the military spending levels for 1941 with alacrity and far outdid Roosevelt's request for an additional $895 million. By the time various revisions were added, the appropriation for the War Department soared to $1.8 billion and passed in the Senate on May 23 by a vote of seventy-four to zero. But that was only army funding.[15] The next day, in a seventy-eight-to-zero vote, the Senate approved a $1.5 billion appropriation for the navy. Congress—which had been the main stumbling block to an ambitious armament program—had unanimously voted to spend $3.3 billion on its military, or almost 40 percent of the $8.4 billion budget FDR had submitted five months earlier. Hitler's spring offensive sank Denmark, Norway, Belgium, the Netherlands, and France in short order, but it mobilized the US government, the most powerful financial apparatus in the world, with the full backing of the American people. Soon, Republican newspaper editor William Allen White, a Kansan known as the spokesman for Middle America, wrote Roosevelt: "As an old friend, let me warn you that maybe you will not be able to lead the American people unless you catch up with them. They are going fast."[16]

The president wanted to resurrect the excess-profits tax, knowing it would play well in an election year. But the Treasury omitted the tax when it proposed increasing personal, corporate, and alcohol taxes by 10 percentage points and adding a few cents to the gasoline tax, aiming to raise an additional $656 million annually. Gallup polls showed the public would accept higher taxes for national defense, so Harrison and Ways and Means Committee Chairman Robert Lee Doughton supported the Treasury plan.[17] Morgenthau appeared before the Ways and Means Committee on May 31 to outline a financing program that called for a $3.7 billion deficit and requested a $3 billion increase in the borrowing limit. "What we had in mind is that the people would like to pay for the extraordinary armament program, that they would like to be taxed," said the secretary at a press conference.[18]

Morgenthau in late May proposed that all manufacturers standardize military aircraft to allow more large-scale production. Problems such as the retooling of secondary plants and the training of skilled labor remained, but production overall was expected to increase dramatically. "Officials of the United Aircraft Corp. state that in their conferences in Washington recently they had found Secretary Morgenthau highly sympathetic to their

problems," said the *Wall Street Journal* on May 24, reporting all major manufacturers supported the proposal.[19] At Morgenthau's suggestion, Roosevelt
on June 3 appointed William B. Knudsen, president of General Motors, as
the coordinator of machine tooling for the defense industries—one of the
key shortfalls in the program. The media speculated Knudsen would eventually take over more of the aircraft and arms production brief. The secretary became so impressed with Knudsen's efficiency that he put his name
forward for War secretary. Roosevelt was dubious, telling Morgenthau the
man spoke "in broken English" (which must have been truly dreadful, as
FDR had tolerated Morgenthau's parlance for so many years).[20] By early
June, automobile companies—which had so far remained sidelined from
the aircraft program—agreed to investigate whether they could manufacture airplane engines. "We moved awful fast in the past 10 days," Morgenthau told a press conference June 3, adding that he had almost taken care
of all the problems associated with aircraft production.[21]

Budget problems occurred when Doughton warned the new budget
would not raise enough money to cover the increased arms production
and Roosevelt wanted the new excess-profits tax included in the revenue
bill. The president had called in New York tax lawyer Randolph Paul—
who he'd tapped previously on tax matters—to devise a "most marvelous
scheme" for a progressive tax on corporate profits based on the declared
value of a company's stock. Profits would be tax-free on the first 4 percent
of the declared value. Then there would be a 1 percent tax imposed on
profits up to 10 percent of the declared value of the stock. Once profits
exceeded 14 percent of the declared value of the stock, the tax rate would
be 99 percent.

Morgenthau explained the scheme to his exhausted staff on the
evening of June 3. The problems extended beyond the fact that it had
come so late in the budget process. The declared value of stock was usually
far less than a stock's actual value. Under Paul's model, almost all profits
would be severely taxed. Even the Treasury's liberal brain trust considered
the plan punitive. It could endanger the entire tax bill in Congress and
could offend arms producers, just as Morgenthau was finally winning over
a broad range of manufacturers to the arms program. The Treasury was

worried about punishing manufacturers when they were needed to win the most mechanized war in history. But Morgenthau intended to follow the chief's orders.

"I am sick and tired of the President giving orders and the people giving him the run around," he told his staff, "and he is entitled to having his wish carried out, and this is the wish, and God damn it I am going to give it to Pat [Harrison] just the way I got it and to old Doughton too, and we will have to shout it four times, and I am going to give it."[22]

As usual, the length of a sentence indicated the strength of his fervor, and the Treasury staff prepared a proposal. Harrison advocated omitting the excess-profits tax for the time being and lowering exemptions on personal income tax instead. Roosevelt agreed but ordered Morgenthau to continue talks on excess profits and—once again—to ensure there were no war millionaires. The bill moved through Congress and passed both houses by overwhelming margins in mid-June, just as the Germans were entering Paris.

The questions about war leadership that summer extended beyond whether Roosevelt would reoffer and encompassed the entire structure of the administration.

"The critical problem at the moment in Washington is the organization of what may be called the high command, where decisions of transcendent political importance will have to be made almost immediately," wrote the syndicated columnist Walter Lippmann. He argued that the presidency was not a man but an office, and without the proper structure the president lacked the power to ensure he carried out his duties.[23] Roosevelt had to replace Harry Woodring and Charles Edison (who had decided to run for governor of New Jersey) and was under pressure to form an effective purchasing commission. There were only the Council of National Defense, which was a group of business executives with little more than titular authority, and the National Defense Advisory Commission, a loosely knit collaboration of cabinet members whose duties were never defined and which rarely met.[24] Frank R. Kent said three critical departments had been effectively headless for two years—the navy because Edison was a stopgap appointment, the War Department because of the internal bickering, and the Commerce Department because Hopkins had been sick so often. He concluded that the situation "clearly cannot continue without lending color to the charges of fumbling incompetency which are made against the administration."[25]

Hopkins had served Roosevelt faithfully through tragedy and crisis. His wife, Barbara, had died of stomach cancer, then he was diagnosed with the same affliction, after which he suffered the effects of malnutrition. Though regarded as Roosevelt's closest adviser, he had never fully performed his role as commerce secretary because he was too sick or he was acting as Roosevelt's personal representative in foreign capitals. After war broke out, Hopkins had moved into the White House to help the chief plan for war. Roosevelt reportedly had considered placing him in charge of military production but scrapped the plan when advisers protested.[26] In the summer of 1940, Roosevelt told Morgenthau that Hopkins would resign in a month, adding, "Well, you know, Hopkins is not well enough to go to the office." When Morgenthau dictated this into his diary, he added, "I felt like saying I had known that for two years."[27] He refrained. He would bad mouth Hull, Woodring, and other insiders in front of the president, but he never did so with Hopkins.

Woodring's career finally ended in early June. The final incident began when Admiral John H. Towers, the chief of naval air, told Morgenthau the navy could spare fifty Curtiss-Wright Scout dive bombers for Britain and France, as it lacked the pilots to fly them. But the army—which was realizing the importance of dive bombers in the French campaign—had asked for them.

"Nuts on the Army!" replied Morgenthau, asking if the navy could ship the planes to the Allies if he reached an arrangement with the manufacturers.

"Of course, you realize we are subject to attack on the Hill," replied Towers.

"So are we all," said the secretary. "Look what I went through a year ago."

Roosevelt signed off on the deal that afternoon and Morgenthau arranged to have the planes shipped to Halifax, Nova Scotia, where they would be picked up by a British aircraft carrier. Then on June 9, Morgenthau located 750 bombs to go with the planes. But Woodring and Johnson refused to release their bombs until they had direct orders from Roosevelt. At 7:25 that night, Morgenthau cabled Roosevelt aboard the USS *Potomac* seeking authorization. "Sorry to bother you at this time but we ought to have an answer tonight," he said. "The French say they need seven-hundred fifty bombs which will be enough to last them for fifteen days."

"It seems obvious that bombs are a necessary part of plane equipment and should go along with the 50 Navy bombers," replied Roosevelt in a cable the next day. "Show this to Woodring as authority to release."[28]

The next night, Morgenthau was able to call Arthur Purvis and tell him the order was going through. "Had the darnedest time," he said.

"You can't tell what this means abroad," said a relieved Purvis. "It just means everything to them."[29]

The partnership of Morgenthau and Purvis was gaining recognition in the British government at this critical juncture in the island nation's history. The "Morgenthau-Purvis channel" was regarded as the most effective means of getting what Britain desperately needed. When Lord Beaverbrook, head of British aircraft production, urged Lord Lothian, the British ambassador in London to go directly to the State Department to speed plane deliveries, Lothian replied that he and Purvis felt they should use "the Morgenthau channel," which had worked so well in the past.[30] And the British came to regard Morgenthau as a unique being in Washington. "He was sometimes referred to in the early correspondence as 'our friend,'" said the British government's official history of the war. "He was prepared to move heaven and earth when approached with a reasonable request." One British official said Morgenthau was always ready "to work far into the night, every day, for us."[31] Even within the establishment circles in Washington, Morgenthau was known as Britain's champion within the cabinet. "The Treasury, under Secretary Henry Morgenthau Jr., has always thought first of the broader aspects of the President's foreign policy," wrote columnists Joseph Alsop and Robert Kintner in the *Wash-*

ington Post. Morgenthau "hates to be taken in, and has never been soft with the British, but his strongest emphasis is on quick aid to Britain."[32] Purvis was also gaining more clout in Britain and was now regarded as something akin to an ambassador, only with greater practical power. "Never have wider powers to commit this country been delegated to any Mission, and indeed it is true to say that no Mission has ever carried so grave a responsibility," one British minister told the House of Lords, referring to Purvis's mission.[33] Morgenthau described Purvis as "one of the rarest persons" he had ever known. "He had a pleasant Scotch burr and a whole chain of anecdotes about the Scot triumphing over the Englishman," said Morgenthau. "'It always takes a Scotsman to pull England out of a hole,' he used to say."[34] They dined together often, and Purvis continually reminded his host that Britain's problems were multiplying.

Roosevelt fired Woodring on June 19 and nominated Republicans to head the War Department and the navy, a bipartisan act unprecedented in American history. The new navy secretary was Col. Frank Knox, a former newspaper editor and a Republican vice presidential candidate who strongly favored naval expansion. The real surprise was the appointment of venerable New York statesman Henry Stimson as War secretary. Stimson had held the same position from 1911 to 1913 and had been Herbert Hoover's secretary of state from 1929 to 1933. Most important, he was an ardent interventionist who shared Morgenthau's hatred of the Nazis and his belief that the United States must help the Allies. Morgenthau met with him before the announcement, advising him to always remember to push the president and to "get rid of Johnson."[35] Roosevelt fired Johnson a month later, hoping to completely clean house in the military. Johnson refused to leave his office until the president made some sort of statement and "broke down and cried like a baby" when Pa Watson told him he was fired.[36] In his place, Stimson brought in two lawyers from Wall Street, Robert Patterson and John J. McCloy.

The Democratic National Convention in Chicago chose Roosevelt, as expected, as its presidential candidate on July 15, and he named as his running mate Henry Wallace, the handsome Iowan who had been Agriculture secretary. Once again, the entire Morgenthau clan fell in line behind

Roosevelt. The elder Henry Morgenthau telegraphed to say: "My sincere commiserations for your having to continue your exhausting task for another four years. May God grant you the health and power it requires."[37]

France fell in early June and was partitioned into an occupied zone in the north and a nominally independent state in the south headed by Marshal Philippe Pétain, a hero of World War I. General Charles de Gaulle, who had been named under secretary of national defense, refused to recognize the government in Vichy and organized the Free French Forces in London. Britain was now defended by a shrunken arsenal, the world's strongest navy, a narrow stretch of water, and historic grit. It had no European ally, and for ammunition it counted on the United States, a neutral country on the far side of a U-boat-infested ocean.

The "Miracle at Dunkirk" had of course been a crushing loss—especially in terms of armaments. The British had forsaken 880 field guns; 330 heavy-caliber guns; 500 light antiaircraft guns; 850 antitank guns; 6,400 antitank rifles; 11,000 machine guns; 690 tanks; 20,000 motorcycles; 5,000 cars; and 40,000 transport vehicles. It was logical to double these numbers because this matériel was now in German hands and added to their existing arsenal, all of which could be used against the desperate Brits.[38]

For the past two years, every time the Germans took another country, they gained the conquest's capacity for manufacturing weapons. For example, Germany's annual steel-production capacity in the summer of 1938 was just over twenty-two million tons, but in the next two years she added about twenty million tons through the occupation of France, Belgium, Luxembourg, Czechoslovakia, and Poland, and by Italy entering the war. In the summer of 1940, Britain expected its own production of steel (including imports from the United States) would amount to about fifteen million tons, compared with more than forty-two million by greater Germany and Italy.[39] That was simply the statistic for raw steel. The British were accelerating their arms program dramatically, but they knew they were outgunned by a vicious foe. "The [British] munitions baby has doubled or trebled its weight in a couple of months," said one British cabinet report. "Yet it is still a very small infant compared to the giant that threatens to attack it."[40]

Purvis came to the corner office on May 29 asking for modern weapons already on order for the US military. The United States would benefit, he argued, because it would allow manufacturers to test their products in battle environments. His list of requests was incomplete, but he knew it would include at least 1,000 to 1,500 medium-sized tanks and 1,000 large tanks; about 1,000 each of thirty-seven-millimeter antiaircraft and anti-tank guns; 300 to 500 ninety-millimeter antiaircraft guns; and 1,000 three-inch antiaircraft guns. They would also need ammunition for all of this artillery and felt a pressing need for motor torpedo boats and nitrocellulose powder.[41]

Morgenthau—who was now being eased out of his responsibilities as aircraft czar in favor of Knudsen—told Purvis he could not deliver motor torpedo boats because there was no way Congress would ever consider this new technology surplus. Although he sympathized with England's plight, General George Marshall told Morgenthau his priority was the prepared-ness of the US Army and Navy and the defense of the Western Hemisphere. He had gone over a number of requests and decided he could offer Britain no further pursuit planes. Fewer planes would mean the training of fewer American pilots, and the military believed the preparation of its own pilots was its priority. The US military also worried about the acute shortage of bombers and specific matériel, like antiaircraft ammunitions. There was no point in shipping antiaircraft guns to the Brits without ammo. What Marshall could release to the British was about 10,000 Browning machine guns; 25,000 automatic rifles; 500,000 Enfield rifles; 500 seventy-five-mil-limeter field guns; and 500 mortars with 50,000 rounds of ammunition. He also said the army could spare 100 million rounds of ammunition for machine guns and rifles.[42] Purvis said the British would take "the whole damned lot," and it was all shipped to Britain as France was a lost cause. "I am delighted to have that list of surplus matériel which is 'ready to roll,'" FDR wrote Morgenthau on June 6. "Give it an extra push every morning and every night until it is on board ship!"[43]

The arms reached Great Britain in July, where the Britons' joy turned to ambivalence. They were expecting a German invasion, so anything was welcome. However, the weapons were old, and the small arms were of a different caliber than those of the British and lacked sufficient ammunition. They were issued to the home guard. The British realized instantly they needed to harmonize their arms program with the Americans'. Since the British were further along in their development, they believed it made sense that the Yanks adapt to meet British requirements.[44]

The British were worried about the shipping losses, which could cost Britain her naval advantage—a disastrous thought for an island nation that needed food imports to survive. Britain would suffer 4.5 million tons of shipping losses in 1940, far more than it could replace domestically. And the French navy was no longer fighting the Germans, having been retained by the officially neutral Vichy government. (The British would virtually destroy the French navy off of French Algeria on July 3, killing 1,297 Frenchmen and ensuring it could not fall into the hands of the Germans.) Purvis asked Morgenthau on June 5 whether Britain could have any US destroyers. The problem was Admiral Stark, the chief of naval operations, had recently testified before Congress that no destroyers could be considered surplus. However, Morgenthau told Purvis that FDR said the United States might be able to part with ten destroyers.[45] Days later, Purvis gave Morgenthau a note from Churchill saying only sixty-eight British destroyers out of 133 in commission were fit for service, and one-third of them had to be kept in Britain to defend against the expected invasion. That compared with 433 British destroyers ready for action in 1918. "We must therefore ask, as a matter of life and death, to be reinforced with these destroyers," Churchill pleaded. "We will carry on the struggle whatever the odds, but it may well be beyond our resources unless we receive every reinforcement and particularly do we need this reinforcement on the sea."[46]

Soon Roosevelt and Morgenthau were both working to deliver destroyers to the British, and their determination intensified once the Luftwaffe began its aerial assaults on shipping points like Portsmouth, on England's south coast. The fact that the Republican presidential candidate was Wendell Willkie, who wanted to support the Allies, meant aid to Britain would not be an election issue. Morgenthau pressured Knudsen to give French aircraft orders to the British. He lobbied to send B-17 Flying Fortresses to Britain until Roosevelt told him to pipe down, lest he upset the negotiations now proceeding with Congress to deliver destroyers to the British.[47] Though there was a lingering concern in Washington that arms sent to Britain would become German arms if Britain fell, Morgenthau fought on to aid the country.

The last half of July 1940 was a seminal period in the career of Henry Morgenthau Jr. as he tackled a host of issues for the Allies. Working excessively hard, he was short-tempered and effective. He had been in cabinet longer than Stimson and Knox, so he held sway with them. His passion burned stronger than that of anyone else in the cabinet, possibly including Roosevelt. And the British air program overlapped with his official role as Treasury secretary because he had to determine how the Brits would pay for their arms.

Sir Frederick Phillips, a ranking British treasury official, told Morgenthau that Britain and its dependencies had about $2.25 billion in gold, dollars, and US securities but expected to run a balance-of-payments deficit of about $1.55 billion with the United States alone in the next year. Morgenthau actually believed Phillips understated the British predicament and urged the British to divest more of their direct holdings.[48]

Morgenthau was walking to work with Knudsen on July 18 when he took the new airplane czar to task for planning to cut back on engine orders for Britain. He was growing frustrated with the problems surrounding the arms program and asked that he and Stimson sit down with Knudsen before any changes were made. "All this defeatism around Washington is terrible and it's just this time that you take the engines away from them [the British]," Morgenthau said. "You can't do it." As they neared their destination, he added. "You have got to pat Purvis on the back and keep up his morale and not undermine him. . . . The man is on the point of a nervous breakdown and he has to have some encouragement." Knudsen promised to do nothing without consulting Morgenthau.

Later that day, Knudsen told the secretary he would divide the airplane orders evenly between the Americans and the British. Though he was skeptical at first, Purvis eventually was convinced it would prove "a solution to my whole problem."[49]

At a dinner at the British embassy that night, Morgenthau learned that the United States was shipping aviation gasoline to the Japanese. Lothian told him the British had asked the United States to stop the shipments, and Stimson, who was also in attendance, said he had argued against such shipments for a year. Dumbfounded, Morgenthau said he would get on it immediately and decided to ask Harold Ickes, who had said he wanted to preserve the US reserves, to stop the fuel shipments.[50] But Morgenthau didn't stop there. He also decided to seek embargoes on petroleum products and scrap metal, which were being used in the Japanese munitions program.

The next day, Morgenthau explained his plan to Roosevelt ahead of a meeting with Ickes, Stimson, Knox, and Welles. The plan could ensure peace in Asia for three to six months, he said. Roosevelt proposed the embargo to the meeting, not mentioning it had come from Morgenthau. Stimson and the Treasury secretary argued strongly in favor. But Welles said it would only lead to Japan declaring war on Britain, and instead he urged that the United States work toward peace between Japan and China.

"Mr. President," Morgenthau objected, "only ten days ago you told me to go ahead with T. V. Soong on a China-Russia-United States deal to keep China going and I think we should keep them going."

The meeting ended without a decision, and Morgenthau, his passions flowing, regaled his staff back at the Treasury about the "beautiful Chamberlain talk that I listened to Sumner Welles give." Japan would not be provoked into a war, he said, if Ickes announced the program as a means of conserving US oil supplies. "We will say no oil can leave the United States and that was the trick in this thing that pulled the main argument away from the State Department," he concluded. "The State Department just drives me crazy."[51]

In the coming days, he persuaded Ickes that the United States should ban all oil exports for reasons of conservation and national defense. Morgenthau then had Edward Stettinius of the Commission for National Defense produce the justification for embargoes on scrap iron and scrap steel products. Morgenthau on July 22 recommended to FDR that petroleum, petroleum products, and scrap metals be added to the list of materials embargoed by the United States. Stimson told him he supported the move and encouraged him to pressure the State Department.

"I'm putting all the pressure on the State Department that I can, and I'm going to continue to," said Morgenthau.

"You're dead right," said Stimson.[52]

The Battle of Britain had begun, the first military conflict in history that took place between rival air forces. The bombings of industrial areas soon spread to residential neighborhoods. When Hitler vowed on July 23 to repay the British bombing tenfold, Morgenthau did not sleep he was so upset about the shortfall in Allied aircraft. He decided the United States could no longer place a ceiling on British requests nor on its own ambitions for production.

Morgenthau's passions boiled over at a July 23 meeting in which Purvis and several US grandees debated what surplus material the Brits could have. Suddenly, Morgenthau halted the discussion, asked that they all hear him out, and delivered a diatribe that was breathtaking in its verbosity and power. The president, he said, had stated the United States would help the Allies. "Furthermore, I also believe it is his belief . . . that just as long as we can keep the English going, and they have the will and the courage to keep going with their own money to buy the stuff they need to keep up this magnificent fight—that if we want to keep out of war . . . that the longer we keep them going, that much longer we stay out of this war." He repeated several times that it would be "the height of stupidity" to do anything now that would interfere with the British armament program.[53]

With a precise and reasoned voice, Purvis told the Americans just how precarious the situation in London really was. "If I were to cable to London today the feeling of discouragement that I had for a moment last week, I think the effect would be very vital on the course of the war." No one had any surpluses, he said, because all the Allies were struggling to catch up with the Axis air program. "There is no plus sign," he said. "They are all minus signs."

Stimson, possibly more eloquent than Purvis, responded that the US

Army had to be prepared for a national crisis and was about three thousand planes short. "I have to consider an emergency when these requirements for 1941 or 1942 seem like iridescent dreams."

Three thousand planes. It took the United States three months to make that many planes—half a year considering that half the US output, at least in theory, was going to the British. In half a year, who knew how many more planes the Germans would have produced? After the meeting broke up, Morgenthau calculated that the proper goal for US production should be six thousand units per month divided evenly between the British and the Americans. It would amount to thirty-six thousand planes a year for the US military—almost two and a half times the unimaginable production figure Roosevelt had proposed in the autumn of 1938.

"You've talked about how the British would like 3,000 planes a month; say to Knudsen you're ready to order them," he told Purvis the next day, adding not to worry about the authorization—he'd get it. "You've got to bluff," he said. "Stick to the 3,000 planes and put it up to Knudsen as though it were an offer you had been thinking about for weeks. After all, part or all of your British production facility will be bombed—this country has got to take care of it." Morgenthau promised to back him up.[54]

Pressured by Morgenthau and Purvis, Knudsen agreed that morning to an additional three thousand planes a month for the British, with the British agreeing to finance the expansion of some plants. Stimson and Roosevelt both supported the plan. Morgenthau told his diary that the president "seems to want my advice and . . . follows the recommendations I make." Lothian told Morgenthau that Purvis had said, "the most marvelous performance he'd ever seen done by anybody was done by you yesterday." He added: "It'll make a terrific difference to the whole future."[55]

Later on July 25, Roosevelt accepted the Treasury recommendations and banned the export of scrap metal, oil, and oil products. The State Department reacted by confining the embargo to high-octane gasoline, airplane motor oil, tetraethyl lead, and No. 1 heavy melting-grade iron and steel scrap, which it said would restrict the Japanese air-force buildup without exciting the government. The department added that a total embargo would be "administratively tremendously difficult." Morgenthau was outraged because the Japanese could still get crude oil, which they could refine into aviation fuel. If the State Department couldn't handle the full embargo, it should "give it to somebody else to do," he said, telling Stimson and Ickes there would be a "big row" on the issue. Stimson said he would "go the limit on it," and Ickes agreed.[56]

Morgenthau attended a cabinet meeting that afternoon with a blunt letter opposing any changes to the president's orders. "May I most respectfully suggest that if the Division of Controls of the State Department and the Administrator of Export Controls cannot administer this proclamation properly the Treasury can," said the letter, adding it would be "comparatively easy." Morgenthau concluded by writing: "The objections raised to the oil and scrap metal control reinforce a growing impression on my part that there is something very seriously wrong with the personnel or system in effect for administering the export control."[57]

Not only did the letter insult the competence of the State Department, it also said the Treasury could do a job the State Department couldn't. Morgenthau and Welles attacked each other as soon as the meeting began. Raising his hands in the air, Roosevelt told the two men to sort it out themselves after the meeting, and they argued harshly with each other later in the hall. Stimson and Morgenthau both considered it a partial victory. But the fact was that the State Department changes remained in force, and the Japanese still had access to most forms of scrap metal and crude oil from the United States.[58] Yet the Japanese understood that the moves were slowly strangling its industry while the Allies grew stronger. The perceptive journalist Edgar Snow wrote in the *Saturday Evening Post* in May 1941 that a war with Japan was almost certain, largely because the Japanese knew its enemies were outpacing its military production.[59] Secretary of State Cordell Hull began talks with Ambassador Kichisaburō Nomura in April 1941 to try to mend their differences, but both sides were intractable. The United States wanted Japan out of China and to renounce designs on other territories. Japan saw no difference between its colonies on mainland Asia and Britain's colonies in Africa and India. Yet Hull and Nomura continued the talks through 1941 in a bid to avert a war.

★ ★ ★

As war raged in Europe, the Morgenthau family was changing with the children reaching adulthood and the adults feeling the ravages of old age. Henry III had graduated from Princeton University and was now working for the Cleveland Metropolitan Housing Authority.[60] Robert, the family's golden boy, was at Amherst College. In July, he warmed his father's heart by enlisting in the US Navy Reserve, though his mother was worried for his safety.[61] He twice invited Eleanor Roosevelt to address the Amherst Political Union, but they had trouble arranging dates.[62] He also was chairman of the Chest Drive, a fundraising campaign for the war effort, at Amherst, which aimed to raise $4,500 that year, of which $1,350 would be used to buy an ambulance for the British.[63]

On Boxing Day, Joan Morgenthau debuted at the White House, believed to be the first time anyone other than a relative of a president had held her coming-out party at the presidential mansion. The Morgenthaus had remained in Washington for the holidays and enjoyed Christmas dinner with the Roosevelts.[64] Then on December 26, Joan, clad in a gown of white tulle embroidered with sprays of silver sequins and wearing a pearl bracelet and necklace, stood beside the president and First Lady to receive several hundred guests who dined at midnight in the State Dining Room. At 3:00 a.m., Morgenthau and a few others decided it was time to go home, so he asked the orchestra to play "Good Night, Ladies," a closing song for dances of the day. It had no effect, so the bandleader had the band play "The Star-Spangled Banner," which forced everyone to stop dancing and sing. That ended the evening.[65]

Though the family remembered Joan as being reluctant to hold the affair at the White House, she was effusive in her thanks to Eleanor Roosevelt. "It was the biggest occasion of my life and I haven't gotten over it and probably never will," she wrote the First Lady. "Everyone was thrilled to be received by you and the President and they seemed delightfully surprised that a party at the White House could be as informal and as much real fun as you made this one."[66]

Josie Morgenthau, the secretary's mother, once so bubbly and gregarious, was growing increasingly vague and needed more attention. "Mama has not been quite well the last few days," Henry Sr. wrote his son in July.[67] Henry Sr. himself was magnificent in old age. "There is no dimming of memory or interest, no sign of great age even in his appearance," the *New York Times* would write on his eighty-fifth birthday in 1941.[68] Elinor Morgenthau's health continued to decline, though she refused to abandon FDR and the Democrats in an election year. "I feel so keenly about this election that I would be the most miserable person if I hadn't been able to do even a very small share of the work," she wrote Eleanor. "I am so glad you asked me this fall to go to headquarters."[69] Henry III noticed his mother was losing sway with her husband, as was the original Henry Morgenthau.

Into this advisory void stepped Henrietta Klotz, whose responsibilities and devotion extended light-years beyond the traditional concept of a secretary. As well as overseeing a large clerical staff and controlling the secretary's appointments, she was privy to Morgenthau's secrets. She lunched with her boss most days in the little dining area whose walls bore framed editorial cartoons depicting Morgenthau. She received dictation for the Morgenthau Diaries, which included the secretary's most intimate thoughts, from the debate on armaments and finance to the discussions with Eleanor Roosevelt on whether he should resign. Klotz was privy to more secrets at the heart of the government than all but a handful of people.

Blonde, intelligent, and ambitious, she was born Henrietta Stein and later married Herman Klotz. She was twenty-one when she joined Morgenthau as an administrative assistant at the *American Agriculturalist*. Morgenthau tested her by hiding money and seeing if she would hand it in. She returned the money and told him she would quit if he tried that again. Morgenthau's trust in her and dependence on her were absolute, which is not to say their relationship was always harmonious. He once threw a fork at her face, drawing blood, when she lobbied on behalf of a colleague for a policy Morgenthau had already rejected. Morgenthau sent her roses the next day as an apology. Their relationship was complicated by Elinor Morgenthau's jealousy of her husband's attractive secretary. Klotz revered the brilliant Mrs. Morgenthau—so much so that she named her only child, a young girl who was almost blind, Elinor Klotz. But when *Fortune* magazine profiled Morgenthau in 1934, it included a photo of Klotz, saying she "keeps large secrets gracefully." Acting on orders from home, Morgenthau forbade Klotz to be photographed by the media again. On another occasion, Elinor received an anonymous letter reading, "Get rid of this woman. She has lunch with your husband. I don't trust her." They later learned it was written by a security guard who had been pestering Klotz to find jobs for his friends.[70] There is no evidence that Klotz's relationship with Morgenthau was anything more than professional, but she revered him. "Henry Morgenthau Jr., is the simplest person I know, full of life and fun," she once said. "He's a very warm person. He hates to make money. He's serving a hundred and thirty million people and the only thing that interests him is what's good for the people."[71]

Klotz wanted Morgenthau to take a greater interest in the European Jews. His father and wife always cautioned him to represent all Americans, not just Jewish Americans. But Klotz understood the massive tragedy developing in Europe, and she wanted the secretary to help end the suffering.

Following a badly needed vacation, Morgenthau returned to his desk on August 5 to find further requests from Purvis and uniformed guards posted at his door as the war raised security concerns. He found the guards annoying. "Why any of them should sit in front of my door, I don't know," Morgenthau told reporters. "It seems very silly to me."[72] Of greater importance was Purvis's memorandum from Churchill asking for aid. "The need of American destroyers is more urgent than ever in view of the losses and the need of coping with the invasion threat as well as keeping the Atlantic approaches open and dealing with Italy," wrote the prime minister. "As I have repeatedly explained the difficulty is to bridge the gap until our new wartime production arrives in a flood."[73]

In Morgenthau's absence, the cabinet had begun to discuss a plan with the British to swap old US destroyers for bases in British possessions in the Western Hemisphere. Morgenthau liked the plan but reminded the cabinet that British needs extended beyond destroyers. He wanted to send Britain every second Allison engine produced and the bombers' new bombsights, considered top secret by the military. With Willkie supporting the bomber agreement, Roosevelt decided to announce the destroyer deal at his August 16 press conference. At a meeting of close advisers, Morgenthau cautioned the president against revealing any discussions on giving the British motor torpedo boats, which Congress had already ruled out. "Hopkins contributed next to nothing but seemed very excited and eager," Morgenthau told his diary.[74]

In early September, the British asked for twenty-three motor torpedo boats, five Flying Fortresses, five flying boats, and 250,000 rifles. The president ruled out the torpedo boats, but Purvis worked with Morgenthau and Stimson on the rest of the request. All three were surprised that the final contract drawn up by the State Department and the British Foreign Office detailed the transfer of fifty destroyers but mentioned no other armaments. Stimson tried to persuade Roosevelt to include the rifles and airplanes, but Hull convinced him that reopening the deal would provoke criticism. Morgenthau therefore tried to strike a separate deal that would meet Britain's needs. "Get what you can, Henry," Roosevelt told him. But the navy ruled it could not spare even five PBY-5 flying boats, though it promised the Brits more in 1941. Morgenthau was astonished, and his despair grew when he learned the United States shipped only seventeen planes to Britain between September 1 and 14, other than training planes and P-40s with no engines.

"The English have got to have more planes," Morgenthau pleaded with the president on the morning of September 19.

"They can have whatever they want," replied the president. "But you had better work this out with the Army, Navy and Knudsen."

Rather than be outraged, Morgenthau warned the president he would likely drag the military to the Oval Office to be told to help the British. "Of course, this is going to be very hard work for me, but if the President will give me his continuous backing on this I will have no trouble," Morgenthau dictated into his diary.[75]

Again Morgenthau proposed to the brass on September 20 that the British get half the production of P-40s and flying boats, and all seemed to support the idea. But five days later, Robert Patterson of the War

Department reported that Marshall needed more equipment for training, including P-40s.[76] By late September, Morgenthau confided to a few close acquaintances that he was no longer able to influence the president. The secretary was frustrated that he wasn't getting the information he needed from the British. Morgenthau spent three hours on September 25 with Roosevelt, who berated him because the figures he had received from Churchill and Lord Beaverbrook did not agree with the figures Morgen-thau had gotten from Purvis. What's more, there were indications the British had not trained enough pilots to fly the few planes they did receive. The next day, Morgenthau demanded Purvis get consistent figures from Churchill and Beaverbrook. "The one person that they ought to take into their confidence is you and me," said Morgenthau, his mood doing nothing to improve his grammar or his math. "You have never heard me talk like this before but here we are in this whole thing, you know, and have worked this thing up and everything, and then for them to treat you and me like this isn't right." Suspicious by nature, Morgenthau was angered that the British brought in two senior officials to assist Purvis and report to London. The secretary preferred working alone with Purvis.[77]

Marshall in late September told the president that the United States had only forty-nine large bombers fit for duty other than those in Panama and Hawaii. And with the Battle of Britain at its apex, Britain continued to ask for more arms. Stimson and Marshall supported a compromise under which the Brits relinquished 120 engines needed for US bombers and in return got twenty-six B-24 bombers as well as the rifles, bombsights, and half the flying boats they had asked for. "Pretty good for one morning," Morgenthau told Purvis. By this time, Morgenthau believed it would be a rule of thumb that the Brits would get half of the US arms production.[78]

Beaverbrook himself cabled Morgenthau to say he had told his pilots the United Kingdom would have a stream of aircraft sufficient to see them through to victory. "This pledge is only possible owing to the help we derive from you," said Beaverbrook. "We cannot acknowledge your assistance but we hope the day will come when you will visit us and receive from our lads the thanks we owe you." To another British colleague, Beaverbrook said the British could never repay Morgenthau. "I have tried to express it to him," he wrote. "We could not have got on so far without his backing."[79] Within the US government, Morgenthau was regarded as the person who kept arms flowing to Britain. Dean Acheson, the State Department official whom Morgenthau had replaced as under secretary of the Treasury in 1933, said Morgenthau was "entirely responsible" for the fact that the British kept fighting from Dunkirk to early 1941.[80] "A great deal of the success of the initial efforts to get airplane production moving was due to his hard, stubborn and concentrated attention to detail in organizing the placement of orders by the British and the French," said Donald Nelson, who would become chairman of the War Production Board.[81]

Increasingly frustrated by the lack of structure, Stimson was now pressuring Roosevelt to define the responsibilities of the various departments and to coordinate the British and American armament needs. But he was skeptical that Roosevelt would ever create "systematic relations, because that is entirely antithetic to his nature and temperament."[82] Morgenthau offered to leave the procurement program at an October 1 lunch, but Stimson said the problem was the way "the President went off half-cocked" without listening to Marshall or the other generals. They both knew Roosevelt was not going to formalize the structure.

The British now warned of an imminent invasion by sixty of the best German divisions and a superior air force and said they needed American help in arming and transporting a large army they were assembling in the Middle East. "The U-boat and air attacks upon our only remaining life line, the northwestern approach, will be repelled only by the strongest concentration of our flotillas," Sir Arthur Salter, an official with the Ministry of Shipping, wrote Morgenthau and Roosevelt on October 27. He pleaded for an accelerated arms program immediately, saying, "The world cause is in your hands."[83]

By late October 1940, Morgenthau was working to deliver an additional 11,700 aircraft, bringing their total for delivery by June 30, 1942, to 26,075. The British wanted 200,000 machine guns for these planes. For ground forces they wanted a combination of British and American weaponry comprising a total of 1.3 million rifles; 4,000 antitank guns; 750 antiaircraft guns; 2,800 field guns; as well as tank guns, mortars, field guns, and machine guns. It was an unimaginably huge arsenal, and much of it would be surplus US production. The task was, however, made easier by the proposed standardized munitions for both the US forces and the British forces.

Roosevelt favored the proposal, and Morgenthau assembled the top military brass in his office on October 29. "The English are not going to win the war without our . . . military help," said Frank Knox at the outset of the meeting, a view they all agreed with. Though worried about stripping the US forces, Stimson listed items that could be spared and promised to work toward meeting the other requests. Morgenthau told the president the military agreed to the order and Roosevelt—criticized by Willkie for not doing enough to help the British—announced the order in Boston the next night. "The British have now asked for permission to negotiate again with American manufacturers for 12,000 additional planes," said FDR. "I have requested the request be given most serious consideration." He said it would bring the British order to twenty-six thousand planes, require plant expansion, and be accompanied by increased orders for land-based weapons. Though falling short of the three thousand planes a month Morgenthau wanted, it was an achievable program and helped Roosevelt win an unprecedented third presidential mandate on November 5, capturing thirty-eight states and almost 55 percent of the popular vote.[84]

The problem of British finances received little attention during the campaign but soon broke into the open and increased the pressure on the United States to provide financial aid. On November 25, Lothian told reporters that Britain was "beginning to come to the end of her financial resources."[85] The British privately estimated they had ordered $2.1 billion in arms and had agreed to invest about $700 million to increase production capacity and to make a down payment of about $500 million.[86] Harry Dexter White estimated the true cost was closer to $5 billion. Morgenthau did not know what the British could raise by selling assets but was certain it didn't add up to $5 billion. The American government and public now understood this would be an expensive war for the United States as well as Britain. Morgenthau had asked Congress in November to extend the debt limit by between $15 billion and $20 billion, and the move drew little notice. Media reports estimated US military expenditures over five to seven years could run as high as $50 billion, compared with annual expenditures of $1.8 billion two years earlier. And there was an acceptance that the British orders created additional US capacity, which would be needed even if Britain did fall.

With Roosevelt vacationing aboard the USS *Tuscaloosa*, Morgenthau called a meeting on December 3 of Hull, Stimson, head of the Export-Import Bank Jesse Jones, and senior military leaders to explain that the president wanted the United States to proceed with the construction of plants to make arms for the British. However, the British simply didn't have the resources to pay for them. The United States could not lend Britain the money without the approval of Congress, which didn't convene until January. Marshall agreed to show Congress that the British orders would allow the military to arm and equip about three million men. British treasury official Sir Frederick Phillips told Morgenthau on December 6 that the British wanted "a free gift of munitions and aircraft." Failing that, Britain would need a loan that could be repaid after the war.[87] On December 11, senior officials led by Morgenthau leaked to the media that Congress would likely be asked to allow the United States to lend money to the United Kingdom.[88]

When Roosevelt and Morgenthau lunched again on December 17, the president lightheartedly told his friend he hadn't looked at a single report while he was away. Morgenthau filled him in on his talks with Phillips and the request for a loan. Roosevelt took it all in and replied by saying, "I have been thinking very hard on this trip about what we should do for England, and it seems to me that the thing to do is to get away from the dollar sign."[89]

CHAPTER SEVEN

LEND-LEASE

★ ★ ★

L
ike Churchill (and Hitler, for that matter), Franklin Roosevelt knew
less about economics than other aspects of government, such as military affairs, diplomacy, and even social policy. Now he wanted to "get
away from the dollar sign" in his program to support war-ravaged Britain.
It was a simple term, elegant and vague, that would serve Roosevelt's goal
of aiding Britain without exciting isolationist sentiment in Congress.

"I don't want to think of this thing in terms of dollars and loans," he told
Morgenthau over lunch on December 17. He wanted to increase production
and let the British take what they needed to use against the Axis and return
it if it survived the war. He would have given the stuff to the English, he told
Morgenthau, but it would be better to have Congress think the White House
was being too stingy and increase the aid rather than the opposite.[1]

Certainly, America was now eager to help Britain. "We have been
paid for every single thing [Britain ordered], and everything we have done
has increased our own powers of production," Eleanor Roosevelt had
said publicly the day before. "I do not see that there is much reason for
talking about loans. I think we might just as well talk about gifts."[2] Morgenthau, Dean Acheson, and others in the administration agreed. The only
dissenters were die-hard isolationists, who were few in number and large
in influence. "Anglophiles, refugees and important financiers" were con-
spiring to "plunge this country into war," charged Senator Rush D. Holt,
who said the United Kingdom had been given enough aid already.[3]

The president repeated to a press conference hours after meeting with
Morgenthau that the United States had to get rid of "that foolish old dollar

sign" in its dealings with Britain. The important thing was that the United States provide Britain with arms, and the president proposed that they be lent or leased to the island nation.[4] Two weeks later, Roosevelt delivered only his third fireside chat, in which he coined the term "arsenal of democracy" to describe the United States' role in arming the countries opposing the Axis. The public at large applauded as the White House received six hundred messages in the first forty minutes after the speech with 99 percent approving of the general tenor.[5] Within a couple of days, another new term entered the political lexicon of the day—*lend-lease*—describing Roosevelt's new policy on supplying Britain and the Allies. John Maynard Keynes would one day write that the Lend-Lease Bill was Franklin Roosevelt's single-greatest act of statesmanship, and it may have also been one of his greatest acts of public relations. The very term *lend-lease* clouded the issue, leaving the public unsure whether the United States was lending the material or the Brits were leasing it. The vagueness meant there was no need to repeal either the Johnson or the Neutrality Acts, which would have given isolationists a huge platform. All that was needed was to get the new Lend-Lease Bill through Congress—no mean feat in itself.

Roosevelt brought in the Treasury to draft the legislation. On Thursday, January 2, three days after the fireside chat, Morgenthau instructed General Counsel Edward Foley and his associate Oscar Cox to write a bill that would concentrate the power to prosecute the war in the office of the president. Roosevelt wanted to be able to increase arms production without going back to Congress repeatedly. By this time, it was obvious lend-lease would apply to all Allies fighting the Axis. So the president wanted complete flexibility in deciding what materials would be allocated to which nations. The war could move to new theaters—maybe the Middle East, or Africa, or even Ireland—and the British would require different weapons in each theater. The president needed the flexibility to speedily deliver the right weapons to the right place. Finally, there was still a vague understanding of whether the material would be lent, leased, or given to the Allies. "I don't know any law, but if the word can be simply 'lend' and leave it up in the air as to how they should be repaid, I think that is what he wants," Morgenthau told the lawyers.[6]

Twelve hours later, Foley and Cox had prepared a rough draft as an amendment to the Neutrality Acts. Over the weekend, the Treasury brought in contributions from a range of supporters such as Arthur Purvis, Dean Acheson, Supreme Court Justice Felix Frankfurter, and senior War Department personnel. Morgenthau and Henry Stimson sat down with a finished bill Monday morning and worked out the fastest way to get it through Congress. They decided to recast it as new legislation rather than a Neutrality Act amendment and to seek a friendly congressional committee in which to introduce it. On Tuesday, January 5, Morgenthau took the finished bill to the president. The Roosevelt circle decided to introduce the bill in the Foreign Affairs Committee, despite worries it was packed with isolationists. On January 10, the bill was introduced in both houses and given the symbolic number of H. R. 1776.[7]

It was a happy, harmonious time in the Roosevelt circle as everyone worked toward the common goal of aiding Britain. (As Elinor told Morgenthau one night, the United States had to "keep England going in order to let us prepare."[8]) In mid-January, the senior members received their customary invitation to FDR's birthday on January 30. In previous years, Eleanor Roosevelt had insisted on a special theme. In 1938, for example, everyone was asked to show up in a costume or bearing a present that represented a special incident, and the president had to guess what the incident was.[9] But this year, it was a simple celebration of the chief's fifty-ninth birthday.

The harmony began to fade as Cordell Hull proved reluctant to lead the legislation through Congress. Morgenthau told Roosevelt of the problem in a phone call on January 13 and said the time had come for the State Department to contribute more to the effort to aid Britain. "The President did not take my suggestion too well," he told his diary, adding that Roosevelt simply said the secretary of state would testify. When Morgenthau complained that the Treasury had done everything so far, up to writing speeches for key members of Congress, FDR said he knew that. "The important thing is that I have planted the seed in his mind," said Morgenthau. The effort to pass these duties on to Hull came two months after Morgenthau tried to persuade Stimson to oversee aid to Britain. He obviously wanted now to focus on major developments within the Treasury.

The second problem arose from Roosevelt's wish that the British should invest a couple billion dollars in arms factories. Though many supporters agreed with the proposal, Morgenthau knew the British simply didn't have the money. In mid-December, a reporter had asked Morgenthau how the US military personnel reacted when they saw the British government's balance sheet, and he drily quipped, "Nobody fainted."[10] But the joke masked a desperate situation. The British government told Morgenthau it had gold and US securities amounting to $1.78 billion and investments outside the United States and the United Kingdom worth $3.89 billion. It also showed that on the operational side, the British Empire, excluding Canada, was due to run a deficit of $1.46 billion in the calendar year of 1941.[11] Yet Morgenthau could not even convince administration insiders— let alone the isolationist congressmen—of Britain's desperate situation. Though the State Department's economic guru Herbert Feis sided with Morgenthau, Hull continued to believe the Brits could put up collateral of $2 billion to $3 billion. Roosevelt himself thought they could come up with $1 billion. The Treasury's preliminary analysis of the British situation showed that the British needed about $15 billion in military aid.[12] The United States' own defense budget for fiscal 1941 was an already-astounding $7.2 billion, more than three times the previous year's figure. A donation of $15 billion was equal to almost 12 percent of the United States' gross domestic product (GDP) in 1941.[13] It's quite possible that no industrialized country in modern history had shown such generosity to another. The entire Marshall Plan, in which the United States helped to pay for Western European reconstruction from 1948 to 1952, cost $13 billion, or roughly 5 percent of the 1948 GDP.

The night before they were to testify, Morgenthau told Hull and Stimson that Britain had been selling down its holdings of US securities, raising $10 million per week. Then Stimson stated Britain should not be bled dry by the war even if it could scrape together a few billion dollars. It was one of the few democracies left in Europe, a country rich in culture and history that shared a common heritage with the United States. It was the type of moral argument that pleased Morgenthau. "I wasn't going up on the Hill as a banker and ask for collateral" from the British, Morgenthau later told his staff. "If the President wanted somebody to do that, he would have to get somebody else to do it."[14]

By the time the Foreign Affairs Committee convened on January 15, the room was packed with spectators, the atmosphere thick with tobacco smoke and conflicting opinions. Alone at the witness table, Hull opened by saying the bill would help the world return to an atmosphere of calm cooperation rather than the perpetual conquest by totalitarians. "Mankind is today face to face, not with regional wars or isolated conflicts, but with an organized, ruthless and implacable movement of steadily expanding conquest," he read in a speech that was partly written by Roosevelt. "The most serious question today for this country is whether the control of the high seas shall pass into the hands of powers conquest."[15]

Flanked by seven underlings, Morgenthau opened by releasing the financial statements the British had given him. It was a considerable gamble because, as Hull told him, it told the Germans just how desperate the British were and increased the chance of an invasion. It might also have convinced Congress that Britain was as good as defeated and could have therefore resulted in a refusal to send it arms. But Morgenthau felt he had to shock the American people into realizing that the British were desperate. He also reminded the committee that the British were financing the war with tax rates far higher than those of the United States. "The British people are not only dodging the bombs and fighting for their existence," he said. "They are also making a stupendous effort to pay for this war by themselves."[16]

Morgenthau had never performed well in testimony on Capitol Hill. (In his first appearance ever, he had introduced himself then asked an under secretary to read his statement.) Now isolationists Hamilton Fish, John Vorys, and George Holden Tinkham tore into him, claiming the bill gave the president excessive powers to arm another country. Vorys got Morgenthau to admit the bill would force the United States to raise its debt limit, then he said the bill should be known as "lend-lose" not "lend-lease." As Morgenthau wore down, Tinkham said to him, "I am very sorry to say I haven't the same confidence in the President that you have."

"If you pardon my saying so," shot back Morgenthau, "you are probably in the minority."[17]

Stimson spent a day and half on the stand, withstanding the isolationist assault and hammering home the point that American defense relied on the survival of the Royal Navy. They also attacked William Knudsen and Frank Knox before the Committee heard from Joseph Kennedy and Charles Lindbergh, both opposing the bill that was broadly supported across the country. "Only a few big isolationist newspapers roared hysterically: the *Chicago Tribune*, the *New York Daily News*, a few others," said *Time* magazine. "The rest of the press mumbled a bit. But most papers said flatly: Pass the bill, and no nonsense."[18]

But Speaker Rayburn told the administration that amendments were needed—especially a reduction of the powers being vested in the presidency. They agreed to limit the time in which the president could approve lend-lease agreements and to require the administration to send a report to Congress on lend-lease activity every ninety days. The House added that Congress could end the president's lend-lease powers before the bill expired and limit the existing order to $1.3 billion. The bill carried the House by 260 votes to 165, complete with amendments that Roosevelt could live with.

A few senators then demanded Congress, not the president, have the final word on how much could be transferred to other countries, arguing that appropriations were the constitutional responsibility of Congress. Morgenthau and Stimson, however, believed this amendment changed the bill's intention of ensuring flexibility in procurement. They wanted to fight the amendment, but the president was ill and Hull said he wanted to back off. Stimson and Morgenthau tried to persuade Hopkins—just returned from a special mission to London—to convince the president to resist the amendments. Morgenthau told his diary his report to Hopkins overall was "discouraging and gloomy." Ed Foley worked out a compromise with the senators. It reversed the wording of the amendment so the president could dispose of any defense articles abroad unless Congress specifically imposed a restriction on them. The amendment was acceptable, and on March 8 the Senate passed the bill sixty to thirty-one.[19]

By this time, Morgenthau—so often criticized for treading on other men's turf—had told Purvis, Stimson, and Roosevelt that he wanted to be freed of any involvement in lend-lease unless the president ordered otherwise. He wanted to focus on Treasury business. The first two told him he was needed in the operation. FDR responded that Morgenthau should probably appoint an assistant secretary to work with Purvis so that he would at least keep a hand on the brief. The suggestion pleased Morgenthau, no doubt because it showed the chief valued the work he had done with Purvis.[20] Roosevelt settled the matter February 25 when he struck a lend-lease committee comprising the secretaries of War, of the navy, and of state and headed by Harry Hopkins.

Morgenthau told Hopkins he could have Philip Young, a Treasury man, if he needed staff. But within the bastions of the Treasury, he told his staff Hopkins was too sick to do the job. He wasn't familiar with the needs of the Chinese, Greeks, or South Americans. "Here is this list of eighteen things the British want," he told his staff one day. "Hopkins has been carrying that around him since Sunday a week ago. The thing could have been mimeographed and everybody have a copy and [be] working on it. That is what would have happened in my shop." He stressed, of course, that he wanted to move away from lend-lease unless the president asked him to help.[21]

Hopkins didn't want Young; rather, he told the president he wanted Oscar Cox, who had done a splendid job assisting Foley on the lend-lease legislation. On March 1, an irate Morgenthau assembled Cox, Foley, and Young and told them explicitly that the president didn't know who Cox was. Hopkins "didn't tell the President that you were in the Treasury," he told Cox. "You're just Oscar Cox. Oh, I have seen that before. That's the way he works." Morgenthau was damned if he would let Hopkins pluck the efficient Cox from his department. "We have a wonderful relationship here, and I am going to keep it that way," he told them.[22] Hopkins won. Cox was soon named general counsel of both the Office of Lend-Lease Administration and the Office of Emergency Management.

A clerk read President Roosevelt's budget message for the 1942 fiscal year to the House of Representatives on January 3. The preamble said this budget was "a reflection of a world at war," and the main feature was increased defense spending. "It is not enough to defend our national existence," read the clerk. "Democracy as a way of life is equally at stake."[23] Then the clerk proceeded to the total expenditures for the year: $17.5 billion. The house was silent, stunned, until one congressman let out a long, slow whistle. Speaker Rayburn pounded his gavel, and the clerk continued.[24]

Seventeen and a half billion dollars. It more than doubled the $8.4 billion figure of a year earlier. What was worse, the figure did not include the lend-lease expenditures, which the administration privately estimated at $7.5 billion. The budget speech stated that between June 1940 and the middle of 1942, the US government would spend about $28.5 billion ($460 billion in 2012 US dollars) on defense, during which time the army (not including the navy) would more than quintuple from 250,000 men to 1.4 million men. The total two-year expenditure amounted to more than one-quarter of the United States' GDP for 1940. It promised to be the greatest buildup of military equipment—in terms of both money spent and the modernity of the technology—the world had ever known. "The President still believes in spending Government money as if it were water," cried Republican senator Robert Taft of Ohio. Senator Alben Barkley, a Kentucky Democrat, countered that it was "a minimum of what we ought to do."[25]

The Treasury now faced an unprecedented task. The government had raised only $7 billion in revenue the year before, and Congress was expected to increase revenue slightly. But Morgenthau wanted to finance two-thirds of the defense expenditures from taxes. He also had to worry about inflation. Prices had been stable for years, but excess industrial capacity was falling and the unemployment rate had dropped from 17.2 percent in 1939 to 14.6 percent in 1940, a low for the Roosevelt administration. Inflationary pressures were building, and the Treasury knew World War I military expenditures were the main reason prices rose 85 percent between 1917 and 1919. Such high inflation in the current war would have driven up the cost of the war materials and military salaries, meaning the government would have to raise even more money. And inflation would drive up interest rates, again increasing war costs.

If that weren't problematic enough, the customary means of raising public money was certain to exacerbate inflation. The process of deficit financing greatly increased money supply because it increased bank deposits for the entire banking system. For example, bank deposits rose from $38 billion in 1933 to $60 billion in 1941. Morgenthau was certain the United States would ignite inflation if the Treasury raised more money by turning again to the nation's banks. Inflation promised to be such a problem that Marriner Eccles came up with an anti-inflationary plan, which would have expanded the powers of the Federal Reserve at the expense of the presidency and the Treasury. Morgenthau was apoplectic, but Roosevelt brushed off his concerns. "Henry, this is so unimportant, the Federal Reserve is so unimportant, nobody believes anything that Marriner Eccles says or pays any attention to him," he said. "The important thing is the war."[26]

Morgenthau believed the best method of financing the war was the sale of war bonds. During World War I, the Treasury had raised $21.5 billion selling what it called "Liberty Bonds," though most of these sales were to financial institutions, not to individuals. The sale of war bonds in the 1940s would simply be an expansion of the popular US savings bonds programs, which continually brought letters of support to the Treasury. "While serious concern—yes, genuine anxiety—is shown over Government spending and the increasing public debt, there is scarcely a word criticizing Savings Bonds, and, almost without exception, our mail reveals only friendship and admiration for the Secretary," said one Treasury official in an April 1939 memo.[27]

On January 22, Morgenthau sent a memo to the president recommending the debt ceiling be raised to $60 billion and that the secretary of the Treasury have greater authority in the savings bonds program. He would be allowed to fix the denominations and the interest rate and to develop them into a security similar to the old Liberty bonds.[28]

"The Treasury wishes to be able to offer securities of a character which would . . . promote thrift and savings," Morgenthau told the Ways and Means Committee on January 29. "We hope that a substantial part of this defense program for which we have to borrow funds can be financed out of the real savings of the people."[29] If successful, the program would raise money without inflating the deposits of the banking system. And it would ease inflation by channeling the earnings of a broad swath of the population to the defense program rather than to consumer goods. Morgenthau also saw a third benefit, one he cherished dearly. It was an opportunity for all Americans—laborers, tradesmen, housewives, seniors, children, or anyone else—to participate in the war effort. It would raise awareness of the great struggle for democracy. Knudsen and others said the United States should follow the British model and impose forced savings on the people, but Morgenthau rejected such a notion forcefully, linking the war-bonds program with a campaign to support democracy. Congress actually raised the debt ceiling to $65 billion and gave Morgenthau full authority on savings bonds.

By late February, the Treasury told the media it was establishing a new unit to handle the "popular" financing of the war effort.[30] Much of the planning and energy for this unit came from Morgenthau himself, and those around him soon noticed he had become obsessed with war bonds. He and Treasury aide Harold Graves decided to offer $5,000 bonds to wealthy people and institutions and war stamps, costing as little as ten cents, to everyone else. They devised a simple album that held $18.75 of stamps and could be cashed in for twenty-five dollars after ten years. Savings bonds could already be purchased at 250,000 outlets, including the fifty-one thousand post offices, but Morgenthau wanted broader distribution. Through the spring of 1941, they enlisted some of the largest corporations in America to institute employee payroll programs so workers could voluntarily pay for bonds through monthly deductions. Many businesses set up the program at their own expense. General Motors, for example, swallowed the $100,000 cost of its workers' program.[31] The *New York Times* would refer to Morgenthau as "the country's No. 1 bond salesman who cannot buy a single war bond because of laws prohibiting Secretaries of the Treasury from making such purchases."[32]

Morgenthau noted glowingly in his diary that the president was pleased with the program. Franklin and Eleanor Roosevelt agreed to be the first to buy the bonds. On April 30, the president joined Morgenthau and the postmaster general on live radio to launch the bonds. "Defense Savings Bonds and Stamps are not for the few; they are for the many," Morgenthau told the radio audience. "Your government . . . is not asking you to buy one bond or one set of stamps and let it go at that; it is inviting you to save regularly and systematically by putting your money into the soundest investment on the face of the Earth—the Unites States."[33]

Morgenthau knew he needed a prolonged promotional campaign to keep people buying the bonds, and that campaign had to be bold and optimistic. He began to ask celebrities to promote his pet project, just as movie stars like Charlie Chaplin and Al Jolson had done in the previous war. On May 20, he asked that liberal refugees, including author Thomas Mann and physicist Albert Einstein, broadcast messages urging immigrants to buy the bonds and stamps. Within two months, Irving Berlin, the toast of Broadway, wrote a jingle for the bond drive called "Any Bonds Today." The song was published in July 1941, with the US Treasury holding the copyright. A year later, it was adapted into an animated short to be played in movie houses before feature movies; the star was a new cartoon character called Bugs Bunny. (The film would later gain notoriety for racial stereotyping as one segment included the rabbit with a blackened face imitating Jolson.) "Any Bonds Today" became the theme song of the CBS radio show *The Treasury Hour*, which began in July 1941. The first episode was written by an unknown writer named Herman Wouk, who would go on to write such bestsellers as *The Caine Mutiny* and *Trilogy*. The show attracted a who's who of show business, from Judy Garland to Mickey Rooney to the comedian Fred Allen to the soprano Grace Moore. And behind it all was Henry Morgenthau Jr., the lurid Treasury secretary, pilloried in Washington as Henry the Morgue. In the first month alone, more than one million Americans bought $3.5 million in stamps and $438 million in bonds.[34]

The media supported the program and would do so throughout the war. In fact, Henry Morgenthau Jr. actually received favorable press throughout his career in Washington. Reporters lampooned him in private but generally respected his candor and efficiency. Of course he'd made mistakes: he once ordered *New York Post* reporter Sylvia Porter out of his office when she jokingly called him Henny Penny. (Henrietta Klotz brought her back in before any permanent damage could be done.[35]) He held weekly press conferences to maintain good relations, and Wall Street reporters gushed about his consistency in selling out large bond issues at low rates. Conservative newspapers, though questioning his qualifications, usually portrayed him as one of the few members of the Roosevelt circle who understood economics. And it didn't hurt that one of his closest friends was the publisher of the most influential newspaper in the world.

Arthur Hays Sulzberger, who had known Henry Morgenthau Jr. since boyhood, became publisher of the *New York Times* on the death of his father-in-law in 1935. He was also one of Morgenthau's few true friends, and their correspondence flowed with bonhomie and affection for each other's families.[36] The publisher wasn't above asking his powerful friend for a favor, as he did in November 1938 on behalf of his friend William Speed, a banker whose failing institution was in trouble with bank regulators. (Morgenthau agreed to meet Speed, but nothing came of the meeting.) And it was well known in Washington circles that Morgenthau would seek favors in return. Herman Oliphant once asked syndicated columnist Joseph Alsop what the prescription was for getting favorable press in the *New York Times*. "The prescription was simple—all I have to do is either mention one of Sulzberger's favorite New York Jewish friends, or merely hint that Sulzberger's taxes might be reduced," said Alsop, making an obvious reference to Morgenthau.[37] Morgenthau often sent representatives to the paper to lobby for good coverage. John Hanes visited the paper when the Treasury was fighting for tax reform in the spring of 1939. On May 5, Arthur Krock personally phoned Morgenthau to tell him Hanes's trip had been "100 percent successful." The result was a few editorials supporting the Treasury secretary and a glowing profile of Morgenthau in the *New York Times Magazine*.[38] Though the New Dealers believed Krock was committed to bringing down their government, Morgenthau enjoyed a relationship with the columnist that often defied journalistic propriety. At one point, Krock phoned Morgenthau to name two congressmen as the anonymous sources for a controversial story. He said he did not want Hanes to be wrongly accused of leaking the story.[39] And Sulzberger would sometimes apologize if the coverage of Morgenthau was not up to scratch. "I am embarrassed at the way *The Times* handled your letter this morning . . . and it was subordinated to what in my judgment was a less important story," Sulzberger wrote on October 11, 1938. "I was sorry also to learn for the first time of the inaccuracy in our Saturday story."[40]

Of course, the *New York Times* would have supported the war-bond program regardless of this relationship. Virtually all organizations and companies backed it. "Almost every bank in the country will participate in the program," reported the *New York Times* on April 30, the day before the official launch. "Newspapers, the motion picture industry and radio stations have also pledged their full support, and cities, towns and villages are scheduled to mark the opening."

Morgenthau would need their support as the defense costs kept on mounting. By the end of April, the defense program for 1941 had added $1.5 billion, pushing total government expenditures for the year up to a record $19 billion. That more than doubled the highest annual expenditure in the New Deal.[41] The Treasury set an aggressive target of raising $6.3 billion in debt that year, hoping all would come through the war-bonds program.[42] And Morgenthau aimed for an extra $3.5 billion from taxation, to bring total tax revenue to $13 billion. The taxes he proposed to raise included surtaxes on individuals' incomes, estate taxes, gift taxes, and excise taxes. And of course, once again, he wanted to tax corporations' "excess" profits. The plan had the support of the Roosevelt circle, Eccles, and the Democratic financial leaders in Congress.[43] But both the House and the Senate needed to pass the plan, and the Treasury was often criticized for its fumbling in Congress. "Its first proposal last April [1941] showed little comprehension of the real requirements of wartime financing, and it was not until after six months of struggle that the tax bill was finally written by the Senate Finance Committee," said the *New York Times*. "The Treasury having opposed broadening the tax base for months only conceded that need after nearly everyone else had become convinced of it."[44]

On April 23, Morgenthau appeared before the Ways and Means Committee to appeal for higher taxes and an excess-profits tax, which he said would protect against defense profiteering. "We are faced with a greater challenge than any in the history of the Republic," Morgenthau said. "It calls for a much greater response than has yet been made."[45] He proposed allowing companies to earn a profit of about 6 to 7 percent of invested capital, after which the government would tax everything. As the committee took a break in June, it appeared he simply could not get the needed support from Republican congressmen.

During the hiatus, Morgenthau won a battle in cabinet to reduce the Work Projects Administration funding by $900 million, six times the amount Roosevelt had proposed, and channel the funding to training in defense industries and the military itself. "They were all breathless when I had said I had arrived at the point where I felt that in order to make this country sufficiently strong against Fascism and Nazism we would have to put every able-bodied man to work and also every woman, doing the jobs which are necessary in case we get into war," he dictated into his diary. "I feel that with the very black days which are ahead of us, we have to take care of the unemployed so that there is one less group for the Nazis and Fascists to appeal to."[46] His public speeches called on all Americans to join the grand struggle against aggressors. "We have seen so much selfishness and greed in high places that we are too apt to take them for granted," he told the graduates of Amherst College, including his son Robert, four days later. "We cannot preserve our freedom without being ready to fight in its defense."[47]

Amid the budget debate, the *New York Times* ran another flattering profile of the Treasury secretary that highlighted his growing position in global finance. "Treasurer to the Democracies," read the headline in the *New York Times Magazine* on June 22, 1941. "The financial nerve centre of the world today lies neither in Wall Street nor in Lombard Street," began the article. "It resides in a huge colonnaded building covering about two square blocks on Pennsylvania Avenue, to the right of the White House. This is the United States Treasury, whose hard-working officials have the responsibility not merely of financing our own defense program, but with the lend-lease law are charged with maintaining the solvency of Britain, Canada, China and the whole international community of democratic nations."[48] (In fact, Canada needed no financial aid during the war.)

Congress passed and Roosevelt signed the Revenue Act of 1941 in September. It raised surtaxes on individuals and corporations and promised to increase total taxation by about $3.7 billion. But it also retained loopholes that allowed corporations to avoid taxes on excess profits.[49] And it was already proving insufficient to meet the demands of the arms program. The Treasury's fiscal report in July had estimated total expenditures for 1942 would be $22.3 billion, and there was already speculation in the media that the figure would exceed $25 billion. Congress had signed off on $33 billion in appropriations in 1941, $26 billion of which was for defense. "These bring defense appropriations, including lend-lease and the authorizations for the two-ocean navy, made since May 1940, to about $43½ billion," said the *Wall Street Journal.* "No one doubts that they will be even greater in the months to come."[50]

Though the lend-lease act passed, the United States and Britain still faced the problem of shipping the donations through the treacherous North Atlantic to Britain, where food shortages were occurring. "There is, I think, no doubt that during the next twelve months Britishers will have to forego a good deal of their traditional diet (which will by no means be all loss) and to reconcile themselves to something much more simple," said the journalist Julian Huxley in February 1941.[51] The British were shipping food from Canada and the United States in convoys, but the U-boats, hunting in wolf packs, were sinking merchant ships and escaping unscathed. "We simply have not got enough escorts to go round, and fight at the same time," Churchill cabled Harry Hopkins on March 28.[52]

Morgenthau, Ickes, Stimson, and Knox wanted the United States to provide escorts, but as of April, Roosevelt would approve only patrols in the Western Hemisphere (extending the boundary so it included Greenland and the west coast of Africa). "My own thought is that it is too much to expect the English people to fight on empty stomachs, and that condition is not very far off," Morgenthau wrote FDR on April 28. "It is my belief that we must transfer a great number of ships to the English flag at once for the transportation of food."[53] At times, the president hinted that American ships would escort the convoys, but he always backed away from the plan. By August, he ordered the US Navy to escort US then British ships as far as Iceland. By September, driven by U-boat attacks on US destroyers, Roosevelt ordered the German subs should be shot on sight.[54]

In essence, the Americans were at war with Germany before Pearl Harbor, but only those Americans sailing on the North Atlantic.

Morgenthau was impressed with the new British ambassador Lord Halifax, who took the post after Philip Kerr, the Marquess of Lothian died suddenly in December 1940. He said the new ambassador made an "excellent impression. He is very simple and very direct and very badly dressed."[55] He was less pleased with another British representative who came to Washington that spring, the famed economist John Maynard Keynes, whom Churchill sent to ask the Americans to write off debts of about $1 billion. Brilliant, self-assured, often abrasive, the Cambridge-educated Keynes had been at the vanguard of political and economic thought in Britain for a quarter century, and his theories of government creating demand with fiscal stimulus had meshed splendidly with Roosevelt's New Deal. However, he and the Americans annoyed each other. He (and other Brits) could never fully accept that the administration had to negotiate with Congress on budgetary and foreign matters. And Keynes, who wrote and spoke magnificent English, dismissed the mumbling of the Americans, describing their speech as "Cherokee." (Keynes's biographer, Robert Skidelsky, compares a discussion between Morgenthau and Harry Hopkins to "a bad B movie" in which the Treasury secretary played the "more or less incoherent stooge."[56]) Morgenthau and even the affable Hopkins wished Keynes would go home. He resisted Morgenthau's recommendation that the two countries establish a committee to oversee the lend-lease operations.

The British continued to sell off assets, including their largest holding in the United States, the American Viscose Corporation, for $40 million plus deferred payments, but they still requested US assistance. At a June 26 meeting, Morgenthau told Keynes that Roosevelt suspected the British were crying wolf about their economic desperation and the Treasury needed specific data. Keynes explained that the British were trying to hold their dollar balances at about $600 million, but some estimates made it appear that they would fall to $200 million within a year.

"If you don't mind," Morgenthau interrupted him, "you work one way and I work another." He explained that the US Treasury had to work in a methodical way, and if Keynes would humor him then he could prove helpful to the British. But he needed accurate statistics. "I have gone to the President once or twice on this," he explained in what must have seemed to Keynes a torrent of Cherokee, "and I have missed it by about six months, and I don't want to go again in your behalf unless I am nearer right than I was before, but he has sort of made fun of me that I have been so bearish on your position." Later that day, British treasury official Sir Frederick Phillips reported back to Morgenthau that Britain's gold and dollar balances had fallen to $161 million. Fortunately, the US military forgave some debts owed by the British, thereby easing its dollar position. The British also agreed to the committee Morgenthau had proposed.[57]

★ ★ ★

On June 22, German forces moved east from Poland, attacking their erstwhile ally, the Soviet Union. In the west, the sea and air battles continued to take their lethal toll, though Britain had gained the upper hand in the Battle of Britain. Her ground troops were fighting in the Mediterranean and in North Africa to prevent the Axis from gaining control of the oil fields in Iraq. The British high command had learned the Germans had given up hope of invading Britain for now. Roosevelt himself guessed that Hitler knew that Britain was out of his reach, though he incorrectly believed the Germans would next invade Spain and Portugal. Morgenthau believed Hitler would try to invade Britain that summer, knowing it would be his last chance to do so.[58]

By midsummer 1941, the Anglo-American partnership that Morgenthau had championed was now official policy in Washington. Its greatest manifestation occurred August 9, when Roosevelt welcomed Churchill aboard the USS *Augusta* on Placentia Bay off Newfoundland. The meetings produced an eight-point joint statement five days later that became known as the Atlantic Charter. The document stipulated that neither country would gain lands through the current war and that all people eventually freed from occupation should live in self-determination. Compared at the time to Woodrow Wilson's Fourteen Points of 1919, it showed that

America, though officially not a belligerent, stood shoulder to shoulder with her British allies.

August 14 should have been a day that Henry Morgenthau Jr. remembered as the fruition of all he had worked for over three years. As well as the announcement of the Atlantic Charter, Knudsen in Buffalo predicted the United States would produce planes at a rate of thirty-six thousand a year by mid-1942. But in Scotland that evening, William Purvis climbed aboard an airplane for a transatlantic flight. The plane took off after dark and immediately lost altitude for some unknown reason. It struck a slight rise in the ground, then smashed through a fence, crashing into a corn field. Its full fuel tanks ignited, and within seconds the craft was engulfed in flames. Everyone on the flight, including Arthur Purvis, was killed.[59]

Morgenthau told newspapermen the next day that he was "shocked and saddened beyond measure," and he did not use the terms lightly. He would later tell his family and biographer that his friendship with Purvis was something that approached his affinity with the president.

Hitler's bloody adventure in the Soviet Union posed a dilemma for the United States. America heartily opposed Communism and had supported Finland following the Soviet invasion. Republicans in Congress were disgusted at the thought of aiding Stalin. But Russia and the Ukraine were the largest military theaters of the war, and defeating Hitler meant forming a partnership with the Soviets.

Morgenthau had long supported the idea of doing business with the Soviets and had been part of Roosevelt's team that opened up negotiations with Moscow in 1933. Since late 1940, the secretary had been developing a relationship with Soviet ambassador Constantin Oumansky. Sumner Welles had delayed a Treasury plan to buy Russian gold, believing it should be the State Department that handled the matter. Now some in Washington wanted Morgenthau to become the Soviet champion in government, just as he had been for the British. "I am not going to rush in to this thing," he told his staff. "Let Mr. Hull come out and kiss the Russians on both cheeks."[60]

Two days after the invasion, Welles drafted a general license allowing the export of munitions to the Soviet Union. The Treasury and Justice Departments approved the license, but the question was how to pay for the $40 million to $50 million of material the Soviets wanted. When the State Department asked if the Treasury could arrange a loan, Morgenthau told Welles to discuss it with loans administrator Jesse Jones. "I burned my heart out and Hull and Welles have gone there consistently, and told the president, 'Morgenthau wants to run the State Department and wants to run foreign affairs,'" Morgenthau told his staff. "Hull told me that himself. And now they want my help." Morgenthau wanted to aid the Soviets but was outraged at what he considered the State Department's gall. "After what they put me through for eight years—they have got to get down on their knees and ask me. I mean I will never forget the tongue lashings that I have had from Mr. Hull about how I want to run his department and the sarcasm and everything else."[61]

Aiding the Soviets was proving difficult due to mutual distrust. The Soviets wanted to receive goods in the Pacific, while the Americans wanted to ship them by way of Britain. And the United States was still ramping up production, so all powers were scrambling for supply that was still quite meager. As for paying for the material, the Lend-Lease Act demanded that Congress approve all appropriations, and now Congress was debating the second lend-lease bill amid vocal opposition to Soviet aid. That meant the Soviets had to pay for the weapons they received in dollars until the administration found a way to have the Soviets included in the lend-lease system. The Treasury began to buy what little gold the Soviets could ship, and Morgenthau helped push through a Soviet request for military supplies, even though the War Department worried such shipments were reducing arms available to Britain. He finally complained to the president.

"I am sick and tired of hearing that they are going to get this and they are going to get that," Roosevelt told his cabinet. "Whatever we are going to give them, it has to be over there by the first of October, and the only answer I want to hear is that it is under way."[62]

Only twenty-four congressmen voted in favor of an amendment to the second lend-lease bill in mid-October excluding the Soviet Union from receiving shipments. Yet the United States still wanted some payback from the Soviets. Hopkins—who had become Roosevelt's personal liaison with the Soviets as well as with the British—proposed that the United States ship equipment to them in exchange for monthly payments of gold and charge 1⅞ interest on surplus shipments. "This is not the way to do the thing," Morgenthau replied. "I think it is a mistake at this time to bother Stalin with any financial arrangements and take his mind off the war."[63] Hopkins agreed, but Hull, always wary of the Soviets and sensitive to Congress, insisted the Soviets pay something. Eventually the United States and Soviet Union agreed that the Americans would extend a $1 billion credit that would carry no interest until the end of the war.

Morgenthau's reforms in aircraft production were now resulting in an unheard-of output as the United States reached peak production of 1,476 units in the month of June 1941. The country was now producing aircraft at a rate of almost seventeen thousand per year, eight times the production of three years earlier and exceeding the wildly optimistic target of fifteen thousand set by the president in late 1938.[64] And a great percentage of that production was being shipped to Britain. In the first seven months of 1941, the United States shipped $248 million in airplanes, engines, and parts to Britain and her outposts in Singapore and Africa, most of it delivered independent of the lend-lease programs. In the second half of 1941, about 60 percent of the American arms output was flowing to the British.[65] "All in all, American aircraft manufacturers in the first seven months of 1941 sent the British almost twice as many planes as the British lost defending the British Isles, according to their own figures, during the entire year 1940," Col. John H. Jouett, president of the Aeronautical Chamber of Commerce of America, told the *New York Times* in October. "At the same time, American manufacturers have shipped tens of millions of dollars worth of extra engines."[66]

Overall, the United States would produce more than 19,400 aircraft in 1941, with the vast majority being produced in the second half of the year. "The extremely trying 'make ready' period of the American Aeronautical Industry is finished," declared an opinion piece in the *New York Times* in October. The article estimated that planes were now being produced at a rate of thirty-five thousand per year and that production would peak at as much as seventy-two thousand per year in the summer of 1942.[67] The administration may not have realized it, but 1941 was the first year in which the American aircraft production exceeded both that of Germany, which produced 12,400 planes that year, and that of Japan, with 5,100.

Still, the hawks in cabinet were dissatisfied with the structure of government procurement in the so-called Victory Program and the fact that government was not bringing in industry, especially the car industry, to boost production. Morgenthau believed production levels had reached 15 percent of their potential.[68] Henry Stimson in particular was astonished that Roosevelt refused to establish a Department of Supply or some similar body to coordinate production, procurement, and shipments to the United Kingdom. Morgenthau sided with Stimson, but even he could not control the president's obsession with control.

On the evening of October 23, Morgenthau called privately at the White House, telling the president he wanted to speak with him not as a cabinet member but as a friend and neighbor. "I am very much worried that when you get down to considering the Victory Program, that the so-called Detroit crowd, who are in charge of production for you, will not be able to take care of the situation," he said. "If that time should come, I want you to have it in the back of your mind that I believe I could do this job for you."[69]

Roosevelt's response was pleasant, encouraging even, and he suggested the two of them discuss the matter with Hopkins, who had to be brought in as the head of lend-lease.

Five days later, Roosevelt received Hopkins, Morgenthau, and an official named Stacy May in his bedroom and listened as Morgenthau and May proposed a production organization. "This isn't the way to do it," Roosevelt responded immediately. "How can anybody tell how big the program should be?" He explained that rather than building from the top down, he wanted the defense program to grow from the bottom up—meaning let the orders come from the military, and the government would find ways to fill them. Morgenthau disagreed on the grounds that any time the government doubled the order for, say, tanks, some other facet of production would suffer. General George Marshall himself had complained about the disorganization of the existing program. The parties ended up agreeing that more American production had to be devoted to military purposes rather than to consumer demands, but the Roosevelt-centric structure remained in place.

In the autumn, Morgenthau suddenly took on a covert mission concerning the country that some feared would become the fourth major member of the Axis—Spain. Though Generalissimo Francisco Franco favored the Nazi cause, his country was officially neutral. If Spain did join the Axis, Britain's naval power in the Mediterranean would be compromised. Now Britain wanted Morgenthau's help to maintain Spain's neutrality.

On November 4, Robert Jemmett Stopford, the second financial secretary to Lord Halifax, called at Morgenthau's home accompanied by John Pehle, a young lawyer from the US Treasury who was working his way into Morgenthau's inner circle. Stopford had written Pehle about something so sensitive that Morgenthau decided it was safer to discuss it at his house rather than at the office. Churchill's cabinet in mid-1940 had set up a secret $10 million fund to bribe key military personnel in Spain to ensure that it remained neutral. But when Morgenthau had recently frozen the accounts of neutral countries, the Swiss bank account used to bribe the Spaniards had been frozen. Stopford now pleaded with the secretary to lift the freeze. Morgenthau agreed, and three weeks later the money was once again greasing Spanish palms.[70]

Soon Morgenthau released revised budget figures for the 1942 fiscal year that the *New York Times* said were "almost breath-taking in their astronomical immensity." The $24.5 billion budget was "equivalent to the total national debt in 1920, after we had fought and won the World War," said the *New York Times*. About $12 billion of the 1942 figure would be paid for by taxes, meaning the Treasury would now have to borrow more than $1 billion each month to cover the shortfall.[71] The only reason Washington insiders were not utterly floored by these numbers was that they had grown used to the Treasury raising spending dramatically.

★ ★ ★

For months, the Hull-Nomura talks aimed at averting a Pacific war had been so secret that not even the Treasury had been apprised of them. In fact, Harry Dexter White, of his own accord, wrote a memorandum recommending a solution to the impasse. Unaware of the two sides' positions, he proposed Japan give up China and leave the Axis in return for financial and trade incentives. Hull received the White memo but took his own path in drafting a final proposal for Japan in mid-November. The Japanese rejected Hull's document and the talks ended.

The secret talks worried Morgenthau greatly. His suspicions of Cordell Hull no doubt plagued him, and he was frightened by rumors that the State Department might appease the Japanese and offer them access to badly needed resources. "Mr. President, I want to explain in language as strong as I can command, my feeling that the need is for iron firmness," he wrote in a draft memo. "No settlement with Japan that in any way seems to the American people, or the rest of the world, to be a retreat, no matter how temporary, from our increasingly clear policy of opposition to aggressors, will be viewed as consistent with the position of our Government or with the leadership that you have established."[72] He did not send the letter, probably because Roosevelt told him in person on December 3 that the Japanese were likely continuing the talks because they needed time to prepare for an invasion somewhere. "The most important thing that the President said is he is talking with the English about war plans as to when and where the U.S.A. and Great Britain should strike, and that is what he is waiting for," Morgenthau dictated into his diary in early December.[73]

The second reason for worry was the Treasury was preparing the largest bond offering in the history of the republic, possibly the world, and the uncertainty over Japan was making markets edgy. Morgenthau had told the media a $1.5 billion offering would probably be launched between December 1 and 5, barring unforeseen events. On December 1, he asked the president whether war might break out and derail the funding, which he had penciled in for December 4. "I cannot guarantee anything," replied the president. "It's in the laps of the Gods." He advised Morgenthau to proceed.[74] To be safe, Morgenthau warned reporters he had never said the offering would definitely come that week. When asked whether it would depend on the Japanese situation, he smiled and replied, "You might say it depended on the weather."[75]

On Thursday, Morgenthau launched the record funding, selling $1 billion in fifteen- to thirty-year bonds at 2.5 percent and $500 million of nine- to thirteen-year paper with a 2 percent coupon. The low interest rates were critical because they showed the market the Treasury would not increase long-term rates to raise even this amount of money during uncertain times. By late afternoon, the Treasury officials closed the book for all except retail investors, having met with an oversubscription of the issue. It notified the media there would be another offering of similar size in January, but Morgenthau would worry about that another day. On Friday, he left the corner office for a well-earned vacation. He and his family were going to spend the weekend in New York and then fly out to Colorado on Sunday, December 7, 1941.

CHAPTER EIGHT

THE SINEWS OF WAR

★ ★ ★

The Morgenthau family (minus Robert, who'd begun his naval service) attended a symphony benefit for war bonds on Saturday night, December 6, 1941, then had lunch the next day at the French restaurant Voisin on Park Avenue in New York City. When they emerged at about 3:00 p.m., their chauffeur, Charles Frazer, told them the Japanese had attacked Pearl Harbor. Morgenthau dashed back to their hotel and learned he had a message from the White House.

"Sir, I have just heard the news," he said when he reached Roosevelt in the Oval Office. "I have my Coast Guard plane standing by. I'll fly right back to Washington."

Roosevelt, always calm in a crisis, responded cheerfully: "Be careful you don't get shot down, Henry."[1]

Japanese aircraft had caught the naval base at Pearl Harbor by complete surprise that morning, sinking four battleships and sinking or damaging three cruisers, three destroyers, an antiaircraft training ship, and one minelayer. Some 188 US aircraft were destroyed. More than two thousand Americans were killed, more than one thousand wounded. The Pacific Fleet was crippled and the nation humiliated. The president had called for a special session of Congress by the time the cabinet held a tense meeting that night. Frank Knox was devastated, and Henry Stimson kept muttering repeatedly that the planes and ships were clustered together, making the attack all the easier. As they discussed the situation, Roosevelt decided he would deliver a brief message the next day declaring war only on Japan.[2]

At 11:00 that night, Morgenthau reached his own office, still numb with disbelief. He found the 9:30 Group—Bell, White, Gaston, Klotz, others—already assembled. Henry III, who accompanied him, realized his father and his team had been preparing for this day for years. "There could have been no Pearl Harbor in the Treasury," he later wrote.[3] By the time the day ended, Morgenthau had impounded $131 million of Japanese investments in the United States and invoked the Trading with the Enemies Act, essentially ceasing all trade between the two countries.[4] The next day, as the secretary responsible for the Secret Service, he increased the protection around the president. And he prepared the American people for the financial reality of what was happening. "I think this means greater expenditures for war purposes which will mean a corresponding increase in taxes," he told reporters gathered in the corner office, adding there may be some controls over capital.[5] In 1943 and after, the United States could be spending $50 billion a year on the war, he said. Sitting on the fringes of the press conference, Henry III noticed that out the high windows he could see the windows of the Oval office, where camera flashes were igniting as photographers captured the president signing the declaration of war.[6]

The next morning, Morgenthau rewarded one of his most stalwart advisers by naming Harry Dexter White an assistant secretary of the Treasury with special responsibilities in foreign affairs.[7] Known as the smartest member of a particularly brainy department, White was a Harvard-trained economist of Jewish Lithuanian extraction who had come to the Treasury in 1934 as a specialist in monetary affairs. A stocky man with a clipped moustache and a brusque manner, he had a colossal capacity for hard work and was known to rub underlings the wrong way. One of the Morgenthau circle, Merle Cochran, asked to be transferred to the State Department when he learned of White's promotion. Even the gentlemanly Dean Acheson would one day write that he was often "outraged by Harry White's capacity for rudeness."[8] But he was also courteous to women, particularly Elinor Morgenthau and Henrietta Klotz, who some noted were the women with the greatest influence on the secretary.

What Morgenthau didn't know was that White was a Soviet spy. According to testimony of former spies later confirmed by the release of

US intelligence, White had begun leaking information to Soviet spies gathered around economist Nathan Gregory Silvermaster as early as 1935. Though he was not a Communist Party member, he clearly favored state involvement in the economy and a stronger position for the Soviet Union in world affairs. The evidence against White is unassailable, though it is not clear how long he continued to leak secrets to the Soviets.[9]

With White's promotion, Morgenthau formalized the status of the two men he relied on the most—White in international affairs and Daniel Bell, the former budget director, in domestic matters. Though Roosevelt, Morgenthau, and others were pleased with the strength of the Treasury team, conservatives worried about the economic team leading the country. "It is clear that there was never a greater need for brains in the Treasury Department, because there has not before been so great a task laid upon it," wrote the *Wall Street Journal* columnist Frank R. Kent. "This is not to say that the Treasury Department lacks brains. Secretary Morgenthau, when he thinks and acts for himself, thinks soundly and acts well. The trouble is that every time he indulges in independent thought and action he discovers either that he is out of line with the White House or finds himself assailed from the rear by the left-wing New Dealers."[10]

Morgenthau was responsible for Foreign Funds Control, and some staff members urged him to seize thousands of small businesses owned by Japanese Americans in the western United States. He refused, preferring instead to ask banks to be extra vigilant in reporting suspicious transactions involving Germans, Italians, and Japanese. "No time to be thinking about civil liberties when the country is at war," said General Counsel Edward Foley at one meeting. Morgenthau insisted his policy was the right one and even opposed Roosevelt's plan to incarcerate Japanese Americans. "When it comes to suddenly mopping up 150,000 Japanese and putting them behind barbed wire, irrespective of their status, and consider doing the same with the Germans, I want at some time to have caught my breath," he said. He supported the incarceration of individuals who would harm the United States but not the indiscriminant imprisoning of an ethnic group. He was appalled when in February 1942 the president ordered the imprisonment of Japanese Americans. He complained to Roosevelt that their properties and businesses were being scattered, but the president replied, "I am not concerned about that."

Confident of an eventual Allied victory, Morgenthau wanted the postwar world to be free of the currency crises that continually erupted in the 1920s and 1930s. One week after Pearl Harbor, he asked White to quietly come up with a plan that would bring this vision to fruition. Morgenthau was looking for something broader than the Tripartite Pact, a multilateral agreement between a range of countries that would prevent competitive devaluations. He and White were both economic nationalists, so it was understood that the plan would demand the dollar replace sterling as the world's dominant currency.[11]

On December 22, 1941, Winston Churchill arrived at the White House for an extended visit to coordinate strategy to win a war that had gone badly thus far. The Japanese had attacked and were gaining ground in Hong Kong, British Malaya, and the Philippines, and they had sunk two important British warships, HMS *Repulse* and HMS *Prince of Wales*. Thailand had formally allied itself with Japan. The only bright spot was that the Soviets had stopped the German advances on Moscow and Leningrad.

Morgenthau attended a Christmas dinner at the White House, sitting across the table from Churchill, whom he considered in "the pink of health." He thought Lord Beaverbrook, also in attendance, "cocky," though he was touched when Beaverbrook, head of British aircraft production, told him that he and Roosevelt were the only friends Britain had in America.[12] Beaverbrook shared with him statistics that showed Britain and the United States produced roughly equivalent amounts of arms in 1941, even though the American population was more than triple that of the island nation. At a Boxing Day cabinet meeting, the president stated repeatedly that the United States had to increase production. Finally Morgenthau said, "Well, Mr. President, if you really want to get production you have to change your setup with the authority divided between OPM, Army and Navy."[13]

FDR paused. He knew Morgenthau and Stimson were unhappy

that the Office of Production Management was hamstrung by its lack of authority over the military departments. But all he said was, "Well, I think the thing is working much better."

Morgenthau noticed the president didn't jump on him for the comment, but he also told his diary: "For the amount of time the President spent on it, I gather it is worrying him considerably." On January 13, Roosevelt established the War Production Board, to be headed by former Treasury executive Donald Nelson, but the new office still did not have authority over the army and navy. Only Roosevelt had such authority.

On the financial side, Morgenthau and congressional leaders agreed in December to raise about $4 billion to $6 billion in additional revenue through a wartime tax. But they did not agree on what form the tax would take. The Ways and Means Committee had previously opposed new taxes because $4 billion had been added in the previous fiscal year though organic economic growth.[14] Morgenthau was still looking for more when he sat down on December 30 with Roosevelt and Budget Director Harold Smith to review their options. Morgenthau disliked and distrusted Smith. "He is like a termite undermining the foundation of the Treasury," he told the president on one occasion. He added: "I have got to raise $19 billion from now until the end of the year, and it is going to take all of my brains, courage and ingenuity, and I don't want a fellow like Harold Smith trying to undermine me."[15] Though Smith believed the United States could produce only $55 billion of war supplies, Morgenthau told Roosevelt he should order manufacturers to produce a certain number of tanks, planes, and other equipment, and it would be up to the country to meet that order. The auto industry, for example, had produced only $218 million in war orders even though its plants had a capacity for $3.5 billion in automobiles. They finally agreed their target would be $9 billion in additional taxes, meaning the deficit would be about $18 billion in the coming year. The economic recovery was helping. Only three years earlier, they had struggled in vain to raise the national income to $80 billion, but now they had $100 billion to work with. FDR said the United States would spend half its national income on the war, or about $50 billion. "I feel I got him to change his attitude, namely, that he is going to set the mark for national defense, and whoever is in charge of supply is going to have to make good, rather than his former attitude of the last cabinet meeting that he would simply take the maximum of tanks and guns which the Army and OPM thought the U.S. could produce," Morgenthau told his diary. "This is of tremendous importance."[16]

The next day, Morgenthau issued a stern New Year's message, warning the public that tax increases were on the way. "The Treasury's job is to provide the sinews of war by taxes and borrowing," he said. "We will try to do it without disrupting society too much, but you can't raise all we are going to need without considerable rearrangement of some people's finances."[17]

Americans were beginning to comprehend the financial demands Morgenthau would make of them. "Never in recorded history has any government raised by national tax levies, in a similar period, an amount of revenue approaching that which will be collected by the United States Treasury in the current fiscal year," said the *New York Times* on January 2, 1942. Federal revenues were expected to reach $13 billion.[18] Roosevelt spelled out quite clearly to the country just how massive the expenditures would be, first with his budget address on January 5 and then with his State of the Union address a day later. He called for the raising of an additional $9 billion in taxes that year, including $2 billion for Social Security. Total military expenditures would rise to $26 billion in the current fiscal year and $56 billion in fiscal 1943, producing deficits of $20.9 billion and $45.4 billion. "We cannot outfight our enemies unless, at the same time, we out-produce our enemies," he told the nation.[19] The State of the Union address spelled out his remarkable ambitions for outproducing the Axis: The United States would produce 60,000 planes in 1942 (10,000 more than the goal set eighteen months earlier) and 125,000 in 1943. It would churn out 45,000 tanks and 20,000 antiaircraft guns in 1942 and 75,000 tanks and 35,000 antiaircraft guns a year later. And finally, in merchant shipping, the nation in 1942 would sextuple its output to six million deadweight tons and increase it again to ten million in 1943.[20] A Nazi spokesman publicly scoffed at the projections, calling them "fantastic," "bombastic," and "skyscraper figures."[21]

Morgenthau had to pay for this fantastic arms program. He now wanted to raise $3 billion—three times the figure he used publicly—by

Henry Morgenthau Jr., Secretary of the Treasury, 1933–1945. During the second-longest tenure as treasury secretary in US history, he financed the Allied war effort, led the creation of the War Refugee Board, and organized the Bretton Woods Conference. *Portrait by David Silvette, 1936. From the Treasury Collection, US Department of Treasury.*

The greatest source of Henry Morgenthau Jr.'s power was his friendship with his Dutchess County neighbor President Franklin Delano Roosevelt. Many in Washington underestimated Morgenthau's abilities and thought the friendship was the only reason he was in cabinet. FDR inscribed this photo to Elinor Morgenthau, signing it, "from one of two of a kind." *Courtesy of the Franklin D. Roosevelt Presidential Library and Museum, Hyde Park, New York.*

Henry and Elinor Morgenthau were known to enjoy a wonderful family life, as shown in this 1937 photo. Elinor (Fatman) Morgenthau was intelligent and level-headed, and she often advised her husband on Treasury business. Their children—from left, Henry III, Joan, and Robert—went on to enjoy great success in their own right. *Courtesy of the Franklin D. Roosevelt Presidential Library and Museum, Hyde Park, New York.*

Henry Morgenthau Jr. and his family all adored First Lady Eleanor Roosevelt, shown viewing an exhibit of war art in Washington with Elinor Morgenthau in 1944. The affection was genuine, but it also buttressed Morgenthau's standing with the president when the two men clashed. *Courtesy of the Franklin D. Roosevelt Presidential Library and Museum, Hyde Park, New York.*

Until the late 1930s, the Treasury secretary relied heavily on the wisdom and connections of his esteemed father, Henry Morgenthau *(center)*. The elder Morgenthau made a fortune in ethical real-estate development and was ambassador to Turkey during the Armenian Genocide. *From the National Archives and Records Administration.*

Henry Morgenthau Jr.'s most trusted aide was his stalwart secretary, Henrietta Klotz. Having worked for Morgenthau years before he came to Washington, she revered him and was instrumental in his work for Jewish refugees as the war progressed. *From the National Archives and Records Administration.*

The magnificent Treasury Building is adjacent to the White House, meaning Henry Morgenthau Jr. was always handy if the president needed him. The secretary's office was at the left of this photo, from which he could see the windows of the Oval Office. *Courtesy of the Franklin D. Roosevelt Presidential Library and Museum, Hyde Park, New York.*

Henry Morgenthau Jr. often spoke of the "Treasury family"—the senior bureaucrats with whom he worked so closely in his corner office. He assembled them for this group shot beneath the portrait of former secretary Salmon Chase when Morgenthau was profiled by *Fortune* magazine in 1934. To the left of Morgenthau *(seated, center)*, in the light suit, is General Counsel Herman Oliphant, whom Morgenthau considered brilliant. *From the Treasury Collection, US Department of the Treasury.*

Henry Morgenthau Jr.'s rivalry with Secretary of State Cordell Hull persisted throughout their time in government. The Tennessean believed—with some justification—that Morgenthau thought he could do a better job of setting foreign policy. *From the National Archives and Records Administration.*

Henry Morgenthau Jr. and Under Secretary of the Treasury John W. Hanes Jr., who inscribed this photo shortly after joining the Treasury in 1938, tried to reform the US tax system before the war. They failed due to opposition from New Dealers, and Hanes left the government. *Courtesy of the Franklin D. Roosevelt Presidential Library and Museum, Hyde Park, New York.*

Daniel Bell added a touch of good humor and moderation to the Treasury deliberations. The career civil servant had served as budget director before becoming under secretary of the Treasury. *From the National Archives and Records Administration.*

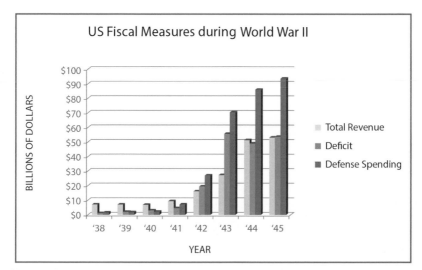

US Fiscal Measures during World War II

Legend:
- Total Revenue
- Deficit
- Defense Spending

As the world was enveloped in war, Henry Morgenthau Jr.'s main priority was to finance the most mechanized war machine the world had ever seen. Though he was never satisfied with the figures, government revenue grew more than sevenfold between 1938 and 1945 to $53.2 billion. Combined with the successful borrowing program, it financed a fifty-five-fold increase in defense spending, which reached $93.7 billion in 1945. *Chart by the author. Based on data from Christopher Chantrill, "Government Spending in the US," http://www.usgovernmentspending.com (accessed November 18, 2011).*

Like millions of American families, the Morgenthaus knew the pride, pain, and worry of having sons in active combat. Henry and Elinor Morgenthau revealed all these emotions when Henry III graduated from cavalry school in 1943. *Courtesy of the Franklin D. Roosevelt Presidential Library and Museum, Hyde Park, New York.*

One aspect of the war financing that Henry Morgenthau Jr. took special pride in was the war-bonds program. He even discovered he had a genius for advertising when he persuaded citizens to buy bonds. Millions of Americans, including those shown here, responded to the call. *Courtesy of the Franklin D. Roosevelt Presidential Library and Museum, Hyde Park, New York.*

The Morgenthau family kept this war-bond poster as a keepsake. It now hangs in the public restrooms at Fishkill Farms, the family's apple farm in Hopewell Junction, New York. *Photo by the author.*

Henry Morgenthau Jr. frequently criticized other cabinet members or White House insiders in his private sessions with Roosevelt, but never Harry Hopkins. He obviously knew the president thought too highly of the man who moved into the White House during the war. Morgenthau dismissed Hopkins as being merely flamboyant. *From the National Archives and Records Administration.*

Henry Morgenthau Jr., more than any other cabinet member, worked to prevent this sort of ghastly scene, from the Auschwitz death camp. Having witnessed his father's work during the Armenian Genocide, Morgenthau had no trouble understanding the enormity of the Nazi's extermination program. He was the driving force behind the War Refugee Board, which is estimated to have saved 200,000 lives. *Courtesy of the Franklin D. Roosevelt Presidential Library and Museum, Hyde Park, New York.*

The Treasury family changed over the war years, though Henrietta Klotz *(seated, third from right)* remained on the Morgenthau team. The man whose star rose the highest was Assistant Secretary Harry Dexter White *(seated, second from right)*. He received huge acclaim as the architect of the Bretton Woods Conference, then infamy when he was accused of being a Soviet spy. *Courtesy of the Franklin D. Roosevelt Presidential Library and Museum, Hyde Park, New York.*

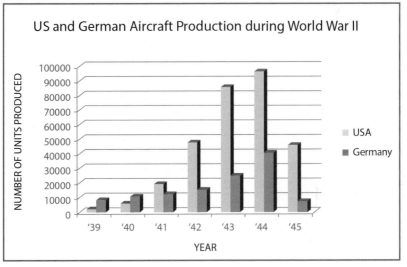

In 1938, there were fears that Germany had such a vast lead in the production of aircraft that the Allies might have difficulty catching up. Henry Morgenthau Jr. played two key roles in ensuring the United States won the aircraft race. He was Roosevelt's aircraft czar" in 1939 and 1940, and his financing ensured America could afford to out-manufacture the Axis. In this six-year period, the United States manufactured 304,000 aircraft, compared with 120,000 by Germany. *Chart by the author. Based on data from David M. Kennedy, ed.,* The Library of Congress World War II Companion *(New York: Simon and Schuster, 2007), p. 202.*

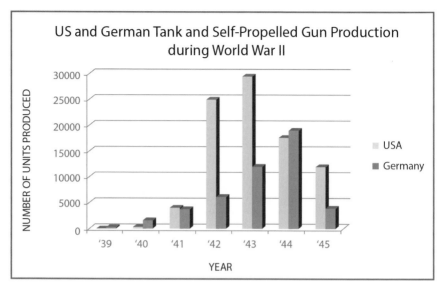

Not a single tank was produced in the United States in 1939, and only 247 tanks and self-propelled guns rolled out of the factories a year later. But the US arms program ramped up quickly and produced almost thirty thousand units in 1943—more than twice the German output. *Chart by the author. Based on data from David M. Kennedy, ed.,* The Library of Congress World War II Companion *(New York: Simon and Schuster, 2007), p. 203.*

Henry Morgenthau Jr. knew his friend, mentor, and president was in failing health late in the war. After this final tour through New York State in the 1944 campaign, Roosevelt's physical abilities and mental awareness both faded. *Courtesy of the Franklin D. Roosevelt Presidential Library and Museum, Hyde Park, New York.*

closing loopholes in corporate taxes. He wanted income taxes to mop up the excess liquidity among consumers but without an undue burden on "the lower one-third," the 33 percent who earned the least.[22] The Treasury was targeting interest rates of lower than 2.5 percent in bonds sold to banks. Bell urged his boss to state publicly that the Treasury would issue no bonds with a coupon of more than 2.5 percent. "Danny, old boy, I love you but I won't say that," said Morgenthau, adding he wouldn't tie his hands in that way. Rather, he convinced the president to say the government could raise the necessary funds without abandoning its low-interest-rate policy.[23] And above all, Morgenthau insisted with a persistent ferocity that the war-bond program should be voluntary so all people understood they were contributing to the fight for liberty and democracy.

On March 3, Morgenthau appeared before the Ways and Means Committee with his tax plan, which sought an additional $7.6 billion—slightly more than Roosevelt had outlined in his budget address—and a $2 billion increase in Social Security payments. "The cost of winning this war is going to affect every resident of America in almost every department and detail of his daily life," said the *New York Times*. "And still no one knows whether the sacrifices demanded will be enough, or for how long they will have to be made."[24] The point of contention in the budget debate was who would bear the burden. Morgenthau and Roosevelt were determined to protect the poor while several congressmen worried about taxing business too heavily. The committee considered a general sales tax or lowering the threshold at which income would be exempt from tax, which then stood at $750 a year for an individual and $1,500 for a married man. The administration opposed both moves. Morgenthau told his March 9 press conference that someone making $750 a year already paid more than 17 percent of his income through other taxes. "Families and individuals below the exemption level are making a fair enough contribution at this time to the government," said the secretary. But an informal poll of the committee showed that the majority favored a sales tax so all Americans would share the cost of the war.[25] The business community backed the committee, and labor backed the administration. Siding with the committee, the *New York Times* argued Americans had earned $61.2 billion in wages and salary the previous year and $7.2 billion in corporate profits, yet Morgenthau wanted to draw $3.06 billion from the first and $3.2 billion from the second.[26]

The pressure to increase taxes was amplified by problems in the war-bond program. The public enthusiasm was overwhelming, but it raised less than the Treasury had hoped. It had brought in $349.8 million in its first month of May 1941, and the sales had tapered downward after that to $232.3 million in September.[27] The total for the six months before the attack on Pearl Harbor had been about $2 billion, but Morgenthau wanted the program to raise $1 billion each month now that the United States was at war. The December figure revealed an improvement to $528.6 million, but it still wasn't enough.

In early January, Morgenthau told a national radio address that the nation "remembers Pearl Harbor" as shown from the fact that sales of war bonds doubled in December.[28] Organizers launched a campaign at major stores in New York asking customers to use their spare change to buy war stamps.[29] When rail workers received $75 million in the settlement of a labor dispute, Morgenthau publicly asked them to invest the payment in war bonds.[30] "Now that the United States is in the war to the eyebrows, we think the advice to buy United States defense savings bonds and stamps is good advice from several points of view," said an editorial from the *New York Daily News* that ran in the anti–New Deal *Chicago Tribune*.[31]

No community did more for the program than entertainers, who were photographed buying bonds and appeared at events promoting them. It was as cool to promote war bonds in 1942 as it would be to protest war a quarter century later. On January 17, the actress Carole Lombard, wife of Clark Gable, died in a plane crash while flying back to Los Angeles from Indianapolis, where she had been promoting war bonds. "Your wife died in the service to her country," Morgenthau wired to Gable.[32] On another day in January, Morgenthau was late for his press conference because he was meeting with Walt Disney to discuss a film promoting war bonds. "Asked to lift the veil which hides his tax plan, Mr. Morgenthau replied that in these matters he was like Mr. Disney's Dumbo, unable to speak," said one report.[33] Disney produced a Donald Duck cartoon urging people to pay their taxes on time. The Treasury was then roundly ridiculed for releasing a two-page, typed release about the short, describing each scene in detail. It left the *Chicago Tribune* wishing the Treasury were as clear in its annual accounts. "As a critic of the drama, if not as a fiscal agent, the treasury suffers from the ailment which psychiatrists have named 'total recall,'" said the editorial. "Once launched on his description, there is no stopping Mr. Morgenthau. Every detail of every scene is recalled."[34] And the songwriter Irving Berlin was back in January with a new song for "Mr. Henry Junior." This song was called "I Paid My Income Tax Today."[35]

Morgenthau enjoyed rubbing shoulders with movie stars, but he never let it overwhelm the importance of his mission. He was quick to chastise Abbott and Costello when the comedians distributed a statement (without the Treasury letterhead) detailing their efforts to promote war bonds. The media accused them of promoting themselves more than the bonds. "I don't like that sort of thing any more than newspapers do," said Morgenthau publicly. "I have been watching this sort of thing and will check it still more closely."[36]

The Treasury met its $1 billion target in January 1942, largely because of the wave of patriotism after the Japanese attack. Morgenthau told the Advertising Club of Baltimore on Valentine's Day that the bond program had reached only one-seventh of the nation's income earners and that even low-income earners could save $11 billion a year through defense stamps.[37] But the enthusiasm was difficult to maintain, and the total dropped to $700 million in February.

By mid-March, with the haggling over taxes dragging on, Morgenthau was feeling pressure to impose compulsory savings even from people in the administration, such as Marriner Eccles and Harold Smith.[38] After meeting with Senator Prentiss M. Brown of Michigan, who wanted to legislate that all overtime be paid in war bonds, Morgenthau said he would wait until July 1 to determine whether the voluntary plan had failed.[39] The president believed a compulsory program could raise only half the potential of the voluntary scheme. "Henry, you and I are the only people who understand it," he said.[40] When the voluntary program raised $564.5 million in March and $243 million in the first fourteen days of April, economists warned of the inflationary impact of the shortfall.[41]

Morgenthau pulled out all the stops when he testified before the Ways and Means Committee on April 16, insisting the voluntary plan would work. "We will ring every doorbell in the country at least once a month in an effort to increase the voluntary purchase of these obligations," said Morgenthau, speaking before a backdrop of posters from a General Motors plant urging workers to buy war bonds. The Treasury organized industry and labor witnesses to come forward to testify about the success of form letters and sales talks at the plants. Morgenthau said the promotion was being rolled out in fifty-four thousand plants where thirty million people worked, roughly 53 percent of the workforce. "If a voluntary system will work, and I am convinced it will, it will be far better for the country," Senator Walter F. George, chairman of the Senate Finance Committee, told reporters.[42] Even the *Wall Street Journal* supported the voluntary savings, saying compulsory savings would reduce take-home pay and therefore make it harder to raise the taxes that were needed to finance the war.[43]

Though still involved in international affairs, Morgenthau's unofficial role as Britain's champion in Washington was now assumed by Under Secretary of State Dean Acheson. He and the British were negotiating a new British-American lend-lease agreement. The countries agreed that the settlement of any debts would wait until after the war, that the United States would not interfere with political structures within the British Empire, and that the US Army would pay for its soldiers billeted in Britain and the empire. Separately, the two treasuries agreed that British dollar holdings would not fall below $600 million.[44]

On December 10, 1941, Maxim Litvinov, the new Soviet ambassador, called on Morgenthau, having been told by his predecessor to see the Treasury secretary if he needed anything. On New Year's Day, the United States agreed to lend the Soviet Union $20 million against deliveries of gold. But the larger problem was the American inefficiency in shipping material to Russia—a huge problem, given the growing importance of the Russian front. The Treasury staff learned that American suppliers could produce only a fraction of what had been promised in such critical supplies as steel wire, steel-alloy tubes, shells, and various tools. "Every promise the English have made to the Russians, they have fallen down on," an infuriated Roosevelt told the secretary in March. "The only reason we stand so well with the Russians is that to date we have kept our promises." He wanted to make sure the United States accelerated its deliveries to keep those promises. "I would rather lose New Zealand, Australia or anything else than have the Russians collapse."[45] The president filled out a written direction for Morgenthau to oversee the remedy. "This is *critical* because (a) we *must* keep our word [and] (b) because Russian resistance counts *most* today."[46]

The next day Morgenthau told such agencies as the Lend-Lease Authority, the Maritime Commission, and the War Production Board that the president wanted this fixed and would tolerate no excuses. Within a day, the War Department changed the authority over inland shipping, which promised to speed up deliveries, and other changes soon fell into place.[47]

The Americans had grown deeply suspicious of General Chiang Kai-shek and his clique, hearing they were growing wealthy from aid shipments and that the army was reluctant to fight the Japanese. No one felt stronger about this than Harry Dexter White. But politics determined that America aid an ally, especially one that had been fighting the Japanese for four years.

On December 30, Chiang officially asked the United States for a loan of $500 million—roughly ten times larger than the previous requests—saying it would bolster the morale of the Chinese people. The president understood the value of backing China, but Morgenthau suggested to his staff that they pay the money slowly and only if Chiang's government fought the Japanese actively. He negotiated, often ferociously, with T. V. Soong, Chiang's brother-in-law and a representative in Washington, during January 1942, and there was always an underlying threat that the Chinese could capitulate, freeing up several Japanese divisions to fight the Americans. Morgenthau compared it to "a hold-up." Litvinov called it "blackmail." The threat of capitulation worked, and Morgenthau agreed on January 29 to lend $500 million to the Chinese government, the repayment of which was deferred until the outcome of the war was clearer. He tried to place caveats on the loan, but the general insisted there be no strings attached.[48]

The reach of the Treasury's war effort even extended to South America when a Treasury report in the spring of 1942 determined Argentina, officially a neutral country, was allowing its banks to do business for Germany. Morgenthau wanted to freeze Argentine funds in the United States. Cordell Hull and the president protested that it would contravene Washington's "good neighbor" policy, which courted Latin American friendship and tried to steer them away from Fascism. Morgenthau said it was only a study at that point, to which Roosevelt replied: "Well, as long as it is a study, that's all right, but I don't want to do anything to upset all the good work that has been done in South America."[49]

White on May 8 submitted his report on an international-stabilization mechanism to Morgenthau that called for two multilateral institutions— one to stabilize currencies and the other to finance reconstruction. The United Nations stabilization fund would have capital of $5 billion provided by its member states, all of whom would agree to liberal trade and commercial policies. The fund would have the ability to buy extra currency of member nations as needed. Gold would be part of its capital, and the United States, which owned most of the world's gold, would have the largest vote. The Bank for Reconstruction and Development would have $10 billion in capital and could make or guarantee loans to governments. White suggested the creation of these two bodies—which came to be known as the International Monetary Fund and the World Bank—would require an international conference to negotiate the terms.[50]

"I am convinced that the launching of such a plan at this time has tremendous strategic as well as economic bearing," Morgenthau wrote to FDR when sharing the plan with him.[51] The president was interested, but he wanted Morgenthau to get financial and foreign-affairs policy makers on board. On May 25, Morgenthau briefed the Board of Economic Warfare, the State Department and the Federal Reserve on White's plan, and they all applauded it warmly. Marriner Eccles called the plan the "most important in the international field from a monetary standpoint." And Herbert Feis of the State Department added: "We, too, think that the time has come to pursue this study, and I don't know of any better way of doing it than the one you suggest." They struck a committee to work on the scheme, and White was named chairman.[52]

By July, Acheson told Morgenthau that the British were worried about a large conference on monetary affairs, likely because it would result in a reduced British role in international finance. He added that the State Department recognized Treasury primacy on the issue but worried about procedure. Morgenthau initially shrugged off the comment by saying the British could kill anything they didn't like, but he worried about the State Department trying to kill the bank and fund. He had a good relationship with Acheson and asked him point-blank to find out whether Hull would back his proposal. Hull recommended the Treasury brief other countries on its plans. If other countries and the president supported the proposal, then they should all proceed with an agenda for an international conference, he said.[53]

★ ★ ★

Morgenthau's personal circle was changing as Purvis was dead and Roosevelt's closest intimate was now Harry Hopkins, who was living in the White House. Occasionally, Morgenthau revealed his jealousy for the man he dismissed as being nothing more than flamboyant. "A couple of years ago the President said, 'You and I will run this war together,' and then it was 'You and I and Hopkins,' and then Hopkins and himself and me out on my ear," he once told his diary.[54]

The Morgenthau family's relationship with Eleanor Roosevelt was as firm and friendly as ever. The senior Morgenthaus still sent special presents (a one-hundred-dollar check for New Year's in 1942 because Henry Sr. didn't know what else to get the First Lady).[55] Even the Morgenthau children would send the Roosevelts gifts from time to time, as Robert sent them cheese in 1942 and Henry III a case of champagne from newly liberated France in 1944.[56] Eleanor Roosevelt still wrote the secretary frequently, asking him to help with her perpetual philanthropy. "Dear Henry," she wrote him. "You were so good about helping to have the tax taken off the theatre tickets given to our Service men in New York City, I wonder if you could consider the possibility of having the tax taken off on the tickets given to the Merchant Marine."[57] She forwarded any suggestions people gave her on the war-bond program, such as Capt. James Gorman's offer to perform the army artillery show on Broadway or a US Navy Band proposal to play Shostakovich's "Hymn to the United Nations" on radio.[58]

Even the 9:30 Group was changing. Stalwarts Daniel Bell, Harry Dexter White, and Henrietta Klotz were still at his side, but General Counsel Edward Foley Jr. resigned to enter the army as a lieutenant colonel. FDR said publicly that Morgenthau was making a sacrifice in releasing Foley. (In 1944, while stationed in Italy, Foley would write Morgenthau asking to return to Washington, claiming his wife was "distressed" and he worried about her health. The secretary responded that he was unable to help, and privately the Treasury gang, most of whom had family at the front, joked about the weak will of Mrs. Foley.[59]) Foley was succeeded by Randolph Paul, a New York tax attorney who had worked with the Treasury on budget matters in the past.[60] Younger men with high ideals were entering the inner circle, such as John Pehle and Josiah DuBois. They had been drawn to the Treasury largely because of Morgenthau's reputation for integrity and his unbending determination to defeat Nazism.

In the Morgenthau household, Robert had joined the navy as an ensign the previous year. Henry III was working for the Office of Emergency Management in Cleveland. (His father arranged to have his salary returned to the Treasury and reimbursed him from Elinor Morgenthau's money.) In the spring of 1942, Henry III enlisted in the army. Morgenthau was photographed in the New York papers seeing him off.[61] The only child left at home was Joan, whose intellect was as keen as her mother's. The Roosevelts and the Morgenthaus now shared the worry and pride of having children in combat. Elinor wrote the First Lady to congratulate her on Elliott Roosevelt receiving the Flying Cross. "He's always been one of my special favorites," she wrote.[62]

Elinor began the war as an enthusiastic lieutenant in her husband's endeavors, as she always had. Early in 1942, they were both in Detroit at a fundraising event at a defense manufacturer. Henry was struck down by one of his migraine headaches, so Elinor, ignoring a sprained ankle, climbed up on a tank and delivered a rousing speech supporting the war-bond program.[63] On April 18, she told 350 executives of the American fashion industry in New York to lead the nation in making frugality fashionable. American women must change their thinking and repair old clothes, appliances, and the like, she said, admitting the war would be hard on the makers of luxury products, like those in the fashion industry. "You could do no greater service than to instruct the women of America how to redesign their old dresses so that they look fresh and attractive; how to recapture the skills by which the pioneer woman made her life not only tolerable but rich and satisfying."[64]

What few outside the family knew was that Elinor Morgenthau, who had always pushed herself to the point of exhaustion, was feeling the cruel effects of age. After a hysterectomy in the early 1940s, her family noticed a decline in her energy, and she resigned from the Office of Civilian Defense in late 1942. Her ailment meant she was less active as an adviser to her husband, and he began to rely more on Henrietta Klotz.[65]

By April, the Ways and Means Committee was writing its own tax bill that apparently would include a sales tax as a means of reaching the $7.6 billion target for new revenue. Chairman of the committee Robert Lee Doughton told the president in April that the target could be met only with a sales tax, but Morgenthau—who knew the country would need more than $8 billion in extra tax revenue—still opposed such a levy.[66] The committee on June 20 decided not to vote on the sales tax, marking a significant victory for Morgenthau. It did, however, lower exemptions from $750 to $500 for a single person and $1,500 to $1,200 for a married person.[67] The committee's final budget raised only $6.25 billion in new revenue—far short of the $8.7 billion the Treasury was now seeking. "Those fellows just don't know there's a war on," said Morgenthau in disgust.[68] As the budget passed from the House, the Senate Finance Committee heard a new proposal that some members found attractive. Beardsley Ruml, the treasurer of R. H. Macy and the chairman of the board of the New York Federal Reserve, proposed that the government start collecting income taxes directly from individuals' paychecks. To ensure that people were not taxed twice in 1942, the previous year's taxes would be forgiven. Though it would relieve the problems of late tax payments and taxpayers' debt, the Treasury worried it would reward the rich, especially arms producers who had had a great year in 1941. The Treasury killed the plan for 1942.[69]

Meanwhile, the shortfalls in the war-bond program persisted. Temporarily scrapping the goal of $1 billion a month, the Treasury said it would work its way up to the $1 billion mark. In May, it achieved its $600 million target and fell just below its $800 million target in June. Though worried that sales might fall off during the summer, Morgenthau set the July target back up to $1 billion.[70] In the spring of 1942, he noted 45 percent of employees were now contributing about 4.8 percent of their monthly wages to war bonds, and he hoped to double that figure.[71] He no longer talked of waiting until July 1 to decide whether there should be a compulsory system. Rather, he declared July 1 would be "War Bond Day" at every store in the country. For fifteen minutes, merchants across the country were to sell nothing but war bonds and stamps. Also in July, the stars and stripes would adorn ninety million magazines. Radio stations throughout July would proclaim the slogan, "Carry the Stamp Book or Carry a Gun."[72] On Independence Day, Morgenthau went to Poughkeepsie to visit International Business Machines Corporation's Plant No. 4, which was working on war contracts, to applaud one thousand workers who worked their regular shift, despite the holiday. "I do not know of any better message to send to Mr. Hitler than to tell him about all you men we see here working on the Fourth of July like any other day," he said, standing before red, white, and blue bunting and American flags.[73] On July 27, Morgenthau announced that 621 radio stations, 70 percent of those in America, had agreed to market war bonds to the public.[74]

In early July, Morgenthau revealed that the government ran a deficit of $19.6 billion in the fiscal year that ended June 30, 1942, largely brought on by $25.95 billion in war expenditures. He called on Congress to raise more revenue, but he personally had to shore up support within the administration.[75] At the end of a fractious cabinet meeting on July 10, the president was talking to one member and without prompting said: "Henry has promised to raise $1 billion a month, and he's got his neck out and let him hang himself if he wants to or else his head goes kaput." The president dragged his finger across his throat as he spoke the final clause. Assembling his staff when he returned to the office, Morgenthau said he could have answered the president in half a dozen ways but did not. "I think you ought to know it so if a week from now I get excited—it may take a week before it boils up to the top—but on the other hand win or lose, nobody could do as good a job as the Treasury is doing and I just wanted to tell you that."[76]

Morgenthau mentioned to the president a week later that he had been a bit rough on the secretary about the war bonds.

"What did I do?" asked FDR. "What did I do?"

"You were unnecessarily rough."

"Well, there isn't a day passes that either Wallace or Miss Perkins does not go after me on compulsory savings." Then he asked, "What did I say?"

"Forget it, but I thought you were pretty rough." They ended the meeting amicably, and Morgenthau told his diary he was pleased the president took the criticism well.[77]

The media continued to publish stories with astronomical figures on the costs of the war. By July 1942, the war had already cost $35 billion— three times as much as all the wars prior to World War I and 83 percent of the total cost of the First World War. The cost was set to rise to $110.5 billion by the end of June 1943, and Congress had already voted to spend $223 billion to buy victory. If that sum was to be met, the United States would have to spend $100 billion just on the war expenses in the year ending June 30, 1944. "Never before has the United States Treasury had to contemplate even remotely the financing of such payments," said the *New York Times*. "If they are to be met in any reasonable degree by taxation Americans must pull their belt to a point hardly dreamed of in the past."[78]

Morgenthau appeared before the Senate Finance Committee in July, stressing that if the Senate went along with the House's plan to increase revenue by only $6.3 billion, the Treasury would have to borrow $53 billion in the current fiscal year—more than $4 billion a month. Even if the Senate increased Social Security levies by $2 billion, the United States would still pay for only 37 percent of its war expenditures through taxation, compared with 70 percent in 1941 in Canada and 44 percent in the United Kingdom.[79] But in early August, Senator George told the media the committee was unlikely to make substantial changes to the budget passed by the House.[80]

George also called for a system of "induced loans," but Morgenthau was unimpressed, saying it was like all the other plans for forced loans. He soon admitted he would not reach the $1 billion mark for war bond sales in July, but he would exceed $900 million, which he described as "a tidy sum."[81] Opposition to voluntary sales was mounting. On August 7, Senator Arthur Vandenberg, a member of the Senate Finance Committee, said the voluntary bond program was totally inadequate, even if it did raise $12 billion a year, because it would result in a $35 billion deficit. He wouldn't say what should happen but noted the Treasury plans to sell $30 billion in bonds to commercial banks. "Everybody seems to agree that while the banks may be able to absorb this deficit, for one more year, it cannot thus be done thereafter and even the immediate effect is highly inflationary."[82]

When Morgenthau appeared in Roanoke, Virginia, in late August to name it the first "Treasury Flag City" of the war-bonds campaign, he sounded a bit petulant. "It should no longer be necessary for the Treasury to come to every American, cap in hand, to ask for subscriptions for war bonds and at 2.9 percent interest. By this time, every American should be coming forward, willingly and gladly, to lend a part of his earnings to his country. After all, we have been at war for more than eight months."[83]

The war was slowly turning. The US Navy won its most decisive victory ever when it defeated Japanese forces at Midway in June. The British finally scored a victory in North Africa in August when a brash general named Bernard Montgomery defeated Erwin Rommel at El Alamein. The Soviets by autumn were holding the Germans in check at Stalingrad and inflicting horrendous losses on the invaders.

Morgenthau fought on for his volunteer program, saying in an opinion piece that he would soon launch a $3 billion bond issue—the largest issue ever. "My problem is not simply one of getting more money," he wrote.

"It is a problem of enlisting the taxes and savings of the American people themselves."[84]

Over lunch on August 25, the president dropped his voice and said, "Henry, now that your War Bonds are not going so well, what are you going to do about it?"

"I am not going to do anything now because I think something will come out of the present tax bill and that will help us with our War Bonds." But it was obvious Roosevelt was losing patience with the shortcomings of the bond program.[85]

In September, the movie industry led a campaign that raised $900 million. "This is a people's war—85,000,000 movie goers are the people," read a poster on the desk of National Campaign Director Si Fabian, who had left his job as a theater-circuit owner and devoted his entire time to the campaign. They planned war-mother nights, war-sweetheart nights, war-bride nights. On September 1, at theaters with a total of eleven million seats, the movies would be stopped for a patriotic ceremony.[86]

As summer gave way to fall, the fiscal deadlock in Washington continued, and Morgenthau was taking a large part of the blame because of his inflexibility on the sales tax, compulsory savings, and the Ruml proposal. "The simple fact is that not in the history of the nation has there been such a tax muddle as now," said columnist Frank R. Kent, who said the colossal job at hand required the best financial minds in the land. "Mr. Morgenthau is an earnest, honest, well-intentioned public man, but to regard him as one of the outstanding financial figures of America is not possible, even for his partial friends," said Kent. "Mr. Bell, a former director of the budget, is an excellent routine career man, but the idea of his coping single handedly with the gigantic war financing problems is not really tenable."[87]

Morgenthau sent FDR a memo proposing a "spending tax." It would be different than a sales tax because it would be progressive, escalating as the price of goods rose, and because there would be exempt items, such as food.[88] He also urged Roosevelt to tell the country in a coming radio address that he had the statutory power to regulate the price of food and other necessities. "Take the bit in your teeth and announce it and get it over with. I know the public will like it," he said.[89] When Roosevelt delivered the fireside chat, he recited much of the Treasury policy but not the spending tax. When Morgenthau questioned him, FDR replied he never made tax recommendations to Congress while a bill was pending. Morgenthau said it completely took his breath away, so much so that he couldn't come up with an example to prove the president wrong. The president tried to joke his way out of it. "Well, you know, Henry, I always have to have a couple of whipping boys."

"Yes, I realize I am one of them and right now I am getting plenty of whippings."[90]

The Senate passed the revenue bill on October 10, producing only $7 billion in new revenue. Arthur Krock praised Senator George's leadership and criticized the administration for not supporting the Ruml plan. "Yet at no time did the Administration, through the Treasury or any other spokesman, give to Senator George any sound assistance in devising a measure that would siphon back into the public funds enough of the swollen payroll billions to turn the fiscal tide strongly against inflation."[91]

The media was criticizing Morgenthau more than it had previously, even when the Treasury Department raised a mammoth $4.1 billion in 1.5 percent notes and 2 percent bonds in October. Though it was as big as a whole year's borrowing a decade earlier, the Treasury held the rate at 2 percent. *Time* magazine called it an "outstanding failure," saying the Treasury had to beg banks to increase their purchases. "Mr. Morgenthau is very high-principled, very modest about his limited financial ability, very timid," it said. The article added Morgenthau's "New Deal advisers . . . are quite sure that the banks will continue to take Government offering, at almost any price, and that they do not have to worry about giving the banks what they want."[92] Marriner Eccles—the most unlikely of defenders—complained to the magazine that the article was unfair to Morgenthau and a disservice to the country.[93]

With US forces slowly entering ground wars in the Pacific at Guadalcanal and in North Africa, the demands of the arms program increased and with them worries about inflation. Roosevelt created the Office of Economic Stabilization to hold down prices and told Morgenthau he was thinking of naming as its head James Byrnes, a former senator from South Carolina who was now on the Supreme Court.[94] In late August, Sam Rosenman, a Roosevelt insider, asked Morgenthau privately if he would be interested in heading the Procurement Division if they could convince the president it was needed. "I insist on sitting at the left of the President where I sit now because I need prestige over the Army and Navy," said Morgenthau, who discussed the matter in privacy with Harry Dexter White, Henrietta Klotz, Herbert Gaston, and Elinor Morgenthau. White warned he would have to be prepared for bad press and powerful enemies. Elinor said the job would be tough, even with the proper authority over loans administrator Jesse Jones. She said Morgenthau would have to continue to align himself with labor because he would be in constant battles with big business.[95]

To escape the endless battles, Morgenthau won the president's approval to visit the United Kingdom. He was still a key player in financing the British war effort, and the British treasury had revealed in August that it too was planning a stabilization instrument. John Maynard Keynes, the architect of the scheme, called it a "clearing union." Though it had many points in common with White's plan, the clearing union called for no capital from the participating countries. Instead, it would offer the members overdraft facilities that they could draw on when they needed it to stabilize their currency.[96] Traveling with White, Morgenthau met in October with Treasury officials, Winston Churchill, and King George VI and was wowed by British courage and the aerial domination of the Royal Air Force. He predicted the war would end in 1943 or 1944 because the British were more advanced than he had thought previously.[97] Sir Kingsley Wood, Chancellor of the Exchequer, introduced him to the Commons on October 20 and said the visit was "a good augury" for confronting current and postwar problems together.[98] The highlight was Churchill taking him and South African prime minister Jan Smuts to Dover to view the coastal defenses. Standing before thousands of cheering British soldiers, Churchill introduced Morgenthau as "the man who gave us 1 million rifles in 1940."[99] When he came home, Morgenthau let the media know the British and Canadians were

paying about twice the taxes that American were. (Over time, this statement was disputed. Noting that the two systems were difficult to compare;
journalist Godfrey N. Nelson said that the British budgetary expenditures
were about 57.5 percent of national income while those of the United
States were about 75 percent.[100]) Morgenthau also noted that the Treasury
raised $6.84 billion in October, a record, including $814 million in the sale
of war bonds, well above the quota of $775 million.[101]

As early as July 1942, the Allies had begun planning for the American-British
invasion of North Africa, and General Dwight Eisenhower, the head of the
invasion force, asked Morgenthau whether the invading troops should use
sterling or dollars once they had secured the territory. International law dictated that the invading force would form the government of the occupied
territory but that the conquered land's inhabitants must pay for that government. Therefore, Allied armies would need a currency that could be used to
pay their troops, and that would become the official currency of the indig-
enous people. Morgenthau immediately ruled out sterling because it would
make US soldiers look like mercenaries, and the Treasury was working to
make the dollar the dominant international currency after the war. What's
more, European governments in exile had told him they wanted dollars after
liberation. White also said liberated jurisdictions like France or the Netherlands that were recognized by the United States should revert to their own
currency as soon as possible, but the dollar—or a special currency linked to
the dollar—should be used in captured Axis zones, like Germany or Italy.

In August, Morgenthau proposed a US committee to oversee the
administration of liberated jurisdictions, and Roosevelt approved, saying it
should include the Treasury, War, and State Departments. Morgenthau told
his staff that in occupying Germany, "I think it had better be the United
States that decides that all of these munitions factories will be leveled to the
ground and destroyed, and the munitions machinery, airplanes that can't
fly more than two or three hundred miles, all the rest of that stuff."[102]

The Allies landed in Morocco and Algeria on November 8, 1942, quickly establishing control of key seaports and airports. François Darlan, a senior Vichy official, happened to be in the area and the Allied forces recognized him as the head of French North Africa. In return, he ordered the French troops to cease all resistance to the Allies. The deal with Darlan absolutely disgusted Morgenthau, who didn't like the army setting foreign policy and hated the thought of the United States dealing with Nazi sympathizers. Over tea with Henry Stimson on November 17, he said lots of rich Americans would deal with Hitler tomorrow and it was wrong to have anything to do with Darlan.[103] Later that day, he told Roosevelt this was a matter "that affects my soul." Roosevelt was sympathetic during their forty-minute discussion. General Marshall had told the president the Darlan deal meant fewer US casualties in a campaign that would otherwise have taken six weeks. Morgenthau was heartened, telling FDR that he was satisfied as long as the president was in charge of everything.[104] As with the issue of imprisoning Japanese Americans, Morgenthau had placed ethics ahead of expediency.

Greater moral issues soon appeared—first in a tiny report on page 10 of the *New York Times* on November 24. It was a five-paragraph story, barely noticeable amid the reports of the war in Russia, North Africa, and the Pacific. It might have been buried because of anti-Semitism or because its contents were so incredible, so disturbing, that editors could not believe it. The United Press report from Jerusalem said Hebrew papers had lined in black borders reports that the Germans were systematically killing Jews in Poland. It estimated 250,000 had been killed so far.

There was more detail the next day, but the *New York Times* still relegated the reports to page 10. There was a large report on a press conference the Polish government in exile had held in London on the mass exterminations of Jews in their homeland. The report said Heinrich Himmler had organized extermination squads to kill as many as half of the Jews in Poland.

Beneath it was another story of a press conference in Washington held by Rabbi Stephen Wise, head of the World Jewish Congress. This five-paragraph story reported that Wise said the State Department, after weeks of badgering, had confirmed that the Germans had killed about half of the Jews in the areas they occupied. About two million people had been murdered, and the number was growing.[105]

CHAPTER NINE

THE JEWS

★ ★ ★

T hough Henry Morgenthau Jr.'s aim in government was to serve all Americans and not just Jews, he was nonetheless the only Jew in the cabinet and therefore the administration's link to the Jewish community. More than any cabinet colleague, he was called on by American Jews, which was a source of pride, heartbreak, and sometimes outrage to him. He knew the joy of reaching the top of society despite being a minority and the angst of being targeted as a minority in spite of his success.

At one point in 1942, Alien Property Custodian Leo Crowley told Morgenthau the president had recently said to him out of the blue, "Leo, you know, this is a Protestant country, and the Catholics and the Jews are here on sufferance. It is up to both of you to go along with anything that I want at this time." Crowley, a Catholic, was shocked, and Morgenthau was appalled his best friend could say such a thing.

"Leo, what are we fighting for?" Morgenthau asked. "What am I killing myself for at this desk if we are just here by sufferance?"

"That's what I want to know," replied Crowley.[1]

The statement was out of character for Roosevelt, whose administration was known for its advancement of Jews. Morgenthau worked closely with the president on refugee matters and knew that FDR wanted deeply to help the persecuted European Jews. That work intensified as the administration became aware of the Nazis' extermination program. Morgenthau was becoming more sympathetic to Zionism and was trying to convince Roosevelt to pressure Britain to let more Jews emigrate to the Holy Land. (The British were worried about an Arab uprising in their Middle Eastern colony, especially at a time when their military was already fighting on three continents.) On July 7, 1942, Morgenthau tried to convince Roosevelt that Jews themselves would make "magnificent fighters." The president said Zionist leader Chaim Weizmann had recently asked him for sixty thousand rifles and ten thousand machine guns, but the Allies simply could not spare them.[2]

The news that the Nazis were exterminating millions of Jews changed Morgenthau's feeling of responsibility. Having witnessed the Armenian Genocide by Germany's ally Turkey during World War I, he had less trouble than his colleagues did believing the reports. Even his wife, who had strongly coaxed him to work for all Americans, could not help but be affected by the plight of the European Jews. After war broke out in Europe, Elinor began to interact with Jewish refugee groups, receiving information from experts on settlements in the Dominican Republic and on the Refugee Economic Corporation.[3] She did what she could, even though she was weakening dramatically. (In May 1943, she would enter the hospital for a hysterectomy. "She had a very bad night but each day she is better, and it is what you would call a successful operation," Morgenthau wrote FDR on May 25. He added she would be in the hospital for three weeks and it would be six months to a year before she would feel like herself again.[4])

Elinor Morgenthau received a call in November from Mrs. David de Sola Pool, the National President of Hadassah, the Women's Zionist Organization of America, telling her of five hundred to eight hundred Polish Jewish children stranded in Tehran. Half of them were starving and in need of clothing and medical aid. The children would be admitted to Palestine as long as the Americans paid for their transportation, living costs, and education. Elinor and Morgenthau both agreed to ask Eleanor Roosevelt to convince the president to help the children. She immediately wrote Eleanor, beginning the letter with a statement that this was not a customary request. "The case of these children is desperate and Palestine can take care of them," she wrote on December 2. "The things that are happening to the Jews in Europe, executions that no longer are in thousands but now mounting to millions, [are so] horrible, that to save 500 children's lives is at least a step in the right direction." She signed the note, "Devotedly always, Elinor."[5]

The next night, a group of people met at the Morgenthau house at the suggestion of presidential adviser Sam Rosenman to discuss how to increase Jewish immigration into Palestine—another indication both Morgenthaus were growing more involved in the Zionist cause. When Morgenthau mentioned the meeting to the president, FDR told him to go easy on Palestine because he already had a plan. "First, I would call Palestine a religious country," he said. "Then I would leave Jerusalem the way it is and have it run by the Orthodox Greek Catholic Church, the Protestants and the Jews—have a joint committee run it." FDR added: "I actually would put a barbed wire around Palestine, and I would begin to move the Arabs out of Palestine." He said he would provide land for the Arabs in some other part of the Middle East and each time a Jewish family moved in, an Arab family would be moved out, so in the end 90 percent of the residents would be Jewish. "There are lots of places to which you could move the Arabs," he said. "All you have to do is drill a well because there is this large underground water supply, and we can move the Arabs to places where they can really live." In the meantime, he had discussed with the government of Colombia the possibility of establishing settlements in the Andes. Morgenthau told him that when they got back to Dutchess County—their euphemism for retirement—he would like to be involved in helping the refugees. "I was surprised to find that the president was studying this thing with so much interest and had gone as far as he had in making up his mind on what he wants to do," he dictated into his diary.[6]

A turning point in Henry Morgenthau Jr.'s relationship with the Jewish community came in November 1942, when Rabbi Stephen Wise came to the corner office to tell the secretary what was happening in Europe. Morgenthau knew of the millions of deaths and the lampshades made from victims' skin, and he asked Wise not to go into excessive details. But Wise went on to tell of the barbarity of the Nazis, how they were making soap out of Jewish flesh. Morgenthau, turning paler, implored him, "Please, Stephen, don't give me the gory details." Wise went on with his list of horrors and Morgenthau repeated his plea again and again. Henrietta Klotz was afraid her boss would keel over.[7] Morgenthau later said the meeting changed his life.

On December 17, the White House finally denounced the slaughter and said the United States would punish anyone guilty of political or racial murder.[8] But that was it. The Western Allies had no beachhead in continental Europe and could do little. The United States did not increase refugee quotas. The government did not work with neutral countries to protect Jews who had escaped from the Nazis and arrange transportation to safe havens. Morgenthau was certain the State Department wasn't up to the task. "The typical foreign services officer lived off paper," Morgenthau would later state in a series of articles ghostwritten by historian Arthur Schlesinger Jr. "The horrors of Dachau and Buchenwald were beyond their conception. They dealt with human lives at the same bureaucratic tempo and with the same lofty manner that they might deal with a not very urgent trade negotiation."[9] The matter weighed heavily on Morgenthau's conscience.

At some point during the winter, Treasury staff member Josiah DuBois learned from a friend at the State Department, Donald Hiss (brother of Alger Hiss, who was spying for the Soviets), that the situation was worse than they had believed. Hiss copied key documents that showed the State Department was not only too passive in its response but also that some key officers were actively working against rescue efforts.[10]

★ ★ ★

As the anniversary of Pearl Harbor approached, Morgenthau issued a statement calling for Americans to pay more taxes. "Today, a year after Pearl Harbor, the nation is engaged in two wars—the war against the Axis and the war against post-war chaos," he said. "Experience has taught us that military victory alone may turn to ashes. We who fight the war have also the duty of paying for the war."[11]

In twelve months, war-bond sales had reached the monthly target of $1 billion only in January 1942. Only 15 percent came from individuals.[12] Roosevelt was growing impatient, and the wisdom of the voluntary program was being challenged by a new powerbroker within the Roosevelt circle, James Byrnes.

For political and economic reasons, the Treasury needed to improve war-bond sales, and by late fall the group devised a plan based on the Liberty-loan drives of the previous war. These raised billions of dollars in brief, targeted campaigns that concentrated the efforts of volunteers, the media, and businesses. By late November, the Treasury was leaking to the media that the coming war-bond drive could exceed even the fourth Liberty-bond drive of 1918, which raised $6.9 billion. Working with its organizing committees in all twelve federal districts, the Treasury brought together 4,400 volunteers working for the Victory Fund committees, who in turn oversaw 300,000 frontline sales people. Through the American Bankers' Association, it asked every bank in the country to contact every customer, asking them to buy war bonds. On November 19, 1942, the Treasury unveiled the Victory Fund drive, with the aim of raising a record $9 billion by the end of January 1943.[13]

Feeling exhausted after such a horrendous year, Morgenthau began the tortuous procedure of preparing a tax bill, but he soon learned he was no longer the only member of the administration negotiating with congressional leaders. Byrnes and his lieutenant Fred Vinson were doing so as well, and Morgenthau began to bicker with Byrnes about who controlled tax policy. He disingenuously told Roosevelt on December 3 that he was "getting along first rate" with Byrnes but wanted to clarify whether the Treasury should prepare the tax bill as it had in the past. "Absolutely," said FDR, adding that he had said nothing to anyone about the Treasury's role changing. "This proves to me that Byrnes is just groping for the power and hasn't got any directive from the President," Morgenthau told his diary. "It also proves I am right in thinking that one should not be scared by anybody like Byrnes."[14]

Soon, Morgenthau's exhaustion gave way to influenza and he was hospitalized. With Morgenthau out of the office, Harold Smith came to acting secretary Daniel Bell with a draft budget that called for compulsory savings, cancellation of some taxes in exchange for a pay-as-you-go system, and a "deterrent tax," which was a euphemism for a sales tax. Bell said such a massive change couldn't be released without the secretary's approval, but Smith responded that the president didn't want Morgenthau bothered in hospital. Suspicious, Bell phoned Elinor Morgenthau, who brought her ailing husband into the discussion so he could approve a counterproposal drafted by his staff.

When Roosevelt finally delivered his budget message to Congress in early January, it made no mention of compulsory savings or a deterrent tax. It said the country needed $16 billion in extra revenue, or a total of $51 billion, and left it to Congress to find ways to raise it. The $109 billion in expenditure was twelve times larger than the biggest New Deal budget. It was such a staggering figure that *Time* magazine placed Morgenthau (then convalescing in a hospital bed) on its cover on January 25, staring out intently in front of a backdrop of dollar bills and coins. The story, titled "U.S. at War: $51,000,000,000-a-Year Man," outlined the horrendous task facing Morgenthau as he worked to cover the costs of the war. It noted that the Civil War (which had taken place eighty years earlier) had cost $3.5 billion; World War I, $35 billion; but the current war would cost $70 billion in 1943 alone. "Some hyperbolic economists, who see fiscal policy as the beginning and end-all of Government planning, say that it is more important in wartime to have a great Treasury Secretary than a great President," it said. "Nobody yet has called Henry Morgenthau a great Treasury Secretary."[15] The Treasury was fraught as budget specialist Daniel Bell was near exhaustion, and Ruml was once again pushing for tax forgiveness in return for a pay-as-you-go system. He said Morgenthau was the one blocking the new system, publicly calling him an "unfortunate man" for the United States.[16]

The saving grace for Morgenthau was that the Victory Fund drive was a smashing success. In its first nineteen days, the campaign raised $10.2 billion, with 55 percent of it from individuals and small businesses. "This is a record that sets a new mark in the financial history of this or any other country," said the *New York Times*.[17] The final tally was $12.9 billion, and only 40 percent of it came from banks. Morgenthau called it a "grand response by the people."[18] Senator Robert Taft, a Republican member of the Finance Committee, dropped his proposal for forced savings after seeing the Treasury raised most of it from individuals and companies other than banks. "In one month then, about as much money was obtained for the Treasury as could be raised in a year from most of the compulsory savings plans that have been suggested to Congress," he said.[19]

Morgenthau was hospitalized with the flu for two weeks, then spent three weeks convalescing in Cuba, relaxing at the Club Kawama on Varadero Beach. He called on dictator Fulgencio Batista, author Ernest Hemingway, and journalist Martha Gellhorn. (In early 1941, Morgenthau and Harry Dexter White had asked the great author to gather intelligence for them when he and Gellhorn traveled to China and Burma.)[20] By the time Morgenthau returned to the corner office in early February, Roosevelt had returned from the Casablanca Conference in North Africa with Churchill. The Germans had now been driven from Africa, and the two leaders agreed that their next move would be to drive north into Sicily and then to Italy itself. At the Brits' insistence, they agreed not to attempt an invasion across the English Channel immediately, opting instead for Churchill's preference for an invasion of Italy. Churchill went along with Roosevelt's proposal that the Allies accept only unconditional surrender from the Axis, ending the possibility of a negotiated settlement that could leave the Nazis in power.

The Treasury now had to administer occupation currencies for North Africa and soon for other jurisdictions, and it proved a delicate affair. If the exchange rates were too strong, domestic businesses would not be able to export, capital would leave the country, and US soldiers would have little spending power. If they were too weak, the country would underprice other European countries, including Britain. In early February, Roosevelt told the cabinet he favored fixing the franc at 43.90 to the pound once France was liberated. The Treasury thought the level was too strong, but the Free French Forces under Charles de Gaulle didn't want it lowered because the franc reflected the glory of France.[21]

The problems in administering the occupied areas were complicated by the residue of class warfare from the New Deal. Henry Stimson, George Marshall, and John McCloy—none of whom had worked on the New Deal—planned to rely on private enterprise to provide supplies and expertise to the occupied zone in Sicily. The thought horrified the Roosevelt circle, including Morgenthau, who believed it would bring in businessmen who had opposed the New Deal. They persuaded FDR to set up a panel to appoint administrators in occupied territories. Stimson was outraged, insisting he was trying to win a war, not squabble over petty ideology. He wrote in his diary on March 28 that Roosevelt was the worst administrator he had ever worked for.[22] Morgenthau asked White to be the Treasury representative on the panel. Soon White was complaining that the State Department had already seized control of economic, monetary, and financial policy and Morgenthau had to step in. "I am glad you are going to pick up the strings," White told the secretary. "You are the only one strong enough to defend our position." The one matter that White did fight for—and won—was a lire valued at one penny, whereas the State Department had originally advocated two per penny.[23]

In early February, Morgenthau began to work with the Federal Reserve on the second Victory Loan drive, set for April with a target of $13 billion. This drive would target small communities.[24] He was growing to adore these bond drives, which brought him rare acclaim and contact with ordinary Americans, including children. On March 5, he presented six-year-old Dickie Laswell of Springfield, Illinois, with a distinguished-services citation for raising nearly $1,000. Dickie suffered from lymphatic leukemia and told his mother he didn't need her to bring him toys in the hospital. But he did want pennies to buy war stamps so the country could win the war. When his mother told the story to a newspaper, pennies flooded in from countless donors.[25] John Anson, six years old, of San Francisco, wrote Morgenthau a scolding letter a month later after the Treasury ran a war-bond advertisement with a caricature of a dachshund with Adolf Hitler's face. "I told him I had two dachshunds and they were nice little dogs and I loved them and that they were good Americans," he told the Associated Press. A secretary replied, saying that the Morgenthaus themselves owned a dachshund and meant no insult to their breed.

When the campaign was launched April 7, the *New York Times* said it would be "the greatest borrowing drive in the history of the world."[26]

A hundred thousand New Yorkers volunteered to sell the bonds, and a quarter million people in the tristate area aimed to raise $3 billion.[27] On April 24, Morgenthau told a crowd in Cedar Rapids, Iowa, that twenty-five million Americans were now buying war bonds through the payroll-reduction plans, but it still wasn't enough. "The interesting thing as we get into the home stretch is that the sales of savings bonds are beginning to increase, and the number of pledges," he said. "That's what we want. The drive wouldn't be a success unless we got the people."[28] By the end of the month, the *New York Times* was already calling the drive "a tremendous success," having already exceeded the target by $500 million and raised $10.5 billion from sources other than banks. The Treasury believed it would be oversubscribed by $2.5 billion by the time the offering closed.[29] It ended up raising $18.5 billion, an oversubscription of $5.5 billion.[30]

By late May, a House committee accepted a bill with 75 percent tax forgiveness as long as the country moved to a pay-as-you-go system, which it did on July 1. Though the rich got a huge tax break in the middle of the most expensive war in history, the new system also raised $4 billion immediately.[31]

★ ★ ★

The Treasury continued to hear rumors about the State Department thwarting efforts to rescue European Jews. They even heard of a State Department cable telling the legation in Bern, Switzerland, not to forward information on the Jewish killings to Washington. The Treasury knew Gerhart Riegner, a representative of the World Jewish Congress in Geneva, had fed information from Jewish refugees to Western authorities, including Leland Harrison, the US minister at the legation. But rather than acting on this information, the State Department had simply referred the matter to the Intergovernmental Committee on Political Refugees.

Morgenthau was aware early in 1943 of opportunities to help the refugees, such as the Romanian government being willing to let seventy thousand Jews go to Palestine. Of course, there were problems: there could have been spies among them; the move could incite Jewish-Arab tensions;

and the Romanians wanted a ransom of £250 per person.[32] Negotiations were needed to bring down the $80 million total, and private and public funds could cover the cost. However, the State Department failed to act.

In April, John Pehle and Josiah DuBois found a document that lent credence to the rumors they'd heard. The two men worked for the Office of Foreign Funds Control, which prevented US funds from leaking to the enemy. They therefore received all correspondence on the refugee issue, since it could involve paying ransom to Axis countries. One cable from Leland Harrison responded to Sumner Welles's request for information from Riegner. It detailed the horrors in the occupied lands and added that such reports should not be subject to Cable 354. Pehle and DuBois immediately assumed Cable 354 was the directive they had heard about. They brought the information to Morgenthau, who authorized them to officially ask for Cable 354. The State Department refused, saying the cable did not concern the Treasury.[33]

Throughout the spring and summer, the World Jewish Congress focused its efforts on trying to rescue Jews in France and Romania. It collected money from private sources in March—enough to rescue as many as seventy thousand people. But the State Department failed to act. Even conscientious State Department officials like Feis and Welles tried to help, but the State Department said it could not let ransom be paid for reasons of economic warfare. The Treasury's foreign-funds division was now becoming more involved.[34]

Stephen Wise and other Jews called on Morgenthau in July to say Romanian officials would allow the evacuation of seventy thousand Jews for $170,000. They needed to be paid in local currency, and the Treasury had to decide whether to release the dollars to pay for it. The Treasury approved the plan because the money would be held in Switzerland until after the war.[35] Wise called on FDR on July 22 to see what was delaying the matter, and the president told Morgenthau he wanted to help the refugees. Morgenthau passed all this on to Cordell Hull, who agreed it should be all right because the money in Switzerland could not pass into the enemy zone. Morgenthau thought the matter was settled, but months passed and there was no action.[36]

When the State Department finally cabled Bern in September with instructions that the Treasury had cleared the payments to Romania, Harrison said he had previously been ordered to pass such matters to the British legation. Nothing was done for seventeen days as the matter was discussed between Bern, London, and Washington. Meanwhile, officials in Washington learned that four thousand children had been taken from their parents in France and were being transported in sealed, window-less boxcars, sixty to a car without food or water.[37] The Treasury officials wanted to force the issue with the State Department. But to complete their case, they knew they had to secure a copy of Cable 354.

In June, Roosevelt created the Office of War Mobilization and named James Byrnes the director, who said publicly he intended to be "Deputy President of the United States." The new agency would have authority over all departments prosecuting the war except the Treasury. The president named five advisers to the office—Henry Stimson, Frank Knox, Harry Hopkins, procurement chief Donald Nelson, and Fred Vinson, head of the office of stabilization—but not Morgenthau. "Secretary of the Treasury Henry M. Morgenthau Jr. was reported to resent Mr. Byrnes's interference in tax matters, on which he has been, until recently at least, the recognized Administration spokesman on Capitol Hill," said a columnist in the *New York Times*.[38] Byrnes then publicly said on June 9 that he would take a hand "in the shaping of future tax policy" and invited Morgenthau, Vinson, and Harold Smith to a session on anti-infla-tion moves.

In public, Morgenthau said little more than the country needed more taxes, protection for the poor, and a voluntary savings program. He chal-lenged Americans to double their investment in war bonds to avoid com-pulsory savings.[39] And he persuaded the president to write a public letter in praise of the bond program. "I am proud of the fact that 27 million patri-otic Americans are regularly investing more than $420 million a month to help pay the cost of the war," said the president's letter. "I do not hesitate to say that the payroll savings plan is the single greatest factor we now have protecting ourselves against inflationary spending."[40]

But in private, the Treasury secretary seethed. One sign of the mounting tension was his severe migraine headaches, which became so bad on June 24 that he was hospitalized and received drugs intravenously.[41]

Morgenthau soon announced publicly that the third war-loan drive would start September 9 with a target of $15 billion—almost half of the $33 billion target for that year.[42] In the corner office, he complained that Byrnes and Vinson were pushing their agenda forward with impunity. "What the President has done, without having the courtesy to tell us, is that he has brought between himself and his cabinet another group that he looks to run it," he said. "He is not going to do it to me and I am not going to take it." Gathering momentum in one of his rants, he called them maneuverers and finaglers, men of personal ambition, and he declared he would not be "a shirt front for Vinson."

"I have been here ten years and your moral fibers begin to weaken after a while," he said. "You can take a rubber band and keep pulling it, and after a while the thing just snaps. The things I could take five years ago . . . I can't take it now."[43]

Morgenthau formally wrote the president on July 27 to complain of a perception that the Treasury was "out of the tax picture," replaced by Byrnes and Vinson. Vinson was negotiating with two congressional committees and had called members of the Treasury staff to meet him. "This creates a situation which makes it very difficult for me and for members of my staff to work effectively on tax matters," he wrote. He enclosed a draft directive to clarify the secretary of the Treasury was in charge of tax policy.[44]

"Aw Hen," responded Roosevelt in a handwritten letter three days later. "The Weather is hot and I'm goin' off fishing. I decline to be serious even when you see 'gremlins' which ain't there. F.D.R."[45]

And with that, the president left Washington and his fuming Treasury secretary. They got together for their regular lunch after FDR returned, and Morgenthau brought up tax policy again.

"Did you get my very snooty note?" asked the president.

"Yes, I did, and I didn't think it was snooty. I thought it was darling and I enjoyed it."

Morgenthau began to raise the issue again, but the president cut him off. "In the first place, Jimmy Byrnes feels in his new position that taxes are part of his overall responsibility as well as other matters." FDR told Morgenthau to go ahead and file a tax plan as the secretary always had and that he wanted a strong tax bill. "So to sum up, the President was very firm in that he wanted me to go ahead as I always have done previously," Morgenthau dictated in his diary. And if Vinson were to cross him again, he said he would go to the president again. "I can't stand it again and I won't stand it."[46]

Yet the next day, FDR told Morgenthau that Byrnes had said Robert Lee Doughton believed Vinson was the only man who could help with the tax bill. Morgenthau said that would be fine.[47] Then a week later, Byrnes in a radio broadcast called for a large compulsory savings program. "I was shocked," Morgenthau wrote Byrnes, who replied Morgenthau had long known his position and shouldn't try to censor tax discussions.[48]

Adhering to the president's previous order, Morgenthau said publicly on August 22 that he hoped to raise $12 billion in additional tax revenue in the next revenue bill. But Doughton and Walter George doubted the economy could bear that much additional taxation. Revenue at the time was about $38 billion (almost four times the level before the war), and the $12 billion addition would raise it by about 30 percent.[49] Morgenthau refused to lower the personal exemption, preferring instead to increase the tax on corporate profits. And to combat inflation, he was preparing privately to propose an increase in Social Security rates, which would have raised $5.5 billion.[50]

By late August, Morgenthau was once again wondering whether he should resign. He prepared a series of documents that showed Byrnes and Vinson had crossed into his portfolio.[51] He discussed the matter with New York governor Herbert Lehman, Elinor's cousin, who believed Byrnes's statement in favor of forced savings constituted weak grounds for Morgenthau to threaten to resign. "However, if the President said to me that I had to take my orders from Jimmy Byrnes then there would be nothing left for me to do but to resign," Morgenthau quoted Lehman as saying. "He was sure, however, that the President wouldn't make any such statement."[52]

On August 29, the two Dutchess County patricians met and briefly discussed the revenue bill. After the president said he was now willing to accept just $10 billion in new revenue, he said to his friend, "You want to talk about Jimmy Byrnes and compulsory savings."

"That is just part of it. Byrnes says he can issue directives to me."

"That is ridiculous," replied the president. "Byrnes can only issue directives through the President."

"Well, I don't think he should issue any directives to the Cabinet," said Morgenthau. FDR agreed. Morgenthau asked him for a note saying so, but FDR declined to put it in writing. He said they would all get together and work it out.

"The trouble is Byrnes believes what he reads in the papers, namely that he is Acting-President," said Morgenthau as a parting shot.[53]

As 1943 ended, one issue that was taking more of Morgenthau's time was White's plan for a stabilization fund and reconstruction bank. American and British technical committees had been trying to find common ground on the White and Keynes proposals. The American side was worried about the technical and political implications of the British plan, not the least of which was suspicion of Keynes among businessmen and congressmen. The parties concentrated on the stabilization instrument rather than the bank, and White had to convince Keynes that he was not trying to give countries with positive balances of payment (which the United States would certainly be for many years) an undue advantage. The British still preferred the Keynes plan, which would reduce the US voting power and place less emphasis on gold.[54]

In March, Morgenthau asked the president if he could brief Senator Arthur Vandenberg on the talks, hoping the Republican from Michigan might become a champion of the proposal. FDR allowed it but advised Morgenthau to speak in generalities and emphasize there had been no commitments. When he heard of the president's response, White asked Morgenthau whether the president supported the fund. "He very seldom, Harry, shows any enthusiasm these days," answered the secretary. "It is very rare. So don't be disappointed."[55]

With a consensus developing in the administration about the proposed fund and bank, the Treasury distributed White's plan to the Allies in April and began to brief Congress. And though details of the Keynes plan had been made public in London, Roosevelt still wouldn't let Morgenthau divulge the entire White plan.

By September, the British realized they would have to subscribe to the White plan simply because the United States had the financial might to impose its will. Throughout that month, White and Keynes negotiated the details, a duel between Keynes's nimble intelligence and White's truculence. Morgenthau, with the president's permission, presented their combined effort to Congress in early October.[56] It called for the United States to commit $10 billion of the $30 billion in capital in the bank and about $2.5 billion to the stabilization fund. Representative Frederick C. Smith, Republican of Ohio, called the plan a "British plot to seize control of United States gold."[57] Wilbert Ward, vice president of the National City Bank of New York, called the World Bank proposal "defective," though he understood the need for reconstruction.[58] So the Treasury still had to win backers for the deal on Capitol Hill and Wall Street, and Morgenthau had been known throughout his career to get on people's nerves in both locations.

★ ★ ★

In January, ninety thousand German troops had surrendered at Stalingrad, marking the turning point of Hitler's eastern campaign. The Allies successfully landed on Sicily on July 9, so Americans were now fighting and dying in Europe. And after the American triumph at Midway in June 1942, the Americans slowly and painfully reclaimed the Pacific. But the leaders in Washington were exhausted and fed up. "I know the President is running foreign affairs and I know the President will not let me help anymore," Hull gloomily told Morgenthau on June 9.[59] Henry Stimson was angry about the lack of a proper procurement structure and the frequent interference of the New Dealers. He confided to his diary that some of Morgenthau's appointments in the Treasury reflected "a narrow political view." Despite their previous alliance in preparing for the war, he and Morgenthau fought openly over the appointment of a US representative to the London-based Combined Civil Affairs Committee, which would install military governments in states recaptured by the Allies. Stimson nominated a Standard Oil executive named Jay Crane, but Morgenthau, suspicious of Crane's business background, went behind Stimson's back to Roosevelt, suggesting instead a bona fide New Dealer like Lauchlin Currie. Stimson was "mad as a boil." Roosevelt eventually appointed a Treasury representative to the committee, William H. Taylor.[60]

Inflation and corruption persisted in China. The Chinese printed 3.5 billion fapi a month—twice the amount of a year earlier. Randolph Paul told Morgenthau in June that the Madame Chiang camp had withdrawn but could not account for $867,000 from the $460 million the United States had deposited for the Chinese.[61] Chinese Finance Minister H. H. Kung asked several times for the United States to transfer more of that money to China, but White urged Morgenthau to be tough. When General Chiang Kai-shek met Roosevelt at the Cairo conference in December 1943, he asked for a further $1 billion loan in gold. Morgenthau told the president the loan was unnecessary, especially since there was still $460 million in the Chinese account that had not been drawn down. The president and Morgenthau wanted to say as much to Chiang, but Hull warned it could only harm such a fragile administration. Morgenthau considered Hull's caution "outrageous." In January, Morgenthau told his staff the billion-dollar loan was definitely not in the works, adding that the Chiang clique are "just a bunch of crooks."[62]

Hull and Morgenthau also battled that autumn over the freezing of Argentine funds. A coup in that country in June had brought to power the pro-Nazi Pedro Ramirez, who wanted to create an anti-Yankee bloc in Latin America. Morgenthau wanted to freeze the country's funds; Hull opposed it and FDR sided with Hull. When Morgenthau was out of the country in October, the Treasury and State Departments, along with the White House, agreed to leak to the media that the Treasury was considering freezing the funds, which had the lone effect of prompting the Argentines to remove funds from the country. When he returned, Morgenthau told his staff he applauded their intent but said it was handled badly.[63]

As the Allied armies advanced, the pressures on the Treasury increased because it had to work on the occupation currencies for several countries—Italy, France, the Low Countries, eventually even Germany. Morgenthau was fighting for a special dollar bill with a yellow seal to be used in occupation zones, but the British and governments in exile opposed the plan. Finally the Treasury insisted the yellow seal be used at least in the early phases of recapturing Europe.[64] As the Allies landed on peninsular Italy in the fall of 1943, the Treasury supplied the forces of General Mark Clark with two currencies—"Allied military currency" and "spearhead currency." Used only by troops advancing at the front, spearhead currency could be used only by US troops so that Germans who captured or killed an American couldn't take it and use it.[65] Even the wording on the currency notes caused problems, as the Treasury planned to have the words "La République Française" printed on the notes for France, but Roosevelt (who was thoroughly sick of de Gaulle) insisted on simply, "La France."[66]

★ ★ ★

The Treasury soon put together a plan for the coming tax bill that would raise the $10 billion that Roosevelt was now asking for to finance the war effort, largely through taxes on business profits and high incomes. And to further mop up inflationary liquidity, the Treasury wanted to increase Social Security payments in increments, so before long the move would raise an additional $5 billion, largely from mainstream Americans. Morgenthau believed the president had to approve the plan in its totality to have a chance before Congress.

Morgenthau and a few staff members arrived at the White House to outline the plan on September 9, 1943, the opening day of the third bond drive. The drive opened in a cloud of confusion, which darkened the secretary's mood. On September 8, the Allies announced publicly that they had signed an armistice with Pietro Badoglio, Mussolini's successor as the head of the Italian government. Immediately, Morgenthau began to field calls from bond-drive organizers, asking if they should bother with the campaign now that the war was winding down. Morgenthau had spent the day telling organizers the war was still raging and would likely do so for some time.[67]

They assembled in the Oval Office, joined by Byrnes and Vinson. Before Morgenthau could present his plan, Byrnes said taxes had to be part of the stabilization program and were therefore under his jurisdiction. Randolph Paul later recounted that Byrnes was "pretty bitter and hot" and continued to talk even after the president tried to get him to stop. Morgenthau merely said it had already been decided he would present and manage the tax bill.

"I am the boss," Roosevelt said, adding that once they all agreed on a policy, he expected "all you fellows to go in and do the work just like soldiers."

But Byrnes insisted he wouldn't support the bill unless he helped to formulate it and stressed he would take no orders from the secretary of the Treasury. "I have never had any trouble getting along with people previously," he said. "I get along with Knox. I get along with Stimson; but I can't get along with the Secretary." Infuriated, FDR pounded the table, yelling, "I am the boss" and that he wanted the Treasury to present the tax bill.

Morgenthau then turned to Byrnes and said, "I think you and I agree on this."

"I wouldn't agree with you on anything," Byrnes shot back. FDR continued to pound the desk, yelling: "I am the boss, I am giving the orders." The meeting soon broke up acrimoniously without Morgenthau so much as removing his proposal from his brief case. It was a problem because the Ways and Means Committee was about to begin discussing the tax bill in less than two weeks.[68]

The story leaked to the Associated Press and the *Wall Street Journal*. The White House tried and failed to find out who had leaked the story, and FDR had to move to quell a very public tiff between two of his senior executives. He summoned all the parties a few days later and told them his plans for Social Security, which were similar to the Treasury plans. Byrnes and

Vinson had both worked on Social Security in 1935 and became engaged with the discussion this time. The group worked on a plan for the next two days and seemed to be making progress on a unified policy.[69] However, after Morgenthau hosted Byrnes, Vinson, and congressional leaders at his office (at which he served them Dutchess County apples), Robert Lee Doughton and Walter George told him the Social Security proposals would never win the support of their committees.[70]

Roosevelt had at least gained temporary unanimity within the administration on the 1944 fiscal proposals, but Morgenthau was disillusioned that FDR let Byrnes get away with such behavior. He warned Roosevelt privately that Byrnes and Vinson may try to convince congressmen that the Treasury secretary couldn't work with them—something, he added, Roosevelt knew was not true. "I don't know how valuable I am to you, but if they keep this thing up you and nobody but you can stop them," he told the president.[71] He was also astonished that the president was beginning to support a compulsory savings program—even though the third loan drive was proving every bit as successful as the previous two.

In deep despair, Morgenthau on October 3 once again sought guidance and solace from Eleanor Roosevelt, whom he continued to help whenever possible. He brought with him a letter he had drafted for the president, which he shared with her as it outlined his position. "In suggesting a form of compulsory saving in the face of the most amazing response to the Third War Loan, on the part of the American people, I feel that I am selling them down the river," it read. He noted that the confidence in American securities was at an all-time low when he took over the job in 1933 and, "by my hard work, I have built up confidence in the Government security market to an all-time high." He added: "So far, I have been able to finance the most costly war in history at the lowest rate of interest ever known."[72]

The First Lady read the letter and listened to Morgenthau say that he had begun to hear from volunteer fundraisers that they would resign if the press reports of a compulsory savings program were true. Eleanor Roosevelt advised him to send the letter to the president.

"So I thought it over and talked it over with Mrs. Morgenthau," he told his diary, "and we decided to do the thing by phoning rather than to send the letter." Morgenthau tried reaching the president's secretary Grace Tully four times before he could ask for an appointment. The only response was that FDR was willing to make a suggestion—rather than a recommendation—of compulsory savings. Privately, Morgenthau said to his press aide Herbert Gaston: "Now, just in this room, isn't that typical of the man?" Gaston agreed.[73]

Morgenthau's fortunes did not improve when he asked Congress for as much as $10.5 billion in additional revenue. Higher Social Security payments were no longer part of the plan, so Morgenthau wanted higher taxes on businesses and the wealthy. In the midst of his testimony, Morgenthau admitted that four-fifths of the "dangerous money," meaning the inflationary oversupply of cash, was in the hands of people who earned less than $5,000 a year. In other words, the inflationary pressures were coming from the people whom Morgenthau was refusing to tax, and the administration's budget plan would do little to ease inflation. *New York Times* columnist Arthur Krock called the proposal one of the "persistent New Deal tax schemes that sought to punish the prosperous and successful."[74] Added the *New York Times* in an editorial three days later: "It seems obvious then that the bulk of new taxes must come from those earning under $5,000 and that they are in a position to pay."[75]

With relief, Morgenthau left Washington on October 10 for a twenty-day tour of the battlefields of North Africa and Italy. In Algiers, he and General Dwight Eisenhower appealed to the American people by radio to buy more war bonds.[76] The Allied forces had moved on to the Italian mainland and were fighting bloody battles as they inched their way up the boot. Morgenthau traveled as far north as the Volturno River, just above Naples. "My only interest in life is to win the war, so I spend a lot of time trying to learn about the war," he told a reporter. "I just want to beat those bastards."[77]

What struck him was the evil of the enemy. "All day I was impressed with the evidences of the ruthlessness of the German enemy—their murder of innocent civilians, the peaceful farm buildings and crops they destroyed, and the homes they ruined. The people at home should see these things.[78] Captured German prisoners told Morgenthau the führer was still in power and the losses in Russia were the fault of bad German generals. "They say their next Fuehrer will win the next great war," he said. "So here they are—these defeated prisoners—already planning another assault on civilization."[79] The three-week tour reinforced Morgenthau's outrage at German brutality. When he returned to the United States, he published a report by Col. Erskine Hume, head of the US government in the Naples area, on the "acts of German cruelty and wanton destruction." It said: "Many people were beaten to make them disclose the whereabouts of supposed valuables. Women as well as men were subjected to such treatment. There were many murders, some of a sadistic nature, with mutilation of dead bodies, particularly those of women."[80]

Morgenthau soon returned to the familiar world of successful bond drives and hard-fought failure with Congress. While he was gone, Daniel Bell had revealed that the third war-loan drive raised $18.9 billion, nearly $4 billion more than planned.[81] That meant there would not be another bond drive in 1943 because the country had already raised $55 billion that year.[82] But the Treasury's relationship with Congress was strained by their disagreements over big economic questions. When it was reported Morgenthau would sell his one hundred head of purebred cattle, Republicans in Congress jeered Morgenthau, a millionaire, for not being able to afford dairy farming. "If all the dairy farmers followed Morgenthau's example, there won't be any more milk," said Representative August H. Andresen of Minnesota.[83] When the budget finally emerged from the Ways and Means Committee, it raised only $2 billion in new revenue and did virtually nothing to mop up the "dangerous money." The Treasury was disgusted with the breaks it preserved for corporations and the wealthy.[84] Morgenthau delivered a strong statement to the Senate Finance Committee, calling for more revenue now rather than asking the returning soldiers to pay off the debt raised to pay for the war—comments the Senate Finance Committee chairman Walter George said represented "exceeding bad grace."[85]

As Morgenthau celebrated his tenth anniversary as head of the Treasury on November 15, he entered a glorious, heart-wrenching period in which he transcended his duties as the country's chief financial officer. He did not seize the duties of other departments; rather, he understood another department was committing a grievous wrong, and he righted it with courage, determination, and efficiency. The State Department was clearly thwarting the efforts to rescue Jews. Under Secretary Sumner Welles, who had been the strongest voice in the department in favor of aiding the Jews, had been forced to resign in August after it became known he had drunkenly propositioned a Pullman porter on a train one night.[86] That left Herbert Feis, the economics head, as the only senior State Department official the Treasury considered an ally.

The State Department signaled its indifference to the tragedy of the Holocaust by telling its officers in official documents that the rescue was a Treasury project. "This file is full of State Department cables which are full of little remarks like the Treasury wants this, the Treasury desires you to do this, and the Treasury this and the Treasury that," complained Pehle at one meeting "[Leland] Harrison, unless he is a dumbbell, can see through that . . . State is, in effect, saying this is [only] what the Treasury wants you to do."[87] The patience of the Treasury staff had run out. They knew French police, under orders from the Nazis, were trying to take a census of six thousand abandoned Jewish children, all of whom the United States could rescue.

Morgenthau's staff urged him to bring Cordell Hull in line, and he must have been tempted to target his old rival. But he resisted. "So far, whenever I have gone to him direct he has been very good," Morgenthau told his staff. He launched into one of his rambling addresses, not angry so much as heartfelt. He told them he wanted the matter in the open as much as anyone, but sadly they were up against a generation of men who felt differently.

"It is only by my happening to be Secretary of the Treasury and being vitally interested in these things, with the help of you people . . . that I can do it," he told them sincerely. "I will do everything I can, and we will get it done, but don't think you will be able to nail anybody in the State Department . . . to the cross." He told Paul, Pehle, and DuBois that they were forthright and courageous and that he would back them. "I will go just as far as you men will let me go."[88]

Paul drafted a letter urging Hull to help the refugees, and Hull replied on December 6 that the State Department sympathized desperately and listed the reasons why Leland Harrison was having difficulty. Then on December 17, the Foreign Office in London let Washington know it was concerned with the difficulty of settling Jews, should they be released from enemy territory. Therefore it was reluctant to approve the preliminary financial arrangements that the Treasury had devised to win the release of condemned Jews. "The letter was a satanic combination of British chill and diplomatic double-talk, cold and correct and adding up to a sentence of death," Morgenthau would later write.[89] The Treasury staff met and realized that the State Department could not do what was needed. They urged Morgenthau to recommend the president remove the file from the State Department.[90] Oscar Cox, formerly of the Treasury and now of the Foreign Economic Administration, privately advised Morgenthau that Roosevelt needed a separate committee that could execute a policy of actively rescuing the Jews. That meant identifying neutral European countries that could provide a safe haven for refugees, finding other countries where they could settle, and arranging transportation between the two. He also thought the United States should relax its own immigration laws.[91]

On December 20, Pehle and Morgenthau visited Hull's office with a Treasury memo saying the British position went beyond the matter under consideration. "If it prevails, it means that we should give up on trying to rescue Jews in enemy territory," said the report. The State Department was represented by Hull, whom Morgenthau thought looked tired, and Breckinridge Long, who had either opposed the Treasury or was dubious to the point of indifference. Long had great powers in issuing visas and ran twenty-three of the forty-two State Department divisions. At this meeting he seemed anxious to please. Before they started, Hull said he had discussed things with Ambassador John Gilbert Winant and replied to the British, striking down all of the British argument forcefully. His reply to the British said their message "has been read with astonishment" and the State

Department was "unable to agree with the point of view set forth."[92] Long told them he had ordered Harrison to issue the license that the Treasury and Hull had asked for five months earlier. "Of course, the people down the line get hold of these things," said Hull. "When I don't know about them, I just can't handle them."

Morgenthau then surprised them by asking to see Cable 354, and Hull, astonished by the request, asked Long to provide the cable to the Treasury.

As they were leaving, Long asked to see Morgenthau privately and said he was troubled by rumors of anti-Semitism in the State Department.

"Well Breck . . . we might be a little frank," said Morgenthau. "The impression is all around you, particularly, are anti-Semitic."

Long said he knew that to be the case and hoped Morgenthau would use his "good offices to correct that impression, because I am not."

"After all Breck, the United States of America was created as a refuge for people who were persecuted the world over, starting with Plymouth. . . . That was the concept of the United States, and as Secretary of the Treasury for one hundred and thirty-five million people—I am carrying this out."

"Well my concept of America as a place of refuge for persecuted people is just the same."

"I am delighted to hear it."

Morgenthau later told his staff it was "Hull at his best," doing the right thing forcefully and effectively. "But the tragic thing is that—dammit!— this thing could have been done last February."[93]

The State Department sent Morgenthau a mimeographed copy of Cable 354 in late December, but it deleted a cross-reference to earlier cables. Morgenthau immediately phoned Long to say he had asked Randolph Paul to get a copy of the original copy as it was sent. Long had to send over a copy of the original cable, which included the reference to a cable on January 21, 1943, and the Treasury's case was now complete.[94] The documentation showed Harrison had been appalled by Gerhart Riegner's intelligence on the death camps and had transmitted the information to the State Department. But on January 21, 1943, the department had asked Harrison not to accept reports from Riegner to be transmitted to other parties except in extraordinary circumstances. That order had been signed by Sumner Welles, but he had no memory of signing it and the Treasury believed it had been slipped to him with a stack of documents he had to sign. The significant point was that the Treasury now had conclusive evidence that the State Department had been thwarting efforts to save European Jews.

Early in 1944, the Treasury learned the British were protesting that the movement of refugees might prove embarrassing to both governments. The Treasury believed they were placing diplomatic niceties ahead of matters of live and death. White wanted Morgenthau to push the president directly to solve the matter, but the secretary continued to work through Hull. When they met on January 12, Morgenthau once again thought his old rival "bewildered," "weary," and badly briefed, not even knowing the names of some staff members who attended the meeting. But Hull agreed with Morgenthau that the record on refugees was shocking.[95]

By the middle of January, Paul presented Morgenthau with a report on refugees to give to the president. Its title was *Report to the Secretary on the Acquiescence of This Government in the Murder of the Jews*. The first sentence read: "One of the greatest crimes in history, the slaughter of the Jewish people in Europe, is continuing unabated." It said State Department officials had willfully failed to act to rescue them.[96] The senior Treasury staff were foursquare behind Paul in presenting it to Roosevelt. DuBois told Morgenthau to tell FDR that if there was no action on the report, he would quit and release it to the press.[97]

Morgenthau changed the title to *Personal Report to the President*, but the document that he, Paul, and Pehle presented at the White House on Sunday, January 20, was nonetheless explosive. It said the State Department utterly failed to "prevent the extermination of Jews in German-controlled Europe." The paper condemned the department's "gross procrastination" and said it had suppressed for two months reports on German atrocities after publication of similar reports intensified public pressure for action. "The matter of rescuing the Jews from extermination is filled with difficulties," read the last paragraph. "Only a fervent will to accomplish, backed by persistent and untiring effort, can succeed where time is so precious."

The president received the report sympathetically. He brought in Edward Stettinius, who had replaced Sumner Welles as under secretary of state and who said he wasn't surprised by the performance of the State Department. Yet he said Long probably wasn't anti-Semitic so much as old and tired.[98]

Within days, the bureaucracy was working on the special agency outside the State Department envisaged by Oscar Cox and Morgenthau. Hull thought it was a great idea.[99] Roosevelt announced the establishment of the War Refugee Board on January 22, 1944. It was created by an executive order, so it would not need congressional approval. The members were to be the secretaries of state, of the Treasury, and of War, and its executive director was to find havens for the refugees. John Pehle was named acting executive director until they could find a higher profile person to run it. Like Morgenthau in 1933, he performed so well that he retained the post.[100]

At the first meeting, Morgenthau congratulated Hull on the "magnificent" cable he'd sent to all embassies instructing them to cooperate with the board.

"What you mean is you are congratulating yourself," said Hull with a smile.

Seeing the two combatants complimenting one another brought a laugh from Stimson. "That is better than throwing brickbats at each other, anyway," he said.[101]

The War Refugee Board was established too late to save the Jews of Romania, yet there was still time to rescue Jews in Hungary and other European countries. And its creation would never have happened without Morgenthau. "Thousands upon thousands will have the cruel hand of suffering and death lifted from them by what you have done," Oscar Cox wrote him on January 22. "To feel with as humans whom you haven't seen in the lands of persecution is one of the marks of your human depth and greatness. Deep in my heart I am warm. Rare individuals like you are what give me, at least, the driving hope to carry on with the war and what comes after."

Eight days later, the senior Treasury staff assembled once again in Morgenthau's office. They presented him with a single sheet of paper, which they had all signed.

Feb. 2, 1944

You have been generous in your praise of the part we played in getting this government to take action designed to forestall Hitler's plan to exterminate the Jews and other persecuted peoples of Europe.

We who have worked toward this goal for months and are intimately acquainted with the facts regarding its achievement take this opportunity to express our deep admiration for the truly great contribution which you and you alone made to this cause—a contribution of courage and statesmanship.

The change which has been brought about in this Government's attitude toward saving the Jews and other persecuted peoples of Europe from extermination as the result of your efforts is, we know, more than sufficient reward for you. Nevertheless, the fact is that the courage and statesmanship you have displayed will live always with those who know what you really did.

Herbert Gaston
Randolph Paul
John W. Pehle
Harry D. White
Ansel F. Luxford
Josiah E. DuBois, Jr.
Henrietta S. Klotz[102]

CHAPTER TEN

BRETTON WOODS

★ ★ ★

I n December 1943, Henry Morgenthau Jr. reached a dubious milestone: he had raised more in taxes during his tenure as secretary of the Treasury than all his predecessors combined. As of December 31, Americans had paid $93.7 billion during the term of the fifty-second secretary of the Treasury, whereas his fifty-one forebears had raised $93.2 billion in total taxes. It was a stunning statistic, given that Morgenthau believed Americans were undertaxed in light of the task at hand. Of course, constitutional authority for taxation rested with Congress, so he had to share the credit or blame, but Morgenthau could claim another record on his own. He had now sold more than $30 billion in government bonds, which meant he had authorized the borrowing of more than any person in the history of the world.[1] He raised this fortune at interest rates of less than 2.5 percent and was intent on raising more. By the end of 1943, he had set the target for the fourth war-bond drive at $14 billion—$3 billion less than the third loan drive—and planned to enlist five million store owners and employees to help sell the securities. He said publicly he hoped for $5.5 billion from individuals—a lofty goal given that $17 billion had been raised in this class since May 1941.[2]

At about this time, Morgenthau began to tell people privately that Wall Street disliked him because he had moved the center of the business world from New York to his own desk. The data justified the claim. The Securities and Exchange Commission in the fiscal year ending June 30, 1944, registered the issuance of securities worth a net $1.8 billion.[3] But in just about the same period (the fifth war-loan drive would end on July 8), the Treasury raised more than $45 billion in just three war-loan drives.

The Senate Finance Committee supported the House of Representatives' budget that raised only $2.1 billion in new money—far short of the $10.5 billion the administration wanted. Senator Walter George told Morgenthau he simply could not muster the votes to back the secretary's demands. Randolph Paul, Herbert Gaston, and Daniel Bell all wanted the secretary to urge the president to veto the tax bill. Morgenthau even consulted Jimmy Byrnes, who pondered the matter then supported a veto. Morgenthau ended up recommending that the president let the bill pass without a presidential signature, as he had in 1938.[4] "I don't know of any time that the Treasury, as far as having influence on the Hill is concerned, was as low as it is right now," he told his staff, attributing the weak standing to their courage in doing what was right.[5]

Roosevelt vetoed the tax bill, which proved an explosive political move. The *New York Times* called it an "obvious blunder" that precipitated a crisis between Congress and the administration. The presidential address on February 22 stated that the bill did not even raise the extra $2.1 billion that Congress advertised. Because it canceled increased Social Security premiums, the real figure was closer to $1 billion. Claiming the bill provided relief "not for the needy but for the greedy," the president said: "The bill is replete with provisions which not only afford indefensible special privileges to favored groups but set dangerous precedents for the future."[6] Alben W. Barkley, a Kentucky Democrat and former Roosevelt ally, resigned as majority leader in the Senate to protest the insult to Congress; but Senator Carter Glass said the president not only had the constitutional power to veto the bill but also the responsibility to strike down "a bill as inadequate as this one."[7] The *New York Times* called on the Senate to override the veto, which it did on February 25. It was the first time that Congress had ever overridden a veto on a tax bill.

A few days later, Roosevelt asked Morgenthau at a cabinet meeting how he'd get the additional $8 billion. The secretary brushed him off by saying he was having productive discussions with congressional leaders, and they dropped the matter.[8] In fact, the Roosevelt administration never again tried to persuade Congress to raise taxes. Morgenthau continued to gnash his teeth about the breaks given to the wealthy and to corporations, but the tax system was producing astonishing revenue gains on its own. In fiscal 1943, government revenues had increased 70 percent to $27.3 billion, and in the year ending June 30, 1944, they would rise a further 88 percent to $51.3 billion. Certainly borrowing increased just as dramatically, but the booming war economy produced enough government revenue to cover the rising borrowing costs.

Meanwhile, the fourth war-loan drive exceeded its target and netted the government $16.7 billion, yet still Morgenthau was pilloried in some circles. "The plain fact is that Secretary Morgenthau is not the master of, he's not even a very apt pupil in, the field of war finance," said the columnist Walter Lippmann. "It is a credit to his modesty that he doesn't pretend to be and he has been, according to his lights, a devoted public servant."[9] Morgenthau was distressed to learn that a book called *Washington Broadcasts*, published anonymously under the pen name "The Man at the Microphone," portrayed him as having nothing more to do than make public appearances with movie stars at war-bond promotions. It upset him so much that he asked the president to mention in public statements how hard it was to run the Treasury. Roosevelt howled with laughter at the book's depiction of his friend.[10]

Though conservative commentators had called for years for Morgenthau to hire bankers from Wall Street to manage the country's finances, what he did do was recruit marketing men to work on the war-loan drives. He brought in Fred Smith, an executive with Young and Rubicon on Madison Avenue, even though Smith had organized the preconvention campaign for Wendell Willkie in 1940. He revered Morgenthau, calling him the second-best advertising mind in Washington, exceeded only by the president himself. The secretary's strength, said Smith, was his ability to cut through distractions to the kernel of any matter. "Henry Morgenthau Jr., has handled more advertising in a shorter period of time than any man in history; but even in the hustle and bustle, nobody gets past him with anything," wrote Smith. "Perhaps the most important advertising decision he ever made was the decision to use *bonds* to sell the *war*, rather than vice-versa."[11] The other was Theodore Gamble, who played the larger role of the two, as he was named national director of the War Finance Division.

Gamble was a self-made millionaire originally from Nevada who owned a chain of five movie theaters in Oregon.

The addition of these two ad men was part of the glamorous aura that Morgenthau brought to the austere halls of the Treasury. He always respected the Treasury and insisted that radio broadcasts promoting war bonds convey the dignity and grandeur of that institution. Yet he dabbled with celebrities and used popular culture to promote the institution's aims. When the *New Yorker* profiled him in two articles in early 1944, it listed the stars he had used to sell bonds: Bing Crosby, Fred Astaire, Bob Burns, Kay Kyser, Mickey Rooney, Judy Garland, and, of course, Irving Berlin.[12] Smith and Gamble—casually called "Fred and Ted" within the Treasury—only added to the modernity of the program.[13] With his own innate inclination for marketing, Morgenthau scoffed at a Senate plan to spend up to $15 million a year for war-bond ads in small newspapers. Morgenthau argued the papers were now promoting the bonds for free.[14] The plan was soon shelved.[15]

Morgenthau planned the fifth war-bond drive with a target of $16 billion for spring 1944 so as not to hold a loan drive when the presidential campaign would be under way in the fall. He lined up Orson Welles to host the launch program on June 12, featuring radio broadcast from the homes of soldiers fighting overseas. Gamble arranged broadcasts by four of the world's leading women—Eleanor Roosevelt, Queen Elizabeth of Great Britain, Madame Chiang of China, and Polina Zhemchuzhina Molotov, the Jewish wife of Soviet foreign minister Vyacheslav Molotov.[16] Morgenthau also convinced the reluctant president to launch the bond drive, which had Gamble and Smith "bubbling over with enthusiasm."[17] When the drive wrapped up on July 8, it had netted a total of $20.6 billion.[18]

As the working groups proceeded with plans for the stabilization fund and world bank, Morgenthau knew he had to schedule an international conference on the plan, despite the woeful track record of such meetings. The Paris Peace Conference's Treaty of Versailles of 1919 had never been ratified by the Senate. Nor were the Lausanne Conferences of 1923 and 1932 or the London Economic Conference of 1933 viewed as successes. Yet the time had come to call an international conference on Harry Dexter White's two-track proposal, despite all the factions, competing interests, and disagreements. Secretary of State Cordell Hull and Roosevelt were working on a similar meeting to solidify plans for a postwar international organization to be called the United Nations, and Morgenthau must have known the success of his conference would have some bearing on the later meeting.

Several factors were working in his favor: the State Department had assigned the file to Dean Acheson, with whom Morgenthau worked well; John Maynard Keynes and Harry Dexter White were close to an agreement on the structure of the bodies; and the new Soviet ambassador Andrei Gromyko voiced support for the plan. But Morgenthau, White, and their team had no guarantee a conference could produce a proposal that would win the support of the American, British, Soviet, and forty-one other governments, as well as the US banking community and Congress.

Republican congressman Charles S. Dewey of Chicago served notice in April that he would introduce a bill outlining a rival plan to White's, adopting some of the details of the world bank and none of the stabilization fund. Dewey was a banker and joined much of the banking community in criticizing White's plan. Benjamin Anderson, a University of California economist who previously worked at Chase National Bank, publicly said that White proposal would drain the US Treasury of billions of dollars.[19] White urged Morgenthau to present the Treasury plan to Congress before hearings on the Dewey bill. Morgenthau couldn't move faster than the British and Soviets would let him, but he let them know nonetheless that he was preparing to testify before Congress about the plan.

On April 12, Morgenthau learned that the White plan faced opposition from the Bank of England, some British cabinet members, and the London banking establishment because it would reduce London's prominence as a banking center, diminish sterling in favor of the US dollar, and impact the economic relationships within the empire. And he still had not heard officially whether Moscow supported the plan. Three days later, the British Treasury agreed to support the proposal, assuming technical points could be ironed out and that the agreements on the bank and fund were part of a broader discussion on international cooperation.

Finally on April 18, Morgenthau "took an awful chance." He had W. Averell Harriman, the US ambassador in Moscow, advise the Soviets that the British had signed off on the American proposal. It was a stretch, but he needed the Soviets at the table. Harriman replied that the Soviets could not go along with White's plan because it demanded members pay gold into the fund. However, Moscow agreed "to instruct its experts to associate itself with Mr. Morgenthau's project." On April 21, Morgenthau was able to announce a broad agreement by the Allies, though no binding commitments.[20]

"Here's where you get a medal, Henry," Roosevelt said as he authorized the Treasury secretary to send out the invitations.[21] On May 25, Roosevelt announced that he had invited forty-two countries and the French Committee on National Liberation to attend the conference in July, titled the United Nations Monetary and Financial Conference. The Treasury decided to hold the conference at a resort in Bretton Woods, New Hampshire, a ski resort whose cool mountain air would be a pleasant spot in the middle of summer. They originally hoped to hold the meeting in May, but it proved difficult to organize on such short notice and the British couldn't travel ahead of the tight security brought on by the Normandy invasion. Morgenthau would head the US delegation.[22]

★ ★ ★

"Henry Morgenthau, who has now been Secretary of the Treasury almost as long as Andrew Mellon, has suffered a heart attack and may have to resign," columnist Drew Pearson reported on his radio show on February 13, when the budget battle was near its climax. "He will take a month's rest to try to recuperate."[23] The report was complete baloney. Morgenthau was in fact exhausted but healthy in the winter of 1944. With the battles over the budget, the conference at Bretton Woods, the occupation currencies, and the War Refugee Board, the pressures on him continued unabated. His battles with Jimmy Byrnes faded away, but he was annoyed by other

Roosevelt insiders. He said Paul McNutt, chairman of the War Manpower Commission, "talks at cabinet the way he would talk to an audience of ten-thousand people."[24] In April, Morgenthau received a document showing that Leo Crowley, the left-leaning head of the Foreign Economic Administration, had been telling people that Roosevelt was abandoning his partnership with Churchill in favor of a closer alliance with Stalin. Morgenthau showed the document to Roosevelt, who encouraged him to bring him more dirt if he heard any.[25]

At home, Elinor was withering away as her heart weakened. (Yet she still worked to further her husband's career. When she heard FDR say at a dinner he'd been unable to find out how much gold the Russians had, she immediately told her husband the president would like him to find out.[26]) Robert Morgenthau, who'd gotten married in December, was sailing the perilous waters of the Atlantic, and Henry III would soon join the invasion force in Western Europe. The greatest shock came when they learned that the USS *Lansdale*, Robert Morgenthau's destroyer, was sunk off the coast of Algeria on April 20. It had just escorted one convoy across the Atlantic and was joining another when it was attacked by Luftwaffe Junkers and Heinkel bombers, striking in two or three waves. Forty-seven seamen lost their lives. The Morgenthaus had anxious hours until the president called on April 21 to say that Bob Morgenthau was among two hundred survivors rescued by nearby ships.[27] Three days after the sinking, Vice Admiral H. K. Hewitt wrote the secretary to say Robert was safe and well. "Not only did he come through it safely, but he demonstrated his fine qualities as a man and an officer," said the letter, which Morgenthau shared with the First Lady. "Since his captain was temporarily hospitalized, it fell to him to report his experiences to me, and also to be in charge of the other officers and the crew. He has been indefatigable in looking out for their welfare. I did not know him before, but I was immediately impressed by him. You have every right to be proud of him."[28]

Morgenthau himself now openly identified himself with the Jewish cause. It would be wrong to say that he'd shown no concern for the Jews before the Holocaust, but the events in Europe created a deeper understanding of his own Judaism. His eldest son called the battles over the refugee issue in 1943 the "initial breakthrough to my father's conscience." Robert Morgenthau said his father at this time began to attend synagogue in Poughkeepsie on the weekends, and he often had to be elbowed awake when he fell asleep.[29] His first effort in furthering the lives of his coreligionists was working with John Pehle on the War Refugee Board.

The task facing Pehle—locating refugees, transporting them to safety, and finding temporary and permanent homes for them—was absolutely staggering. The surviving Jews were, for the most part, in territory occupied by the Nazis or their allies, and the Western Allies at first had only one European beachhead in southern Italy. Working with a small staff in Washington, Pehle often had to negotiate with hostile or indifferent governments. Then he had to find at least one more government to offer refugees sanctuary, often a temporary haven, which meant another country would have to be found for a permanent home. He had to use American influence to persuade foreign governments to cooperate, even though all parties knew the American government itself was not accepting many refugees. And he had to arrange financing to pay for the transportation and initial support. Pehle and his staff knew they were combatting one of the most heinous crimes in human history, yet society as a whole and the media in particular seemed almost oblivious to the enormity taking place in the Nazi territories. Even when Roosevelt created the War Refugee Board, the *New York Times* ran only a small story on page 11. That prompted Morgenthau to phone Arthur Sulzberger on January 29 to complain about the coverage. Sulzberger was sympathetic, and a front page story on the War Refugee Board appeared the following day.[30]

Pehle worked especially closely with missions in neutral European countries, like Spain, Sweden, Switzerland, and Turkey, which were key in the initial stages of bringing refugees out of harm's way. He established contacts with the International Red Cross and the Vatican, and in the early months he secured private contributions of $100,000. Within days of its establishment, the board agreed with the World Jewish Congress on a program to remove Jews from Vichy France to transport them to Spain, Switzerland, and North Africa. Soon there was an agreement to remove five thousand to six thousand Jewish children from France. The board also initiated plans to remove Jews from Poland (which had had the largest Jewish population in Europe) and Hungary (a Nazi puppet whose Jewish community was the last in Europe to face mass deportation to the death camps).[31]

By mid-March, the American administration began to succeed in placing more Jewish refugees in Palestine, largely at the behest of Roosevelt himself. During a March 7 meeting with Morgenthau, Roosevelt repeatedly said he wanted to pressure the British to state publicly they would allow Jewish refugees into Palestine. "I want them to say it now that any Jews that we are successful in getting out, they will let them go to Palestine," Morgenthau quoted him as saying later.[32] In the middle of the month, the board began to transport 150 Jewish children every ten days from Bulgaria, through Turkey, to Palestine. The British said nothing about it.[33]

Both Pehle and Morgenthau felt there should be at least one United States safe haven for Jews and other persecuted people, though that was impossible under existing quotas for immigration. Their first line of opposition was War Secretary Henry Stimson. "I pointed out the dangers," Stimson wrote in his diary after a March 21 meeting at the White House. He detailed "how it was impossible to be sure they would be taken back and that, if they weren't, it would be a violation of our quota policy, which I support."[34] At the very least, he wanted the president to consult Congress on the matter.

Pehle, Stimson, Morgenthau, and Hull pondered a range of options, from establishing a "free port" for refugees by executive order, to an executive order with some consultation, to asking Congress to frame legislation allowing the free port. Morgenthau and Hull warned executive action could jeopardize the president's standing with Congress. Pehle presented his plans to Roosevelt on May 16, and the president liked the proposal, though he wanted the name of the camps to reflect the temporary nature of the refugees' stay in America. He was willing to sidestep congressional approval as long as they began slowly, by admitting five hundred to one thousand refugees on a temporary basis, and then explaining to Congress the reasons.

Pehle didn't believe there was time for Congress to debate the matter. On May 18, they learned of overcrowded camps in southern Italy, where an estimated 1,800 refugees were arriving each week. Roosevelt instructed the War Department "under no circumstances to turn these people back."

As they examined the issue, Pehle furnished Roosevelt with evidence that 70 percent of the American public supported temporary havens, as did a range of religious groups and newspaper editorial boards. Roosevelt was ready to move forward with "Emergency Refugee Shelters," and John McCloy, under secretary of the War Department, told Morgenthau on June 2 that he might have a perfect site for a pilot project—Fort Ontario, a former army base at Oswego, New York. Roosevelt ordered that arrangements be made for about one thousand refugees to be housed at the camp beginning that summer.

Working with other departments, the Treasury had to plan occupation currencies in the liberated countries that met the approval of these countries' governments in exile while ensuring an efficient occupation by the Allied armies. Then it would have to work with the conquering Allies, including the Soviets, at a functional occupation currency for Germany. Each created complexities for the Treasury, and any diplomatic misstep would have jeopardized the outcome of the monetary conference.

In January, Morgenthau was facing domestic pressure to cut aid to Britain, but he and Dean Acheson both believed it was not the time to create conflicts with Allies. The Treasury had wanted to cut about $500 million in lend-lease payments but ended up cutting $288 million—a move that enraged Churchill. Throughout the winter and spring, the US government had negotiated with the Chinese on the exchange rate that should be paid for the airfields and other military installations that Americans had been financing in China. The official rate was still twenty yuan to the US dollar, though the true rate had deteriorated to a level closer to 220 to 1 because of Chinese hyperinflation. The official rate greatly favored the Chungking government—and therefore the Chiang clique—so Roosevelt suggested in January that they renegotiate the rate. The Chinese flatly refused. The two governments negotiated in the lead-up to the Bretton Woods Conference, and the Chinese would lower the rate only to 60 to 1. The matter was unresolved in June, when United States officials faced the unsettling prospect of not only Finance Minister H. H. Kung but also his excessively demanding wife coming to the United States.[35]

These were mere spats compared with the disagreements on occupation currencies, especially for France and Germany. Throughout 1943, Morgenthau had fought to issue the yellow-seal dollars as the initial currency when invasions began in Western European countries then to issue a supplementary military currency in each country until a government was in place. However, the British told him—quite correctly—that governments in exile would never agree to the United States or Britain printing money for their country. So arrangements were made for the governments in exile from Belgium, Norway, and the Netherlands to supply the US government with currency that could be used in the early stages of the advance into these countries.

France was a special case—a big country, strategically positioned, with a large population and historic power. Most important, France had no government in exile. Northern France had been annexed by Germany, and southern France was overseen by the puppet government at Vichy, with which the Roosevelt administration had maintained diplomatic relations. There was the French Committee of National Liberation, a London-based quasi-government-in-exile headed by Charles de Gaulle, but none of its members, not even de Gaulle, had been elected to the committee. He personally believed his mandate was not only to liberate his country but also to restore its glory—a mission that often interfered with the mission of the Allies. The US Treasury, for example, wanted to set the franc's exchange rate at about one cent to reflect its reconstruction, but the French committee shuddered at the thought of devaluing the franc. The committee wanted the words "La République Française" printed on the bills but had to bend to Roosevelt's insistence that they say simply "La France." By late May, they agreed the Americans would print francs—valued at two cents each—for the committee.[36]

The planning for the German occupation currency began in early 1944 and required the cooperation of the three major powers that would invade Germany. The Treasury and War Departments both favored producing Allied Military Marks, a single currency used by all the occupation forces. The British and Americans wanted identical bills printed by the Allies and used by all occupation forces. By February, the Soviets supported the broad terms of the plan but wanted to print some of them in the Soviet Union so they could deliver them to the Red Army. That meant the Soviets would need the list of available serial numbers, details of paper and color, and access to the plates to print the notes.[37]

"To acquiesce to such an unprecedented request would create serious complications," Alvin W. Hall, the director of the Bureau of Engraving and Printing, wrote Daniel Bell as soon as he heard of the proposal. It would make accountability impossible and violate the global practice of governments retaining the plates used to print their currency and bonds. Hall said his outfit used special papers and dyes to prevent counterfeiting, and the Treasury would lose any ability to prevent counterfeiting if it surrendered the plates. The Forbes Company, which was to print the notes, said it would not accept the contract if the plates were given to the Russians. Within the Treasury, Bell agreed with Hall, but Harry Dexter White forcefully supported the Soviets. Bell drafted a letter refusing the Soviet request, but Morgenthau declined to send it, preferring instead to discuss the matter personally with the Soviet ambassador. Andrei Gromyko stood his ground at the meeting on March 18. That deadlock lasted for the next month, the stakes raised by the Soviets' advance in the east and the Americans' need for an agreement in Bretton Woods. "In order to convince the Soviet Government of our sincerity in the desire to have the closest collaboration in these military operations against Germany, it becomes essential that we make every effort within our possibility to furnish the plates to that government," said Morgenthau.[38] Hall and Bell lost the battle. The Soviets received the duplicate plates. The Soviets would eventually flood occupied Germany with printed money, complicating the occupation.

On the morning of June 6, American, British, and Canadian troops landed on the coast of Normandy, establishing the second front that Stalin had sought for four years. About 160,000 Allied troops landed that day, aided by almost 200,000 naval and merchant-navy personnel, making it the largest amphibious operation in history. The once-feared Luftwaffe was barely a factor. The Allies controlled the skies, partly because of the success of the Allied armaments program, aided by Morgenthau's early work in the aircraft program. The American aircraft industry, which had barely produced 2,000 planes in 1939, had churned out 86,000 planes in 1943 and would build 96,000 in 1944, more than double the German production in both latter years.[39] The Allies advanced steadily, and within days one million Allied soldiers were on French soil.

For Henry Morgenthau, it meant his eldest son would soon be in France, and it meant the dynamics of the all-important monetary conference would change. De Gaulle felt slighted by being excluded from the D-Day operation, so the French were upset. But the Soviets could no longer complain about the lack of a second front. Technical experts from several countries had worked out many of their differences during negotiations held in Atlantic City. FDR had long said that he'd never seen an international conference that accomplished anything, but now a deal was within reach.[40]

The British and American camps were now firmly committed to the multinational institutions, and the British accepted they should be backed by gold, as the Americans had demanded. The fund, with $8 billion in capital, including $2 billion in gold, would provide short-term stability for countries whose currencies were under pressure. The contributions of gold would be in relation to each country's quota for drawing money from the fund. If a country other than the United States were forced to draw dollars from the fund, it would repay the amount in dollars. The United States could occasionally buy that country's currency from the fund to pay for imports. If the fund had too much of any one currency, it would use that currency to buy gold. The World Bank, with $10 billion in capital, would promote investment in more long-term reconstruction projects. The bank's primary function would be to guarantee loans made by private lenders for development projects, though it would also make direct loans itself.[41]

Accompanied by his wife, his daughter (who spent the time working on a college history paper) and Henrietta Klotz, Morgenthau left Washington for the Mount Washington Hotel in Bretton Woods in late June. Nestled in the foothills of northern New Hampshire, the hotel offered a pleasant respite from the oppressive heat of Washington, especially at night, and there were enough hotels nearby to house support staff and reporters. But the revered hotel had grown shabby, so the government assembled what men could be found during war and had them paint the hotel white. A week before the delegates were to arrive, they realized the workers had painted everything— walls, wooden trim, gold fixtures. They managed to stop the work before the painters reached the ballroom, where the main conference was held. The Morgenthaus stayed in one of the finest suites, though they had trouble sleeping because the Keyneses were above them and Lady Keynes kept them awake all night as she practiced her ballet steps.

There were key countries whose support Morgenthau, the conference chairman, needed: the Soviet Union, which was essential to build a new global order in trade; Britain, because delegates from the empire would follow its lead and because the United States needed its acceptance of the dollar as a reserve currency, even within the empire; and the United States itself, which was not guaranteed. There was no guarantee Congress would support an agreement, even if the conference produced one. So Morgenthau ensured the US delegation included representatives from both parties in both the House and the Senate and members of the financial community. These included Republicans Senator Tobey and Representative Wolcott, and Chicago banker Ned Brown. "This has no party politics," Morgenthau told the US delegation when they arrived. "It is bigger than either the Republican or Democratic Party."[42]

The conference got down to work on July 1 and divided into two working groups: White chaired the group dealing with the International Monetary Fund (IMF), and Keynes chaired the International Bank for Reconstruction and Development group. Acheson headed the US delegation in the negotiations on the World Bank. The first crisis of the conference occurred on the third day, when the Soviet delegation protested the quota they were allotted for the IMF—which represented the amount it could withdraw from the fund and the voting power it would receive. White and Keynes had allotted the country a quota of about $800 million, but the Soviet delegation, headed by Finance Commissar Mikhail Stepanov, complained they had been promised a quota of 10 percent, worth about $1 billion. They were also angry their quota was below that of Britain, which had $1.25 billion. Aiming to be fair to all sides, Morgenthau discussed the matter with the US delegation, and Acheson proposed raising the Soviet quota to $900 million. But White protested that adjusting the Soviet quota would open up discussions on all the quotas.[43]

After a few days, Morgenthau had to return to Washington to help smooth relations between Roosevelt and de Gaulle, who was in the United States to protest the treatment of his country, his committee, and himself. His demand to be treated as the head of a sovereign nation was matched by Roosevelt's determination not to regard an unelected body as a country's government. Morgenthau and McCloy recommended that the United States deal with the committee as a "de facto authority" so the Allies could jointly establish a civil administration as they captured France. With de Gaulle in the capital, a more conciliatory Roosevelt accepted the new wording.[44]

Meanwhile, Fred Vinson, the lieutenant to Morgenthau's archenemy Jimmy Byrnes, substituted as chairman of the conference and worked with White to achieve a Soviet quota of $850 million and a British quota of $900 million. Stepanov said his country would never agree, and he doubted the British would either. The Soviets increased their demand to a quota of $1.2 billion, Vinson told Morgenthau on July 6.

"They're doing such a magnificent job in the war . . . that I've got a weak spot for them," Morgenthau said.

"We feel the same way," said Vinson.[45]

By the end of the first week, Morgenthau said publicly that the parties agreed to raise the Soviet quota to $1.2 billion, compared with $1.3 billion for Britain and $2.75 billion for the United States. However, he was careful to note that the United States vote on the fund would exceed that of the entire British empire.[46] When Morgenthau returned to Bretton Woods, he learned that the Soviets had yet to respond to the US proposal. They were now also demanding that countries that had been overrun by the Nazis, including the Soviet Union, be required to put up 25 percent less gold (relative to their quota) than other countries. If that wasn't enough, Morgenthau also learned that the discussions on the International Bank for Reconstruction and Development were running into problems.

As he often had, Morgenthau personally pushed through bureaucratic tangles that ensnared his underlings. He told the Soviet delegation on July 11 that he had always had good relations with their government, but now there was a problem. Apologizing for using a vernacular they may not understand, he said they were now "horse-trading" with him. "I must ask the Russian Delegation please to reconsider," he said. "I feel that very deeply because I have only one desire, and that is the continued friendly relations side by side of our two Governments."

Stepanov replied that the Soviets had originally hoped for a 50 percent reduction in the gold contribution. Morgenthau would understand their concerns better if he had a clearer understanding of their gold holdings and national income. The Soviets had never revealed their gold holdings (in part because they didn't want the world to estimate how many political prisoners were forced into mining), but Morgenthau decided to push the issue. He said he had heard gossip that the Soviets held $4 billion in gold and were producing $300 million to $400 million a year.

"Well, you can't stop the gossiping," said Stepanov.

He was obviously trying to dismiss the remark, but Morgenthau let him know the bottom line. "We have made you an ultimate proposal," he said. "We have honestly gone as far as we can go." He said there would be more deals between the governments in the future—an obvious reference to the Soviet ambition to secure a postwar loan from the United States—but on this issue the United States had given all it could give. If they didn't agree to the terms for the IMF, the Bretton Woods Conference would collapse. Their meeting broke up, and Morgenthau briefed the American delegation on what had been said.[47]

On July 14, the *New York Times* reported there were now five areas of disagreement between the Americans and the Soviets, including quotas and how the gold would be paid. Someone on the US team had obviously leaked the story, and Morgenthau had to call Stepanov and apologize. The report infuriated the Morgenthau team, who were convinced the two *New York Times* reporters at Bretton Woods were trying to derail the conference. Reporters Russell Porter and John H. Criders seemed to highlight the financial community's worries about the fund and bank. As Morgenthau wrote in a letter to Arthur Sulzberger that he decided not to send, "I think they have been influenced too much by the opinions of a few hardshell New York bankers whose thought processes have been frozen for a good many years."[48] A July 8 editorial—possibly written by the two reporters—chastised the American team for ignoring the country's balance of payments in their deliberations. Dollars were expected to be in high demand after the war, as reconstructing countries needed them to import American goods, and these countries could buy dollars from the fund in exchange for their "worthless" paper money, said the editorial. The United States could use that money only if it adopted a policy to encourage imports, but that didn't seem likely. The editorial said that "indicates a fundamental weakness in our approach to currency stabilization."[49]

Negotiations on the International Bank began to get bogged down over the ratio of loans to capital—the fundamental measure of the strength of a lending institution. A high capital ratio would stabilize the institution during financial shocks, but it would also restrict the amount of money that could be lent. The committee had agreed the new institution would have an initial capital of $10 billion, but only 20 percent would have to be paid in at the outset. The bank could issue loans and loan guarantees (known as assets) against the entire amount, including the committed capital that had not yet been paid in. The Dutch delegation recommended the loans and guarantees amount to only 75 percent of fully committed capital. Some members of the American team, especially the bankers, supported this conservative view, but White wanted to let the assets reach 200 percent of capital so the bank could make a significant impact in the critical job of reconstruction. "There is nothing that will serve to drive these countries into some kind of ism—Communism or something else—faster than having inadequate capital to construct their railways, their port facilities, their power development, things which have been destroyed during the war, or things which have deteriorated," said White. He added the United States would need a market for all that it would produce after the war.[50]

One thing that complicated the negotiations was that the quotas for the bank differed greatly from the fund's quota system. The Soviets were greatly interested in the bank because their need for reconstruction was so profound. Whereas they were negotiating for an increase in their quota in the IMF, Stepanov insisted they would pay no more than $900 million into the bank, only three-quarters of the $1.2 billion Morgenthau was hoping for. Sick of waiting for approval from Moscow, Morgenthau was tempted to unilaterally put the Russians down for $1.2 billion. Acheson warned him against it, saying there was no way the war-weary Soviets could contribute more than $1 billion. It mattered little, said Ned Brown, since no one in the financial world would accept a loan guarantee backed by Russia.[51]

Amid the huge issues being debated by the United States, Britain, and Russia, the other countries were haggling about matters that interested them specifically. The United States had to make concessions to the Latin Americans, especially to Mexico, Brazil, and Cuba, on stabilization funds. Britain championed small nations like Poland and feebly argued the headquarters of the institutions should be in London, though everyone knew they'd be based in the United States. France complained about the reduction in its IMF quota from $500 million to $450 million and the ensuing loss in prestige. Chinese finance minister H. H. Kung was worried about saving face and wanted China to announce it took less so Russia could have more. The Soviets would not allow it, so Morgenthau turned Kung down.[52]

Through it all, the delegates grew exhausted and impatient. The days were hot, and the nights packed with late meetings. Many delegates negotiated in a language and on issues they little understood. Morgenthau worried aloud to Acheson that the bankers, especially Ned Brown, might be too conservative and could scupper the negotiations. But Acheson replied that Brown had worked incredibly hard on the brief for a long time. "He is a big fat man and that takes a lot," he said. "He is really simply exhausted." Many delegates believed Keynes was moving too quickly, calling for votes before they understood the issues. Keynes was frustrated the proceedings were too slow. Morgenthau had to diplomatically tell the economist to slow down, advice he received with good humor.[53] Keynes actually wrote to a friend that for the "first time in my life I am really getting on with Morgy."[54]

The delegates narrowed their differences. They agreed the institutions would be headquartered in the member with the largest quotas, referring to the United States without actually naming it. They agreed to a total subscription for the World Bank of $8.8 billion—$800 million more than the figure at the start, even though the original figure had outraged the conservative banking community. On July 22, one hour before the final plenary session, Stepanov called Morgenthau to say that Moscow had agreed to a $1.2 billion quota for the IMF with no reduction in the gold contribution. Morgenthau was ecstatic, telling the minister to thank Molotov from the bottom of his heart. He rushed to the final session, at which the forty-four countries were able to sign an agreement on the creation of the two institutions. "And I do make bold to say Mr. President that under your wise and kindly guidance we have been successful," Keynes told Morgenthau in his closing remarks. "International conferences have not a good record. I am certain that no similar conference within memory has achieved such a bulk of lucid, solid construction. We owe this not least to the indomitable will and energy, always tempered by good temper and humor, of Harry White."[55] At the final banquet, the bone-weary delegates toasted one another before dashing out to catch the final train. Keynes arrived late, and as he shuffled to the head table, the hall rose spontaneously in applause.[56]

"This has been the great lesson taught by the war, and is, I think, the greatest lesson of contemporary life—that the peoples of the earth are inseparably linked to one another by a deep, underlying community of purpose," Morgenthau told the United States in a radio broadcast that night. "To seek achievement of our aims separately through the planless, senseless rivalry that divided us in the past, or through the outright economic aggression which turned neighbors into enemies would be to invite ruin again upon us all."[57]

Morgenthau knew the agreement would have to be approved by several governments. Such passage was far from assured in Britain, which had suffered a huge blow in prestige as the Bretton Woods Accord officially established the United States' financial preeminence. And in the United States, the conservative press and Republican caucuses were no less suspicious of the plan than they had been before.

That might be why Henry Morgenthau Jr. took extraordinary steps to chastise the *New York Times* for its coverage. He assured Sulzberger in a phone call he was not questioning his patriotism but wanted to send a representative to New York to explain the deal to the *New York Times*'s editors. He did so, and Sulzberger had reporter Russell Porter prepare a memo for the Treasury secretary on the coverage. "The *Times* does not set out to 'torpedo' any meeting, even though we would be following high example were we to do so," said Porter's memo. "Please realize that I, too, love my country and that I, too, fight for a stable world in which my children and theirs may live in peace." Porter said his reports were constructive and helped to bring public opinion to bear on the conference, stiffening the resolve of the US delegation in negotiating with the foreign parties. "It seemed to me that this was a highly valuable contribution, especially in view of the noticeable weakness of our delegation on the diplomatic side, and its need for some stiffening influence when dealing with skilled foreign diplomats and negotiators."[58]

Morgenthau's spat with the *New York Times* was a bagatelle compared with the radiating success of the agreement. Bretton Woods was the first international conference in living memory to succeed, despite the need to work closely with the Soviet Union. It gave the United States financial prestige the country had never known, and it created optimism for the conference establishing the United Nations. Though White was obviously the intellectual creator of the fund, Morgenthau helped to conceive of the idea, sold it to Roosevelt, and oversaw the process to create it. He contained the opposition in Congress and negotiated effectively with the Soviet Union. As Morgenthau left for a badly needed vacation at the end of July, laudatory international press reports and congratulatory letters from dignitaries poured into his office. The London *Times* editorial hailed the World Bank and IMF as "a new phase in the collaboration of the United Nations." The *Financial Times* called it "the launching of the biggest financial scheme the world has ever known."[59] Across enemy lines, the German press called the agreement the exploitation of other countries by Jewish Wall Street capital and attacked Roosevelt, Morgenthau, and the "Jewish world currency plan."[60] Dean Acheson wrote Morgenthau: "The complete success of the Conference in arriving at these results was due to the skillful direction which you gave to the Conference and to the excellent preparatory work of Dr. White and his staff." And Malcolm Bryan of the Federal Reserve of Atlanta wrote: "I want to say that the agreements reached at Bretton Woods are a great tribute to you and your colleagues at the Treasury Department."[61]

During the conference, Roosevelt had confirmed that he would run again and chose as his running mate a little-known senator from Missouri named Harry Truman. The beachhead in Western Europe was expanding. Henry Morgenthau was entering the endgame of World War II and the postwar world as the architect of the emerging global economic order.

CHAPTER ELEVEN

OCTAGON

★ ★ ★

Harry Dexter White could probably sense his boss was ready for a new challenge as they winged their way toward Scotland in a C-54 Skymaster on August 5. The monetary conference had been an unqualified triumph, and the Allies were advancing on all fronts. Mussolini had been imprisoned, and Hitler almost killed in an assassination attempt. The Soviets were on the verge of Romania and Lithuania. In the Pacific, the Americans continued their tortuous island-hopping. Roosevelt would likely win another four-year term. Now Morgenthau, White, and a few staff members were flying to Britain and France to assess Allied needs in the next stage of the war. Wanting to steer his boss toward one particular aspect of the victory, White handed Morgenthau the State Department document he'd secured a few days earlier.

Written by Secretary of State Cordell Hull's underling Leo Pasvolsky, the memorandum on the postwar strategy for Germany highlighted the need to rebuild the country. It argued that German goods would be needed after the war, so the Allies would have to rebuild German industry and make them pay short-term reparations. Germany, it said, should remain a unified country and retain sufficient factories to maintain a comfortable standard of living. White had gotten hold of a copy of the document through an interdepartmental committee he served on and strongly disagreed with it. Morgenthau read the paper silently, growing more and more furious.[1] White obviously wanted to lure the secretary into the planning for postwar Germany, but he probably had no idea the forces he was unleashing. By the time the plane landed in Scotland, Morgenthau was obsessed with postwar Germany.

Soon they were on a train heading south with Col. Bernard Bernstein, a former Treasury lawyer now serving with the Civil Affairs section of SHAEF, the Supreme Headquarters Allied Expeditionary Force. He told them the SHAEF staff believed they should bolster the German economy after the war to "keep our troops from bogging down in a morass of economic wreckage."[2]

By noon, they had arrived at Portsmouth, where Morgenthau and White wasted no time in asking their host, Supreme Allied Commander General Dwight Eisenhower, his position on the treatment of defeated Germany. Still fighting a war, Eisenhower had given little thought to the coming occupation. But he had just learned that morning of the Nazi barbarity at some of the death camps and made it clear the Germans would have to make amends for starting the war and committing crimes against humanity. "I am not interested in the German economy and personally would not like to bolster it if that will make it any easier for the Germans," one Treasury member remembered him saying.[3]

"He was very positive that he was going to treat them rough," Morgenthau said weeks later, pleased with what he had heard. "He was perfectly willing to let them stew in their own juice at the beginning," even though such thoughts were contrary to the official document.[4] Morgenthau continued to investigate the matter as he met with military leaders like Chief of Staff Bedell Smith and General Omar Bradley. In all these meetings, he sought reassurance that the military would be tough on Germany, and his impressions were no doubt shaped by the fervency of his own position.

The next day he flew under fighter escort to Cherbourg, France, where he was awestruck by the wooden pilings and concrete breakwaters being thrown up to handle the massive import of men and equipment. "I mean, I have never seen any place where the electricity is so in the air and the drive behind this thing, you just can't understand it until you see it and feel it," he later told his colleagues. Standing amid the stacks of ordnance and supplies, he learned that 500,000 men had come ashore through one beach alone. He had an emotional reunion with Henry III, who later noted his father put on his dark glasses when they parted so no one would see the tears in his eyes. After sleeping in a French farmhouse, Morgenthau met Bradley, whose military bearing impressed the secretary. Morgenthau was allowed within five hundred yards of the front, where the US troops faced a German force that included three SS divisions. On his last night in France, he visited an evacuation hospital, where men injured only hours earlier awaited transportation to England or back home. He boarded one evacuation plane and had to battle nausea from the smell of the wounded. "There were sixty boys and I shook hands with every one of them, and some of them are very, very sick," he said later.[5]

He settled into London, where buzz bombs (unmanned craft that flew across the channel and exploded on impact) had replaced the Luftwaffe as the main threat. He wrote his wife from his hotel room at Claridge's, saying: "I have returned from France where both Henrys were well." (Censors actually eliminated the word "where" presumably because it identified the location of a soldier.)[6] Morgenthau wanted to meet common people as well as decision makers, so Clementine Churchill, the prime minister's wife, and Lady Edwina Mountbatten, wife of the head of the British forces in India, led him one night to converted tube stations to visit the homeless. Morgenthau adored Mrs. Churchill, who reminded him of Eleanor Roosevelt, and had sent her through US ambassador John Gilbert Winant a selection of eggs and ham from his farm.[7]

Morgenthau was moved by the people in the shelters—which ranged from a new, clean tube station to a grotto by the Thames. The warmth and spirit of the people dissolved his natural shyness, and he reveled in chatting with whole families that had moved into these bunkers. "You see a family—there was one family there that had no home and they had been there for six weeks, living there," he later told his staff. "That was their home. I saw one mother with five children. I saw another mother with an eight-months-old baby. . . . You go in and see these people—this is London—and see the spirit."[8]

His main duty was to meet government officials, so he spent about two hours with Churchill in his subterranean map room near Whitehall and with Chancellor of the Exchequer John Anderson and Foreign Secretary Anthony Eden. Churchill kept driving home the point that Britain was broke and needed financial aid. Morgenthau sympathized but also wanted to probe the German question. He got the impression that Churchill favored a harsh policy, but he also learned many Conservatives wanted to rebuild Germany to provide a market for British goods and a bulwark against the Soviet Union. He came away believing that Anthony Eden wanted to dismember Germany. Eden revealed to him that Stalin, Roosevelt, and Churchill had all agreed at Tehran that Germany should be partitioned, which demonstrated to Morgenthau that Pasvolsky's document contradicted the president's wishes. Morgenthau later told his staff Eden "wants to take Germany apart. Completely apart. He is very good on this thing."[9]

During their meeting, Churchill said he'd heard Morgenthau was "unfriendly" toward Britain—a surprising statement given that the "Morgenthau-Purvis Channel" was three years earlier the best way to get support in Washington. Morgenthau said it wasn't so but that he didn't like the way the British would play one party against another. He suggested the prime minister be frank with the president about the country's position and proposed a committee to study the financial matters. The British had been surviving on phase one lend-lease, which the United States had authorized to prosecute the war up to victory in Europe. The Allies had yet to finalize lend-lease arrangements for phase 2 (between the fall of Germany and victory over Japan) and phase 3 (after the fall of Japan). Britain believed it was only fair that the United States, with its financial might, continue the program through reconstruction. But powerful people within Congress believed the program was designed for military action, not reconstruction. The lend-lease payments were substantial, amounting by August 1944 to $26.9 billion over three years.[10] To put that in perspective, the entire US government expenditures in 1944 were $100 billion. The matter was further complicated because Britain wanted a role in providing aid to mainland Europe while receiving aid from the United States. The Americans believed Churchill wanted to use the aid to garner support for reestablishing monarchs in countries like Greece and Italy in spite of American opposition.[11]

On August 12, Morgenthau invited Ambassador Winant and several of his advisers to lunch at a country house in Wiltshire, where the secretary was now staying. Winant had been serving with British and Soviet representatives on the Europe Advisory Commission, which was drawing up surrender documents for the coming victory. He favored a magnanimous peace. After lunch, they sat out on the broad lawn, and Morgenthau, with backing from White, outlined his position on the German question for the first time. He said Germany should never again be in a position to wage war, so it might be necessary to reduce Germany to a fifth-rate power. He failed to convince Winant and the other guests, one of whom said White came close to "clothing a bad thesis with an appearance of intellectual respectability." Philip Mosely said Morgenthau's plan would simply drive Germany to Russia and give the Soviets control of central Europe.[12]

As the trip wound down, Morgenthau told the British people in a radio broadcast that the Allies had to do more than defeat Germany and hope it remained disarmed. They had to permanently disarm the Nazis.[13] The Germans, meanwhile, broadcast their own propaganda, saying Morgenthau during his trip to Normandy had "appropriated" the historic 230-foot Bayeux Tapestry, showing William the Conqueror's preparations for his invasion of England. (It had previously been reported that Reich Marshall Hermann Göring had taken the tapestry for his own art collection, though it was later found in the Louvre in Paris.)[14]

By the time Morgenthau returned to Washington on August 16, he had formulated the framework of a plan for postwar Germany. Though Morgenthau is often portrayed as a lone voice crying for retribution against Germany, he was no doubt influenced by the volumes of books and articles published during the war warning that Germany unchecked would grow bellicose again. On the weekend that Morgenthau flew to England, the *New York Times Magazine* had run a feature titled "The Nazis Dig In for World War III." It noted that the Nazis for five years had seen people in their occupied territories fight an underground war against the Reich. The article postulated that the Germans were now preparing similar tactics to employ when they were occupied by the Allies. It was why they were fighting so furiously even though they knew they had lost the war. "They are playing for time to complete their 'post-war plans' for the survival of Nazism," said the article.[15] So officials debated not only how to prevent the Nazis from becoming a guerilla force but also how to ensure Germany lacked the power ever to wage war again. As early as 1942, British author

Paul Einzig had published *Can We Win the Peace?*, which advocated the abolition of German military production. It said Germany's arms buildup in 1933 to 1939 was one of the most spectacular economic and technical achievements in history. "To prevent Germany after this war from preparing for another war of aggression, it is vitally important for us to realise the importance of the economic factor among the factors that enabled Germany to rearm in record time," wrote Einzig, who wanted to remove its capacity for producing arms and ordnance.[16] Books on the postwar world were popular in the early 1940s, and several argued for some means of suppressing Germany's potential for waging war. In *What to Do with Germany*, Col. T. H. Minshall argued that international commissions would be needed to monitor German factories, including airplane factories, to make sure only domestic planes were built.[17] C. J. Hambro, in *How to Win the Peace*, advocated "public control" in the armament industries.[18] But many supported rebuilding Germany. "To dismantle German industry would be to leave in the heart of Europe a cancer that would eventually destroy not only the Germans but the Continent itself," said Vera Micheles Dean in *On the Threshold of World Order*. "And it would be a great waste of skills, energies and ingenuity that the Germans have in so large a scale."[19] In his own book, Sumner Welles agreed that the Nazis were already planning to rise again after losing the current war, but he warned against punishing Germany. "The Policy to be followed should be designed not to destroy Germany, but to construct out of Germany a safe and co-operative member of world society."[20]

The day before Morgenthau left for Europe, Arthur Krock noted that several plans for postwar Germany had circulated within the administration, but attention was being centered on an economic solution. "To prepare for, make and sustain war, a nation must depend on heavy industry," wrote Krock. "This suggestion is to internationalize the areas in Germany proper on which heavy industry depends. The Germans would be allowed to share in the products of these areas up to a point where they could begin to pile up reserves sufficient to start another war." The column said that when occupied land was returned to original countries, the German industrial capacity would have shrunk dramatically.[21]

Polls showed 81 percent of Americans supported the notion of unconditional surrender. Most believed Germany would start planning a new
war soon after the current one ended and wanted Germany reduced to
a third-rate power.[22] But Morgenthau, the strongest hawk in the administration, took the idea of German suppression further than anyone else
and devised a plan to put it into action. On his return to Washington, he
met first with the 9:30 Group to brief them on his discussions in Europe.
(Daniel Bell's first question was, "Do you have this tapestry with you?"[23])
Morgenthau said the president "will have to get awfully busy. It took me
days, and days, and days, but I got the story. There isn't anything in regard
to Germany which is being carried out [as the president wants]. I am going
to tell Hull so, because his boys are the worst."[24]

Morgenthau visited Hull's office on August 17 and found him exhausted
and confused about what the three powers had agreed to. "I have never
been permitted to see the minutes of the Tehran Conference," Hull said.
"I have asked, and I have not been allowed to see them, and what you have
told me is the first time I have heard this." He described the European
Advisory Committee as a "complete failure" and left Morgenthau with the
impression that he too favored a harsh settlement for Germany. Morgenthau ended the meeting by asking him definitively what he would like to do
with Germany, "I don't have a chance to do anything," he said. "I am not
told what's going on."[25]

Two days later, Morgenthau complained again to the president about
the State Department, detailing the Pasvolsky report and what Hull had
said. "The President didn't like it, but he didn't say anything," he later
dictated into his diary. "He looked very embarrassed, and I repeated it
so that he would be sure to get it." Morgenthau then told him about the
work of Winant and the European Advisory Committee and concluded
that nobody "has been studying how to treat Germany roughly along the
lines you wanted."

"Give me thirty minutes with Churchill and I can correct this," Roo-
sevelt finally said. He added the Allies had to be tough not just with the
Nazis but also with the German people. "We either have to castrate the
German people or you have got to treat them in such a manner so they

can't just go on reproducing people who want to continue the way they have in the past."

"Well Mr. President, nobody is considering the question along those lines," said Morgenthau. "In England they want to build up Germany so she can pay reparations." He left the meeting convinced that the president "personally wants to be rough with the Germans."[26]

Morgenthau immediately formed a Treasury committee with John Pehle, Harry Dexter White, and Ansel Luxford—men he believed shared his views on Germany. He wanted them to write a memo proposing policy on Germany. Historian John Morton Blum later wrote that Morgenthau dominated this committee, and the members did his bidding even when they disagreed with him. They collected materials far and wide, even from John Maynard Keynes, who had opposed the harsh peace settlement of the previous war.[27]

Henry Stimson invited Morgenthau to lunch with John J. McCloy a few days later, and the atmosphere among the administration's leading hawks was convivial. When the talk turned to Germany, McCloy revealed he was focused on the short-term problem of how the army would oversee Germany and the period after the armistice, but Stimson was worried mainly about long-term considerations. He said the Allies may need to patrol Germany for decades, until another generation grew, and seemed to support a proposal by French statesman Jean Monnet to make the industrialized Saar Basin an international zone.

"Well, if you let the young children of today be brought up by SS Troopers who are indoctrinated with Hitlerism, aren't you simply going to raise another generation of Germans who will want to wage war?" asked Morgenthau. "Don't you think the thing to do is to take a leaf from Hitler's book and completely remove these children from their parents and make them wards of the state, and have ex–US Army officers, English Army officers and Russian Army officers run these schools and have these children raised in the true spirit of democracy?"

He also said the Allies should remove industry from Germany. Stimson replied that would mean removing a lot of people from the country because agriculture could not support the current German population.

"Well, that is not nearly as bad as sending them to gas chambers," said Morgenthau, who proposed a committee made up of himself, Stimson, and Hull to draw up proposals for the president on a policy for postwar Germany.[28]

The German policy soon occupied more and more of the secretary's time because he was involved in postwar planning, occupation currencies, and the efforts to help Jewish refugees. The refugee issue itself could only have amplified Morgenthau's hatred of the Nazis as he received several briefings a week from Pehle proving the tyrannical evil of the regime. Most Jews in Nazi-occupied Europe had been murdered, and the Germans were now turning their attention to the remaining pockets in Bulgaria, Romania, and especially Hungary. On August 23, for example, Morgenthau learned of twenty thousand Jewish men, women, and children, sleeping for four or five days in a field in Hungary, who were then herded into boxcars for transportation. Sixty people were packed into each car, which was then nailed shut. "The people are packed in the cars like sardines with no possibility of sitting or moving," said one report from Pehle. "Many must have been dead on arrival." Though the Allies were certain 400,000 Hungarian Jews had already been deported and murdered, Admiral Miklós Horthy, the Hungarian leader, had offered to release surviving Jews as long as the Allies accepted responsibility for their resettlement. Yet the Gestapo was actively trying to prevent any Jewish escape, especially to Palestine.[29]

On the currency issue, the Treasury favored a weak occupation mark, a rate of twenty marks to the dollar, so US soldiers would have a lot of buying power. However, the British favored a stronger mark at an exchange rate of about five, while the State Department backed an exchange rate of eight. The stronger rate would protect British industry once the countries began to trade again. Roosevelt, Morgenthau knew, wanted the exchange rate left open so every soldier could negotiate when buying goods in Germany.

On the morning of August 25, Morgenthau called on the president, whom he saw less frequently than before. He knew Roosevelt was aging with disturbing speed. Just the night before at a dinner for the president of Iceland, FDR toasted the visiting dignitary, then waited while the guest responded with his own toast. Then Roosevelt toasted his guest again, having completely forgotten he had already done so. On this particular morning, the president's appearance shocked Morgenthau. "I really was shocked for the first time because he is a very sick man and seems to have wasted away," he dictated to his diary hours later.[30]

Morgenthau bore a memorandum pushing for a twenty-mark exchange rate, which FDR again turned down in favor of having no official rate. And Morgenthau voiced his concerns about another official document that signaled magnanimity toward Germany. *The Handbook of Military Government* had been prepared by the Supreme Headquarters Allied Expeditionary Force as a guide for British and American forces overseeing the coming occupation government in Germany. The handbook instructed the military to install an efficient government as quickly as possible, to organize a working police force to maintain order, and to convert industrial plants to the manufacture of consumer goods. Regulations affecting industrial production and the methods of extracting raw materials from the earth should be maintained, unless specifically ordered otherwise. "The highly centralized German administrative system is to be retained unless otherwise directed by higher authorities," said the handbook, which Morgenthau denounced strongly.[31]

After a rambling conversation on Germany and other matters, Morgenthau blurted out, "Mr. President, some time when you have time I would like to talk to you about myself because, looking forward to the next four years, I am kind of getting bored over at the Treasury, and I don't think you are making use of all my talents." The president responded with the old bromide about the two of them one day retiring to Dutchess County and added they may find a role in the United Nations. Morgenthau persisted in discussing his own role in the administration, stressing that, like FDR, he believed the postwar foreign policy must focus on collaboration with Moscow. "I was able to work with Russia at Bretton Woods, and Dean Acheson said I seemed to have a sixth sense on those things," he told the president.[32]

It seems obvious Morgenthau was lobbying to become the next secretary of state. He was the longest-serving Treasury secretary since the Madison administration, and the only promotion available was the State

Department. (As a Jew, he could not realistically seek the presidency.) He had scored unlikely foreign-policy victories in the Tripartite Pact and Bretton Woods Accord. And there were few other candidates. Sumner Welles had resigned; Harry Hopkins was sick; Hull was exhausted; seventy-six-year-old Stimson was a Republican with ties to Wall Street. Morgenthau alone was robust, experienced, and ambitious. Even his migraine headaches had been held in abeyance recently, and through the end of August he had not missed a single day of work that year.[33]

"This so-called 'Handbook' is pretty bad," Roosevelt wrote to Stimson the next day, siding with Morgenthau. "I should like to know how it came to be written and who approved it down the line. If it has not been sent out as approved, all copies should be withdrawn until you get a chance to go over it." He wanted the German population to understand they were a defeated nation. They could be fed by US Army soup kitchens, he said, to keep the people healthy. "There exists a school of thought both in London and here which would, in effect, do for Germany what this Government did for its own citizens in 1933 when they were flat on their backs," said the memo. "I see no reason for starting a WPA, PWA or a CCC for Germany when we go in with our Army of Occupation."[34] At a cabinet meeting that day, FDR struck a committee of Hull, Morgenthau, and Stimson and chaired by Hopkins (all of whom were given a copy of the handbook memo) to review the question of the treatment of Germany. Hull was characteristically bitter that the others were encroaching on his turf. As they departed for the Labor Day weekend, it was already becoming apparent that the main combatants would be Morgenthau and Stimson.

Trying to relax in Saranac, New York, Stimson recorded in his diary he was very concerned about "Morgenthau's very bitter atmosphere of personal resentment against the entire German people without regard to individual guilt and I am very much afraid that it will result in our taking mass vengeance." He added that such a clumsy economic policy would produce a "dangerous reaction and probably a new war."[35]

Morgenthau retreated to Fishkill Farm but pressed his staff by phone to take an ever tougher line in their memo. "I wish that your men would attack the problem from this angle, that they take the Ruhr and completely put it out of business," he said in a phone conversation with White and Pehle on August 31. "That's one thing—and also the Saar." He wanted them to research coal production and industry in the Ruhr and Saar— Germany's industrial hub—and consider how Britain might benefit from the elimination of competition from these regions.

"This Ruhr thing is the most difficult problem," said White. He was obviously uncomfortable with Morgenthau's demands, even though he had weeks earlier initiated his boss's interest in the German issue. "Crushing it, as you say, presents us with about fifteen million out of eighteen million people who—who will have absolutely nothing to do, and it's trying to . . ." Uncharacteristically stumbling on his words, he explained the Ruhr was too big to give to another country, leave with Germany, or guard under an international mandate. "It's—it's the most difficult problem, and we'll— we'll work along the lines you're suggesting."

Morgenthau had no patience with White's squeamishness, saying again that the Ruhr would be shut down. "I can tell you this," he said. "That if the Ruhr was put out of business, the coal mines and the steel mills of England would flourish for many years."[36]

Morgenthau had always respected his staff and worked with them to formulate policy, but now he alone was dictating the Treasury position, which he believed the president supported. On September 2, Franklin and Eleanor Roosevelt drove out to Fishkill Farm for tea, where they ended up discussing the German situation for a full hour. Morgenthau showed FDR a draft outline of the Treasury proposal. When they studied a map showing the proposed postwar partition of Germany, Roosevelt wasn't sure it represented the boundaries agreed to at Tehran. After some reflection, the president said the memo should include three paramount stipulations: first, that Germany should be allowed no aircraft of any kind; second, that no German be allowed to wear a uniform; and third, that no Germans be allowed to march in a parade. That, he said, would teach the Germans they were a defeated people.

"That's very interesting," said Morgenthau, who could only have been aghast that the aging president's reaction to German brutality was to outlaw uniforms and parades. "But I don't think it goes far enough." He

urged the Ruhr be shut down as an industrial area. Making it an international zone would mean only that the Germans could seize it once again
the next time they rearmed, he said. He agreed eighteen million to twenty
million people may be put out of work, but they could be sent to other
parts of the world, Central Africa, for example. The president supported
Morgenthau's proposal, as did Eleanor.[37]

Morgenthau was getting close to the proposal he wanted and assembled his staff one final time to refine the wording and add in stipulations on
aircraft, uniforms, and parades. Again, White protested the loss of fifteen
million jobs and suggested the Ruhr be placed under international control.

"Harry, you can't sell it to me at all," rebuked Morgenthau. "The only
thing you can sell me, or I will have any part of, is the complete shutdown
of the Ruhr." He wanted mines flooded and army engineers to blow up
every steel mill, synthetic gas business, and chemical plant. "Just strip it. I
don't care what happens to the population. . . . I am for destroying first and
we will worry about the population second." Herbert Gaston and adviser
Robert McConnell also objected to the severity of the plan, but Morgenthau shot them down. "I am not going to budge an inch," he said. "Why
the hell should I worry about what happens to their people?" Gathering his
fury he added: "We didn't ask for this war; we didn't put millions of people
through gas chambers, we didn't do any of these things. They have asked
for it." He concluded by saying the president would go even further than
he would. FDR was "crazy for something to work with," he said, though it
would be difficult to sell the plan to Churchill.[38]

On the evening of September 4, Morgenthau hosted a dinner with
Stimson, McCloy, and White, at which he revealed his final plan for
Germany. It was officially titled "Program to Prevent Germany from Starting
World War III," though it instantly became known as the Morgenthau Plan.
Its dominant theme was the complete and immediate deindustrialization
of Germany, but it delved into far greater detail. It wanted to dismember
Germany, give Poland part of East Prussia and Southern Silesia, and give
France the Saar and nearby territories. The Ruhr and its surrounding territo-
ries were to become an international zone. The remaining parts of Germany
were to be divided into north and south sectors.

The German industrial heartland—the Ruhr, the Rhineland, the Kiel Canal, and the land north of the canal—would be stripped of all industry and mines so they could never be used by the Germans again. The plan did not demand reparations, other than the transfer of industrial equipment to the victorious powers.

Schools and universities were to be shut down until an Allied commission on education could write a new curriculum. All news media were to be discontinued until adequate controls on information could be imposed. All national-government officials were to be dismissed, and the occupying forces would deal only with local governments. The occupying military government was not to worry about such economic matters as price controls, rationing, or unemployment. For at least twenty years after surrender, the United Nations was to maintain controls over foreign trade and capital imports, with the aim of ensuring there would be no new industrialization. It banned—as Roosevelt had asked—German-owned aircraft, uniforms, and parades. It requested that continental armies police Germany, allowing American troops to return home soon.[39]

Stimson was polite, but his rebuttal was firm and immediate. He said Morgenthau's proposal would mean the starvation of thirty million people. Morgenthau was surprised by the number, which was roughly double the figure of fifteen million people White had used earlier in the day. Stimson explained it was the difference between the population now supported by the industrial economy and the last time Germany relied on agriculture for its sustenance. He did not disagree with dividing territory or punishing war criminals, but he maintained that the deindustrialization of Germany would not prevent future wars.[40]

The venerable War secretary was even more emphatic the next day, when the cabinet committee chaired by Hopkins met. "More and more Stimson came out very emphatically, very, very, positively, that he didn't want any production stopped," Morgenthau told his staff. "He said it was an unnatural thing to do, it ran in the face of the economy." Stimson also used a term that he would use a few times in discussing postwar Germany. He said the Allies needed a policy of "kindness and Christianity." Morgenthau apparently didn't say anything, but the implications and insensitivity of the word *Christianity* were not lost on him as Stimson mentioned it a few times.[41]

Though Stimson was immovable, Morgenthau held sway. Hopkins and Hull favored a tough policy. Stimson even wrote in his diary that Hull was "as bitter as Morgenthau."[42] Hopkins told Morgenthau that Stimson—the only participant who had not worked on the New Deal—didn't want to shut down German plants because "it hurts [him] so much to think of the non-use of property. . . . He's grown up in that school so long that property, God, becomes so sacred."[43]

The cabinet members brought their case before the president on September 6. FDR started off by saying they didn't need to make a decision in the first six months of occupation. Then he digressed to talk of how people lived in Dutchess County in 1810, in homespun wool, and there was no reason that Germans couldn't live that way. "He expounded on that at great length," wrote Morgenthau. The meeting lasted only half an hour, and Morgenthau believed Stimson won the session.[44]

In the next few days, the War Department brought Morgenthau into the discussion on altering the handbook. The officials discussing the matter included Major John Boettiger, FDR's son-in-law who had been living with his wife, Anna, at the White House and was working for the Civil Affairs Section of the Joint Chiefs of Staff. A journalist by trade, Boettiger had once written that FDR had appointed Morgenthau Treasury secretary because he knew Morgenthau would always do the president's bidding. But he and his wife frequently wrote Morgenthau over the years to ask for favors, from advice on preparing their income tax in 1936, to Secret Service protection for their children in 1937. They later complained that the Secret Service had gone "somewhat haywire" and were considering protecting the family with tear gas and shotguns.[45] Yet Anna Boettiger did not like Morgenthau and privately complained that he used her mother to fight his battles. There was speculation within Washington that she was planning a sort of latter-day regency, in which she and her husband would have key positions in aiding the president, who was too feeble to bear the burden of office alone.[46]

White and Bell were encouraging Morgenthau to be more assertive about the occupation marks, but Morgenthau brushed them aside, saying he had bigger fish to fry. He did however negotiate throughout the first week of September with Robert Brand of the British Treasury on the exchange rate. After several days, Morgenthau and Brand agreed to the level of ten marks to the dollar. Before the deal was signed, Brand needled the secretary to make sure the president was fully briefed on the discussions and had agreed on the ten-mark level. Morgenthau was utterly incensed by the man's impudence. "A couple more like that," he told White after Brand had left the office, "and he is going to be hoisted out of the window. I am not going to take much more of his—if you don't mind—God damned lip." White dismissed Brand as a fool.[47]

But the truth was that Morgenthau had given Roosevelt scant details about the talks and didn't inform him fully that the British wanted a 12.5-cent exchange rate. "Now I told the President at Cabinet about the ten-cent mark," he told his staff, referring to the meeting after he had met with Brand. "Just for the record, because I forgot, when I took it up with the President, I didn't tell him about the twelve and a half cent, because I remember his saying, 'I don't like the twelve and a half-cent mark. I want a ten-cent mark.'"[48] Morgenthau was for the first time acting beyond the authority of the president. Just a few years earlier, he would never have concluded an agreement with a foreign government without the full approval of Roosevelt.

Morgenthau also had a hand in writing the proclamation Eisenhower would read on entering Germany. He wanted the supreme commander to say: "We come as militant victors to insure [sic] that Germany shall never again drench the world with blood. The German people must never again become the carriers of death, horror and wanton destruction of civilization." When he read it to McCloy, the under secretary of war said he wasn't too sure about the "drench the world with blood" part. Morgenthau assured him the president would love it. It was yet another indication that Morgenthau's judgment was failing him. No doubt, he was suffering from hubris after the roaring success of Bretton Woods. He was now ignoring the advice of his staff and subtly manipulating the president. He was abandoning his successful formula as an administrator—develop policy with a great staff, sell it to a superior, and implement it.[49]

The three secretaries finally submitted their respective proposals to the president on September 9 at a wrap-up session before Roosevelt left to meet Churchill in Quebec City. Roosevelt had privately assured Morgenthau not to worry, though the German plants might have to be closed gradually.[50] FDR kept checking the Treasury's document to make sure it included rules against uniforms and parades. When the president asked what would happen if the Soviets wanted reparations while the British and Americans didn't, Morgenthau responded that he had found the Russians to be "intelligent and reasonable" and would likely forsake reparations as long as there was something else in return. The meeting reached no conclusions. Hull, who seemed to be siding more with Stimson now, declined Roosevelt's invitation to come to Quebec, insisting he was too exhausted. Since the Quebec Conference would deal with the British fiscal position, Roosevelt told the meeting he might invite Morgenthau.[51]

Morgenthau was nevertheless surprised when Roosevelt sent word on September 12 that he should be in Quebec City two days later. He and White quickly flew up to the ancient French Canadian city perched on a rocky outcrop overlooking the St. Lawrence River. It was the second time in thirteen months that Churchill and Roosevelt had met there. On August 1, 1943, the Chateau Frontenac, the Canadian Pacific hotel dominating the skyline, suddenly canceled three thousand reservations and posted armed guards. It sparked rumors that the edifice was either to become a military hospital or that Pope Pius XII was fleeing Italy and would set up a headquarters in the Chateau Frontenac. It turned out just to be a meeting of the great democratic leaders. Now they were returning, accompanied by their wives and advisers—even Roosevelt's dog Fala—in September 1944.[52]

When Churchill and Roosevelt met, the prime minister immediately stressed that Britain was in perilous financial straits and needed assistance to carry out phase 2 of the war. He handed Roosevelt a document that asked for military donations in the first year of phase 2 to be maintained at their 1944 level and that foodstuffs and raw materials be added. In all, it would amount to $3 billion in additional contribution from the United States, over and above the $3.9 billion payment of 1944.[53]

Morgenthau enjoyed tea with Eleanor Roosevelt when he arrived, then met with the president. "Say hello to your Uncle Henry," Roosevelt told Fala when Morgenthau entered. He asked the secretary to meet with Lord Cherwell, Churchill's science adviser and confidant, to discuss economic matters and invited him to a dinner of the senior delegates that night. The discussion over dinner began on economic matters, and Churchill again tried to persuade the president that Britain was in dire need of funds. Roosevelt would commit to nothing. "What do you want me to do, stand up and beg like Fala?" Churchill cried in desperation. As the evening wore on, Roosevelt finally asked Morgenthau to outline his plan for Germany, which the secretary was more than eager to do. Soon after he started, the prime minister began to mutter under his breath about the problems and scowl at some of Morgenthau's points. "After I finished my piece he turned loose on me the full flood of his rhetoric, sarcasm and violence," Morgenthau dictated into his diary. "He looked on the Treasury Plan, he said, as he would on chaining himself to a dead German. He was slumped in his chair, his language biting, his flow incessant, his manner merciless. I never have had such a verbal lashing in my life."[54]

The president said nothing until Churchill had finished, when he tried to lighten the atmosphere with a joke. Morgenthau believed it suited Roosevelt's purposes to have his secretary draw Churchill's wrath, thereby sparing the president himself. Morgenthau said little else and was later unable to sleep, certain he had failed in his effort to demilitarize Germany.

However, things changed the next day. Morgenthau met Cherwell as instructed and found in him an unlikely ally. An eccentric Oxford don who often served as Churchill's scientific adviser, Cherwell was known in London to be anti-Semitic, but Morgenthau found him "wonderful to work with."[55] "The Prof," as he was known, said the prime minister obviously didn't understand Morgenthau's point and that he himself had been surprised by the prime minister's response. The Prof supported the Treasury position on Germany, and Morgenthau found they soon reached common ground on the financial questions. The British would receive $3.5 billion in munitions and $3 billion in other material in the first year, all under lend-lease (meaning it didn't have to be repaid).

At noon, Morgenthau, Cherwell, Eden, and the two leaders met again.

No doubt Cherwell had briefed the prime minister on the tentative agreement on financing, and it is likely that Churchill was more pleasant to Morgenthau because of it. Roosevelt lightened the atmosphere with a joke or two, and Churchill allowed Cherwell and Morgenthau to present a policy for Germany together. They produced a framework based on the Treasury proposal, and soon Churchill was dictating a policy in his own words based on Morgenthau's plan. When he dictated the segment about deindustrializing the Ruhr, Roosevelt insisted he specify that the policy apply to all of Germany, not just the Ruhr.

"You can't do this," a shocked Eden said to Churchill. "After all, you and I publicly have said quite the opposite. Furthermore, we have a lot of things in London which are quite different."

Churchill and Eden argued about their policy while Morgenthau interjected to back up his newfound comrade, Churchill. FDR sat silently. The prime minister was suddenly adopting Morgenthau's line that Britain would export more if it no longer had to compete with Germany. "The future of my people is at stake, and when I have to choose between my people and the German people, I am going to choose my people," Churchill said. Morgenthau was surprised just how nasty he was with the foreign minister, but he himself was delighted. Churchill and Roosevelt initialed the draft, after which Eden sulked for the rest of the day. "Of course, the fact that Churchill has dictated this himself strengthens the whole matter tremendously," Morgenthau said in his diary. "Naturally, I am terrifically happy over it as we got just what we started out to get."[56]

The next day, the two leaders also signed an agreement that Britain would receive $6.5 billion in aid under lend-lease phase 2. White understood that Churchill had backed the Morgenthau Plan only because he needed the secretary's support for the lend-lease payments. Morgenthau deluded himself that there was only a slight link between the two agreements. After sitting in the president's room and chatting with Roosevelt as they had over the years, Morgenthau returned to Washington the next day, where he proudly reported to his staff that the Quebec meeting was the crowning achievement of his career. He had guaranteed that German industrial capacity would be eradicated.

CHAPTER TWELVE

THE MORGENTHAU PLAN

★ ★ ★

F our days after the Quebec Conference, Morgenthau's triumph began to crumble as *Washington Post* columnist Drew Pearson wrote the cabinet was divided over *The Handbook of Military Government* and Roosevelt had reprimanded Henry Stimson about the document. Soon, the Washington press corps was focusing on the German policy and the Treasury secretary's role in the matter. With his office fielding phone inquiries into whether Morgenthau was now overseeing foreign policy, Arthur Krock told his readers the secretary was responsible only for financial matters and the planning for postwar Germany.[1]

The *Wall Street Journal* soon reported the details of the Morgenthau Plan, adding it was not yet official policy and it was creating division within and outside the cabinet. Stimson privately told people that it amounted to Jewish retribution—a view shared by many. "Such a plan as that attributed to Mr. Morgenthau would shatter whatever economic balance will remain in Europe when peace comes," said Raymond Moley, a former New Dealer who had become a bitter critic of the administration.[2] *Wall Street Journal* columnist Frank R. Kent said Morgenthau has "no conceivable business whatever" dictating policy on what was obviously a military and foreign-affairs brief. A *Washington Post* editorial called it "the product of a fevered mind."

In Berlin, Joseph Goebbels considered the Morgenthau Plan proof the Jews were planning to harm Germany if the country fell. "Roosevelt and Churchill Agree to Jewish Murder Plan!" screamed a headline in the *Völkischer Beobachter* newspaper. German radio broadcast that Roosevelt's bosom friend Morgenthau, the "spokesman for world Judaism," was "singing the same tune as the Jews in the Kremlin"—dismember Germany, destroy her industry and "exterminate forty-three million Germans."[3] Even after it was clear the Morgenthau Plan was not official policy, Goebbels publicized it. "Germany will obtain a peace deserving of the name only if she defeats the plans of an enemy who is determined to convert Europe into a colony of Jewish high finance and bolshevism by crippling and depopulating the heart of the continent," said the *Völkischer Beobachter* on October 8, warning that Germany was in a life-and-death struggle against "these cannibals."[4]

In Washington, it was soon clear that Roosevelt was wavering. "Familiar signs point to the abandonment by the President of Secretary Morgenthau's Carthaginian post-war plan for Germany, which was briefly ascendant here and got much encouragement at Quebec," said Krock on September 29. The "usual high sources" were passing out word that FDR didn't like the plan after all, he said, and foreign and military policies would be retained by the State and War Departments, respectively.[5]

Morgenthau tried for a month to find the source of the leaks with no success. He and Hopkins both believed they came from Stimson and the War Office. The secretary was also furious the president wasn't sticking by him. "This isn't the first time that I have been the whipping boy for the President," he told his staff after the second story by Krock appeared. Yet he was also confident that the president still agreed with him.

In no mood to back down, he took his press clippings on the matter and went to the White House, where he was asked to wait outside the Oval Office. A few minutes later Anna Boettiger appeared and said her father was unable to see him. He pushed the point with the woman he had known since her childhood, asking her to show the clippings to the president. She led him out saying the president didn't want to see him.[6]

Later that day, the president told a press conference that there was no breech within cabinet and he had asked trusted New Dealer Leo Crowley to look into postwar Germany. He then told Cordell Hull privately that the State Department alone would deal with the matter. And when he met Stimson on October 3, the president said with a cheeky smirk, "Henry

Morgenthau pulled a boner." According to Stimson's diary, the president said he had never intended Germany to become a pastoral society. Stimson showed him the paper from Quebec he had initialed, and an astonished Roosevelt said he didn't know how he could have signed it.[7]

Morgenthau believed the president had told the press about Crowley simply to quiet things down and decided to remain silent until after the election. "I'd like to mark time and see what happens," he told his staff on October 5. "I don't want to do much between now and the seventh of November."[8] But he wanted to be prepared, so he ordered Harry Dexter White, Ansel F. Luxford, and Josiah DuBois to draft a book explaining his position and rebutting the perception he was acting out of Jewish vengeance and had bought off Churchill with $6 billion in taxpayer funds.[9]

As the Western Allies' advance toward Germany began to slow, some observers said the Germans were fighting with renewed vigor because they feared defeat would lead to the implementation of the Morgenthau Plan. Republican presidential candidate Thomas Dewey charged the plan "put the fight back into the German Army" and was worth as much as "ten fresh German divisions." He added that "the blood of our fighting men is paying for this improvised meddling."[10]

The charge shocked Morgenthau. Not only was he a raging patriot, but also his son and namesake was then with Eisenhower's advance camp heading toward Germany. Henry III had begun to volunteer for dangerous missions whenever possible to prove his mettle and fight his image of being the son of privilege. The Morgenthaus had almost lost Robert with the sinking of the *Lansdale*, and now young Henry—who bore the same name as the author of the Morgenthau Plan—was in an active theater. Morgenthau worried about what would happen if the boy were captured and what effect the stress of having boys in combat was having on his feeble wife.

On November 13, Morgenthau asked General Edward Greenbaum if there was any way to change the name on Henry III's dog tags. "If the Germans captured Henry they undoubtedly would be extremely cruel to him," he recorded in his diary. The general at first said it would be impossible, that it would contravene the Geneva Convention, but he discussed it with Assistant Secretary of War John J. McCloy. Together, they warned

Morgenthau the army would have to disown Henry if he were captured and the Germans realized he had false identification. They proposed transferring him to a less dangerous location. "I said that I would unalterably oppose any such procedure, that Henry would never forgive me and that I would have no part of it," Morgenthau said, making them promise they would not transfer the lad.[11]

Franklin Roosevelt won an unprecedented fourth term as president of the United States on November 7, 1944, defeating Thomas Dewey 432 to 99 in the Electoral College. On November 30, Cordell Hull resigned as the longest-serving secretary of state in the country's history and claimed the Nobel Peace Prize the next year for his role in the founding of the United Nations. He was succeeded by Edward Stettinius, the former US Steel executive. Morgenthau told Roosevelt that Stettinius was the best man to succeed Hull, and the new secretary of state wrote with profuse thanks when he learned of it.[12]

With the election decided, Morgenthau launched his sixth war-bond drive on November 20, aiming to raise $14 billion at interest rates of 2.5 percent or less.[13] He had to keep on raising money because the unimaginable costs of World War II would continue mounting for at least another year and a half. "During the first six months following the armistice in World War I, expenditures were slightly greater than in the six months preceding the armistice," he told the public.[14] It was the first Christmas-season bond drive and it was a smashing success, raising $20.4 billion by Christmas Eve. The secretary himself announced the success by calling three wire-service reporters into the corner office to thank them for their diligence in covering the bond drives.[15] The final tally in the drive was $21.6 billion—54 percent more than the target.[16]

The president's budget address on January 9, 1945, predicted $70 billion in war expenditures in the fiscal year that would end June 30, 1946, down $19 billion from the previous fiscal year. "The overall cost of the war to this country from 1941 through the 1946 fiscal year was estimated by Mr. Roosevelt at $450 billion," said the *New York Times* the next day.[17] Morgenthau, days after the address, said the war had already cost $238 billion, a figure due to reach $289 billion by June 30. He noted that 46 percent of the cost was paid through taxes, and the number of taxpayers had increased from four million before the defense program to fifty million in 1945. That means that it went from 3 percent of the total population to 36 percent. "Never before has a democracy taxed itself on such a broad base," he said, adding more taxes were still needed.[18]

Morgenthau pleaded so strongly for more taxation because his office and Congress were once again negotiating a revenue bill. In the middle of these talks, Jimmy Byrnes, head of the Office of Economic Stabilization, introduced his own tax proposal without consulting the Treasury. This time, Byrnes was roundly criticized for interfering when the parties were making progress. "We sincerely hope that Director Byrnes' ill-timed and unwarranted attempts to put over a tax plan of his own will not upset the new entente cordiale," said a *Washington Post* editorial.[19]

It was apparent that the war would endure into 1945, so many of the suppositions of the Quebec agreement, which assumed phase 2 of lend-lease would begin in 1944, were no longer valid. That meant Britain and America once again negotiated on lend-lease financing, and Morgenthau in November met with his old antagonist John Maynard Keynes to discuss the matter. Morgenthau told White—who warned of the limitless demands of the British for financial aid—that the United Kingdom had proved a "good moral risk" and it was necessary to help a neighbor who had fought so valiantly. Morgenthau's vision of the postwar world called for a strong United Kingdom, but the president was growing uncomfortable with the "Spirit of Quebec" and annoyed at Churchill for propping up southern European monarchs. Morgenthau told Stettinius the president was acting as if he had never heard of the Quebec agreement. He vowed to send a delegation to the White House to establish firmly what the Quebec agreement meant.[20]

In mid-November, Keynes wrote Morgenthau complaining that no country in the empire except Canada contributed to the British finances, yet the United Kingdom had to support a large military presence in India and in the Middle East. (It was not the best opening argument, for Congress and the administration both cringed at the thought of lend-lease payments supporting the empire.) Keynes argued that these forces had shown their value in North Africa. Meanwhile, the United Kingdom squandered its gold reserves before the United States began lend-lease and withdrew from export markets under the terms of lend-lease. "No doubt, the above makes collectively a story of financial imprudence that has no parallel in history," wrote Keynes. "Nevertheless, that imprudence may have been a facet of that single-minded devotion, without which the war would have been lost. So we beg leave to think that it was worthwhile—for us, and also for you."[21] But many in Washington called for restraint in helping the Allies, especially the British, who were using their precious finances to maintain the empire. Arthur Krock reported that financier Bernard Baruch had warned the president that Americans may be "weakening ourselves while trying to help the rest of the world."[22]

On November 22, the United States said it would give the British about $5.5 billion in the first year of phase 2, a reduction from the $7 billion agreed to at Quebec. What's more, it demanded the British maintain their export ban, though the two countries had agreed at Quebec it would be relaxed. As part of lend-lease, the British had agreed not to export goods and compete with American industry while the country was receiving US aid. The British obviously wanted the ban ended as soon as possible, and the Quebec talks had produced a relaxation in the policy. But now that looser policy would be delayed. Some in the British government, like Lord Cherwell and John Anderson, nonetheless thanked Morgenthau for his support. Keynes understood that Morgenthau had done his best but failed to budge Roosevelt. "Mr. Morgenthau has easier access to [the president's] presence than to his mind," he said.[23]

The dubious regime of General Chiang Kai-shek, meanwhile, continued to badger Morgenthau and the military for money for such things as its alleged military efforts. In particular, the two sides disputed what the United States owed for the Chengtu airfield, about one hundred miles west of Chungking, and whether the Americans should pay at the official exchange rate. Under Secretary of the Treasury Daniel Bell in July 1944 calculated a $115 million payment would be fair, or a net $90 million since the US Army had already paid $25 million. But Finance Minister H. H. Kung insisted his government had been promised $25 million a month in aid, and that did not include the cost of airfields. In fact, he said Roosevelt had personally promised at Cairo to pay for the Chengtu airstrip, which the Chinese valued at $200 million. The Americans raised their offer to $100 million, then $125 million, then to $185 million in late October. The negotiations became acrimonious and extended for months as economic conditions deteriorated in China. They agreed to the last American offer in December 1944.[24]

But in October 1944, Kung had begun to demand an additional $20 million in gold to soak up the additional fapi that was stoking inflation. Kung said it was part of a $500 million loan approved in 1942. White advised against it because Chiang Kai-shek and his in-laws, the Soongs, could end up pocketing profits from the deal. Patrick Hurley, the US ambassador to Chungking, warned Morgenthau that Chinese officials thought the American taxpayer was "a sucker" and added that T. V. Soong was "a crook." Early in 1945, the Chinese increased the request to $180 million in gold and gave notice that they wanted an additional $100 million in the near future. Morgenthau delayed. He didn't want to deprive an ally, but he was worried about being swindled and agreed that even $200 million in gold would be insufficient to halt Chinese inflation. In the end, Morgenthau approved a shipment of $7 million in gold and said all future shipments would need the approval of Hurley.[25]

John Pehle and his War Refugee Board continued to work with partners to find homes for the displaced Jews, and Morgenthau continued to take an active interest. In April 1944, three rabbis visited the Treasury to complain that the State Department refused to help 240 French Jews who had been given permission to leave France but whose passports the United States didn't recognize. DuBois leaked the story to Drew Pearson at the *Washington Post*, and the State Department was forced to act. Though Hull bawled out the rabbis afterward, Morgenthau silently approved of DuBois's actions. On another occasion, some Polish Jews came in to ask Morgenthau to free funds needed to liberate Jews from Poland. The rabbis knew Morgenthau didn't speak Yiddish. What they didn't know was that Henrietta Klotz could understand it. She sat silently as they stage-managed the presentation in Yiddish, with one demanding of the other to make his pleading more hysterical. One worked himself into such a frenzy that he collapsed. As he was helped up, he asked in the ancient language if he had cried well enough. Klotz revealed none of this to her boss because she wanted him to act.[26]

The War Refugee Board is estimated to have saved the lives of about 200,000 Jews. It was created tragically late in the war, but it is impossible to overstate in human terms the good it performed. As well as allowing these people to survive the horrors of Nazi Germany, it preserved to some extent the honor of the United States, which had been shamed by its immigration policy, the *St. Louis* affair, and the conduct of the State Department. And Morgenthau was instrumental in creating the board. As historian Robert N. Rosen has written, "Had Morgenthau not taken the lead when he did, it is doubtful the rescue agency proponents would have succeeded."[27]

Disagreements on the policy for postwar Germany persisted into 1945, focusing on whether to fire or retain German officials who had worked for the Nazis. Morgenthau's position that they must be fired was supported by such groups as the Senate Subcommittee on War Mobilization. But the State Department warned that the British and Soviets would likely want to retain existing administrators, and the United States would jeopardize tripartite cooperation by opposing such a plan. Stimson had distanced himself from the debate, disgusted that the president had even considered the Morgenthau Plan. Now representing the War Department, McCloy sought a magnanimous policy mainly because the army wanted something that it could implement with the resources available. The key decision was Franklin Roosevelt's, and his mental faculties were diminishing rapidly. He privately let both Stettinius and Morgenthau believe he supported them. He told all of the cabinet he would make no decision on the big questions until Germany was defeated, leaving them months to quarrel.[28]

Soon the debate focused on JCS 1067, a War Department document overseen by McCloy to guide the operations of the US occupation forces. Morgenthau contributed liberally to the document, which was shaped largely by Roosevelt's desire for a tough policy on Germany. It stated Germany was a defeated power, and there would be no effort to resurrect the nation. Though his efforts to fire all government employees failed, Morgenthau ensured JCS 1067 stated that even low-level officials must be assumed to be Nazis or Nazi sympathizers. Roosevelt asked his friend Samuel Rosenman to script a policy on war criminals. Morgenthau would later tell historian John Morton Blum that he would have preferred to see them simply shot, but he realized they needed to be tried. The Treasury secretary and DuBois drafted a memo advocating that all members of organizations like the SS should be considered guilty of crimes against humanity.[29]

On December 19, McCloy sent Major John Boettiger to Morgenthau's office to explain what he had witnessed during a recent trip to Aachen, the first German city occupied by the Americans. Boettiger said the city had been 70 percent destroyed by aerial bombing and no building still had the roof on it. The Germans were utterly hostile to the Allies. He believed the Allies would have to control administration of such cities and use local production facilities to supply such areas and other parts of Europe. Otherwise, he warned, the entire continent could erupt in revolution. "You can tell McCloy I will be delighted to see him, but as of today my position hasn't changed one iota," Morgenthau responded. "I don't want to destroy Germany, I want them to take care of themselves as we leave it."[30]

When Morgenthau told his staff of the meeting, the pragmatic Daniel Bell suggested the Treasury position might be too extreme. Morgenthau rejected the statement, saying the State and War Departments were being too soft. In January 1945, a group of Treasury men, including the closet Communist White and the fervent anti-Nazi DuBois, tried again to persuade him to dilute his position. White suggested he be vague on the fate of German coal mines, as his opponents' harshest criticism was his plan to close down mines and industry. "I am not going to change on that," snapped Morgenthau. "There is no use pounding me on it." [31]

The stress of his professional and family problems was mounting, and

Morgenthau sought more medical attention for his migraine headaches than ever before. On December 12, he asked Klotz to find the name of a Philadelphia doctor he'd heard of who specialized in headaches, and on Sunday, February 17, he took a train to Philly to meet Dr. Harold Palmer. The doctor prescribed pills of potassium chloride and calcium lactate that Morgenthau found helpful. Later that month, he also corresponded with Dr. Harold Hyman of New York, who also suffered from migraine headaches. He recommended Morgenthau each morning take a teaspoon of bicarbonate of soda and two glasses of hot water. "I regulate the bicarbonate dose so that I take enough to give me one or two fluid evacuations immediately after my breakfast," Hyman wrote the secretary. "I think this morning emptying out of the cesspool has been a factor in the reduction of my headaches and in giving me a sense of well-being." (He also sent congratulations on the birth of Robert Morgenthau's first child, the first grandchild for Elinor and Henry. "Did it come with or without a tassel?" he asked of the child, who happened to be a girl.) Morgenthau preferred the advice of Palmer, continuing the consultations and, in June, ordering five hundred more of his pills.[32]

From February 4 to 11, Roosevelt met with Churchill and Stalin at the Crimean resort city of Yalta to finalize plans for Europe after the inevitable surrender of Germany. Roosevelt wanted support for the war on Japan and for the new United Nations, and he was now more interested in ties to the Soviet Union than bankrupt Britain. Churchill was intent on preserving Britain's empire and standing in the world. Stalin was determined to make sure he held sway over Eastern Europe in general and Poland in particular to provide a buffer between Germany and the Soviet Union in the future. They agreed to partition Germany into four zones—one administered by each of the three great powers and a fourth by France. Their communiqué was vague, and it said their inalterable goal was to destroy German militarism and Nazism, but not to destroy the German people.

Roosevelt returned to Washington in early March as the Allies were inching toward Berlin in the face of savage German resistance. The president then made his most decisive move in the debate over postwar Germany by secretly asking Stettinius to prepare a report in keeping with the decisions reached at Yalta. He also appointed a working group called the Informal Policy Committee on Germany, or IPCOG, which comprised representatives from several departments, including White from the Treasury. It set in train two weeks of double-dealing and intrigue, in which the competing factions tried to impose their views on the final policy.

Stettinius handed the "Draft Directive for the Treatment of Germany" to Roosevelt on March 10, which FDR signed. He told Stimson and Morgenthau two days later only that Stettinius was working on the matter. McCloy was infuriated to learn not only that the draft directive had been submitted and signed but also that Stettinius told the president that the War Department supported it. McCloy and Morgenthau—who generally liked and respected each other—kept in touch with one another, though they both had different priorities. Morgenthau was actually encouraged that John and Anna Boettiger also opposed the draft directive. With Roosevelt so weak, one or both of them attended virtually all of the president's meetings, and Morgenthau was pleased they were going "to go to work on this with the President." [33] Such feelings faded quickly, and Morgenthau grew annoyed that the pair kept insisting that the Allies manage every aspect of the German economy.

When Morgenthau pressed his concerns about the directive over lunch on March 21, the president had "absolutely no recollection of having seen it or signed it."[34] He now demanded that IPCOG prepare a new document to take the place of the draft directive. Morgenthau phoned the State Department as soon as he left the lunch to relay the president's decision.

When the committee met the next day, the State Department tried to simply rework the draft directive, but McCloy, the strongest voice at the meeting, insisted they start over and adopt a flexible, centralized policy that the military could implement. Morgenthau was satisfied with the report, surprising his own staff, who thought he opposed a centralized authority. He explained that the generals in the central council would include Soviet, American, and French generals, who would override any British attempt to build up the German economy.

The State Department—possibly with the concurrence of the Boet-tigers—had Morgenthau excluded from other meetings in the next few days. "The cards are stacked against us," Morgenthau said to White. Finally, Joseph Grew of the State Department went behind Morgenthau's back to try again to get the president at a private meeting to sign a rewritten draft directive. What they were not expecting was that the president had invited McCloy to attend. Roosevelt told Grew he'd been sold a bill of goods and added that the new paper placed too much emphasis on cen-tralization. Then he rambled on, discussing his boyhood visits to Germany and the need for public services in Germany and to change the character of German industry. He agreed there may be some need for centralized authority, but they would have to see how much.

"Well, then I think . . . we're very close," said Grew, according to McCloy's account later. He added: "You agree generally with the paper that Mr. Stettinius submitted to you."

"Why yes, I guess so," said the president. Then he caught himself and asked: "Oh, you mean the March 10 paper?" Yes, Grew said, that paper. "No, that will have to be rewritten."

Roosevelt agreed to take a look at the new paper the State Department had penned, but the meeting adjourned without him signing it. Morgenthau was delighted to hear the news when McCloy phoned him later. "It may sound silly to say thank you because when I'm treated squarely it is so unusual that I have to say thank you," he said. "It has happened so rarely in Washington."[35]

All the parties were tired of the intrigue, so officials from the three departments gathered at the corner office of the Treasury Building to reach a final agreement on March 23. They quickly agreed on a War Department document called "Summary of U.S. Initial Post-Defeat Policy Relating to Germany." It said a central council would formulate broad policies, but local governments in the various zones would interpret and apply the policies. The economic policy was to prevent starvation, but it should not raise the German standards of living above its neighbors. As well as outlawing the Nazi party, the policy included vague calls for demili-tarization and disarmament of Germany and controls to prevent her from "developing a war potential" again.[36]

Stimson was pleased the zone commanders would have the flexibility to administer their regions. Morgenthau was willing to tolerate the central authority given the other demands of the document. They all knew JCS 1067 was still the document that would govern the occupation troops, and the parties would still have to negotiate to ensure that document adhered to the one Roosevelt had just signed. Morgenthau also believed the American people needed more information on Germany and why the United States had adopted its policy. He proposed writing a book on the matter. Roosevelt at first approved, as long as publication was withheld until after the war. But then he told Morgenthau he would have to give the subject more thought.[37]

After Roosevelt signed the War Department paper, Morgenthau and his enfeebled wife took a much-needed vacation in Florida. They attended a seder, a ritual feast that marks the beginning of Passover. It was the first time that Henry Morgenthau Jr. had ever attended such a ceremony. The calm of the holiday was shattered on April 5 when Elinor suffered a heart attack and was hospitalized. After Morgenthau phoned the First Lady, she immediately wrote, urging Elinor to rest. "I know that in spite of the brave front you put up that there is constant anxiety in your heart and the long strain wears on your whole physical condition," wrote Eleanor Roosevelt. "All the operations have taken their toll and the mental anxiety when you cannot be active is always harder to bear. Henry has the satisfaction of his accomplishments in his work but I know that you've grieved that your physical strength did not permit you to do more."[38] Eleanor Roosevelt checked regularly with Klotz to see how Elinor was doing, and the president, vacationing in the resort he frequented in Warm Springs, Georgia, sent Morgenthau a note asking to be kept up to date on Elinor's condition. A few days later, in a barely legible hand, he wrote:

Ellie Dear,

It's great that all is getting along so well—See you very soon. Affec. FDR.[39]

Morgenthau was at his wife's bedside for six days as she convalesced in an oxygen tent, and she gradually showed signs of improvement. So he left her in the care of trusted servants and doctors and took the train north. On the evening of April 11, he stopped by Warm Springs to talk with the president about the proposed book on Germany.

He found the president enjoying his evening drink with a small group of women that included Anna Boettiger and Lucy Rutherford, the true love of Roosevelt's life, with whom he'd carried on an affair of sorts for years. Morgenthau was shocked at how terribly his friend, propped up in a chair with his feet on a large footstool, had aged. But the old man was charming, joking that he was going to pinch the candies Morgenthau had brought and asking after Elinor. At a dinner of veal and noodles, the two men sat at opposite ends of the table, and Morgenthau noticed that the president's hearing was so bad that he couldn't hear what the Treasury secretary was saying.

After dinner, Morgenthau took the president aside and explained his book would educate the American people on Germany. For example, he said sixty million Germans could feed themselves from their own produce. Now Roosevelt said he thought it was a grand idea, and he rambled on, telling Morgenthau about the time Hjalmar Schacht, the former German central banker, came to the White House and cried on the presidential desk because of the poverty in Germany. "This is a story that I have heard the President tell about three different times, but he seems to enjoy telling it," said Morgenthau in his diary. He warned the president about the misconduct and incompetence of a few men working on the German matter and was glad when the president said he was pleased with McCloy. When Morgenthau asked whether he should be involved in the German matter, Roosevelt was noncommittal.

When the four ladies joined them, Morgenthau excused himself to make a phone call. "Then I came back and said good-bye to the President and his company, and when I left them they were sitting around laughing and chatting, and I must say the President seemed to be happy and enjoying himself," dictated Morgenthau.[40]

Morgenthau caught the next train to Washington, arriving early in the morning of April 12. He dictated a lengthy description of his evening with the president (never naming Lucy Rutherford). He was at work early that morning, writing to the president about Bretton Woods and to H. H. Kung about a gold shipment. In the late morning, the First Lady summoned him to the White House. He went immediately, and she told him the president had died. It turned out he had suffered a massive cerebral hemorrhage. Eleanor Roosevelt said her husband had known he was weakening, but he had acted as a good soldier and he should serve as an example to them all. Morgenthau was the first person she had called to tell the news so that he could tell his ailing wife and make sure she received the news gently. She didn't want the shock to cause a setback in Elinor's recovery.[41]

Morgenthau was already exhausted from more than eleven years in cabinet, the bruising battle over the Morgenthau Plan, and worrying about his sons and ailing wife. And now he had lost the one man to whom he had devoted his career. "For Henry Morgenthau Jr., the President's death was a catastrophe," wrote Blum. "He had lost his sponsor, his chief, his closest friend."[42]

The president of the United States called a cabinet meeting that afternoon, and all the secretaries, recovering from their shock, had to realize that the president was now Harry S. Truman, a man they barely knew. "I want every one of you to stay and carry on, and I want to do everything just the way President Roosevelt wanted it," he told them. There was an uncomfortable silence, and then Stettinius said they would all back the president. Then Morgenthau spoke: "Mr. Truman, I will do all I can do to help, but I want you to be free to call on anyone else in my place." He obviously could not bring himself to call the new chief "Mr. President."[43]

Morgenthau took his daughter, Joan, then a student at Vassar, to the funeral in Hyde Park. He said the flowers were like jewels, and he was overcome with emotion when a trumpeter blew taps. He was worried about Joan, who couldn't stop crying, so he took her back to the train and gave her tea and a sandwich.[44]

The Morgenthaus and Roosevelts slowly adjusted to the new life. Eleanor Roosevelt left the White House and moved into the Morgenthau apartment in New York for a short time. "You and Henry are good to let me go to your apartment and he made it seem so simple and easy," the former First Lady wrote to Elinor on April 25.[45] "What wonderful friends you both are." She had not only to adjust to the grief of widowhood but also to the knowledge that she was now officially just another citizen. "I went out and did my first marketing this morning, thinking I had better acquaint myself with stamps and prices etc.," she wrote. "The first time in 12 years I've actually been to market and enjoyed it."[46]

Morgenthau held his first meeting with his new boss on April 14. The president opened the meeting by saying how terrible he felt and that he was sure he admired Roosevelt as much as Morgenthau had. "I don't think that's possible," replied the secretary.

Doing much of the talking, Morgenthau said Roosevelt had asked him to do jobs that were not strictly Treasury business and that he hoped to explain the Morgenthau Plan to him at some point. He warned he had difficulty working with some people lower down in the State Department and that "the big boys" on Wall Street would target him. "In my job, I am very vulnerable because we have moved the financial capital from London and Wall Street right to my desk at the Treasury," he said.[47]

Truman said he wanted to maintain Morgenthau's desk as the center of the financial world. "Now I want you to stay with me," he told Morgenthau as he escorted him to the door."

"I will stay just as long as I think I can serve you."

"When the time comes that you can't, you will hear from me first direct."[48]

Overcoming his grief, Morgenthau continued to work on major projects. The Bretton Woods agreement still had to be approved by Congress, so Morgenthau called on its disparate supporters to speak out in favor of the deal. He wanted to counter the opposition of the banking community, conservative media, and isolationists in the Senate. He launched an extensive public-relations exercise, persuading influential publications from the *New York Times* to *Reader's Digest* to write complimentary articles. He tried to broker a deal with the American Bankers' Association, but the talks proved difficult. Truman publicly supported the legislation as it worked its way through the House in mid-April.[49]

Morgenthau still had to raise money. In the seventh war financing, whose deadline was June 30, 1945, the Treasury set a target of $14 billion, of which it hoped $4 billion would come from wage earners. Morgenthau noted to Federal Reserve Chairman Marriner Eccles that World War II was the costliest war in history. From July 1940 to July 1945, they had raised $211 billion in interest-bearing debt, of which $122 billion came from nonfinancial lenders.[50]

In the final days of the war against Germany, three issues proved to be tortuous and created harsh conflicts with the staff Morgenthau so cherished.

First, the government had to decide what to do with lend-lease shipments for the United Kingdom because the victory in Europe was changing the dynamics of the special relationship. The Joint Chiefs of Staff were now saying they believed the military requirements for Britain were different than what they had estimated just five months earlier. Morgenthau told Truman the whole lend-lease system had to be overhauled, and the president agreed.[51]

Second, the mendicant family of Chiang Kai-shek said they were still owed a massive gold shipment—$240 million of a previously approved $500 million. But Treasury officials believed that $27 million already shipped to China had been horribly wasted to the benefit of speculators. Frank Coe, a monetary-unit official, said the main beneficiaries of Soong's request would be speculators close to the Chiang clique. Morgenthau was conflicted. The State Department told him the Chinese were now fighting the Japanese, and the army wanted the Treasury to support a stabilization program, even though the Chiangs, Kungs and Soongs couldn't be trusted.[52]

Finally, the entire policy toward Germany was dogging the administration. There were disagreements over reparations and whether German authorities should control prices and wages. Morgenthau continued to press for tough policies, and he still wanted to publish a book on Germany. He even showed a few draft chapters to Truman. Morgenthau had told his diary several times that Truman seemed to have confidence in him. But on

May 4 the president asked him to stay after a cabinet meeting and said he was uneasy about Morgenthau's book. He asked him not to do anything with it for the time being.[53]

Adolf Hitler shot himself after his lover, Eva Braun, poisoned herself with cyanide on April 30. He had come to power thirty-four days before Roosevelt had taken office and outlived the president by eighteen days. In the same compound, Josef Goebbels, who had so publicly vilified Morgenthau over the years, and his wife poisoned their six children before taking their own lives. On May 7, the Nazi government finally declared the unconditional surrender that Roosevelt had insisted on. In Washington, Morgenthau interrupted his hectic schedule to assemble his staff in the corner office. "I think that those of you who have been associated with me since Pearl Harbor or before . . . can all feel we have had a little share of this victory," he said, obviously understating his message. He noted the French orders for airplane engines advanced the air force's development by at least a year and the Treasury's role in developing lend-lease and writing the legislation. "Certainly we have raised the money that the war cost from the people. It has been the people's financing." He noted that they still had an extremely tough opponent in the Japanese. "And when the last phase is through and the Japanese quit, then I think for the first time in my life—I have never really been drunk—I think I will get drunk then."[54]

The celebration was short-lived. Within twenty-four hours of the armistice and without consulting the Treasury, Truman signed an order cutting back the shipment of supplies to Great Britain under lend-lease. And T. V. Soong held a meeting with several US officials, including Morgenthau, protesting stridently that the Treasury was not letting China have gold it had previously been promised. Focusing his wrath on Morgenthau, he said the Treasury had not honored an April 27, 1943, commitment to deliver $200 million in gold. He produced and read the letter aloud for all to hear. Morgenthau was unprepared for the request and didn't even remember signing the letter. He was furious his staff hadn't prepared him better, and he scolded them in one of his disjointed rants the next day. "Look, you people, I think, should be severely criticized for letting me go into court and try my case before T.V. Soong, and the letter . . . where I gave the Chinese Government a firm commitment . . . I think it's inexcusable." He railed at them for putting him in a dishonorable position and ordered them to make sure the Chinese got the gold they were owed.[55]

Morgenthau was working hard to develop a working relationship with Truman. On the day he scolded his staff, he went to the Oval Office to once again explain the Morgenthau Plan. He noted the president was surprised to learn that Germany was among the world's top four producers in several food categories. Asked if he supported the plan, Truman said he was "by and large" for it. But when Morgenthau said he could help in negotiations with the Soviets, the president was noncommittal. "I went away with the distinct feeling that the man likes me and has confidence in me," he told his diary.[56] He had always highlighted in his diary how Roosevelt had treated him during their meetings, but now Morgenthau spoke as a man trying to convince himself that he had the new president's support. He was pleased the next day when the president signed the revised version of JSC 1067 and the documents outlining a policy on reparations.

The angst over China did not let up, largely because the staff resented Morgenthau's blaming them for the difficulties with a corrupt administration. Coe on May 15 recommended Morgenthau write the new president, outlining the Chinese gold scandals and advising that the United States should ask China to withdraw its request. White reminded Morgenthau that the 1943 negotiations had stipulated that gold shipments would depend on their being used prudently. "These people own this gold," Morgenthau reminded them harshly. In another meandering diatribe, he said the Chinese were beginning to fight and must be given support to carry on the war. What's more, he had given written assurances that the gold would be shipped to Chungking. What was at stake, he said, was "my written word and the promise of Franklin Roosevelt."

A day later, May 16, he bawled his staff out again, this time because he had just been told that Soong and Kung had not profited directly from gold sales. "You boys have been telling me right along that Soong owns most of this stuff, and that's misleading," he told them bluntly. Morgenthau assured Soong that day that the gold would be shipped, though the United States wanted assurances there would be none of the mistakes made in the past—a diplomatic reference to the profiteering off speculative sales. The Treasury secretary even persuaded the State Department to write a letter supporting the sales. Yet Ambassador Hurley in Chungking was livid when he heard about the shipments. He said the gold sales were useless in preventing inflation, and he was upset by the "vicious speculation" and the "so-called gold scandals." Above all, he was upset the United States had "reserved no power to control the situation in its gold commitment to China."[57]

As friction with his staff mounted, Morgenthau's relationship with the new president began to strain. Truman made it clear that Morgenthau would not be the main person interpreting American commitments agreed to with Britain at Quebec. "I don't want to give them everything they ask for," Truman told him.

"I never have," Morgenthau responded. "In fact, they have complained about it."

Morgenthau recommended an interdepartmental committee examine the matter; Truman said he would think about it but never approved it.[58] The British, naturally, were distressed that American support was being reduced, and Churchill cabled Truman to complain on May 28. Morgenthau declined a British request for his help. "I am waiting for the President to tell me whether he wants me in on it," he told his staff—the same men he'd chastised over the Chinese file days before. He said he wanted it stated publicly in writing that he was involved or he wouldn't do it. He was tired of being blamed for all the problems in foreign affairs. "The French are starving and freezing, and I'm the one who is holding this up?" he asked sardonically. "And this is wrong and that is wrong, and Churchill gets on the floor in Parliament and thanks Lord Keynes for the wonderful job he did, and I never get a line. I'm not going to take it. I was willing to take it from Roosevelt because I was his friend, but I want a little more now."[59]

Rather than Morgenthau, Truman asked Fred Vinson—Jimmy Byrnes's former deputy and now the head of the Office of War Mobilization—to head the dealings with Britain. Vinson's team—which included

Treasury representative Frank Coe—drafted a letter for Truman to send to Churchill explaining that the Quebec decision was based on many strategic and economic assumptions that no longer held true. It asked for the British government to relax its position on certain items.

"I am not going to go along with that," Morgenthau told White and Coe in the sanctity of the corner office. He complained that Vinson's letter gave no reason for "welching," and the United States and Britain should both honor their obligations made at Quebec. He ordered Coe to write another draft letter saying the United States would honor its commitment, which Coe did and gave to Vinson. In June, Morgenthau again overruled Harry Dexter White and refused to back a State Department plan to lend—not give—the United Kingdom $3 billion with a 2.5 percent interest rate during phase 3 of lend-lease.[60]

When he heard that Byrnes would be named secretary of state, Morgenthau asked Truman if the rumors were true, warning, "I can't get along with him." Truman would say only that he was studying the situation.[61] While Morgenthau wanted to focus almost exclusively on postwar Germany, Truman wanted him to concentrate on economic matters and leave Germany alone. He told Stimson that neither Morgenthau nor Bernard Baruch could keep his hands off German policy. And when Stimson heard that Morgenthau would be attending the Potsdam Conference and checked it with the president, Truman replied, "Neither Morgenthau nor Baruch nor any of the Jew boys will be going to Potsdam."[62]

In mid-June, the French government invited Morgenthau to open an exhibit of war bonds in July. (The seventh war-bond drive—known in the Treasury as "The Mighty Seventh"—would wrap up June 30 and bring in $26.3 billion. Investments by working people came in just below the $4 billion target. Overall, it was the most successful drive yet, exceeding the target by 88 percent even though the population knew the war was won.[63]) One of the authors of the invitation was Jean Monnet, the colorful businessman who had created so much controversy with his plane-engine purchases in 1938. Morgenthau told Truman of the invitation and mentioned to Joseph Grew of the State Department that he hoped to visit the Ruhr and Saar after Paris to "see what is going on."[64]

Morgenthau sat down with the president to discuss the invitation on June 13, and Truman seemed to search for the right response. He was unable to sit still and constantly paced around the Oval Office. "Well, the French feel that it would help to teach democracy to their people, and that is important to them," said Morgenthau. Truman kept repeating that he needed time to think about it.[65] Five days later, Truman told Morgenthau he did not want him to go to Paris. The president would be at the Potsdam Conference, and he didn't want them both out of Washington. Morgenthau eventually understood that Truman was worried Morgenthau might "mess around" in European affairs while the president was negotiating with Churchill and Stalin at a conference from which the French had been excluded. Truman also told Morgenthau he was like a brother to him and hoped the secretary felt the same way.[66]

Morgenthau's feelings were less than fraternal when the president named Jimmy Byrnes secretary of state in early July. Byrnes would be the one to accompany the president to Potsdam. He would determine foreign policy as the war with Japan wound down. Worse still, Washington was abuzz with rumors that Morgenthau would soon be replaced by Fred Vinson.

On the morning of July 5, Morgenthau sat with the president again and asked flatly where he stood. Was he being replaced? Would he be able to stay through the victory over Japan? How could he exercise authority in Washington while Truman and Byrnes were in Europe?

"Well, I don't know," said Truman, after a few minutes without assuring or dissuading Morgenthau. "I may want a new Secretary of the Treasury."

"Well, Mr. President, if you have any doubts in your mind after my record of twelve years here, and after several months with you and when I have given you my loyal support, you ought to know your mind now, and if you don't know it, I want to get it out now."

"Well," said the president, "Let me think it over."

Morgenthau took matters into his own hands and offered to write a letter of resignation and a draft response by the president. Truman wanted him to remain during the Potsdam sojourn, and Morgenthau said he was willing to stay only until the president returned. Truman told him several times, "You are rushing it."

Though the president wanted time to think about it, Morgenthau was fed up and simply said either Truman wanted him or he didn't. "After all, Mr. President, I don't think it is conceited to say that I am at least as good or better than some of the five new people you appointed in the cabinet, and on some of them I think you definitely made a mistake."[67]

He offered to break in Vinson—whom he generally liked—while the president was away, but Truman said Vinson would be traveling with him to Potsdam. They parted amicably, and Truman reassured him that he liked and agreed with the Morgenthau Plan. Back at the corner office, Morgenthau told what had happened first to Henrietta Klotz, Daniel Bell, and Herbert Gaston and then to the broader staff, including Harry Dexter White, Frank Coe, John Pehle and Ansel Luxford. He then wrote both the letters he had proposed to the president and dated them July 5.[68]

Truman set sail for Europe the next day, but first the White House issued a statement saying Vinson would be appointed secretary of the Treasury, though it did not say when. The White House was starting to feel pressure from its supporters to replace Morgenthau because of worries about succession. There was no vice president, so if the president and secretary of state were killed in still-perilous Germany, then Morgenthau, a Jew, would become president. (The succession order changed with the 1947 Presidential Succession Act.) On July 11, Truman asked Sam Rosenman to sound out Morgenthau about resigning immediately. In an easygoing chat at the Treasury, Rosenman suggested Morgenthau could be appointed the governor of the new World Bank. Morgenthau said he would think things over and then got together with Rosenman two days later.[69] He wrote a new letter of resignation and two possible replies from the president. One thanked Morgenthau for his service, and the other added that the president would like him to become the governor of the World Bank and International Monetary Fund. Rosenman was leery of sending the second letter because Byrnes might try to dissuade the president, but Morgenthau thought it was as good a time as any to see where Byrnes stood. Morgenthau wanted Vinson to approve the letters, but his successor—who had ended up staying in Washington rather than going to Potsdam—wanted nothing to do with the discussions, in spite of pressure from Morgenthau.[70]

Rosenman cabled the letters to Truman, who accepted the resignation. He sent Morgenthau the letter thanking him for his service, which was how Morgenthau learned he would not be the governor of the institutions he had helped to create.[71]

Vinson was sworn in as Treasury secretary on July 23, 1945. Morgenthau stood alone at the back of the room, looking completely dejected and alone. He had no family there. His wife was still recuperating in Florida, and his sons were overseas. Only Henrietta Klotz was there to comfort him.

One week later, the Senate approved the Bretton Woods legislation, which had already passed the House of Representatives. On the same day, Morgenthau received one of his few wholehearted endorsements on leaving office. In a column in the *Washington Post*, Drew Pearson, one of the most influential journalists in the country, blamed Morgenthau's shabby dismissal on Byrnes and said Morgenthau deserved to be remembered for his contributions. He predicted that historians would forget the doleful face that spawned the nickname "Henry the Morgue" and instead recall that Morgenthau hammered at the army and navy to build more planes and ship arms to Britain. Congressmen, he added, would forget they had been continually goaded into raising taxes by a man constantly worried about "the problem of financing the biggest government spending program in history."

Going back to the prewar days, Pearson recalled that Morgenthau "made life miserable" for the State Department when it wanted to sell scrap iron to Japan and cut red tape to get arms to Russia. In short, Pearson said Morgenthau had a habit of being unbearable to anyone who detracted from the war effort.

"He was the most constant interferer with other people's business in Cabinet—especially the business of slow-moving Cabinet colleagues," said Pearson. "But he did it. Nobody who does that can be popular. But when the final history of the Roosevelt Administration is written, it will be said that Henry Morgenthau, next to his chief, did more for the war than any other one man in Washington."[72]

EPILOGUE

★ ★ ★

Drew Pearson was wrong. History has remembered few of Henry Morgenthau Jr.'s astonishing accomplishments. When he is remembered, it is usually for his eponymous plan that was a complete failure and never implemented. Other than that, he sometimes receives the credit he deserves for creating the War Refugee Board, but only within the circles familiar with the history of the Holocaust. He rarely, if ever, is celebrated for his leadership in the key phases of the airplane program or in supporting Britain when it was the lone European opponent of Hitler's tyranny. And there is no recognition for his greatest accomplishment—leading the biggest economic program in history to combat the greatest evil the world has ever known. The late British-military historian John Keegan called World War II "the largest single event in human history,"[1] and financing the winning side was undoubtedly the biggest economic program ever.

This epic snub began in 1945, immediately after he left the Treasury. He had been the second-longest-serving secretary of the Treasury ever, but he had never developed strong relations with the financial community. He was known to be ostracized by the Truman camp and represented the anti-business leanings of the New Deal. So he was offered only a single directorship after he left government—the chairmanship of the New York–based Modern Industrial Bank, a ridiculously low position for a man who had recently considered himself the vortex of the financial world. He inched back into public life when Zionists in the United States persuaded him to use his abilities in fundraising to help the victims of Nazism settling in the Holy Land. Morgenthau in 1946 became the director general of the United Jewish Fund, which sought funds from private individuals to help the displaced people settling in what was then Palestine. It raised $124 million in 1947. The next year, when the new state of Israel was founded, it raised $148 million.[2]

His relative obscurity ended briefly in 1948 when Harry Dexter White was accused publicly of being a Soviet spy. Two former Communists, Whittaker Chambers and Elizabeth Bentley, testified before the House Un-American Activities Committee that White had delivered to them classified information while he worked at the Treasury. White vehemently denied the charges and testified before the committee that they were false and he lived by the American credos of freedom, liberty, and the capitalist system. Three days after the testimony, he suffered a fatal heart attack. Morgenthau, to the resentment of the White family, never rushed to his former lieutenant's defense and did not attend the funeral. White's family continued to deny the allegations for decades, though the release in 1997 of the Verona decrypts, the transcriptions of American taps of secret Soviet cables, established beyond a reasonable doubt that White did indeed give information to the Communist government.

Morgenthau's personal life was infused with melancholy after the war. His dearest friend, Franklin Roosevelt, had died in 1945, followed by the original Henry Morgenthau in 1946. Elinor Morgenthau grew frailer and finally passed away in 1949. Morgenthau chose as his second wife a French widow Marcelle Puthon Hirsch. The three Morgenthau children disliked her, and the marriage created a rift in the family until Henry Morgenthau Jr.'s death in 1967. His children provided a legacy that would make any man proud. Henry III became a successful television producer, and Joan a physician. Robert received a law degree after the war and carried on the family tradition of public service, serving as the district attorney for Manhattan for thirty-four years.

But Morgenthau had always hoped for a larger legacy. That's why he compiled one million pages of the Morgenthau Diaries, initiated biographical projects, and worked with historians like Arthur Schlesinger Jr. and John Morton Blum. He always had an eye on history, yet history has rarely returned his amorous gaze. He had the misfortune of competing for posterity's attention with such eminent contemporaries as Franklin and Eleanor Roosevelt, Winston Churchill, and Dwight Eisenhower, and men of action like General George Patton and Field Marshal Bernard Montgomery. Yet his body of achievement places him in the ranks of such giants, despite his obvious flaws.

Obviously, the Morgenthau Plan was bad policy and fortunately was never implemented. Germany has grown into a moderate, successful nation and Israel's strongest ally in Europe. Less obviously, Morgenthau must accept some blame for the failed economic policies of the Roosevelt administration, especially in the 1930s. As secretary of the Treasury, Henry Morgenthau Jr. produced a punitive fiscal framework from 1934 to about 1940 that discouraged private investment, added virtually no industrial capacity to the economy, and perpetuated high unemployment. The excess-profits tax, which starved the economy of investment, originated in his department. The best that could be said of his efforts before the war is that he frequently—though not always—muted the liberal excesses of Roosevelt and the New Dealers and scored several scattered triumphs in exchange-rate policy. Working with John Hanes, he tried to reform the tax system, but their efforts were diminished by the zeal of the New Dealers.

He often engaged in the class warfare that epitomized the worst aspects of the New Deal. He understood the need to develop business as the engine of a healthy economy, especially during a war. But too often this rational economic axiom was lost when he was swept up in the antibusiness ethos of the administration. This was particularly troublesome during the war, when the Roosevelt circle's suspicion of business interfered with the smooth operation of the War Department.

He had blind spots in foreign policy. He trusted the Soviet Union— even during Stalin's tenure—far more than he should have. And he was never able to fully accept the rot at the core of the government of Chiang Kai-shek, which drained US coffers of hundreds of millions of dollars. (Ironically, one of the finest chronicles of the Chinese government's corruption was penned by Morgenthau's own niece, the historian Barbara Tuchman, in her 1972 Pulitzer Prize winner *Stilwell and the American Experience in China, 1911–45.*)

Those were legitimate marks against Morgenthau, which should not be overlooked. Yet we should correct the criticisms he did not deserve and applaud his accomplishments that were too quickly forgotten. The most unfair slight against the man was that he was a yes-man to Roosevelt. The record shows he frequently stood up to his boss—courageously so, because Roosevelt had the power to devastate Morgenthau with his disapproval.

Morgenthau's record in prosecuting the war was exemplary. He consistently fought for military efficiency and often steered the president away from economic disaster. It's been all but forgotten that Morgenthau led the airplane program for about two years. In that time, US aircraft production rose from 2,141 units in 1939 to 19,443 in 1941. More important, Morgenthau took the initial steps to increase machine-tool production, bring in foreign orders and investment, and enlist private manufacturers. The result was that airplane production in the United States peaked at 96,318 in 1944. In that year, the Allies (including those receiving aid from the United States) produced 165,000 aircraft compared with 69,000 by the Axis.[3] Morgenthau understood the importance of industrial power in modern warfare. "Any country's war potential these days can be measured in its heavy industries much more accurately than by the size of its army, navy, and air force at any given moment," he wrote in his 1945 book, *Germany Is Our Problem*.[4] And no one during World War II worked more successfully to convert America's industrial might into military power.

Second, he was the essential link in helping the United Kingdom tap into this American industrial might in 1940 and 1941. It's largely recognized that securing American aid was Churchill's greatest foreign-policy objective, and Morgenthau aided the task immeasurably. He worked with Arthur Purvis to channel arms to Britain, which received a substantial portion of American output. Then he pushed to improve the efficiency and maintain the funding of the lend-lease program. The British Empire is estimated to have received $30.1 billion in lend-lease deliveries between 1941 and 1945, or about 60 percent of the total lend-lease deliveries.[5] To put that in perspective, $30 billion was about 15 percent of the American GDP in 1943. Converted to sterling, it averaged almost £1.9 billion per year over four years, or equivalent to almost 30 percent of the total expenditures by the British government in 1942 to 1945.[6] Morgenthau was an essential cog in the machinery that kept Britain fighting, especially through its most critical phase in 1940 to 1942.

He raised the money to fight the most mechanized war the world had ever seen. Estimates of the cost of the US war effort vary, but in 2010 the Congressional Research Service produced a paper showing the total military costs of the war between 1941 and 1945 were $296 billion at the time, or $4.1 trillion in 2010 US dollars. Obviously that figure understates the total because the war expenditures began before the United States officially entered the war in December 1941. Even at $4 trillion, the US war effort was very likely the largest economic program in the history of the world. The only US military event that could compare was the actions in Iraq, Afghanistan, and other countries following the terrorist actions of September 11, 2001, which totaled $1.15 trillion in 2010 dollars.[7] The economic stimulus package of 2009 (including the Troubled Asset Relief Program, most of which was repaid) was about $1.5 trillion. The cost in 2010 dollars of putting a man on the moon was about $165 billion; of the Marshall Plan, $117 billion; the Interstate Highway System, about $460 billion over thirty-five years. Some believe the cost of converting the world's energy complex from hydrocarbons to renewables may exceed the cost of World War II, but that will be carried out by governments and industry around the world. The United States' Victory Program of 1939 to 1945 was undoubtedly the largest economic program ever, and the keystone in its structure was a dyslexic college dropout named Henry Morgenthau Jr.

Conservative contemporaries frequently complained that Morgenthau was too unsophisticated a financier to carry out such a task, but the evidence destroys this a theory. The tools needed to raise such huge amounts of money were simply taxation and a variety of bonds. No other financial mechanism could raise such vast sums of money. Morgenthau could have done a better job negotiating with Congress, but the wartime boom still produced an increase of seventeenfold in income tax revenue. The two main worries about Morgenthau's program were that it would be inflationary and would generate higher interest rates. Consumer-price inflation peaked at about 10.8 percent in 1942 then trended downward.[8] Throughout the war-bond program, interest rates were consistently held comfortably below 3 percent—a staggering achievement, considering the amount of money the Treasury had to raise. When the *New York Times* summed up Morgenthau's career in August 1945, it was muted in its praise, noting mainly that he conducted himself with consistent rectitude. But it also noted that his Treasury had to raise volumes of money that had previously been unimaginable: "The machinery set up to handle millions of dollars has to deal with billions."[9] Tax revenue rose from $7 billion in 1940 to $53.2 billion in 1945. During that time, individual income tax revenue rose from $2 billion to $34.4 billion, and tens of millions of citizens paid taxes for the first time, broadening the financing of government.[10] The war-bond program, including the eighth bond drive that took place after Morgenthau resigned, raised more than $156 billion, about four times the total government debt in 1940. Simple logic dictates that an issuer could only raise such unprecedented amounts of money by offering higher interest rates. But the Treasury held interest rates down throughout the program. Had the buy-side of the bond markets been as worried about the Morgenthau Treasury's stewardship as his public critics, they would have demanded higher rates to compensate for the risks of lending money to such incompetents. Morgenthau was able to raise so much money so cheaply because his Treasury was masterful in the debt market.

That capitalized on the Allies' industrial advantage over the Axis, which was a prime factor in winning the war. It was not a given that Morgenthau would raise so much money so smoothly. He had to battle enemies in cabinet, in the administration, in Congress, and on Wall Street. He had to overcome the legacy of the New Deal and start from a weak industrial base. He was constantly drawn to other important duties, from running the Secret Service to negotiating occupation currencies, to freezing or releasing foreign funds.

Through it all, he was plagued by crippling migraine headaches and worries about his sons in combat zones and the failing health of his wife, parents, and best friend. And he was always beyond reproach in his ethics. His was a clarion voice for morality on such matters as the incarceration of Japanese Americans, the deal with Darlan, and aid to European refugees. Henry Morgenthau Jr. led a group that rescued 200,000 refugees, and he financed the destruction of the Third Reich. In the end, he was indeed the Jew who defeated Hitler.

ACKNOWLEDGMENTS

★ ★ ★

T his book would not have been possible without countless acts of kindness by a range of people. I know I will be omitting people who should be thanked here, but there are several individuals and groups that need to be recognized. Above all, I'd like to thank Steven L. Mitchell and his staff at Prometheus Books for their faith in this project. In particular, Mariel Bard's patience, knowledge, and insight greatly improved this book. And I wouldn't have connected with my publisher had it not been for the enduring support and patience of Roger Williams at New England Publishing Associates. I also had the honor of working with Roger's predecessors at NEPA, the late Edward W. Knappman and Elizabeth Knappman-Frost. A consummate gentleman, Ed was taken from us too soon, and I wish he had lived to read this book.

Robert Morgenthau was incredibly kind to take the time to grant an interview, and his insights and memories were invaluable. I would also like to thank Robert Morgenthau's assistant, Ida Van Lindt, Henry Morgenthau III, and the staff at Fishkill Farms.

Every modern study of Henry Morgenthau Jr. owes a huge debt of gratitude to the pioneering work of John Morton Blum, whose three-volume *From the Morgenthau Diaries* provides a magnificent roadmap to the labyrinthine Morgenthau archive. Blum spent a decade and a half going through these papers, and this book would not have been possible without his great organization and precision.

Robert Clark, Matthew Hanson, and the staff at the archives at the Franklin D. Roosevelt Presidential Library and Museum in Hyde Park, New York, were a tremendous help. I'd also like to thank Richard Cole, curator of the US Treasury, and Registrar Merrill Lavine for their assistance. Other librarians and archivists that aided this project included: Karen Smith, Killam Memorial Library, Dalhousie University; Barry Cahill, Public Archives of Nova Scotia; Clare Kavanagh, The Library, Nuffield College, Oxford; the staffs of the New York Public Library, Forty-Second Street; and the Toronto Reference Library.

I'd also like to thank Craig Clemmer, the head of media relations at the Omni Mount Washington Resort, for an entertaining and fascinating tour of the site of the Bretton Woods Conference.

Dozens of friends, family members, and acquaintances have offered support, encouragement, and advice, including: Catharine Axley; Paul Bennett; Chris Bucci; Stephen Patrick Clare; Stephen Harding, Max Lewkowicz, Melissa Ladenheim, Alison MacKeen, James Moreira, John Morris, Ed Paisley, Scott Shapiro, Robert Teitelman. Many thanks to them all.

My family members have shown the patience of Job as their husband or father has used his vacation time to sit in libraries in New York State to feed his weird obsession. Many thanks to Cat, Scott, and above all my greatest friend, editor, and love, Carol.

NOTES

★ ★ ★

Henry Morgenthau Jr. donated his papers, comprising more than one million pages of documents, to the Franklin D. Roosevelt Presidential Library and Museum in Hyde Park, NY. These documents, which are the principal sources of all Morgenthau studies, are classified in three different sets:

- The Morgenthau Diaries, which comprise Morgenthau's correspondence, Treasury reports, and transcripts of phone conversations and meetings during his tenure as secretary of the Treasury. The Morgenthau Diaries are classified by the book and page number.
- The Morgenthau Papers, which comprise the family's personal papers. The Morgenthau papers are classified by the box in which the documents are contained.
- The Presidential Diaries, which are a condensed grouping of many of the most important documents of Morgenthau's tenure as secretary of the Treasury. The Presidential Diaries are classified by the date on which the document was written.

As well as the Morgenthau documents, this work has relied extensively on the papers of Eleanor Roosevelt, which is also found in the Roosevelt Library. Like the Morgenthau Papers, they are arranged according to the box in which the documents are found.

PROLOGUE

1. Henry Morgenthau III, *Mostly Morgenthaus: A Family History* (New York: Ticknor and Fields, 1991), pp. 286–90.

2. Morgenthau Papers, box 829.

3. Elinor Morgenthau, letter to her parents, August 10, 1938, Morgenthau Papers, box 452.

4. Henry Morgenthau Sr., letter to Henry Morgenthau Jr., July 24, 1938, Morgenthau Papers, box 442.

5. Henry Morgenthau Jr., letter to Henry Morgenthau Sr., August 2, 1938, Morgenthau Papers, box 442.

6. Robert Morgenthau, interview with the author, October 1, 2013.

7. Morgenthau Papers, box 829.

8. "Rome Irked by Jewish League," *New York Times*, October 19, 1938, p. 10.

9. Conrad Black, *Franklin Delano Roosevelt: Champion of Freedom* (New York: Public Affairs, 2003), p. 344.

10. Paul Kennedy, *The Rise and Fall of the Great Powers* (New York: Random House, 1987), p. 355.

11. Harry Dexter Whiter, letter to Henry Morgenthau Jr., May 1, 1941, Morgenthau Papers, box 453.

12. "Table 1.1—Summary of Receipts, Outlays, and Surpluses or Deficits, 1789–2009," Office of Management and Budget, http://www.whitehouse.gov/omb/budget/historicals (accessed July 21, 2014).

CHAPTER ONE. BATTLING THE AGGRESSORS

1. Morgenthau Diaries, book 145, p. 259.

2. Arthur M. Schlesinger Jr., *Journals 1952–2000* (New York: Penguin, 2007), p. 160.

3. Joseph Alsop and Robert Kintner, "Henny Penny: Farmer at the Treasury," *Saturday Evening Post*, April 1, 1939, p. 8.

4. "$51,000,000,000-a-Year Man," *Time*, January 25, 1943, pp. 18–20.

5. John Kennedy Ohl, *Hugh S. Johnson and the New Deal* (DeKalb: Northern Illinois University Press, 1985), p. 291.

6. "Stands by His Shower," *New York Times*, December 15, 1933, p. 7.

7. Morgenthau Papers, box 519; Henry Morgenthau III, *Mostly Morgenthaus: A Family History* (New York: Ticknor and Fields, 1991), p. 297.

8. Morgenthau Papers, box 99.

9. Morgenthau Diaries, book 145, p. 260.

10. Ibid., p. 262.

11. Morgenthau Papers, box 673.

12. "President Sounds Cabinet on Crisis," *New York Times*, September 17, 1938, p. 2.

13. Cordell Hull, *The Memoirs of Cordell Hull* (New York: MacMillan, 1948), p. 207.

14. Morgenthau Diaries, book 145, pp. 263–67.

15. Ibid.

16. Ibid., pp. 275–85.

17. Ibid., p. 288.

18. Morgenthau, *Mostly Morgenthaus*, p. 214.

19. Ibid., p. 47.

20. "High-Priced Real Estate," *New York Times*, May 27, 1891, p. 8.

21. "Big Realty Merger Plans Developed," *New York Times*, August 1, 1902, p. 1.

22. Henry Morgenthau Jr., letter to parents, January 28, 1906, Morgenthau Papers, box 442.

23. "One of Two of a Kind," *Fortune*, May 1934, pp. 61 ff.

24. Morgenthau Papers, box 979.

25. Morgenthau, *Mostly Morgenthaus*, p. 257.

26. Morgenthau Papers, box 979.

27. Morgenthau Papers, box 442; "Hatry Group Held in $50,000,000 Crash," *New York Times*, September 22, 1939, p. 6.

28. Henry Morgenthau Sr., letter to Henry Morgenthau Jr., January 1, 1939, Morgenthau Papers, box 442.

29. Morgenthau, *Mostly Morgenthaus*, p. 250.

30. Morgenthau Papers, box 513.

31. Frank R. Kent, The Great Game of Politics, *Wall Street Journal*, March 6, 1939, p. 4, and March 28, 1939, p. 4.

32. Morgenthau Diaries, book 155, pp. 84–85.

33. John Morton Blum, *From the Morgenthau Diaries: Years of Crisis, 1928–1938* (Boston: Houghton Mifflin, 1959), p. 49.

34. Ibid., pp. 69–70.

35. "One of Two of a Kind," p. 61.

36. John Boettiger, "Morgenthau Jr. Will Be Acting Treasury Head," *Chicago Tribune*, November 16, 1933, p. 1.

37. "$51,000,000,000-a-Year Man," pp. 18–20.

38. *Chicago Tribune*, January 7, 1934, p. 5.

39. Carlisle Bargeron, "Along the Potomac," *Washington Post*, November 22, 1933, p. 6.

40. Presidential Diaries, November 13, 1938.

41. Harold L. Ickes, *The Secret Diary of Harold L. Ickes, Vol. II: The Inside Struggle 1936–1939* (New York: Simon and Schuster, 1954), p. 272.

42. "Levy on Profits Halts Expansion," *New York Times*, August 27, 1937, p. 24.

43. "Herman Oliphant of Treasury Dies," *New York Times*, January 12, 1938, p. 19.

44. Joseph Alsop and Robert Kintner, "The Great World Money Play," *Saturday Evening Post*, April 8, 1939, p. 74.

45. Bernard Kilgore, "Secretary Morgenthau," *Wall Street Journal*, November 20, 1937, p. 4.

46. Blum, *From the Morgenthau Diaries: Years of Crisis*, pp. 420–21.

47. Presidential Diaries, April 13, 1939; see also ibid., pp. 424–25.

48. Blum, *From the Morgenthau Diaries: Years of Crisis*, p. 205.

49. Morgenthau Diaries, book 141, p. 115.

50. Ibid., pp. 176, 182.

51. Morgenthau Diaries, book 146, p. 284.

52. Jim Bishop, *FDR's Last Year, April 1944–April 1945* (New York: William Morrow, 1974), p. 40.

53. Morgenthau Diaries, book 146, pp. 108–37.

54. Ibid., p. 106.

55. Ibid., p. 254.

56. Ibid.

57. "Britain-Germany: Tit for Tat?" *Time*, October 28, 1934, pp. 18–20.

58. Morgenthau Diaries, book 150, p. 337.

59. Morgenthau Diaries, book 146, p. 279.

CHAPTER TWO. THE FRENCH MISSION

1. Morgenthau Diaries, book 146, pp. 279–80.

2. L. H. Robbins, "Financial Guide of Our Recovery Tsar," *New York Times*, January 14, 1934; Henry Morgenthau III, *Mostly Morgenthaus: A Family History* (New York: Ticknor and Fields, 1991), p. 299.

3. Morgenthau Diaries, book 146, pp. 282–83.

4. Ibid.

5. Morgenthau Diaries, book 151, p. 353.

6. Ibid., p. 166.

7. Corinne Reid Frazier, "Two Wives of Cabinet Members," *Christian Science Monitor*, found in the Morgenthau Papers, box 511.

8. Morgenthau, *Mostly Morgenthaus*, pp. 220–37.

9. Morgenthau Papers, box 452.

10. Morgenthau Papers, box 512.

11. Morgenthau, *Mostly Morgenthaus*, pp. 257–60; Morgenthau Papers, box 512.

12. "On the Distaff Side of Cabinet," *New York Times*, January 9, 1938, p. D5.

13. Ibid.

14. "Morgenthau Hits Liberty Ban Here," *New York Times*, June 17, 1938, p. 22.

15. Morgenthau Diaries, book 171, pp. 13–14.

16. Morgenthau Diaries, book 149, pp. 213–14.

17. Morgenthau Diaries, book 215, p. 33.

18. Morgenthau Diaries, book 147, pp. 185–204.

19. Ibid.

20. Ibid.

21. Morgenthau Diaries, book 150, pp. 10, 28.

22. J. Fred Essary, "Roosevelt Denounces Nazis," *Baltimore Sun*, November 16, 1938, p. 1; Bertram D. Hulen, "Roosevelt Condemns Nazi Outbreak," *New York Times*, November 16, 1938, p. 1.

23. Robert N. Rosen, *Saving the Jews: Franklin D. Roosevelt and the Holocaust* (New York: Thunder's Mouth Press, 2006), p. 440.

24. Sander L. Gilman and Steven T. Katz, eds., *Anti-Semitism in Times of Crisis* (New York: New York University Press, 1991), p. 221.

25. Adam Cohen, *Nothing to Fear: FDR's Inner Circle and the Hundred Days That Created Modern America* (New York: Penguin, 2009), p. 520.

26. Henry Morgenthau Sr., letter to Henry Morgenthau Jr., September 29, 1937, Morgenthau Papers, box 442.

27. Morgenthau, *Mostly Morgenthaus*, p. xiv.

28. "Former State Employee Raked over the Fire," *Troy Observer*, December 20, 1931, found in Morgenthau Papers, box 452.

29. John Morton Blum, *From the Morgenthau Diaries: Years of Crisis, 1928–1938* (Boston: Houghton Mifflin, 1959), p. 241.

30. Morgenthau Diaries, book 151, pp. 32–34.

31. Morgenthau Diaries, book 152, pp. 21–22, 88; Morgenthau Diaries, book 155, pp. 41–44.

32. Morgenthau Diaries, book 150, pp. 338–41.

33. Ibid., p. 347.

34. Morgenthau Diaries, book 146, pp. 394–98.

35. Morgenthau Diaries, book 147, p. 436.

36. Morgenthau Diaries, book 150, p. 200.

37. Morgenthau Diaries, book 172, p. 65.

38. Morgenthau Diaries, book 180, p. 223.

39. Morgenthau Diaries, book 150, p. 47; Morgenthau Diaries, book 151, p. 123; Morgenthau Diaries, book 153, p. 364.

40. Morgenthau Diaries, book 172, pp. 12–15.

41. Ibid.

42. John Morton Blum, *From the Morgenthau Diaries: Years of Urgency, 1938–1941* (Boston: Houghton Mifflin, 1965), pp. 68–69.

43. Morgenthau Diaries, book 172, p. 12.

44. Ibid., p. 16.

45. Morgenthau Diaries, book 157, p. 230.

46. Morgenthau Diaries, book 172, p. 27.

47. Ibid., pp. 31–32.

48. Ibid., pp. 38–54.

49. Ibid.

50. Ibid., p. 57.

51. Ibid., p. 62.

52. Ibid., pp. 78, 80.

53. Ibid., pp. 80–87.

54. Morgenthau Diaries, book 159, pp.7–11.

55. Ibid., pp. 102–20.

56. "Daniel Bell, 80, Retired Banker," *New York Times*, October 5, 1971, p. 44.

57. "Big Increase in the National Defense Program Marks the New Roosevelt Budget," *New York Times*, January 6, 1939, p. 13.

58. Paul Fredericksen, "Hanes—Student of Taxes," *New York Times*, April 9, 1939, p. SM2.

59. Morgenthau Diaries, book 159, p. 219.

60. Morgenthau Diaries, book 160, pp.1–17.

61. Morgenthau Diaries, book 173, pp. 9–10.

62. Ibid., pp. 11–22.

63. Ibid., p.39.

64. Ibid., p. 46, 49.

65. Ibid., pp. 62, 76–142.

CHAPTER THREE. THE GATHERING STORM

1. Morgenthau Diaries, book 163, pp. 185–88.

2. Ibid., p. 183; Morgenthau Diaries, book 173, pp. 69–71.

3. Morgenthau Diaries, book 173, pp. 66–68.

4. "Roosevelt Lets French Buy Planes," *New York Times*, January 28, 1939, p. 1.

5. Morgenthau Diaries, book 173, pp. 76–142.

6. Presidential Diaries, July 31, 1939.

7. Morgenthau Diaries, book 164, pp. 133–50.

8. Ibid., pp. 47–51.

9. Cordell Hull, *The Memoirs of Cordell Hull* (New York: MacMillan, 1948), p. 207.

10. Morgenthau Diaries, book 138, p. 152.

11. Herbert Levy, *Henry Morgenthau, Jr.: The Remarkable Life of FDR's Secretary of the Treasury* (New York: Skyhorse Publishing, 2010), p. 350.

12. Henry Morgenthau III, *Mostly Morgenthaus: A Family History* (New York: Ticknor and Fields, 1991), p. 313.

13. Morgenthau Diaries, book 165, pp. 184–85.

14. Morgenthau Diaries, book 160, p. 1.

15. "National Debt Nears the 45 Billion Limit," *New York Times*, January 6, 1939, p. 13.

16. Morgenthau Diaries, book 165, pp. 128–29.

17. Morgenthau Diaries, book 182, pp. 9, 178.

18. Ibid., p. 135.

19. Ibid., p. 191.

20. "U.S. Policies Block Upturn, N.A.M. Finds," *New York Herald Tribune*, February 12, 1939, p. 13.

21. "Mr. Morgenthau's Pledge," *Chicago Tribune*, February 28, 1939, p. 12.

22. John Hanes Jr., letter to Elinor Morgenthau, September 26, 1940, Morgenthau Papers, box 116; Henry Morgenthau Jr., letter to Henry Morgenthau Sr., May 3, 1939, Morgenthau Papers, box 442.

23. Morgenthau Diaries, book 189, p. 59.

24. Morgenthau Diaries, book 154, pp. 349–50.

25. Ibid.

26. Morgenthau Diaries, book 168, pp. 27–31.

27. Ibid., p. 31.

28. Ibid., pp. 29–31.

29. John Morton Blum, *From the Morgenthau Diaries: Years of Urgency, 1938–1941* (Boston: Houghton Mifflin, 1965), pp. 79–80.

30. Morgenthau Diaries, book 200, p. 100.

31. Morgenthau Diaries, book 142, p. 176.

32. Ibid., pp. 269–83.

33. Presidential Diaries, April 11, 1939.

34. Blum, *From the Morgenthau Diaries: Years of Urgency*, pp. 83–86.

35. Morgenthau Diaries, book 170, pp. 263–67.

36. Morgenthau Diaries, book 169, p. 124.

37. Morgenthau Diaries, book 178, pp. 82–128.

38. Morgenthau Diaries, book 168, pp. 27–31.

39. "The Nation," *New York Times*, March 12, 1939, p. 63.

40. Arthur Krock, "New Deal Die-Hards Fight for Survival," *New York Times*, March 12, 1939, p. 65.

41. Walter Lippmann, "The Necessity for American Recovery," *New York Herald Tribune*, March 7, 1939, found in Morgenthau Diaries, book 168, p. 111.

42. Frank R. Kent, The Great Game of Politics, *Wall Street Journal*, March 28, 1939, p. 4.

43. Paul Fredericksen, "Hanes—Student of Taxes," *New York Times*, April 9, 1939, p. SM2; Turner Catledge, "Does It Contribute to Recovery?," *New York Times*, June 4, 1939, p. SM2.

44. Morgenthau Diaries, book 188, pp. 137–38.

45. Catledge, "Does It Contribute to Recovery?," p. SM2.

46. Morgenthau Diaries, book 187, p. 140.

47. Ibid., p. 204.

48. Morgenthau Diaries, book 188, pp. 170–89.

49. Morgenthau Diaries, book 189, pp. 39–61.

50. Frank R. Kent, The Great Game of Politics, *Wall Street Journal*, May 12, 1939, p. 4.

51. Morgenthau Diaries, book 189, pp. 39–61.

52. "Morgenthau Vexed at President over Tax Parley Slight," *Chicago Tribune*, May 17, 1939, p. 27.

53. Presidential Diaries, May 16, 1939.

54. Morgenthau Diaries, book 189, p. 190.

55. Ibid.

56. Morgenthau Papers, boxes 287 and 332.

57. Ibid., box 618.

58. Ibid., box 769.

59. Presidential Diaries, May 18, 1939.

60. Frank R. Kent, The Great Game of Politics, *Wall Street Journal*, May 12, 1939, p. 4.

61. Arthur Krock, In the Nation, *New York Times*, December 26, 1939, p. 17.

62. Morgenthau Diaries, book 192, p. 11.

63. Frank R. Kent, The Great Game of Politics, *Wall Street Journal*, June 8, 1939, p. 4.

64. "Protocol Rules at State Dinner," *New York Times*, June 9, 1939, p. 9; "King Tries Hot Dogs and Asks for More," *New York Times*, June 11, 1939, p. 1.

65. Morgenthau Papers, box 175.

66. Morgenthau Diaries, book 194, pp. 1–5.

67. Ibid., p. 114.

CHAPTER FOUR. THE PHONY WAR

1. Presidential Diaries, August 31, 1939.

2. Ibid., September 1, 1939.

3. "Morgenthau Busy after Rush Home," *New York Times*, September 5, 1939, p. 26.

4. Arthur Krock, In the Nation, *New York Times*, August 30, 1939, p. 14.

5. "Morgenthau on Way back on Coast Guard Cutter," *New York Times*, August 30, 1939, p. 4; Morgenthau Diaries, book 209, p. 176; Robert Morgenthau, interview with the author, October 1, 2013.

6. Presidential Diaries, October 5, 1939.

7. Ibid., September 11, 1939.

8. Ibid., September 18, 1939; Morgenthau Diaries, book 210, p. 12.

9. "Army & Navy: Scandalous Spats," *Time*, October 9, 1939, p. 16.

10. Morgenthau Diaries, book 210, p. 224.

11. Presidential Diaries, September 18, 1939.

12. Ibid., October 14, 1939.

13. David M. Kennedy, ed., *The Library of Congress World War II Companion* (New York: Simon and Schuster, 2007), p. 202.

14. Presidential Diaries, October 6, 1939.

15. Morgenthau Diaries, book 221, p. 154.

16. John Morton Blum, *From the Morgenthau Diaries: Years of Urgency, 1938–1941* (Boston: Houghton Mifflin, 1965), p. 104.

17. Ibid., p. 103.

18. Morgenthau Diaries, book 209, pp. 140–42.

19. Ibid., p. 142.

20. Ibid., pp. 140, 178.

21. Blum, *From the Morgenthau Diaries: Years of Urgency*, p. 106.

22. Presidential Diaries, October 9, 1939.

23. Morgenthau Diaries, book 216, pp. 206a–206b.

24. Morgenthau Diaries, book 220, p. 132a.

25. Morgenthau Diaries, book 221, p. 365.

26. Ibid., p. 150.

27. Blum, *From the Morgenthau Diaries: Years of Urgency*, p. 110.

28. Morgenthau Diaries, book 222, p. 18.

29. Morgenthau Diaries, book 225, p. 41.

30. Presidential Diaries, December 12, 1939.

31. Morgenthau Papers, boxes 106, 166, and 237.

32. Morgenthau Diaries, book 216, p. 206.

33. Stephen Wise, letter to Henry Morgenthau Jr., December 12, 1939, Morgenthau Papers, box 106.

34. Presidential Diaries, September 18, 1939.

35. Frank R. Kent, The Great Game of Politics, *Wall Street Journal*, March 10, 1939, p. 4.

36. Morgenthau Diaries, book 87, pp. 421–55.

37. Presidential Diaries, September 25, 1939.

38. "Tax on Small Man Sought by Eccles," Associated Press, found in *New York Times*, November 9, 1939.

39. Presidential Diaries, November 21, 1939.

40. "Wall Street Comment," *New York Herald Tribune*, December 6, 1938, found in Morgenthau Diaries, book 155, p. 46.

41. Presidential Diaries, October 9, 1939; "Treasury to Lift Its Bill Offering," *New York Times*, October 10, 1939, p. 38.

42. Presidential Diaries, November 21, 1939.

43. "Treasury Offers $500,000,000 of 2s" *New York Times*, November 28, 1939, p. 37.

44. Morgenthau Diaries, book 212, p. 47.

45. Ibid., p. 216e.

46. Presidential Diaries, September 20, 1939.

47. Ibid., September 25, 1939.

48. Ibid.

49. Ibid., December 12, 1941.

50. Ibid.

51. Ibid.

52. Ibid.

53. Arthur Krock, In the Nation, *New York Times*, December 26, 1939, p. 17.

54. Frank R. Kent, The Great Game of Politics, *Wall Street Journal*, December 26, 1939, p. 4.

55. "Republic Gains in Congress Seen," *New York Times*, October 24, 1940, found in Morgenthau Papers, box 116.

CHAPTER FIVE. THE ASSISTANT PRESIDENT

1. Harold L. Ickes, *The Secret Diary of Harold L. Ickes: The First Thousand Days 1933–1936* (New York: Simon and Schuster, 1953), p. 700.

2. "Army & Navy: Scandalous Spats," *Time*, October 9, 1939, p. 16.

3. Morgenthau Diaries, book 221, pp. 358–64.

4. Morgenthau Diaries, book 228, p. 200.

5. John Morton Blum, *From the Morgenthau Diaries: Years of Urgency, 1938–1941* (Boston: Houghton Mifflin, 1965), p. 114.

6. Morgenthau Diaries, book 212, pp. 23, 27.

7. Blum, *From the Morgenthau Diaries: Years of Urgency*, p. 112.

8. Presidential Diaries, January 24, 1940.

9. Blum, *From the Morgenthau Diaries: Years of Urgency*, pp. 123–25.

10. "Elevated by Treasury," *New York Times*, January 18, 1940, p. 40.

11. Presidential Diaries, January 25, 1940.

12. Franklin D. Roosevelt, "Annual Budget Message," January 3, 1940, from *The American Presidency Project*, John T. Woolley and Gerhard Peters, http://www.presidency.ucsb.edu/ws/?pid=15922 (accessed August 14, 2014).

13. Presidential Diaries, January 8, 1940.

14. Ibid.

15. Morgenthau Diaries, book 235, pp. 96–101.

16. Morgenthau Diaries, book 237, pp. 2–4.

17. Ibid., pp. 153–55, 284–88.

18. "Plane Purchasing up to Morgenthau," *New York Times*, January 22, 1940, p. 3.

19. Blum, *From the Morgenthau Diaries: Years of Urgency*, p. 108.

20. "Morgenthau Talks Machine Tool and Arms Coordination," *Wall Street Journal*, February 1, 1940, p. 3.

21. Morgenthau Diaries, book 238, pp. 185, 295–302, 357–61.

22. "Morgenthau Commends Handling of Aircraft Expansion Programs," *Wall Street Journal*, February 6, 1940, p. 3.

23. Presidential Diaries, March 3, 1940.

24. Franklin D. Roosevelt, "Excerpts from the Press Conference," March 19, 1940, from Woolley and Peters, *American Presidency Project*, http://www.presidency.ucsb.edu/ws/?pid=15925 (accessed August 14, 2014).

25. "The Best Bargain We Can Jolly Well Make," *Fortune*, April 1940, p. 70.

26. Presidential Diaries, March 4, 1940.

27. Ibid.

28. Ibid.

29. Ibid., March 12, 1940.

30. Ibid.

31. Ibid., March 12, 1940.

32. Ibid.

33. Hanson W. Baldwin, "Plane Exports Stir Capital Tempest," *New York Times*, March 13, 1940, p. 8.

34. "Plane Exports Stir Capital Tempest," *New York Times*, March 13, 1940, p. 8;

"Treasury Denies War Buying Hitch," *New York Times*, March 19, 1940, p. 11; "President Praises Air Export Policy," *New York Times*, March 20, 1940, p. 13; "Roosevelt Stand Halts Air Inquiry," *New York Times*, March 12, 1940, p. 12.

35. Associated Press, "Allies Contract for 1500 Planes," found in *New York Times*, April 19, 1940, p. 8.

36. Morgenthau Diaries, book 234, pp. 208–209.

37. Presidential Diaries, March 19, 1940.

38. Ibid., March 21, 1940.

39. Ibid., March 31, 1940.

40. Ibid., April 9, 10, and 16, 1940.

41. "Mrs. Morgenthau Jr. in Hospital," *New York Times*, April 25, 1940, p. 16.

42. Presidential Diaries, April 18, 1940.

43. Ibid., April 29, 1940.

44. Ibid., May 10, 1940.

45. Ibid.

46. Ibid., May 13, 1940.

47. Ibid.

48. Morgenthau Diaries, book 262, pp. 172–76, 257.

49. Martin Gilbert, *Second World War* (London: Stoddard, 1989), p. 64.

50. Franklin D. Roosevelt, "Message to Congress on Appropriations for National Defense," May 16, 1940, from Woolley and Peters, *American Presidency Project*, http://www.presidency.ucsb.edu/ws/?pid=15954 (accessed August 14, 2014).

51. Morgenthau Diaries, book 263, p. 321.

52. Presidential Diaries, May 16, 1940.

CHAPTER SIX. AIDING BRITAIN

1. "Confusion Marks Battle of France," *New York Times*, May 21, 1940, p. 2.

2. Presidential Diaries, May 20, 1940.

3. Ibid.

4. Ibid., May 16, 1940.

5. Ibid.

6. Raymond Clapper, "Western Isolationists Altering Defense Views," found in *Syracuse Herald-Journal*, June 17, 1940, p. 26.

7. "Reaction Is Varied to Lindbergh Talk," *New York Times*, May 21, 1940, p. 12.

8. Presidential Diaries, May 20, 1940.

9. Louis P. Lochner, "On the Attack," Associated Press, found in *New York Times*, May 21, 1940, p. 1.

10. "Pepper Urges Sale of Our War Planes," *New York Times*, May 22, 1940, p. 10.

11. Arthur Krock, "National Unity a Fact on the Security Front," *New York Times*, May 26, 1940, p. E3.

12. Presidential Diaries, May 20, 1940.

13. Morgenthau Diaries, book 264, pp. 244–47.

14. Morgenthau Diaries, book 263, pp. 297–98.

15. "Senate Rushes Action," *New York Times*, May 24, 1940, p. 1.

16. John Morton Blum, *From the Morgenthau Diaries: Years of Urgency, 1938–1941* (Boston: Houghton Mifflin, 1965), p. 157.

17. Morgenthau Diaries, book 266, pp. 281–83; Morgenthau Diaries, book 267, pp. 1–4.

18. "Tax Rise Essential, Says Morgenthau," *New York Times*, June 1, 1940, p. 6.

19. "Aircraft Engine Makers Welcome Morgenthau Plan," *Wall Street Journal*, May 24, 1940, p. 3.

20. Presidential Diaries, June 19, 1940.

21. "Knudsen to Direct Defense Tooling," *New York Times*, June 4, 1940, p. 12; "Mass Building of Plane Engines by Automobile Industry Being Studied," *Wall Street Journal*, June 4, 1940, p. 1.

22. Morgenthau Diaries, book 268, pp. 82–94, 218–19.

23. Walter Lippmann, "Western Isolationists Altering Defense Views," June 3, 1940, found in *Salt Lake Tribune*, p. 5.

24. William L. Langer and S. Everett Gleason, *The Undeclared War 1940–1941: The World Crisis and American Foreign Policy* (New York: Harper and Brothers, 1953), p. 185.

25. Frank R. Kent, The Great Game of Politics, June 6, 1940, found in *Charleston Daily Mail*, p. 6.

26. Ibid.

27. Presidential Diaries, July 25, 1940.

28. Ibid., June 9, 1940.

29. Ibid., June 10, 1940.

30. H. Duncan Hall, *North American Supply* (London: HMSO, 1955), p. 77.

31. Ibid., p. 73.

32. Ibid.

33. Ibid., p. 76.

34. Ibid.

35. Morgenthau Diaries, book 283, pp. 184–85.

36. Presidential Diaries, July 24 and 25, 1940.

37. Henry Morgenthau Sr., letter to Henry Morgenthau Jr., July 21, 1940, Morgenthau Papers, box 442.

38. Herbert Morrison, "The Munitions Situation," report to the British War Cabinet, August 29, 1940, p. 3, found in the Public Records Office, London.

39. Ibid.

40. Ibid., p. 4.

41. Morgenthau Diaries, book 267, pp. 165–67.

42. Morgenthau Diaries, book 265, pp. 83–89.

43. Blum, *From the Morgenthau Diaries: Years of Urgency*, p. 155.

44. Morrison, "Munitions Situation," p. 2.

45. Morgenthau Diaries, book 269, p. 58.

46. Presidential Diaries, June 18, 1940.

47. Blum, *From the Morgenthau Diaries: Years of Urgency*, pp. 163, 164.

48. Presidential Diaries, July 17, 1940; Blum, *From the Morgenthau Diaries: Years of Urgency*, p. 170.

49. Blum, *From the Morgenthau Diaries: Years of Urgency*, p. 172.

50. Ibid., p. 349.

51. Ibid., pp. 350–51.

52. Morgenthau Diaries, book 285, pp. 317 ff.

53. Blum, *From the Morgenthau Diaries: Years of Urgency*, p. 173.

54. Morgenthau Diaries, book 286, pp. 122–26.

55. Ibid., p. 284.

56. Morgenthau Diaries, book 287, pp. 153–64.

57. Morgenthau Diaries, book 287, p. 173.

58. Blum, *From the Morgenthau Diaries: Years of Urgency*, p. 353.

59. Edgar Snow, "Showdown in the Pacific," *Saturday Evening Post*, May 31, 1941, pp. 27 ff.

60. Henry Morgenthau III, *Mostly Morgenthaus: A Family History* (New York: Ticknor and Fields, 1991), p. 292.

61. Presidential Diaries, July 12, 1940.

62. Eleanor Roosevelt, letters to Robert Morgenthau, October 5 and November 19, 1940, Eleanor Roosevelt Papers, box 723.

63. "Amherst Aids Campaign," *New York Times*, November 1, 1940, p. 26.

64. Eleanor Roosevelt, letter to Elinor Morgenthau, December 19, 1940, Eleanor Roosevelt Papers, box 723.

65. "Party for Joan," *Time*, January 6, 1941.

66. Joan Morgenthau, letter to Eleanor Roosevelt, December 28, 1940, Morgenthau Papers, box 723.

67. Henry Morgenthau Sr., letter to Henry Morgenthau Jr., July 11, 1940, Morgenthau Papers, box 442.

68. S. L. Woolf, "Morgenthau at 85 Recalls a Full Life," *New York Times*, April 27, 1941, p. SM13.

69. Elinor Morgenthau, letter to Eleanor Roosevelt, undated, Morgenthau Papers, box 723.

70. Morgenthau, *Mostly Morgenthaus*, pp. 251, 304–306.

71. Geoffrey T. Hellman, "Any Bonds Today? Part II," *New Yorker*, January 29, 1944, p. 30.

72. "Guards Irk Morgenthau," *New York Times*, August 9, 1940, p. 4.

73. Morgenthau Diaries, book 290, p. 35.

74. Presidential Diaries, August 16, 1940.

75. Ibid., September 19, 1940.

76. Blum, *From the Morgenthau Diaries: Years of Urgency*, pp. 184–85.

77. Ibid., p. 183.

78. Ibid., p. 187.

79. Ibid.

80. Morgenthau, *Mostly Morgenthaus*, p. 338.

81. Donald M. Nelson, *Arsenal of Democracy: The Story of American War Production* (New York: Harcourt, Brace, 1946), pp. 68–69.

82. Blum, *From the Morgenthau Diaries: Years of Urgency*, p. 187.

83. Presidential Diaries, October 27, 1940.

84. Blum, *From the Morgenthau Diaries: Years of Urgency*, pp. 193–95.

85. Ibid., p. 199.

86. Presidential Diaries, November 30, 1940.

87. Blum, *From the Morgenthau Diaries: Years of Urgency*, p. 203.

88. Turner Catledge, "British Loan Issue to Go to Congress," *New York Times*, December 12, 1940, p. 6.

89. Presidential Diaries, December 17, 1940.

CHAPTER SEVEN. LEND-LEASE

1. Presidential Diaries, December 17, 1940.

2. "Issue for Congress," *New York Times*, December 17, 1940, p. 8.

3. Ibid.

4. Frank L. Kluckhohn, "Roosevelt Would Lend Arms to Britain," *New York Times*, December 18, 1940, pp. 1, 4.

5. Ibid.

6. Morgenthau Diaries, book 344, pp. 91, 149–55.

7. John Morton Blum, *From the Morgenthau Diaries: Years of Urgency, 1938–1941* (Boston: Houghton Mifflin, 1965), pp. 212–17.

8. Ibid., p. 220.

9. Eleanor Roosevelt, letter to the Morgenthaus, January 13, 1938, Eleanor Roosevelt Papers, box 322.

10. Kluckhohn, "Roosevelt Would Lend Arms to Britain," p. 4.

11. "Treasury's Summary of Britain's Financial Position," *New York Times*, January 16, 1941, p. 10.

12. Blum, *From the Morgenthau Diaries: Years of Urgency*, p. 211.

13. Figures from "Government Spending in the US," www.usgovernmentspending.com (accessed August 16, 2014).

14. Blum, *From the Morgenthau Diaries: Years of Urgency*, pp. 219–20.

15. "The Congress: Matter of Faith," *Time*, January 27, 1941, p. 28.

16. Blum, *From the Morgenthau Diaries: Years of Urgency*, pp. 220–21.

17. Ibid., p. 222.

18. "The Congress: Matter of Faith," p. 28.

19. Blum, *From the Morgenthau Diaries: Years of Urgency*, pp. 227–29.

20. Presidential Diaries, February 10, 1941.

21. Morgenthau Diaries, book 376, p. 169.

22. Presidential Diaries, March 1, 1941.

23. Franklin D. Roosevelt, "Annual Budget Message," January 3, 1941, from *The American Presidency Project*, John T. Woolley and Gerhard Peters, http://www.presidency.ucsb.edu/ws/index.php?pid=16081&st=budget&st1=#ixzz1YsIaApNu (accessed August 16, 2014).

24. "Fiscal: Up the Rollercoaster," *Time*, January 21, 1941, p. 27.

25. Ibid.

26. Morgenthau Diaries, book 344, p. 28.

27. Morgenthau Diaries, book 177, pp. 87–88.

28. Presidential Diaries, January 22, 1941.

29. Morgenthau Diaries, book 352, pp. 159 ff.

30. "New Treasury Unit to Run Defense Issues, to Range from 25-Cent Stamps Upward," *New York Times*, February 28, 1941, p. 7.

31. Blum, *From the Morgenthau Diaries: Years of Urgency*, pp. 300, 302–303.

32. "U.S. Not to Be Bound by Money Parley, Morgenthau Says," *New York Times*, June 20, 1944, p. 1.

33. Blum, *From the Morgenthau Diaries: Years of Urgency*, p. 301.

34. Ibid., p. 303.

35. Henry Morgenthau III, *Mostly Morgenthaus: A Family History* (New York: Ticknor and Fields, 1991), p. 307.

36. Morgenthau Papers, box 277.

37. Morgenthau Diaries, book 155, p. 75.

38. Morgenthau Diaries, book 188, pp. 137–38.

39. Morgenthau Diaries, book 189, p. 184.

40. Morgenthau Papers, box 277.

41. Elliott V. Bell, "Framing New Tax Bill Is Two-Fold Problem," *New York Times*, April 27, 1941, p. E12.

42. "Saving Being Stressed in Defense Financing," *New York Times*, May 4, 1941, p. E10.

43. Blum, *From the Morgenthau Diaries: Years of Urgency*, pp. 304–305.

44. "Time for a Tax Program," *New York Times*, February 4, 1942, p. 18.

45. Morgenthau Diaries, book 391, p. 3.

46. Presidential Diaries, June 10, 1941.

47. "Amherst Hears Challenge of Day," *New York Times*, June 15, 1941, p. 39.

48. Elliott V. Bell, "Treasurer to the Democracies," *New York Times Magazine*, June 22, 1941, p. SM10.

49. Blum, *From the Morgenthau Diaries: Years of Urgency*, pp. 309–11.

50. "U.S. Deficit for 1941 Fiscal Year $5,103,000,000, Third Highest," *Wall Street Journal*, July 3, 1941, p. 7.

51. Julian Huxley, "Food for Britain," *New Republic*, February 17, 1941, pp. 200–201.

52. Martin Gilbert, *The Second World War* (London: Stoddard, 1989), p. 167.

53. Presidential Diaries, April 28, 1941.

54. Blum, *From the Morgenthau Diaries: Years of Urgency*, p. 254.

55. Ibid., pp. 236–37.

56. Robert Skidelsky, *John Maynard Keynes, 1883–1946: Economist, Philosopher, Statesman* (London: Penguin, 2005), p. 631.

57. Ibid., pp. 244–48.

58. Presidential Diaries, June 14, 1941.

59. "11 U.S. Ferry Pilots Die in Crash," *New York Times*, August 16, 1941, p. 4.

60. Blum, *From the Morgenthau Diaries: Years of Urgency*, p. 260.

61. Ibid., p. 261.

62. Presidential Diaries, August 4, 1941.

63. Ibid., October 28, 1941.

64. "June Plane Output Reaches 1,476 Peak," *New York Times*, July 10, 1941, p. 1.

65. Blum, *From the Morgenthau Diaries: Years of Urgency*, p. 265.

66. "Air Aid to British Put at $284,000,000," *New York Times*, October 8, 1941, p. 2.

67. Frederick Graham, "Vast Plane Output Starts," *New York Times*, October 19, 1941, p. E5.

68. Blum, *From the Morgenthau Diaries: Years of Urgency*, p. 275.

69. Presidential Diaries, October 23, 1941.

70. David Stafford, *Roosevelt and Churchill: Men of Secrets* (Woodstock, NY: Overlook Press, 2000), pp. 79–100.

71. Frederick R. Barkley, "Revised Budget Raises This Year's Big Figures," *New York Times*, October 11, 1941, p. E7.

72. Presidential Diaries, undated (likely late November 1941).

73. Ibid., December 3, 1941.

74. Ibid., December 1, 1941.

75. Associated Press, "Pacific Crisis May Delay Record U.S. Borrowing," December 2, 1941, found in *New York Times*, p. 4.

CHAPTER EIGHT. THE SINEWS OF WAR

1. Henry Morgenthau III, *Mostly Morgenthaus: A Family History* (New York: Ticknor and Fields, 1991), p. 297.

2. Conrad Black, *Franklin Delano Roosevelt: Champion of Freedom* (New York: Public Affairs, 2003), p. 686; John Morton Blum, *From the Morgenthau Diaries: Years of War, 1941–1945* (Boston: Houghton Mifflin, 1967), p. 1.

3. Morgenthau, *Mostly Morgenthaus*, p. 298.

4. "Japan's Holdings Here Impounded," *New York Times*, December 8, 1941, p. 7.

5. "Morgenthau's Big Job," *Wall Street Journal*, December 9, 1941, p. 2.

6. Morgenthau, *Mostly Morgenthaus*, pp. 298–99.

7. Blum, *From the Morgenthau Diaries: Years of War*, p. 89.

8. Benn Steil, *The Battle of Bretton Woods: John Maynard Keynes, Harry Dexter White, and the Making of the New World Order* (Princeton, NJ: Princeton University Press, 2013), p. 225.

9. Ibid., pp. 36–46.

10. Frank R. Kent, The Great Game of Politics, *Wall Street Journal*, December 12, 1941, p. 4.

11. Blum, *From the Morgenthau Diaries: Years of War*, pp. 228–30.

12. Morgenthau Diaries, book 478, p. 5.

13. Presidential Diaries, December 26, 1941.

14. Henry N. Dorris, "4 to 6 Billion Rise Likely in Tax Bill," *New York Times*, December 13, 1941, p. 11.

15. Presidential Diaries, April 15, 1942.

16. Ibid., December 30, 1941.

17. "Morgenthau Warns Taxpayers to Be Ready," *New York Times*, December 30, 1941, p. 21.

18. Godfrey N. Nelson, "Nation Surpassing All Tax Records," *New York Times*, January 2, 1942, p. 42.

19. Franklin D. Roosevelt, "Annual Budget Message," January 5, 1942, from *The American Presidency Project*, John T. Woolley and Gerhard Peters, found at www.presidency.ucsb.edu/ws/index.php?pid=16231&st=&st1=#ixzz1pShbsC5B (accessed August 17, 2014).

20. Ibid.

21. Charles E. Egan, "Fantastic Arms Yield Held Sure," *New York Times*, January 11, 1942, p. E5.

22. Blum, *From the Morgenthau Diaries: Years of War*, p. 35.

23. Ibid., p. 15.

24. Frederick R. Barkley, "War Tax Plans Spare No Wallets," *New York Times*, March 8, 1942, p. E7.

25. Henry N. Dorris, "Says Tax Exempts 'Can't Stand More,'" *New York Times*, March 10, 1942, p. 14.

26. "Where the Income Is," *New York Times*, March 10, 1942, p. 18.

27. "Morgenthau Urges New Speed-Up in Defense Bond Sale Campaign," *New York Times*, December 10, 1941, p. 39.

28. "Morgenthau Hails Defense Bond Sale," *New York Times*, January 5, 1942, p. 10.

29. "Shoppers Buying Defense Stamps," *New York Times*, January 3, 1942, p. 16.

30. "Rail Workers Asked to Invest," *New York Times*, December 17, 1941, p. 27.

31. "Buy Defense Bonds," *Chicago Tribune*, December 21, 1941, p. 14.

32. "Plane Tragedy Stuns Hollywood," *New York Times*, January 18, 1942, p. 38.

33. "Disney Sees Morgenthau on Film for War Bonds," *New York Times*, January 6, 1942, p. 27.

34. "Donald Duck Totally Recalled," *Chicago Tribune*, February 9, 1942, p. 14.

35. "Berlin Writes Song for Treasury," *New York Times*, January 26, 1942, p. 17.

36. "Scores Publicity for Bond Sellers," *New York Times*, July 17, 1942, p. 11.

37. "Morgenthau Gives War Savings Plan," *New York Times*, February 15, 1942, p. 29.

38. Blum, *From the Morgenthau Diaries: Years of War*, pp. 17–18.

39. "Treasury to Study Compulsory Savings," *New York Times*, March 20, 1942, p. 32.

40. Presidential Diaries, April 15, 1942.

41. Howard W. Calkins, "Demand Increases for Forced Saving," *New York Times*, April 19, 1942, p. F1.

42. "Treasury Opposes Compulsory Saving," *New York Times*, April 17, 1942, p. 32.

43. "Financing a People's War," *Wall Street Journal*, April 18, 1942, p. 4.

44. Blum, *From the Morgenthau Diaries: Years of War*, pp. 125–26.

45. Ibid., pp. 81–82.

46. Ibid., p. 82.

47. Ibid., pp. 84–86.

48. Ibid., pp. 87–95; "U.S. and China Sign Financial Accord," *New York Times*, March 22, 1942, p. 34.

49. Presidential Diaries, May 14, 1942.

50. Blum, *From the Morgenthau Diaries: Years of War*, p. 232.

51. Presidential Diaries, May 15, 1942.

52. Morgenthau Papers, box 909.

53. Blum, *From the Morgenthau Diaries: Years of War*, pp. 232–36.

54. Presidential Diaries, August 25, 1944.

55. Henry Morgenthau Sr., letter to Eleanor Roosevelt, December 27, 1941, Eleanor Roosevelt Papers, box 769.

56. Eleanor Roosevelt, letter to Robert Morgenthau, May 29, 1942, Eleanor Roosevelt Papers, box 769; Morgenthau, *Mostly Morgenthaus*, p. 396.

57. Eleanor Roosevelt, letter to Henry Morgenthau Jr., January 5, 1943, Eleanor Roosevelt Papers, box 393.

58. Eleanor Roosevelt, letter to Henry Morgenthau Jr., September 8, 1942, Eleanor Roosevelt Papers, box 374.

59. Morgenthau Diaries, book 760, pp. 167, 171–72; Morgenthau Diaries, book 763, p. 114.

60. "Foley Joins Army, Leaving Treasury," *New York Times*, August 2, 1942, p. 38.

61. Morgenthau, *Mostly Morgenthaus*, p. 300.

62. Elinor Morgenthau, letter to Eleanor Roosevelt, undated, Eleanor Roosevelt Papers, box 769.

63. Morgenthau, *Mostly Morgenthaus*, caption for photograph on p. 23.

64. "Mrs. Morgenthau Stresses Thrift," *New York Times*, April 18, 1942, p. 8.

65. Morgenthau, *Mostly Morgenthaus*, pp. 302–303.

66. "Takes Tax Problem to the White House," *New York Times*, April 16, 1942, p. 34; Blum, *From the Morgenthau Diaries: Years of War*, p. 40.

67. "Sales Levy Killed; Hold-Out Tax Wins," *New York Times*, June 21, 1942, p. 25.

68. Blum, *From the Morgenthau Diaries: Years of War*, p. 42.

69. Ibid., pp. 29–30.

70. John MacCormac, "War Bond Sales Goal Looms," *New York Times*, June 21, 1942, p. E6; "War Bond Quota Is Billion in July," *New York Times*, June 30, 1942, p. 12.

71. Blum, *From the Morgenthau Diaries: Years of War*, p. 19.

72. "War Bond Day Set by Nation's Stores," *New York Times*, May 26, 1942, p. 19.

73. "Morgenthau Hails Holiday Workers," *New York Times*, July 5, 1942, p. 25.

74. "621 Radio Stations Back War Bond Drive," *New York Times*, July 28, 1942, p. 14.

75. Henry N. Dorris, "Deficit for '42 put at $19,598,000,000," *New York Times*, July 3, 1942, p. 10.

76. Presidential Diaries, July 10, 1942.

77. Ibid., July 16, 1942.

78. John MacCormac, "War Outlay Soars Dizzily," *New York Times*, July 26, 1942, p. E4.

79. John MacCormac, "War Outlay Soars Dizzily," *New York Times*, July 26, 1942, p. E4.

80. Thomas J. Hamilton, "Senators Oppose Higher Income Tax," *New York Times*, August 6, 1942, p. 20.

81. "Morgenthau Cool to 'Forced Loans,'" *New York Times*, July 31, 1942, p. 24.

82. United Press, "Bond Plan Fails, Vandenberg Says," August 8, 1942, found in *New York Times*, August 9, 1942, p. 46.

83. "Morgenthau Asks More Bond Buying," *New York Times*, August 21, 1942, p. 14.

84. Henry Morgenthau Jr., "Morgenthau on Spending Tax," *New York Times*, September 6, 1942, p. 26.

85. Presidential Diaries, August 25, 1942.

86. "Movies Will Lead in Big Bond Drive," *New York Times*, August 23, 1942, p. 39.

87. Frank R. Kent, The Great Game of Politics, *Wall Street Journal*, September 8, 1942, p. 4.

88. Presidential Diaries, August 25, 1942.

89. Ibid., September 2, 1942.

90. Ibid., September 7, 1942.

91. Arthur Krock, In the Nation, *New York Times*, October 13, 1942, p. 27.

92. "Greatest Flop since Mellon," *Time*, October 26, 1942, p. 85.

93. Morgenthau Papers, box 909.

94. Presidential Diaries, September 4, 1942.

95. Ibid., August 25, 1942.

96. Blum, *From the Morgenthau Diaries: Years of War*, pp. 234–36.

97. Ibid., pp. 128–30.

98. "Morgenthau Visit Hailed in Commons," *New York Times*, October 21, 1942, p. 5.

99. "Morgenthau, Smuts on Visit to Dover," *New York Times*, October 24, 1942, p. 8.

100. Godfrey N. Nelson, "Income and Taxes in the U.S. and Britain," *New York Times*, October 17, 1943, p. S7.

101. "Morgenthau Cites British Taxation," *New York Times*, November 3, 1942, p. 25.

102. Blum, *From the Morgenthau Diaries: Years of War*, pp. 141–44.

103. Ibid., p. 150.

104. Presidential Diaries, November 17, 1942.

105. "Wise Gets Confirmation: Checks with State Department on Nazis' 'Extermination Campaign,'" *New York Times*, November 25, 1942, p. 10.

CHAPTER NINE. THE JEWS

1. Presidential Diaries, January 27, 1942.

2. Ibid., July 7, 1942.

3. Morgenthau Papers, box 237.

4. Presidential Diaries, May 25, 1943.

5. Elinor Morgenthau, letter to Eleanor Roosevelt, December 2, 1942, Eleanor Roosevelt Papers, box 769.

6. Presidential Diaries, December 3, 1942.

7. Henry Morgenthau III, *Mostly Morgenthaus: A Family History* (New York: Ticknor and Fields, 1991), p. 323.

8. "11 Allies Condemn Nazi War on Jews: United Nations Issue Joint Declaration of Protest on 'Cold-Blooded Extermination,'" *New York Times*, December 18, 1942, pp. 1, 10.

9. Henry Morgenthau Jr., "The Morgenthau Diaries, VI—The Refugee Run-Around," *Collier's*, November 1, 1947, pp. 22 ff.

10. Ibid.; Morgenthau, *Mostly Morgenthaus*, p. 324.

11. "We Must Pay More, Morgenthau Says," *New York Times*, December 6, 1942, p. 66.

12. Edward J. Conlon, "War Bond Sales Continue to Lag," *New York Times*, September 6, 1942, p. F1.

13. Edward J. Conlon, "Treasury Plans War Bond Drive," *New York Times*, November 15, 1942, p. F2; "9,000,000,000 Goal of New War Loan; Treasury Record," *New York Times*, November 20, 1942, p. 1.

14. Presidential Diaries, December 3, 1942.

15. "U.S. at War: $51,000,000,000-a-Year Man," *Time*, January 25, 1943, pp. 18–20.

16. John Morton Blum, *From the Morgenthau Diaries: Years of War, 1941–1945* (Boston: Houghton Mifflin, 1967), p. 59.

17. "Over the Top," *New York Times*, December 23, 1942, p. 18.

18. Blum, *From the Morgenthau Diaries: Years of War*, p. 22; "Victory Loan Over Goal by 3 Billions," *New York Times*, December 29, 1942, p. 17.

19. Associated Press, "Taft Drops Move to Force Savings," January 2, 1943, found in *New York Times*, p. 21.

20. "Morgenthau Returning," *New York Times*, February 6, 1943, p. 3; "Morgenthau Returns to Office" *New York Times*, February 9, 1943, p. 21.

21. Blum, *From the Morgenthau Diaries: Years of War*, pp. 155–56.

22. Morgenthau, *Mostly Morgenthaus*, p. 373.

23. Blum, *From the Morgenthau Diaries: Years of War*, pp. 156–58.

24. "Morgenthau Maps April Bond Drive," *New York Times*, February 17, 1943, p. 29.

25. Associated Press, "Treasury Honors 'Penny Bond' Youth," March 6, 1943, found in *New York Times*, p. 14.

26. "Meeting to Launch War Loan Drive," *New York Times*, April 8, 1943, p. 29.

27. "100,000 Enrolled as Bond Sellers," *New York Times*, April 11, 1943, p. 44.

28. Associated Press, "Morgenthau Urges Rise in Bond Buying," April 25, 1943, found in *New York Times*, p. 3.

29. "Backing the Armed Forces," *New York Times*, April 30, 1943, p. 20.

30. James J. Kimble, *Mobilizing the Home Front: War Bonds and Domestic Propaganda* (College Station: Texas A&M University Press, 2006), p. 44.

31. Blum, *From the Morgenthau Diaries: Years of War*, p. 63.

32. Ibid., p. 210.

33. Morgenthau, "Morgenthau Diaries, VI—The Refugee Run-Around."

34. Ibid.

35. Blum, *From the Morgenthau Diaries: Years of War*, p. 211.

36. Morgenthau, "Morgenthau Diaries, VI—The Refugee Run-Around."

37. Ibid.

38. W. H. Lawrence, "Byrnes Moves to Use Powers on Many Fronts," *New York Times*, June 13, 1943, p. E6.

39. "Morgenthau Asks Double Bond Rate," *New York Times*, June 13, 1943, p. 32.

40. Franklin Roosevelt, letter to Henry Morgenthau Jr., June 24, 1943, Morgenthau Papers, box 519.

41. Morgenthau Papers, box 500.

42. "U.S. Must Borrow 33 Billion More," *New York Times*, July 23, 1943, p. 25.

43. Blum, *From the Morgenthau Diaries: Years of War*, p. 66.

44. Presidential Diaries, July 27, 1943.

45. Ibid., July 30, 1943.

46. Ibid., August 10, 1943.

47. Ibid., August 11, 1943.

48. Blum, *From the Morgenthau Diaries: Years of War*, pp. 60–69.

49. John MacCormac, "New and Heavier Load Ahead for Taxpayers," *New York Times*, August 22, 1943, p. E6.

50. Blum, *From the Morgenthau Diaries: Years of War*, p. 68.

51. Presidential Diaries, August 24, 1943.

52. Ibid.

53. Ibid., August 29, 1943.

54. Associated Press, "Keynes Plan Sets No Fixed Capital," April 8, 1943, found in *New York Times*, p. 8.

55. Blum, *From the Morgenthau Diaries: Years of War*, p. 238.

56. Ibid., pp. 243–45; Morgenthau, *Mostly Morgenthaus*, p. 343.

57. "Assails World Bank Plan," *New York Times*, November 2, 1943, p. 18.

58. "World Bank Plan Called Defective," *New York Times*, December 2, 1943, p. 35.

59. Blum, *From the Morgenthau Diaries: Years of War*, pp. 241–42.

60. Ibid., pp. 163–65.

61. Ibid., p. 107.

62. Ibid., pp. 111–16.

63. Ibid., pp. 197–99.

64. Ibid., pp. 159–60.

65. John H. Crider, "Occupation Money Issue," *New York Times*, October 25, 1943, p. 4.

66. Blum, *From the Morgenthau Diaries: Years of War*, pp. 167–68.

67. Geoffrey T. Hellman, "Any Bonds Today?" *New Yorker*, January 22, 1944, pp. 24 ff.

68. "Tax Program Delayed as Byrnes and Vinson Oppose Morgenthau," *Wall Street Journal*, September 11, 1943, found in Presidential Diaries, September 13, 1943.

69. Blum, *From the Morgenthau Diaries: Years of War*, pp. 70–71.

70. Presidential Diaries, September 20, 1943; "Tax Plan Revealed to Congress Group," *New York Times*, September 30, 1943, p. 17.

71. Presidential Diaries, September 18, 1943.

72. Ibid., October 3, 1943.

73. Ibid.

74. Arthur Krock, In the Nation, *New York Times*, October 8, 1943, p. 18.

75. "Problem of Higher Income," *New York Times*, October 11, 1943, p. 18.

76. "Eisenhower Bids US Buy More War Bonds," *New York Times*, October 24, 1943, p. 36.

77. Blum, *From the Morgenthau Diaries: Years of War*, p. 25.

78. United Press, "Morgenthau Visits Volturno Front," October 22, 1943, found in *New York Times*, p. 9.

79. "Morgenthau Asks Advertisers' Help," *New York Times*, November 19, 1943, p. 29.

80. "Morgenthau Lists Naples Atrocities," *New York Times*, November 5, 1943, p. 5.

81. "War Loan Goal Exceeded by Nearly $4 Billions," *New York Times*, October 19, 1943, p. 25.

82. "No New Loan Drive before Next Year," *New York Times*, October 8, 1943, p. 27.

83. Associated Press, "Morgenthau Dairy Sale Deplored in Congress," October 20, 1943, found in *New York Times*, p. 12.

84. Blum, *From the Morgenthau Diaries: Years of War*, p. 73.

85. Ibid., p. 75.

86. Morgenthau, Mostly Morgenthaus, p. 325.

87. Morgenthau, "Morgenthau Diaries, VI—Refugee Run-Around."

88. Blum, *From the Morgenthau Diaries: Years of War*, p. 213.

89. Morgenthau, "Morgenthau Diaries, VI—Refugee Run-Around."

90. Blum, *From the Morgenthau Diaries: Years of War*, p. 216.

91. Ibid., pp. 216–17.

92. Morgenthau, "Morgenthau Diaries, VI—Refugee Run-Around."

93. Ibid.

94. Ibid.

95. Ibid.

96. Blum, *From the Morgenthau Diaries: Years of War*, p. 220.

97. Morgenthau, *Mostly Morgenthaus*, p. 327.

98. Ibid.

99. Ibid.

100. Ibid.

101. Ibid.

102. Presidential Diaries, February 2, 1944.

CHAPTER TEN. BRETTON WOODS

1. Geoffrey T. Hellman, "Any Bonds Today?" *New Yorker*, January 22, 1944, pp. 24 ff.

2. "4th War Loan Goal Set at 14 Billions," *New York Times*, November 22, 1943, p. 29; "Stores Enlisted in 4th Bond Drive," *New York Times*, December 30, 1943, p. 6.

3. Ganson Purcell, Robert E. Healy, Sumner T. Pike, and Robert K. McCon-

naughey, *Tenth Annual Report of the Securities and Exchange Commission, Fiscal Year Ended June 30, 1944* (Philadelphia: US Securities and Exchange Commission, 1944), p. xix.

4. John Morton Blum, *From the Morgenthau Diaries: Years of War, 1941–1945* (Boston: Houghton Mifflin, 1967), p. 75.

5. Ibid.

6. Franklin D. Roosevelt, "Veto of a Revenue Bill," February 22, 1944, from *The American Presidency Project*, John T. Woolley and Gerhard Peters, http://www.presidency.ucsb.edu/ws/?pid=16490#ixzz1wljDxPLS (accessed August 20, 2014).

7. Drew Pearson, "Carter Glass, Extolling Tax Veto, Gets Warm Letter from President," *St. Petersburg (FL) Times*, March 14, 1944, p. 4.

8. Presidential Diaries, March 3, 1944.

9. Walter Lippmann, "New Deal Needs Resignations, Lippmann Says," *Portsmouth Times*, February 26, 1944, p. 14.

10. Presidential Diaries, March 7, 1944.

11. Fred Smith, "Washington's No. 2 Advertising Man," *Advertising & Selling*, March 1945, found in Morgenthau Papers, box 511.

12. Hellman, "Any Bonds Today?"

13. Ibid.

14. Associated Press, "War Bond 'Ad' Bill Hit by Morgenthau," December 3, 1943, found in *New York Times*, p. 11.

15. "War Bond Ad Bill Shelved in House," *New York Times*, December 9, 1943, p. 15.

16. United Press, "'Big 4' Women to Back Loan Drive on Radio," May 19, 1944, found in *New York Times*, p. 4.

17. Presidential Diaries, June 8, 1944.

18. James J. Kimble, *Mobilizing the Home Front: War Bonds and Domestic Propaganda* (College Station: Texas A&M University Press, 2006), p. 69.

19. "Is This Uncle Sam or Good Time Charlie?" *Chicago Tribune*, March 20, 1944, p. 14.

20. Blum, *From the Morgenthau Diaries: Years of War*, pp. 247–49.

21. Ibid., p. 251.

22. Associated Press, "Foreign Nations to Discuss Post War Financial Items at Bretton Woods Meeting," May 26, 1944, found in *Telegraph*, p. 1.

23. Morgenthau Papers, box 500.

24. Presidential Diaries, March 17, 1944.

25. Ibid., April 17, 1944.

26. Ibid., July 6, 1944.

27. Morgenthau, *Mostly Morgenthaus*, p. 351; Presidential Diaries, April 22, 1944.

28. Eleanor Roosevelt Papers, box 414.

29. Robert Morgenthau, interview with the author, October 1, 2013.

30. "Roosevelt Sets Up War Refugee Board," *New York Times*, January 23, 1944, p, 11; "Roosevelt Board Is Negotiating to Save Refugees from Nazis," *New York Times*, January 30, 1944, p. 1.

31. Blum, *From the Morgenthau Diaries: Years of War*, p. 223.

32. Presidential Diaries, March 7, 1944.

33. Blum, *From the Morgenthau Diaries: Years of War*, p. 224.

34. Ibid., p. 225.

35. Ibid., pp. 117–20, 285–86.

36. Ibid., pp. 165–70.

37. Ibid., p. 179.

38. Ibid., p. 187.

39. David M. Kennedy, ed., *The Library of Congress World War II Companion* (New York: Simon and Schuster, 2007), p. 202.

40. Conrad Black, *Franklin Delano Roosevelt: Champion of Freedom* (New York: Public Affairs, 2003), p. 444.

41. Morgenthau Diaries, book 747, pp. 141a–141l, 232–41.

42. Benn Steil, *The Battle of Bretton Woods: John Maynard Keynes, Harry Dexter White, and the Making of the New World Order* (Princeton, NJ: Princeton University Press, 2013), pp. 206–207; Blum, *From the Morgenthau Diaries: Years of War*, p. 258.

43. Morgenthau Diaries, book 749, pp. 254–88.

44. Blum, *From the Morgenthau Diaries: Years of War*, pp. 175–76.

45. Ibid., p. 262.

46. Russell Porter, "Morgenthau Sees Monetary Accord," *New York Times*, July 9, 1944, p. 23.

47. Morgenthau Diaries, book 752, pp. 202–16.

48. Morgenthau Diaries, box 761, p. 3.

49. "At Bretton Woods," *New York Times*, July 8, 1944, p. 10.

50. Blum, *From the Morgenthau Diaries: Years of War*, p. 272.

51. Ibid., p. 275.

52. Ibid., pp. 265–67.

53. Ibid., pp. 274.

54. Morgenthau, *Mostly Morgenthaus*, p. 343.

55. Morgenthau Papers, box 395.

56. Robert Skidelsky, *John Maynard Keynes, 1883–1946: Economist, Philosopher, Statesman* (London: Penguin, 2005), p. 766.

57. Henry Morgenthau Jr., "Analysis by Morgenthau of Monetary Agreements," *New York Times*, July 23, 1944, p. 25.

58. Morgenthau Diaries, book 761, pp. 1–12.

59. Ibid., pp. 43, 47.

60. Ibid., p. 114.

61. Morgenthau Diaries, book 762, pp. 77–78.

CHAPTER ELEVEN. OCTAGON

1. Henry Morgenthau III, *Mostly Morgenthaus: A Family History* (New York: Ticknor and Fields, 1991), pp. 352–53.

2. Ibid., p. 354.

3. Ibid.

4. Morgenthau Diaries, book 763, p. 93.

5. Ibid., pp. 94–102.

6. Ibid.

7. Ibid.; Clementine Churchill, letter to Henry Morgenthau Jr., August 15, 1944, found in Morgenthau Papers, box 289.

8. Morgenthau Diaries, book 763, p. 104.

9. Ibid., p. 106; John Morton Blum, *From the Morgenthau Diaries: Years of War, 1941–1945* (Boston: Houghton Mifflin, 1967), p. 338.

10. Bertram D. Hulen, "Lend-Lease after War Still an Open Question," *New York Times*, August 13, 1944, p. 6E.

11. Blum, *From the Morgenthau Diaries: Years of War*, pp. 307–308.

12. Ibid.

13. Ibid.

14. "Berlin Says Morgenthau Took Bayeux Tapestry," *New York Times*, August 13, 1944, p. 4.

15. Curt Ress, "The Nazis Dig In for World War III," *New York Times Magazine*, August 6, 1944.

16. Paul Einzig, *Can We Win the Peace?* (London: MacMillan, 1942), pp. 62–63.

17. T. H. Minshall, *What to Do with Germany* (London: George Allen and Unwin, 1941), pp. 147–48.

18. C. J. Hambro, *How to Win the Peace* (Philadelphia: J. B. Lippincott, 1942), p. 363.

19. Vera Micheles Dean, *On the Threshold of World Order*, Headline Series no. 44 (New York: Foreign Policy Association, 1944), p. 37.

20. Sumner Welles, *The Time for Decision* (New York: Harper and Brothers Publishers, 1944), pp. 342–43, 360.

21. Arthur Krock, In the Nation, *New York Times*, August 4, 1944, p. 12.

22. Blum, *From the Morgenthau Diaries: Years of War*, p. 328.

23. Morgenthau Diaries, book 763, p. 107.

24. Ibid., p. 108.

25. Ibid., pp. 202–205.

26. Presidential Diaries, August 19, 1944.

27. Blum, *From the Morgenthau Diaries: Years of War*, p. 343; Morgenthau Diaries, book 764, p. 120.

28. Morgenthau Diaries, book 765, pp. 14–16.

29. Morgenthau Diaries, book 766, p. 157; Morgenthau Diaries, book 767, pp. 36–45.

30. Presidential Diaries, August 25, 1944.

31. Morgenthau Diaries, book 766, pp. 13–16.

32. Presidential Diaries, August 25, 1944.

33. Morgenthau Diaries, book 769, pp. 105–107.

34. Morgenthau Diaries, book 766, pp. 167–70.

35. Blum, *From the Morgenthau Diaries: Years of War*, p. 350.

36. Morgenthau Diaries, book 767, pp. 159–68.

37. Presidential Diaries, September 2, 1944.

38. Morgenthau Diaries, book 768, pp. 104–27.

39. Ibid., pp. 158–65.

40. Ibid., p. 156.

41. Morgenthau Diaries, book 769, pp. 1–19.

42. Blum, *From the Morgenthau Diaries: Years of War*, p. 359.

43. Ibid., p. 360.

44. Morgenthau Diaries, book 769, pp. 118–45.

45. Morgenthau Papers, box 36.

46. Michael Beschloss, *The Conquerors: Roosevelt, Truman and the Destruction of Hitler's Germany, 1941–1945* (New York: Simon and Schuster, 2002), p. 196.

47. Morgenthau Diaries, book 770, pp. 70–71.

48. Ibid., pp. 68–71, 140.

49. Ibid., p. 84.

50. Blum, *From the Morgenthau Diaries: Years of War*, pp. 365–66.

51. Presidential Diaries, September 9, 1944.

52. Archives of the Chateau Frontenac, Quebec, Canada.

53. Morgenthau Diaries, book 771, pp. 223–25.

54. Presidential Diaries, September 15, 1944.

55. Blum, *From the Morgenthau Diaries: Years of War*, p. 312.

56. Presidential Diaries, September 15, 1944.

CHAPTER TWELVE. THE MORGENTHAU PLAN

1. Arthur Krock, "Why Secretary Morgenthau Went to Quebec," *New York Times*, September 22, 1944, p. 18.

2. Raymond Moley, "Too Many Surgeons," *Wall Street Journal*, October 2, 1944, p. 6.

3. Michael Beschloss, *The Conquerors: Roosevelt, Truman and the Destruction of Hitler's Germany, 1941–1945* (New York: Simon and Schuster, 2002), p. 144.

4. "Nazis Still Attack Morgenthau Project," *New York Times*, October 9, 1944, p. 3.

5. Arthur Krock, "A Good Example of the Value of Publicity," *New York Times*, September 29, 1944, p. 20.

6. John Morton Blum, *From the Morgenthau Diaries: Years of War, 1941–1945* (Boston: Houghton Mifflin, 1967), pp. 378–79.

7. Ibid., pp. 380–81.

8. Morgenthau Diaries, book 779, pp. 291–301.

9. Blum, *From the Morgenthau Diaries: Years of War*, p. 381; Henry Morgenthau III, *Mostly Morgenthaus: A Family History* (New York: Ticknor and Fields, 1991), p. 289.

10. "Mr. Dewey's Accusation," *New York Times*, November 6, 1944, p. 18.

11. Morgenthau Papers, box 500.

12. Presidential Diaries, November 27, 1944.

13. "New Issues Slated for 6th Loan Drive," *New York Times*, October 23, 1944, p. 23.

14. "War Costs Continuing," *New York Times*, December 15, 1944, p. 8.

15. Associated Press, "War Loan Exceeds Goal by 6 Billion," December 25, 1944, found in *New York Times*, p. 24.

16. James J. Kimble, *Mobilizing the Home Front: War Bonds and Domestic Propaganda* (College Station: Texas A&M University Press, 2006), pp. 70–71.

17. "70 Billion for War," *New York Times*, January 10, 1945, p. 1.

18. "Our Costs in War Reach 238 Billion," *New York Times*, February 12, 1945, p. 5.

19. *Washington Post*, January 5, 1945, found in Eleanor Roosevelt Papers, box 425.

20. Blum, *From the Morgenthau Diaries: Years of War*, p. 319.

21. Ibid.

22. Arthur Krock, "The Clouds Gathering over Dumbarton Oaks," *New York Times*, December 12, 1944, p. 22.

23. Robert Skidelsky, *John Maynard Keynes, 1883–1946: Economist, Philosopher, Statesman* (London: Penguin, 2005), p. 774.

24. Blum, *From the Morgenthau Diaries: Years of War*, pp. 285–95.

25. Ibid., pp. 296–303.

26. Morgenthau, *Mostly Morgenthaus*, pp. 328–31.

27. Robert N. Rosen, *Saving the Jews: Franklin D. Roosevelt and the Holocaust* (New York: Thunder's Mouth Press, 2006), pp. 344, 465.

28. Blum, *From the Morgenthau Diaries: Years of War*, pp. 390–91.

29. Ibid., p. 397.

30. Morgenthau Diaries, book 804, pp. 13–28.

31. Blum, *From the Morgenthau Diaries: Years of War*, pp. 388, 395.

32. Henry Morgenthau Jr., letter to Henrietta Klotz, December 12, 1944, in Morgenthau Papers, box 500; Henry Morgenthau Jr., letter to Harold Palmer, February 17, 1945, in Morgenthau Papers, box 500; Harold Hyman, letter to Henry Morgenthau Jr., February 26, 1945, in Morgenthau Papers, box 500; and Harold Palmer, letter to Henry Morgenthau Jr., June 1, 1945, in Morgenthau Papers, box 500.

33. Presidential Diaries, March 17, 1944.

34. Morgenthau Diaries, book 830, pp. 19–20.

35. Blum, *From the Morgenthau Diaries: Years of War*, pp. 409–12.

36. Morgenthau Diaries, book 831, pp. 183–224; Morgenthau Diaries, book 835, pp. 87–94.

37. Blum, *From the Morgenthau Diaries: Years of War*, p. 415.

38. Eleanor Roosevelt, letters to Elinor Morgenthau, April 1945, Eleanor Roosevelt Papers, box 2.

39. Franklin D. Roosevelt, letter to Elinor Morgenthau, April 1945, Morgenthau Papers, box 513.

40. Presidential Diaries, April 11, 1945.

41. Morgenthau Papers, box 519; Presidential Diaries, April 12, 1945; Morgenthau, *Mostly Morgenthaus*, p. 403.

42. Blum, *From the Morgenthau Diaries: Years of War*, pp. 419–20.

43. Presidential Diaries, April 12, 1945.

44. Ibid., April 16, 1945.

45. Eleanor Roosevelt, letter to Elinor Morgenthau, April 25, 1945, Eleanor Roosevelt Papers, box 2.

46. Ibid., May 5, 1945.

47. Presidential Diaries, April 14, 1945.

48. Ibid.

49. Blum, *From the Morgenthau Diaries: Years of War*, pp. 428–34.

50. Ibid., pp. 29–30.

51. Ibid., pp. 446–47.

52. Ibid., pp. 436–38.

53. Presidential Diaries, May 4, 1945.

54. Morgenthau Diaries, book 845, pp. 12–14.

55. Blum, *From the Morgenthau Diaries: Years of War*, pp. 439–41.

56. Presidential Diaries, May 9, 1945.

57. Blum, *From the Morgenthau Diaries: Years of War*, p. 445.

58. Presidential Diaries, May 23, 1945.

59. Morgenthau Diaries, book 850, pp. 45–46.

60. Blum, *From the Morgenthau Diaries: Years of War*, pp. 450–51.

61. Presidential Diaries, June 1, 1945.

62. Blum, *From the Morgenthau Diaries: Years of War*, p. 464; Morgenthau, *Mostly Morgenthaus*, p. 435.

63. Kimble, *Mobilizing the Home Front*, p. 101.

64. Blum, *From the Morgenthau Diaries: Years of War*, p. 461.

65. Presidential Diaries, June 13, 1945.

66. Ibid., June 18, 1945.

67. Ibid., July 5, 1945.

68. Blum, *From the Morgenthau Diaries: Years of War*, pp. 467–68.

69. Presidential Diaries, July 11, 1945.

70. Ibid., July 13, 1945.

71. Blum, *From the Morgenthau Diaries: Years of War*, p. 473.

72. Drew Pearson, "Washington Merry-Go-Round," *Washington Post*, July 30, 1945, found in Morgenthau Papers, box 805.

EPILOGUE

1. John Keegan, *The Second World War* (London: Penguin Book, 1990), p. 6.

2. Henry Morgenthau III, Mostly Morgenthaus*: A Family History* (New York: Ticknor and Fields, 1991), pp. 410–14.

3. David M. Kennedy, ed., *The Library of Congress World War II Companion* (New York: Simon and Schuster, 2007), p. 202.

4. Henry Morgenthau Jr., *Germany Is Our Problem* (New York: Harper and Brothers, 1945), p. 17.

5. W. K. Hancock and M. M. Gowing, *British War Economy* (London: HMSO, 1949), p. 375.

6. Mark Harrison, ed., *The Economics of World War II: Six Great Powers in International Comparison* (Cambridge: Cambridge University Press, 1998), p. 51.

7. Stephen Daggett, *Costs of Major U.S. Wars* (Washington, DC: Congressional Research Service, 2010).

8. Harrison, *Economics of World War II*, p. 86.

9. "Mr. Morgenthau's Resignation," *New York Times*, July 6, 1945, p. 10.

10. Christopher Chantrill, "Government Spending in the US," http://www.usgovernmentspending.com (accessed August 16, 2014).

SELECT BIBLIOGRAPHY

★ ★ ★

Ahamed, Liaquat. *Lords of Finance: The Bankers Who Broke the World.* New York: Penguin, 2009.

Barnett, Correlli. *The Lost Victory: British Dreams, British Realities, 1945–1950.* London: MacMillan, 1995.

Beschloss, Michael. *The Conquerors: Roosevelt, Truman and the Destruction of Hitler's Germany, 1941–1945.* New York: Simon and Schuster, 2003.

Bishop, Jim. *FDR's Last Year, April 1944–April 1945.* New York: William Morrow, 1974.

Black, Conrad. *Franklin Delano Roosevelt: Champion of Freedom.* New York: Public Affairs, 2003.

Blum, John Morton. *From the Morgenthau Diaries: Years of Crisis, 1928–1938.* Boston: Houghton Mifflin, 1959.

———. *From the Morgenthau Diaries, Years of Urgency, 1938–1941.* Boston: Houghton Mifflin, 1965.

———. *From the Morgenthau Diaries, Years of War, 1941–1945.* Boston: Houghton Mifflin, 1967.

Brands, H. W. *Traitor to His Class: The Privileged Life and Radical Presidency of Franklin Delano Roosevelt.* New York: Doubleday, 2008.

Cohen, Adam. *Nothing to Fear: FDR's Inner Circle and the Hundred Days That Created Modern America.* New York: Penguin, 2009.

Craig, R. Bruce. *Treasonable Doubt: The Harry Dexter White Spy Case.* Lawrence: University of Kansas Press, 2004.

Dwork, Debórah, and Robert Jan Van Pelt. *Flight from the Reich: Refugee Jews, 1933–1946.* New York: W. W. Norton, 2009.

Einzig, Paul. *Can We Win the Peace?* London: MacMillan, 1942.

Feingold, Henry L. *The Politics of Rescue: The Roosevelt Administration and the Holocaust.* New Brunswick, NJ: Rutgers University Press, 1970.

Feis, Herbert. *1933: Characters in Crisis.* New York: Little, Brown, 1966.

Gilbert, Martin. *Second World War.* London: Stoddard, 1989.

Gilman, Sander L., and Steven T. Katz, eds. *Antisemitism in Times of Crisis in the United States.* New York: New York University Press, 1991.

Hall, H. Duncan. *North American Supply.* London: HMSO, 1955.

Hancock, W. K., and M. M. Gowing. *British War Economy.* London: HMSO, 1949.

Harrison, Mark, ed. *The Economics of World War II: Six Great Powers in International Comparison*. Cambridge: Cambridge University Press, 1998.

Hastings, Max. *Winston's War: Churchill, 1940–1945*. New York: Alfred A. Knopf, 2010.

Herf, Jeffrey. *The Jewish Enemy: Nazi Propaganda during World War II and the Holocaust*. New York: Belknap, 2006.

Hull, Cordell. *The Memoirs of Cordell Hull*. New York: MacMillan, 1948.

Ickes, Harold L. *The Secret Diary of Harold L. Ickes: The First Thousand Days 1933–1936*. New York: Simon and Schuster, 1953.

Kearns Goodwin, Doris. *No Ordinary Time: Franklin and Eleanor Roosevelt: The Home Front in World War II*. New York: Simon and Schuster, 1994.

Kennedy, David M., ed. *The Library of Congress World War II Companion*. New York: Simon and Schuster, 2007.

Kennedy, Paul. *The Rise and Fall of the Great Powers*. New York: Random House, 1987.

Langer, William L., and S. Everett Gleason. *The Undeclared War, 1940–1941*. New York: Harper and Brothers Publishers, 1953.

Levy, Herbert. *Henry Morgenthau Jr.: The Remarkable Life of FDR's Secretary of the Treasury*. New York: Skyhorse Publishing, 2010.

MacIver, R. M. *Towards an Abiding Peace*. New York: MacMillan, 1943.

Minshall, Col. T. H. *What to Do with Germany*. London: George Allen and Unwin, 1941.

Morgenthau, Henry, Jr. *Germany Is Our Problem*. New York: Harper and Brothers, 1945.

Morgenthau, Henry, III. *Mostly Morgenthau: A Family History*. New York: Ticknor and Fields, 1991.

Mukerjee, Madhusree. *Churchill's Secret War: The British Empire and the Ravaging of India during World War II*. London: Basic Books, 2010.

Nelson, Donald M. *Arsenal of Democracy: The Story of American War Production*. New York: Harcourt, Brace, 1946.

Ohl, John Kennedy. *Hugh S. Johnson and the New Deal*. DeKalb: Northern Illinois University Press, 1985.

Plokhy, S. M. *Yalta: The Price of Peace*. New York: Viking, 2010.

Rees, David. *Harry Dexter White: A Study in Paradox*. London: MacMillan, 1973.

Rosen, Robert N. *Saving the Jews: Franklin D. Roosevelt and the Holocaust*. New York: Thunder's Mouth Press, 2006.

Schlesinger, Arthur M., Jr. *Journals 1952–2000*. New York: Penguin, 2007.

Shirer, William. *The Rise and Fall of the Third Reich: A History of Nazi Germany*. New York: Simon and Schuster, 1960.

Shirlaw, G. B., and L. E. Jones. *You and the Peace*. London: MacMillan, 1944.

Shlaes, Amity. *The Forgotten Man: A New History of the Great Depression*. New York: HarperCollins, 2007.

Skidelsky, Robert. *John Maynard Keynes, 1883–1946: Economist, Philosopher, Statesman.* London: Penguin, 2005.

Smith, Jean Edward. *FDR.* New York: Random House, 2007.

Stafford, David. *Roosevelt and Churchill: Men of Secrets.* London: Overlook, 2000.

Steil, Benn. *The Battle of Bretton Woods: John Maynard Keynes, Harry Dexter White, and the Making of the New World Order.* Princeton, NJ: Princeton University Press, 2013.

Visson, Andre. *The Coming Struggle for Peace.* New York: Viking, 1944.

Wyman, David S. *The Abandonment of the Jews.* New York: New Press, 1998.

INDEX

★ ★ ★